Angel on my arm

The Prison Letters

SEAN LIZÉE

This book contains scans of original, handwritten prison letters, preserved in their original form, including handwriting, spelling, grammar, and style. To protect privacy and safety, some names, identifying details, or sensitive information have been changed or removed.

Content Notice: These letters may include strong language, mature themes, and sensitive subject matter. Reader discretion is advised.

Published by SummerNova Publishing Inc.

For more information :
https://www.angelonmyarm.com

ISBN: 978-1-0698958-1-3

Book and Cover design © SummerNova Publishing Inc.

10 9 8 7 6 5 4 3 2 1

First Hardcover Edition 2025

"It is what it is."

Note to the reader

Before you get into these pages, there's a few things you should know.

Everything in here was written by hand, one page at a time, from inside my prison cell. Nothing's been rewritten or polished up. The only things that changed were a few names and details—some were blanked out to protect people's privacy. The rest is how it came out, raw and real.

You'll see small numbers written at the top of some pages. Those were mine. I used them to count how many sheets I could fit in an envelope without folding them too tight or leaving creases. It was my way of keeping track—how much could go out at once, how much I could send of myself that day.

You'll also notice this symbol: ==> That just means I stopped writing for a bit and came back later. Sometimes it was hours, sometimes a whole day. Life inside moves strange, and that little arrow was how I marked the breaks between moments—like hitting pause and then unpausing again when my head cleared.

These letters weren't meant to be read by the world. They were me trying to stay human. Everything in here was written by my hand from my mind—the way I lived it and felt it.

If you're holding this now, just know it's all real. Every line, every pause, every breath between words—that's me.

— Sean

1

Intake

"Learning to breath."

These letters started because I needed somewhere to put my mind. The hours dragged, the nights got long, and that place could swallow you whole. Days blurred until I needed something—anything—to keep my head from slipping. Writing became survival.

But the reason the words had somewhere to go began before I ever picked up a pen. It started with her. I met her at an AA meeting before I went inside. I hadn't planned on saying a word, but when she spoke, it hit me—the honesty, the way she carried herself—it was real. From that moment on, she stayed with me, even after I was behind those walls.

And then one day, after weeks of trying to hold myself together, I remembered her number. I called her, and that one conversation became the spark that lit all of this.

At first, the writing was just to her. Every time I put pen to paper, it felt like reaching through the walls for something real—something that reminded me there was a world beyond the one I was trapped in.

But these letters weren't just about me and her. My daughters were why I kept trying to be better in there. I wanted them to know their dad was still fighting to hold on to the good in him. They were the heartbeat behind every word.

So this is where it began: me in a cell, trying to make sense of my life and not lose myself in it. The pages that follow are raw and real—love, pain, hope—written so I wouldn't forget who I was.

(1)

DEAR ANGEL 2022-01-18

I JUST WANTED TO SAY THANK YOU FOR BEING YOU. JUST HEARING YOUR VOICE MAKES ME SO HAPPY. THE WAY YOU SPEAK MAKES ME SMILE. YOU ARE ABSOLUTELY ADORABLE.
A WHILE AGO YOU DIBS PICKING ME UP. I REALLY HOPE I WALK OUT OF HERE TO YOU WAITING FOR ME. YOU SAID YOUD GIVE ME ONE OF THOSE HUGS WHERE YOU JUMP INTO MY ARMS AND WRAP YOUR LEGS AROUND ME. IF YOU DO IM HOLDING ON TO YOU FOR AS LONG AS YOULL LET ME. TO BE COMPL-ETELY HONEST ANGEL THE MORE I GET TO KNOW HOW AWESOME YOU ARE THE MORE YOU INTIMIDATE ME (IN A GOOD WAY). I HAVE SO MUCH RESPECT FOR YOU AND WHO YOU ARE.
ASK ME SOME QUESTIONS IF YOU'D LIKE. ANYTHING YOU'D LIKE. I'LL ANSWER :) TODAY I AM GRATEFUL AND APPRECIATIVE TO THIS PROCESS. EVEN THOUGH ITS A STRUGGLE THERE IS ALWAYS A LESSON TO BE LEARNED.
I AM A DENSE PERSON AND THIS IS THE ROUGHEST WAY TO LEARN HOW TO LOVE THE LITTLE THINGS IN LIFE. I LOOK FORWARD TO LIVING LIFE FROM A FRESH START. FRESH SOBER PERSPECTIVE. DEFINATELY GETTING SOME TATT-OOS IMMEDIATELY. CHEESE PLATE IS 100% NEEDED ON DAY ONE OF FREEDOM. DINNER DATE? UP TO YOU. :)

(2)

2022-01-19

WELL ITS MORNING. APPROX 10AM. THE SHORTAGE OF INMATE KITCHEN STAFF LET US SLEEP IN. WE GOT BRUNCH INSTEAD OF BREAKFAST. IT WAS POTATO SALAD, EGGS, AND "CHICKEN". ONCE AGAIN I WAS VERY HAPPY TO TALK TO YOU LAST NIGHT AND SUPER STOKED FOR THE EXTRA 15 MINS. 8:30-9:15. I HAD A GOOD SLEEP W/ CLEAN SHEETS AND FOR THE FIRST TIME IN MONTHS I USED TIDE PODS WHICH SMELLED LIKE HOME. I'M GETTING A HAIRCUT THIS AFTERNOON WHICH IS SWEET. MY WORKOUT BUDDY IS WORKING THE KITCHEN SO WE WILL WORKOUT LATER. I FEEL GOOD TODAY. HOW ARE YOU? I LOVE HEARING YOU TALKING ABOUT YOUR DAY LAST NIGHT. LISTENING TO YOU IS VERY CALMING. 3 NEW GUYS SHOWED UP ON OUR UNIT AND IT APPEARS I AM THE ONE WHO IS TO ASK ABOUT HOW RRAC WORKS. "FRESH FISH" LOL (SHAWSHANK). 2 OF THE 3 WALKED IN LIKE THE DANNY DEVITO & ARNOLD MOVIE "TWINS". WE LAUGHED A BIT. OUR DUO LOGO "SUBTLE 28" IS BEING DRAWN TODAY. I ALREADY GAVE THE PEANUTS ☺ HAHA. IM WATCHING DANE COOK ON COMEDY NETWORK WHILE I WRITE YOU. I CANT WAIT FOR EVERYONE TO SEE HOW MUCH I WILL HAVE CHANGED PHYSICALLY AND MENTALLY WHILE IM AWAY. THANKS FOR SHOWING ME SO MUCH LOVE EVERYDAY AND TELLING ME YOU LOVE ME. NORMALLY I HAVE A HARD TIME BELIEVING PEOPLE BUT FOR SOME REASON I TRULY BELIEVE YOU. THIS IS A VERY LOVELESS PLACE/ENVIRONMENT FULL OF PEOPLE WHO THINK

(3)

YOU HAVE TO BE "HARD". WELL YOU DONT. I FIND IT EASIER TO JUST BE MYSELF. I CRACK JOKES, BE NICE, AND KEEP THINGS LIGHT. IVE GOT LOTS OF RESPECT FOR MY PRIDE IN SOBRIETY, AND LOTS OF PEOPLE IN HERE NEED TO SEE/HEAR MY STORY ABOUT CHANGE AS I GET ASKED MORE AND MORE AND PASS OUT LITERATURE. IT MAKES ME FEEL NORMAL. I'M LOOKING FORWARD TO CALLING YOU LATER AS IT MAKES THE DAY. I THINK ABOUT YOU OFTEN AND MISS YOU CONSTANTLY. SOMETIMES I WONDER IF THATS WEIRD FOR YOU OR NOT. IS IT? THE MORE I LEARN ABOUT YOU I REALIZE HOW MUCH WE HAVE IN COMMON. I TALKED TO MY GIRLS LAST NIGHT. DAUGHTER HADNT BEEN TO SCHOOL IN AWHILE AND TALKED ABOUT HOW EXCITED SHE WAS TO GO BACK. AND DAUGHTER LOVES SCHOOL. I AM SO PROUD OF THEM BOTH. I CANT WAIT TO HAVE THEM AND DAUGHTER TOGETHER ONCE IM OUT. ALSO EXCITED TO RELAX AND ENJOY SOME ME TIME. IF YOU HAVENT HAD A BEACH ~~FIRE BY THEN WOULD YOU LIKE TO DO THAT TOGETHER?~~ OR GO TO THAT VIEW SPOT? TIME HERE IS BI POLAR. SOMETIMES FAST SOMETIMES SLOW. 2.5 MONTHS ALREADY ITS CRAZY. SO MANY MOVIES TO WATCH WHEN THIS IS DONE. THE MAIN C.O. REFERS TO ME AS "THE ANGRY GUY" LOL. LIKE CALLING SOMEONE TALL/BIG "TINY" HAHA BIENG GOOD AT BEING IN PRISON ISNT A SKILL I KNEW I HAD HAHAHA. OR NEEDED. :) FYI ⇒ I MIGHT CRY WHEN I SEE YOU. TEARS OF JOY OF COURSE. CAN YOU TELL GORD, ALLEN, AND DON ⟹ THEY BETTER

4

BE AT MY RETURN GATHERING IF THERE IS ONE. THEY MISSED THE LAST ONES. CAN YOU TELL [redacted] I WILL CALL HIM AS SOON AS I MOVE. AND THAT I THINK ABOUT HIM ALOT AND I LOVE HIM PLEASE? - DO YOU LIKE CAMPING? JEREMY HOTZ IS ON COMEDY NOW... HILARIOUS. I CANNOT WAIT FOR MY OLD CLOTHES & UNERWEAR. ESPECIALLY THE UNDERWEAR. I MEAN TIGHTY WHITIES LOOK SUPER SHEYSHAY ON ME! (OF COURSE) BUT THEY ARE NOT ALL THAT COMFY LOL. LIKE A MODEL. NOT MARKY MARK. BUT SCANY SEAN... HAHAHAHA... I REALLY HOPE YOU LAUGHED AT THAT [redacted]. PLEASE DONT PICTURE IT UNTIL YOU SEE THE CHANGE LOL ☺. ⇒ WELL IM OFF OF WORK NOW AND ITS 10PM. I DIDNT GET TO TALK TO YOU WHICH WAS A BUMMER. THE LODGE BURNER GOT ON THE PHONE JUST BEFORE I GOT THERE. SO I REMINDED OUR UNIT + THE NEW GUYS ITS MY PHONE TIME TO CALL [redacted] FROM 845-915. NOW THERES A SIGN ON THE PHONE. MY WORKOUT WAS AWESOME. WE RAN STAIRS DID TRIANGLE PUSH UPS AND FILLED A SMALL GARBAGE CAN W/ WATER AND WORKED UPPER CENTER CHEST. OUR SUBTLE DRAWING WAS DONE TODAY. THE SKULLS ARE A BIT SKULLIER (IF THATS A WORD) THAN I WANTED BUT ITS PRETTY SWEET. A PRESENT FOR YOU. COST A BOWL OF SALTED PEANUTS. 50$ PRISON MONEY HAHAHA! HE WOULDVE DONE IT FOR FREE HE SAID BUT PEANUTS IS PEANUTS (PUN INTENDED HOPE YOU LAUGHED)

(5)

TELL ME ABOUT YOURSELF SO I CAN GET TO KNOW YOU EVEN BETTER. ANYTHING AT ALL. LIKES, DISLIKES, PAST, PRESENT, FUTURE, LOVE, HATE, INTERESTS, WHAT MAKES YOU HAPPY, WHAT MAKES YOU UPSET, FAV FOOD, RESTAURANT, BOOKS, MUSIC, MOVIES, TATTOO YOU HAVE, TATTOOS YOU WANT, SOME JOKES, QUOTES, POEMS ETC. I KNOW YOURE BUSY AND WRITTING TAKES SO DONT FEEL PRESSURED TO WRITE BACK. I HAVE ALL THE TIME IN THE WORLD AND THIS IS LIKE THERAPY. PLUS ITS GOOD TO DO. MY WRITTING MAY BE ALL OVER THE PLACE BUT IM WRITTING THROUGHOUT THE DAY OF WHATEVER COMES TO MIND WHEN THE PENCIL IS IN MY HAND. I WRITE IN ALL CAPS BECAUSE This is what my writing looks like when I write normally. Super girly dont you think? I used to get teased for it. All sisters for me so I adapted bubble writing from them. well I'm going to have a cookies n cream protien shake and some bran cereal then watch t.v. and lay in bed. Sweet dreams lovely lady. night.

2022 01-20 GOOD MORNING ANGEL TODAY WE GOT ANOTHER NEW GUY IN THE CELL NEXT TO ME, WEVE BEEN ON LOCKDOWNS THIS MORNING. OUR UNIT IS FILLING UP SO HOPEFULLY I GET MOVED ASAP. TODAY IS A GOOD DAY. I AM IN FAIRLY HIGH SPIRITS AND HAPPY. TODAY IM NOTICING HOW MUCH ID LOVE A HUG. ILL NEVER TAKE ONE FORGRANTED AGAIN. PHYSICAL CONTACT/CONNECTION IS A HUG PART OF WHAT MAKES ME, ME. ILL DEFINATELY

(6)

BE ALOT MORE RESERVED W/ WHO I HUG OR CON-
-NECT W/. IVE WASTED ALOT OF TIME ON PEOPLE
TO LEARN THIS LESSON. MY LOVE IS FOR THOSE
WHO TRULY LOVE ME AS MUCH AS I DO THEM.
UNCONDITIONALLY. CONDITIONAL LOVE IVE LEARNED
IS NOT TRUE LOVE. ITS MANIPULATION. THE WORD
LOVE IS SO SPECIAL. ON ANOTHER NOTE, TODAY
I FEEL CONFIDENT AND HUMBLE TO THIS PROCESS
OF LIFE IM IN. ITS GREAT IN THE WAY THAT → IT
SEPARATES WHO IS WHO IN MY LIFE. IT HAS STRIPPED
MY LIFE BARE AND IM EXCITED TO GET BACK TO
CRUSHING LIFE LIKE BEFORE BUT W A SUPER HEALTHY
AND POSITIVE SOBER OUTLOOK. I MISS YOU ANGEL ♡
I TRULY DO LOVE YOU. SARA SILVERMAN IS ON COMEDY
RIGHT NOW. SO FUNNY. 2 NEW GUYS NOW ITS 1 15PM
I DIDNT EAT THE LUNCH BECAUSE IT LOOKED LIKE
SLOP. OH WELL. THE NEW GUYS LOOKED TO ME FOR
INFO. THEY DIDNT EVEN KNOW HOW TO BE RELEASED
FROM THIER CELLS. SUPER GREEN. MAYBE I JUST
FIGURE STUFF LIKE THIS OUT FASTER THAN OTHERS.
I GOT TOLD BY AN INMATE ON ANOTHER UNIT THAT HE
SAW HOW FAST I CHANGED PHYSICALLY AND IT INSPIRED
HIM TO DO THE SAME. THAT MADE ME FEEL GOOD.
I DECIDED IM GOING TO GET 11:11 TATTOOD ON MY
EYE LIDS. ITS MY LUCKY NUMBER. ITS ALWAYS PROMI-
-NENT WHEN I AM WHERE IM SUPPOSED TO BE.
TODAY I FEEL SOME EXCITEMENT IN MY STOMACH
BECAUSE ITS FILLING UP IN HERE AND I AM SOME-
ONE WHO HAS BEEN HERE FOR AWHILE. ANYDAY
NOW.  ← THATS NOT A DOOBIE. (SUPPOSED TO BE
A PARTY EMOJI HAHA)

2

Close Enough To Touch

"The kind of distance you feel in your bones."

There were nights when I could almost feel her beside me—the weight of her head on my chest, the warmth of her breath, the quiet rhythm of her sleeping. It wasn't real, but my mind made it real enough to get through another night. In a place built to strip you of feeling, memory becomes its own kind of mercy.

That was the distance I lived with. Close enough to remember every detail, too far to reach any of it. The smell of her hair, the sound of her laugh, the way her voice softened when she said my name—I chased them like echoes down a hallway that never ended. Sometimes it hurt, but that hurt reminded me I was still alive.

I wrote to her every day. Some letters were strong; others barely held together. I told her how the thought of her kept me steady, how love became the only thing that still felt real. It's strange how a few sheets of paper could hold more warmth than a whole room.

Even now, when I think back, I can still feel that pull—the need to reach for something I couldn't touch. Those words became my hands, my heartbeat, my proof that I hadn't gone numb. So I kept writing, again and again, until the pen gave out but the feeling didn't.

①

2022-01-28

ITS 10PM AND IM ALL DONE WORK. IT WAS AWESOME. I GOT A PRESENT WHILE ON THE PHONE W/ YOU (PEANUT BUTTER CUPS) AND WHEN I WAS DONE WORK A BUNCH OF DUDES WERE UP TO YELL GOODNIGHT. I GOT ANOTHER 12x12 A.A BOOK FROM ANOTHER UNIT AND SLID IT UNDER THE DOOR OF AN OLDER DUDES CELL. HE WAS STOKED. WHEN I GOT TO MY CELL/HOUSE YET ANOTHER GIFT. A HALF BAG OF SPICED POPCORN. IT ADDED TO AN ALREADY STELLAR DAY. THE INMATES AND GUARDS TREAT ME REALLY WELL IN HERE. IM FINALLY FEEL--ING LIKE MY TRUE SELF LATELY. I GET TO LOOK AT YOU WHILE I WRITE YOU AND IT MAKES ME FEEL NORM--ALIZED CONSIDERING MY CEMENT SURROUNDINGS. YOU ARE SO BEAUTIFUL. TODAY I FEEL BLESSED. ITS LIKE A DREAM TO FEEL AT HOME ANYWHERE AND EVERYWHERE AS LONG AS THERE IS LOVE, FAITH, HOPE, AND HAPPINESS. EVEN HERE THERE IS LOTS OF LAUGHS AND REALNESS. PRISON STRIPS PEOPLE BARE AND THE RAWNESS IS UNCANNY TO ANYTHING IVE EVER KNOWN. I LOOK FORWARD TO BEING IN PERSON W/ YOU AND TELLING YOU ALL THE STORIES AND HEAR ALL ABOUT WHAT YOUVE BEEN UP TO AND ALL ABOUT YOU FOR THAT MATTER. THERE IS SO MUCH TO OFFER THIS WORLD, THIS LIFE, AND IT HAS ONLY JUST BEGAN. EVERY SINGLE DAY IS NEW AND ILL CONTINUE TO LIVE IN THAT VERY MANNER. ID LOVE MORE PHOTOS OF YOU ♡ WHEN WE HAVE A VIDEO CHAT YOU CAN SCREENSHOT ME IF YOUD LIKE ONE OF WHAT I LOOK LIKE NOW. STILL THE SAME JUST A BIT LIGHTER IN WEIGHT AND MORE MUSCLES LOL. WAIT THREE MONTHS

(2)

AND THE TRANFORMATION WILL SHOCK YOU I HOPE. ITS GOING TO SHOCK MY DAUGHTERS. MY HEAD IS SHAVED TO THE SKIN AND READY FOR A HEAD TA--TTOO. I FEEL LIKE THIS WEEKEND IS GOING TO GO BY VERY QUICKLY. I HOPE THAT IT DOES. TALKING TO YOU IS SO CALMING. SOMETHING ABOUT YOUR VOICE CAN SOFTEN ME EVEN IN A PLACE LIKE THIS. ♡ WELL IM OFF TO BED NOW. GOODNIGHT ANGEL. LOVE YOU.

ZZZZZZZZZZ

2022-01-29

GOOD MORNING LOVELY LADY. YOU ARE THE VERY FIRST PERSON I SAW THIS MORNING. I AM GRATEFUL FOR THAT IN SO MANY WAYS. IM HAVING PEANUT BUTTER MIXED PLAIN YOGURT AND SLICED BANANAS FOR BREAKFAST. WE GOT OUR CONDEMENTS BAGS SO I TRADED MINE FOR MORE P.B. ♥. LIKE HALLOWEEN AGAIN. WE GET THE YARD ONCE TODAY SO ILL DO MY JOGGING AT 1:15PM WHEN WE HAVE IT. IM STOKED TO CALL YOU TODAY ANGEL. THE DAYS ARE GOING BY QUICKLY AND MY TRANSFER TIME IS GETTING CLOSER AND CLOSER. ONCE AGAIN I CANNOT WAIT. I FEEL IM GOING TO MISS THIS PLACE AND THE PEOPLE IVE MET BUT IM SURE ILL REALLY ENJOY MY NEXT PHASE. THERE IS ONE GOAL IN MIND AND THAT IS TO GET HOME TO EVERYONE ♡. ⟹ MORNING SOCIAL TIME WENT FAST. THE WHOLE UNIT WAS UP EARLY AND IN FAIRLY GOOD SPIRITS WHICH WAS NICE. WE DID AN AB WORKOUT AND THERE FOOD BEING PREPPED FOR DINNER WHICH SMELLED DELICIOUS AND LOTS OF LAUGHTER. THE TWO GUYS WHO LIKE TO COOK ARE COMPETING EACH NIGHT AND IM GOING TO REMEMBER IT ALL BEFORE I LEAVE. IT ALMOST FEELS LIKE A MULTI-DAY GOING AWAY CELEBRATION. I TALKED THE GIRLS TODAY ARE SO ADORABLE. "UMMM.. DADDY... GUESS WHAT?.. →

(3)

WE ARE GOING TO FIGHT THE GOVERNMENT YAAAAY!! AND WE MADE SO MANY SIGNS". THEY ARE SO EXCITED. WE ARE RAISING FREETHINKERS. SUCH BEAUTIFUL KIND SOULS THOSE GIRLS ARE. THEY ARE FILLED W/ SO MUCH LOVE IT MELTS MY HEART. IM SUCH A PROUD DAD. I DEFINATELY LOVE KIDS AND WILL 100% HAVE MORE. LOL. I LOVE BEING A DAD AND ONCE IM OUT OF HERE I WILL FOREVER BE A BETTER DAD. ILL BE STOKED TO GIVE EVERYONE HUGS. ESPECIALLY YOU. ITS A GORGEOUS DAY OUTSIDE SO IM GOING TO SPEND IT IN THE YARD AFTER LUNCH. IF I WASNT IN HERE I WOULD HAVE ASKED YOU IF YOUD LIKE TO GO ON A WALK AND HAVE A FIRE AT THE VIEW SPOT. AND IT BEING SATURDAY ID HAVE THE GIRLS BROUGHT UP TO JOIN. THEY LOVE YOU SO MUCH ITS SO CUTE. ⇒ WHAT A DAY. I THINK RRAC IS NOT SUPPOSED TO BE THIS HAPPY/POSITIVE BUT I REFUSE TO LET ANY SCENARIO BRING NEGATIVITY INTO MY HEART. IF IT DOES ILL PROCESS IT AND FILTER IT INTO POSITIVE™ AND LIGHT. I SPENT TOO MUCH OF MY LIFE IN A DARK PLACE. I MOVED YOUR PHOTO NEAR/BESIDE MY DOOR SO I COULD LOOK AT YOU WHEN I LEAVE MY SPACE. I WISH I HAD MORE FOR BESIDE MY DESK & BED. YOU BRING SO MUCH COMFORT TO THESE WALLS. WHAT A GREAT MOOD IM IN ANGEL :) ♡ ⇒ BACK IN MY CELL AGAIN. JUST ORGANIZING MY THINGS (DRAWERS SHELVES, SINK AREA, CANTEEN CLOTHES ETC.) IT FEELS FRESH IN HERE. SOMEONE SPIT ON THE GROUND IN THE YARD TODAY AND I TOLD THE WHOLE UNIT THATS NOT GOING TO FLY. NOT ON THE GROUND OR FENCE. EVERYONE AGREED :). WE ARE NOT ANIMALS WE CAN BE

4

GENTLEMEN AND SHOW SOME CLASS WHERE/WHEN WE CAN. WE CAN HAVE DIGNITY AND RESPECT AS WELL. I HOPE YOUR DAY HAS BEEN CALMING AND RELAXED. THE WEEKEND IS ALMOST HALF OVER ☺. WHEN YOU GET THIS LETTER PUT ON THE SONG "WHEN THE NIGHT" BY BEDOVIN SOUNDCLASH. IM NOT SURE IF THATS AC- -TUALLY THE SONG TITLE BUT IT WILL COME UP ON YOUTUBE. ITS A FEEL GOOD SONG AND ALWAYS MAKES ME HAPPY. HOPEFULLY ITLL MAKE YOU HAPPY TOO. I LIKE MAKING YOU LAUGH AND SMILE. WHATS GOOD W/ YOU?

⇒ I HAD MY FIRST WHISTLE MISTAKE. PEOPLE WERE ALL OVER ME LMAO. I ALWAYS GET FREE PASSES HAHAHAHAHA. EVERYONE ACTS SO HARD AND THEN DO NOTHING. WHY ACT. LIFE IS TOO SHORT TO HAVE NEGATIVITY. I JUST LAUGHED AND SAID CALM DOWN. DINNER IS OVER AND IT WAS AMAZING. THOSE BOYS KNOW WHATS UP W/ JAIL COOKING. ~~AR~~ ME AND ANOTHER GUY MADE NAAN BREAD BY GARLIC BUTTERING BOTH SIDES OF A WRAP THEN FOLDING IT INTO THE TOASTER. IT WORKED PERFECTLY. I GOT THE UNIT EXTRA PEARS FOR THE WHISTLE LOL. IM SO GLAD I GOT MAIL YESTERDAY SO IM NOT HAVING TO HOPE FOR SOME. PICS OF THE GIRLS (ALL THREE) ARE ON ROUTE (THANX TO THEIR MOM). HOPEFULLY ILL GET MORE OF YOU AS WELL ☺. MY ROOM IN MY NEXT HOME WILL BE FULL OF LOVE. IM REALLY EXCITED FOR THAT. I JUST FILLED OUT A FORM TO VIDEO CALL YOU. HOPEFULLY THAT HAPPENS. ID LOVE TO SEE YOU.

⇒

2022-01-30

GOOD MORNING ANGEL

ITS 6:30AM AND I AM AWAKE. I WOKE UP AND YOU WERE THE FIRST FACE I SAW. I SMILED AND WAS

(5)

VERY HAPPY TO SEE YOU. MY FIRST THOUGHT WAS I WONDER HOW LATE YOU WERE AWAKE PLAYING ZELDA AND DID YOU GET THE HORSE SO LINK COULD TRAVEL FASTER. ITS SUNDAY AND IM BEGINNING TO REFLECT ON MY TIME IN RRAC. SOMETIMES IT WENT BY SLOW BUT OVERALL ITS BEEN FAIRLY FAST. WHAT AN EXPE--RIANCE. I MANAGED TO KEEP A SOUL IN SUCH A SOUL--ESS PLACE. I TRIED TO BRING JOY, HAPPINESS, CARING, AND COMPASSION WHERE I COULD. I LEFT THE A.A. MESSAGE EVERYWHERE I COULD. THIS PLACE IS DESIGNED TO PUSH BUTTONS BUT I MANAGE TO STAY HAPPY TO A POINT A C.O CALLS ME "ANGRY GUY". BECAUSE OF PRISON I FEEL LOVE ON A WHOLE OTHER LEVEL. A.A. BROUGHT THAT LOVE TO LIGHT AND THIS PLACE HIGHTENED IT. I HOPE YOU HAVE A LAZY SUNDAY, SLEEP IN, EAT GOOD FOOD, AND STAY IN YOUR PAJAMAS ALL DAY AND PLAY VIDEO GAMES ALL DAY AND DONT FEEL ONE BIT GUILTY FOR IT. TBH. I WISH I WAS SITTING RIGHT BESIDE YOU WATCHING AND ANNOYING YOU LOL ALSO MAKING YOU SMILE & LAUGH. IM FEELING EXCITEMENT TODAY KNOW IM SO INCEDIBLY CLOSE TO MY MOVE NOW AND HAPPY KNOWING I LEFT MY MARK ON RRAC INMATES & STAFF. I WISH I COULD HUG YOU RIGHT NOW. I HAVENT BEEN THIS HAPPY IN HERE YET. IVE HAPPY BUT NOT ON A LEVEL LIKE TODAY. UP EARLY TALKING (THROUGH A PEN) TO YOU AND YOUR PHOTO MAKES ME FEEL AT PEACE AND AT HOME IN HERE. YOU ARE SO BEAUTIFUL DUDE. PLEASE DO SEND ME MORE ASAP. TODAY IS THE DAY WE GET REAL EGGS AND THEY ARE BOILED. IM STOKED. IM NOT SURE IF THIS QUESTION WILL BREACH OUR FRIENDSHIP BUT I WOULD REALLY LIKE TO TAKE YOU ON A DATE.

(6)

WOULD YOU GO ON ONE DATE W/ ME ANGEL ? IF YES TELL ME ON THE PHONE. IF NO JUST IGNORE THAT QUESTION. LOL. DINNER - MOVIE - AND WALK IN DAVIS BAY. REMEMBER I AM DENSE AND DO NOT PICK UP ON SUBLETY WHATSOEVER. IVE NEVER MET ANOTHER PERSON LIKE YOU BEFORE. ⇒ I DECIDED TO SAVE THE EGGS FOR A SNACK LATER AND 3 DICED BANA-NAS AND YOGURT. IT WAS GOOD. I WENT AND WALKED THE TRASH OUT TO THE DUMPSTER IN THE PARKING LOT (A.K.A. MY MORNING OUTING LOL). TODAY IS OVERCAST. SOME OF THE GUYS WERE GRUMPY THIS MORNING AND OTHERS AS HAPPY AS CAN BE. DOESNT BOTHER ME, EITHER WAY IM STOKED. ⇒ ITS 1:00PM. LAUGHING AND JOKING AROUND FILL THE GP (GENERAL POPULATION) AREA W/ SOUND. IT SMELLS LIKE GOOD FOOD. I TRADED SOME PROTEIN POWDER FOR AN ERASER FOR THE TATTOO ARTIST SO HE COULD FINISH A DRAWING FOR HIS DAUGHTER. HE DREW ON AN ENVELOPE SO I COULD SEND IT TO YOU AS HE KNOWS IM ALWAYS WRITING TO YOU AND CALL YOU EVERY NIGHT. WE ARENT SUPPOSED TO TRADE BUT I FIGURE ITS ALL FOR HONEST AND MORAL REASONS. I AM SO GLAD IM SOBER. THAT IS ONE THING I TAKE ZERO PART IN, IN LIFE AND AM GRATEFUL I GOT MYSELF BACK IN ONE PIECE. EVERYONE TEASES THAT RRAC IS KEEPING ME FOR GOOD LOL. GUARDS & INMATES BOTH. ⇒ DINNER IS OVER. IN CELLS UNTIL 7:15 SO IM SITTING DOWN AND WRITING / HANGING OUT W/ YOU ☺. I GOT TO MY GRANDMA WHO HAS SERIOUS DIMENTIA. SHE ASKED WHERE I WAS SO I TOLD HER I WAS IN FEDERAL PRISON LOL. SHE ASKED ME IF I HAD KILLED SOMEONE SO I SAID NO GRANDMA. SHE TOLD ME I DID NOT MATTER BECAUSE

(7)

I AM HER SPECIAL BABY BOY AND IM A GOOD BOY. THAT GRANDMA LOVES ME SO MUCH AND THAT I'M HER LITTLE ANGEL ♡. SHE PROBABLY FORGOT ALREADY LOL. MY G-MA IS SUCH A SWEETHEART. SHE WAS MY ROCK GROWING UP AND I WAS ALWAYS HER BABY BOY. I LOVE HER AND MISS HER. I REALLY HOPE SHE IS STILL ALIVE WHEN I AM FREE. SHE IS SUCH A PERFECT LADY/HUMAN BEING. SHE ALWAYS USED TO MAKE SAUSAGE ROLLS FOR ME BECAUSE SHE KNEW HOW MUCH I LOVED THE ONES SHE MADE. HER BAKED BREAD WAS SO DELICIOUS AND ITS A LEGACY. ALL MY SISTERS KNOW HOW TO BAKE IT PERFECTLY. I LOOK FORWARD TO TALKING W/ YOU TONIGHT ☺. RIGHT NOW IM THINKING OF WATCHING MOVIES SITTING ON A COUCH IN SWEATPANTS AND A HOODIE. IT HAS BEEN TOO TOO LONG. IN HERE ITS BLUE JEANS AND A BLUE T-SHIRT. ITS SO DRY THAT IF I DONT MOISTURIZE I GET REALLY ITCHY. IM NOT USED TO MOISTURIZING SO USUALLY BY THE TIME I REM- -EMBER TO I AM STARTING TO ITCH. EVERYTHING HERE DRIES A PERSON OUT. THE AIR, CLOTHES, SOAP, BLANKETS ETC. ALL ADD TO THE DRYNESS. AH WELL ONLY A DAY OR TWO AWAY NOW. WE GOT 2 NEW DUDES TODAY AND NOW OUR UNIT IS 100% FULL CAPACITY. THIS WEEKEND FLEW RIGHT ON BY. TOMORROW IS A NEW DAY. IS THERE ANYTHING YOU'D LIKE TO KNOW ABOUT ME? IF SO JUST ASK, I AM AN OPEN BOOK. ⟹ ALL DONE WORK. IT WAS SWEEEET. GOT GIVEN COFFEE, POPCORN, AND GRANOLA BARS FROM DIF. PEOPLE IN DIFFERENT UNITS. I FEEL VERY BLESSED. I WAS ASKED ABOUT GETTING SOMEONE A.A. LITERATURE WHICH ME FEEL ON THE RIGHT PATH AND DOING WHAT I SET OUT TO DO. I DID A DRAWING FOR MY FRIEND AND

(8)

HE WALKED AROUND HIS UNIT SHOWING EVERYONE. WE HAD ANOTHER BANANA CAKE W/ HOT CHOCOLATE DRIZZLE FOR AN EVENING SNACK. THIS UNIT IS A REALLY AMAZING PLACE. LOTS OF LOVE & BROMANCE HAPPENING. UNIT BRAVO IS VERY BROMANTIC LOL AFTER WORK I HAD A SHOWER AND DID A SHOULDER WORKOUT IN MY ROOM. NOW IM SITTING AT MY DESK LOOKING AT PHOTOS OF DAVIS BAY AND WATCHING SHARK TANK WRITING YOU THEN GOING TO DRAW FOR A LITTLE BIT. IM SO GLAD TO HAVE THE SERENITY PRAYER AND 12 STEPS ON MY WALL. I WISH I HAD MORE SO I COULD HAND THEM OUT. I DRANK SOME COFFEE AT 10PM AND GOING TO STAY UP LATE AND ENJOY MYSELF AND THE TIME I HAVE LEFT. AS GLAD AS I AM TO MOVE FORWARD I MUST SAY A PART OF ME WILL MISS RRAC. IT WILL BE A PART OF MY STORY FOREVER. I HOPE YOU HAD AN EPIC EVENING ANGEL. GOODNIGHT. ♡ ZZZZZZZZZZZ

2022-01-31

ANOTHER GREAT MORNING LOVELY ANGEL ☺ I HAD AN AWESOME SLEEP. WOKE UP AT 6AM HAPPY & GRATEFUL ONCE AGAIN. IS TODAY MY DAY? WHO KNOWS. I KEEP TELLING THE GUYS IT SURE IS. THEY SAY NOPE AND I KEEP TELLING THEM ONE OF THESE ILL BE ABLE TO SAY I TOLD YOU SO LOL I MAY BE WRONG 14 TIMES BUT THE DAY I LEAVE I WILL HAVE BEEN RIGHT. I DIDNT GET TO CHAT W/ YOU LAST NIGHT AND I HOPE YOUR NIGHT WAS GREAT. I WONDER HOW LONG YOU PLAYED VIDS FOR THIS WEEKEND. I HOPE THE WHOLE WEEKEND W/ ZERO GUILT ☺ IM HAVING A P.B & COOKIES N CREAM PROTEIN SHAKE FOR BREAKFAST. I SLACKED ON THE DIET A TINY BIT THIS WEEKEND SO ILL BE STRICT ON IT THIS WEEKEND. THE GOAL IS TO GET TO 200-215PDS AND LOOK LIKE A PIT BULL LIKE I USE TO BEFORE I HAD KIDS.

9

AND LIKE ONE TOO. A BIG SWEETHEART WHO WILL PRO-
-TECT HIS LOVED ONES AND LOVE TO SNUGGLE, EAT FOOD,
AND BE W/ HIS PERSON, AND HANDSOME OF COURSE.
⇒ I PAID MY ICBC FINE TODAY AND NOW HAVE MY
~~LICENCE AGAIN~~ LICENSE AGAIN. IM HAPPY. I WILL LEAVE
PRISON W/ MONEY IN THE BANK, CHILD SUPPORTS PAID
FOR A YEAR, NO DEBT, NO MONTHLY PAYMENTS, A
DRIVERS LICENSE, AND GREAT CREDIT. THAT'LL MAKE
FOR A GREAT START AND IM SOBER W AN AMAZING
SUPPORT NETWORK AND FRIENDS. HAPPY HAPPY JOY JOY
ITS THE FIRST OF FEBRUARY TOMORROW. THATSCRAZ-
-INESS. HALF WAY TO A DAY PAROLE HEARING. I FOUND
THE PERFECT BOX TO TRANSPORT MY ORIGAMI IN SO
IT DOESNT GET DAMAGED. YOULL LAUGH WHEN YOU SEE
THEM. SOME OF THE CRAZIEST MULTI-PAPER ORIGAMI IVE
EVER SEEN. ITS SLOW ON THE UNIT TODAY. MY 3 MAIN
HOMIES ARE WORKING IN THE KITCHEN TODAY SO ITS A
TAD BORING. I JUST CAME TO MY ROOM AND AM WAT-
-CHING PEARL HARBOR AND STARTED WRITING YOU. LAST
BREAK I DREW FOR TWO HOURS. I THINK ILL TAKE A NAP
FROM 4-530 TODAY. ⇒ YEP WAS OUT COLD. THAT WAS
A NICE NAP. OUT FOR AN HOUR AND A HALF ALMOST
EXACTLY. IVE BEEN COLORING MY OWL PICTURE AND GET-
-TING MORE DRAWINGS TO COLOR THIS EVENING AT WORK.
IM ALSO GETTING MORE PAPER. IM EXCITED. NEVER IN A
MILLION YEARS DID I IMAGINE BEING EXTATIC OVER LINED
PAPER AND CHILDRENS COLORING BOOK OF NATIVE & SPIRI
-TUAL ART. ⇒ DONE WORK. THE C.O. TOLD ME HE THINKS
THIS IS ONE OF THE BEST GROUPS RRAC HAS SEEN. MY
BUDDY AND BOTH THOUGHT THEY SPLIT THE 3 OF US UP
TO HAVE ORDER AMONG THE INMATES AND UNITS.

(10)

IM NOT SURE IF THATS TRUE BUT IF IT IS, IT 100% IS WORKING. THERE ARE ZERO BEEFS IN HERE AND EVERYONE IS GETTING ALONG. RRAC IS TO SAY THE LEAST A FAIRLY CALM PLACE. WORK WAS GOOD. I GOT TO CHAT W/ THE OTHER CLEANERS AND MY BUDDIES WHICH WAS NICE. TONIGHT IM GOING TO DO A QUICK WORKOUT THEN LAY IN BED. FIRST IM GOING TO SMASH DOWN 2 CUPS OF COFFEE LOL. IM SO HAPPY ABOUT MY TRAD- -ITIONAL NURSE TATTOO HAVING A SEXY 28 ON HER SHOULDER. IM STOKED YOU THOUGHT IT WAS AWESOME TOO BECAUSE IM THRILLED ABOUT IT. I HEARD FROM SOMEONE WHO WAS JUST RELEASE FROM MISSION MIN AND TOLD MY BUDDY THAT IT IS ABSOLUTELY PHENOMENAL THERE. THEY SAID I MAY NOT WANT TO LEAVE ONCE IM THERE. I AM CONTENT IN LIFE ATM. THIS PROCESS HAS HELPED KNOW WHO I AM AND EXACTLY WHAT I WANT IN LIFE. I WISH I COULDVE DONE THIS WHEN I WAS YOUNGER W/ THE EXEPTION OF COMMITING A TERRIBLE ACT TO GET HERE. ITS ALL APART OF MY STORY AND I ASPIRE TO INSPIRE OTHERS TO MAKE BETTER CHOICES. GOODNIGHT SWEET GIRL.. ZZZZZZZZZZZZZZZZ 28

2022-02-01

ITS AFTERNOON ALREADY. THIS AM WAS A BIT HECTIC. I HAD THE OPTION TO MOVE TO CORD UNIT TODAY BUT DECLINED. I ENJOY BRAVO UNIT TOO MUCH AND THERES TOO MUCH EGO OUT THERE. I DONT WANT TO SIT AROUND AND HEAR HOW COOL EVERYONE IS LOL. IF WE WERE "COOL" WE WOULDNT BE IN HERE. I SLEPT GOOD LAST NIGHT AND STAYED IN BED UNTIL GAR- -BAGE TIME THIS MORN. ITS A FAIRLY NICE DAY TODAY. THE WEATHER CHANNEL CALLS FOR SNOW TOMORROW. I HOPE

(11)

IT DOES SNOW A LOT. DOES NOT SEEM PROMISING ABOUT MY MOVE THIS WEEK. DAMN COVID. FINGERS STILL CROSSED THOUGH. I GOT A TIDE POD FOR TODAYS LAUNDRY :). IT NICE WHEN CLOTHING SMELLS NICE IN HERE. ITS ALL THE THE LITTLE THINGS IN HERE THAT NORMALIZE A PERSON. WHAT ARE UP TO? YOUR DRIVE YESTERDAY SOUNDED AMAZING. I COULD USE A NICE DRIVE SOUNDS CALMING ⇒ I HAVE BEEN MOVED GROUND LEVEL CHARLIE UNIT NEXT DOOR TO MY GOOD BUDDY. AT FIRST I DIDN'T WANT TO MOVE BUT NOW THAT IM MOVED IM REFRESHED AND HAPPY. SOME NEW SCENERY AND THE YARD IS OPEN FULL TIME WHEN WE ARE OUT OF OUR CELLS. ITS THE T.D. UNITS (TEMPORARY DETENTION). MY NEW CELL IS NICE BESIDES THE RACISM ON THE WALLS. I FIND SOME RACIST JOKES FUNNY BUT RACISM NOT FUNNY. I WILL WASH MOST OF IT OFF TONIGHT. THE CARVED STUFF I HAVE COVERED W/ SCENIC PRINTOUTS MY BUDDY HAD. YOU ARE ONCE AGAIN RIGHT NEXT TO WHERE I SIT AT THE DESK. SO PRETTY. I LOVE LOOKING AT YOU ANGEL. DONT BE OFFENDED (LOL) IF I LOOK AT YOU FOR A MINUTE WHEN I FINALLY GET OUT OF HERE AND SEE YOU. IM IN MY CELL UNTIL 5:30 NOW. ⇒ HELLO :) TONIGHT WAS A GOOD NIGHT. THE NEW UNIT IS MORE CHILL THAN I EXPECTED I ENJOYED EVENING 1 IN CHARLIE UNIT MORE THAN I THOUGHT I WOULD. AT WORK I GOT TO TALK TO THE DUDES I LIKED BEST IN BRAVO W/OUT THE OTHER RIFF RAFF. I WAS SAD TO HEAR YOUR VOICE IN PAIN. I WOULD'VE TAKEN THAT HEADACHE FROM YOU IF I COULD. I SINCERELY HOPE IT PASSED ENOUGH FOR YOU TO REST AND SLEEP WELL. TONIGHT ILL DRAW & WRITE & WATCH TV UNTIL IM TIRED THEN GO TO BED. GOODNIGHT ♡:) ZZZZZZZZZ Z Z Z Z Z Z Z Z Z.

(12)

2022-01-02

GOOOOOOOD MORNING SUNSHINE. I HOPE YOUR HEADACHE IS GONE THIS MORNING. IM SURE THAT WAS NOT FUN. TODAY IS A NEW DAY. APPARENTLY MISSION IS FULL ATM SO I HAVE TO WAIT FOR AN OPENING UNFORTUNATELY. MY FIRST NIGHT ON THE NEW UNIT WAS DECENT AND MY NEW CELL IS ALL ORGANIZED AND SET UP NICE. I ENJOYED THE DAY IN HERE YESTERDAY MEETING SOME NEW DUDES. IM MISSING YOU AND MY KIDS A LOT RIGHT NOW. ALSO MISS THE ROOMS AND THE NOONER REGULARS. I ALWAYS ENJOYED SHOWING UP EARLY AND WATCHING PEOPLE SHOW UP. I GOT TOLD TODAY FOR THE SECOND TIME BY A DIFFERENT PER--SON THAT BRAVO ISNT THE SAME W/OUT ME. HOW NICE LOL. ONE OF THE C.O.S (A STRICT ONE) MADE A POINT TO SAY HI TO ME THIS MORN AND EVEN CALLED ME BY MY NAME WHICH WAS A FIRST. ⟹ I AM WIRED FOR SOUND RIGHT NOW FROM A SUPER STRONG COFFEE. I GOT GIVEN A BLUE ROSARY TODAY WHICH WAS SUPER NICE. IM EXCITED TO CALL YOU TONIGHT AGAIN. TODAY IS HALF OVER AND WENT BY QUICKLY. ITS MY BABY SISTER COURTNEYS BIRTHDAY TODAY. SHE TURNED 31. I MISS HER. ⟹ ITS THE END OF THE DAY NOW AND IM SHOWERED AND DONE WORK. TODAY WENT FAST AND WAS A GOOD DAY. I MISSED TALKING TO YOU AGAIN TONIGHT. I DID GET A CONFIRMATION ABOUT A VIDEO CALL W/ YOU ON SUNDAY @ 12:30. I AM SO EXCITED. FOR THAT REASON ALONE I HOPE I STAY IN RRAC FOR ANOTHER WEEK SO I CAN SEE YOU ANGEL. TONIGHT IM GOING TO HAVE A CAN OF COCA COLA AND DO A QUICK WORKOUT BEFORE BED. I WAS ALSO GIVEN A ROSARY BY A FRIEND WHICH ILL WEAR AND CHERISH. IT WAS THE ONE HE WORE EVERYDAY IN RRAC. IM HONORED. GOODNIGHT ANGEL OZZZZZZZ Z Z Z Z Z Z Z Z Z

(13)

2022-02-03

WELL HELLO BROOOOO. MY GOOD FRIEND COOPER IS LEAVING HERE TODAY. WHAT A GOOD MAN. I REALLY ENJOYED MY TIME W/ HIM. HE GAVE ME HIS ROSARY AND DREW HIM TONS ART FOR HIS ROOM. HE IS THE BEST/CLEANEST CLEANER IN THIS PLACE. HE READ THE LITERATURE I GAVE HIM AND WE WOULD TALK ABOUT SOBER LIVING. HE WAS A HEROIN ADDICT AND I REALLY HOPE HE STAYS SOBER. MY PRAYERS WILL BE W/ HIM. THIS MORNING I ATE PEACH YOGURT FOR BREAKFAST. YESTERDAY I WAS GIVEN 2 CROSSWORD PUZZLES AND COMPLETED THEM IN RECORD TIME EVEN I WAS SHOCKED. OH MAN ⇒ THEY HAD HIM ALL PACKED, ROOM CLEAN, AND READY TO GO AND CALLED IT OFF. DUDE IS NOT HA-PPY. I GAVE HIM A BILL SEES IT TO CALM HIM DOWN TODAY. BESIDES THAT THINGS ARE GOOD TODAY. IVE BEEN IN RRAC JUST OVER 2 MONTHS NOW AND 3 MONTHS INCARCERATED. I MISS YOU DUDE ♡. WHAT'RE YOU UP TO FOR VALENTINES DAY TOMORROW ANGEL? IM NOT DOIN MUCH LOL. THIS UNIT IS A LOT MORE SITTING AROUND AND DOING NOTHING. I THINK I LIKED THE OTHER UNIT BETTER. WAY LESS EGO AND MORE OF A GROUP OF POSITIVE VIBE IN-STEAD OF CLIQUES. I LIKED BEING ON MY OWN AS WELL. ON BRAVO WE WOULD PLAY CHESS, WORKOUT, COOK, LAUGH, JUST GENERALLY HAPPY. ON CHARLIE THERE MORE BUGS AND HATERS. I AM STILL GRATEFUL FOR THE LIFE EXP-ERIENCES. ITS SPAGHETTI FOR DINNER AND I'M GETTING DOUBLE TONIGHT. IM TRADING MY FRUIT & VEGGIES FOR IT. IM STOKED. SPAG IS MY FAV. TOMORROW FOR LUNCH IS HAMBURGERS. ☺ ⇒ IT WAS GREAT TO HEAR YOUR VOICE TONIGHT. THANKS FOR ANSWERING ALTHOUGH YOU HAVE A HEADACHE. I TRIED TO SPEAK SOFT AND GENTLE FOR YOU. YOU SOUNDED SO SWEET. I TRULY DO LOVE YOU DUDE.

(14)

I AM SO GRATEFUL THAT YOU ARE IN MY LIFE. EVEN WHEN TIMES ARE TOUGH IN HERE WHEN I THINK ABOUT YOU IT MAKES ME SUPER HAPPY. I ADDED MORE WATER BOTTLES TO MY MAKESHIFT DUMBELL AND ADDED APPROX 5pds.. IM MOVING UP IN THE WORLD LOL. I AM SO EXCITED FOR OUR CALL ON SUNDAY. FOR ME ITS LIKE A VACATION TO SEE SUCH A BEAUTIFUL FACE LIKE YOURS. IM GOING TO DRESS IN MY NICEST CLOTHES (ALL MY CLOTHES ARE THE SAME LOL). JUST GOT MY HAIR DID SO ILL LOOK LIKE IM IN PRISON ☺. MY 28 IS PRETTY MUCH ALL HEALED UP ON MY NURSES SHOULDER ATM ITS MY FAVORITE TATTOO. ITS A FUNNY STORY AS WELL. ~~[illegible]~~ I KNOW WE HAVENT KNOWN EACHOTHER FOR THAT LONG BUT I THINK YOU ARE MY FAVORITE PERSON IN THE WORLD. YOU ARE SUCH A BLESSING AND ILL NEVER TAKE YOU FORGRANTED. YOU HAVE BEEN MY ROCK WHILE IVE BEEN AWAY AND SOMETIMES I WONDER WHY YOU HAVE BEEN SO GOOD TO ME ANGEL ♡ IM GOING TO WORKOUT THEN GO TO BED. GOODNIGHT. YOU ARE SUCH A SWEETHEART. I MISS YOU LOTS

Z Z Z Z Z Z Z Z Z Z

2022-02-04

GOOD MORNING SWEET GIRL. BUSY MORNING THIS A.M. I WAS ASKED ABOUT TRAINING THE NEXT GUY FOR MY JOB AND I KNEW EXACTLY WHO IT SHOULD BE. A 5'2" GUY NAMED DENT WHO LOOKS LIKE WE COULD BE RELATED (LIKE AN UNCLE OR OLD COUSIN). THAT MEANS I MOST LIKELY AM BOOKED TO LEAVE MON, TUES, OR WED. ☺ ♡♡ IM VERY VERY VERY HAPPY (HENSE THE 3 VERYS LOL) I THOUGHT ABOUT YOU MORE THAN USUAL LAST NIGHT BECAUSE I KNEW YOU WERE IN PAIN AND WISH I COULDVE HELPED GET/FEEL BETTER OR BRING FOOD/COOK FOR YOU SO YOU COULD JUST REST. ILL BE ALLOWED VIDEOS OFTEN IN MINIMUM SO →

(15)

HOPEFULLY WE CAN SEE ONE ANOTHER MORE OFTEN. ONLY IF YOU'D LIKE TO THOUGH. I SURE WOULD (OBVIOUSLY) YOU ARE SO DOPE DUDE. I TRADED AN ERASER TO HAVE THIS ENVELOPE MADE FOR YOU. (☺) THE DIAMOND IS BECAUSE TO ME YOU HAVE BEEN SUCH A PRECIOUS GEM AND THE WINGS ARE TO SHOW THAT ANGEL IS AN ABS- -OLUTE ANGEL. XOXO ⇒ THE GEESE OUTSIDE MUST BE HORNY LOL. THEY ARE NONSTOP HONKING AT EACHOTHER AND CHASING BACK AND FORTH SUPER AGGRESIVELY. I KNOW EXACTLY HOW THEY FEEL SOMETIMES LOL HAHAHAHAHA H O N K HONK HAHAHAHA (I HOPE YOU THO- -UGHT THAT WAS HUMOROUS AT LEAST A LITTLE BIT) HONK ITS HAS BEEN A MINUTE. YIKES. I WAS ASSURED THAT THIS IS MY LAST WEEKEND HERE. ILL BELIEVE WHEN IT HAPPEN AND JUST BE HAPPY TO WAKE UP SOBER EVERY SINGLE DAY. ⇒ I JUST SIGNED PAPERWORK SO I CAN GET THE PAPERWORK FROM WHEN I GRADUATED HIGH- -SCHOOL. THAT'LL BE NEAT TO HAVE. JUST ANOTHER STEP CLOSER. ⇒ WELL THAT WAS FUN. ⇒ THEY MOVED US ALL TO ALPHA UNIT FOR A BIT IN FREEZING COLD EMPTY CELLS AFTER THEY LINED US UP AND LET THE DOG SNIFF US ALL FRONT TO BACK (SHWAER SHEXSHAY LOL) THEN PROCEEDED TO TOSS OUR CELLS. NOT ALL THAT FUN PERSAY BUT KIND OF A FUNNY EXPERIENCE. NOW WE ARE BACK IN OUR CELLS UNTIL 5:30PM DINNER TIME. INTERESTING FRIDAY AND START TO THE WEEK- END. LUCKY IM A MINIMALIST AND DONT KEEP JUNK IN MY CELL. ITS ORGANIZED REALLY WELL. THEY WENT THROUGH MY PROTEIN POWDER IN SEARCH OF COOKIES N CREAMCAIN LOL HAHAHAHAHA. OVERALL IT WAS LAUGHWORTHY. 2 MORE DAYS UNTIL OUR VIDEO CHAT. I AM SO EXCITED TO SEE YOU. IM GLAD THAT DURING OUR CELL TOSS THEY DIDNT

(16)

TAKE MY WEIGHT BAG. HOPEFULLY THERES SOME DECENT SHOWS/MOVIES ON AFTER 10PM TONIGHT. MAYBE THAT ONE MOVIE (:-) ITS BEEN AWHILE HAHA HAHAHA TOO MUCH INFO I KNOW LOL. ITS TRUE THOUGH. THIS PLACE SURE DOES HAVE A WAY OF TURNING A DUDE OFF. MAYBE THE BLEEK CONCRETE INTERIOR, OR THE SINGLE COLOR DÉCOR, POSSIBLY UMMM YA KNOW... THE FACT THAT ITS ALL MEN IN HERE.. WELL EXEPT THAT ON "HER/SHE" BUT "SHE'S" GONE AND NOT MY TYPE... JUST A LITTLE TOO MUCH PENIS ON HER. NOT THE FEEL/LOOK IM INTO (I REALLY HOPE YOU ARE LAUGHING BECAUSE IT IS BOTH FUNNY AND 100% TRUE) ⇒ BACK IN MY HOUSE UNTIL 7:20 EXCHANGE. THE GIRLS WROTE ME LETTERS AND THEIR MOM SENT PHOTOS OF THEM AWHILE AGO. I REALLY HOPE I GET THEM TONIGHT. IM MISSING ALL MY KIDS RIGHT NOW. IM SUPER GLAD I DO HAVE ONE PHOTO IN HERE OF SOMEONE AND ESPECIALLY GLAD ITS YOU. DEFINATELY NEED MORE (HINT HINT LOL) (KNUDGE KNUDGE). WE HAD HAM & POTATOES FOR DINNER. I ATE THE HAM ONLY (X2). IT WAS PRETTY DECENT FOR PRISON MEAT. MY MIND KEEPS JUMPING TO JUST ONE MORE DAY AND ITS SUNDAY AND I GET TO SEE YOUR FACE. I LOOK UP ABOVE WHERE I AM WRITING THIS VERY SECOND AND THERE YOU ARE SMILING AND ADORABLE. MAKES ME SMILE EVERY TIME. ITS HARD TO DESCRIBE WHY BUT FOR SOME REASON WHEN I LOOK AT YOU IM FILLED W/ JOY. ⇒ BED TIME FOR ME. I HOPE YOU DID NOT SUFFER YET ANOTHER MIGRAINE TONIGHT. SLEEP WELL ZZZZ

2022-02-05

MAN O MAN ANGEL TODAY WAS QUITE THE DAY. ITS 10PM AND I JUST SAT DOWN TO WRITE TO YOU →

(7)

MOST IMPORTANT THINGS FIRST. I WAS UPSET TO HEAR THAT YOU ARE STILL SUFFERING. I DO WISH THERE WAS SOMETHING I COULD DO TO HELP YOU. IM NOT SURE IF IM BEING OVERBEARING WHEN I TELL YOU THAT I WOULD TAKE CARE OF YOU OR GET YOU WHAT YOU NEEDED IF I WAS NOT AWAY. ITS JUST WHO I AM AND HOW I FEEL A FRIEND SHOULD TREAT A FRIEND. YOU SAID YOU WERE IN THE BATH. I CANNOT WAIT TO SOAK IN A BATH WHEN I AM OUT. I JOKED ABOUT TELLING ME LOL HOPEFULLY I DIDNT COME ACROSS CREEPY AND YOU LAUGHED. NORMALLY I COULD CRACK THOSE KINDS OF JOKES W/ ANYONE BUT FOR SOME REASON W/ YOU ITS DIFFERENT. I HONESTLY THINK ITS BECAUSE HOW MUCH RESPECT I HAVE FOR YOU AND YOU INTIMIDATE ME A BIT (WHICH IM NOT AT ALL USED TO). TODAY I GOT AGGRESIVELY SEARCHED BY A DOG SNIFFING ME AND MY CELL & WORK CLOSET THOROUGHLY RIPPED APART. HONESTLY I WAS ONLY UPSET WHEN A C.O. WAS EXTREMELY RUDE AND CONDESCENDING TOWARDS ME WHEN I KNEW I HAD DONE ABSOLUTELY ZERO WRONG. ALL IN ALL ITLL BE A FUNNY STORY LATER IN LIFE. TALKING TO YOU ALWAYS CHEERS ME UP AND IF I DONT NEED CHEERING IT MAKES MY HEART VERY FULL AND HAPPY. IN HERE I FIND A LOT OF TIMES I COUNT EVERY MINUTE. 14HRS 18MINS TIL WE HANGOUT ON CCTV FACETIME. IM SUPER HAPPY ABOUT AND A LITTLE NERVOUS (BUTTERFLIES) FOR SOME REASON. ALMOST LIKE WE ARE MEETING FOR THE VERY FIRST TIME ALTHOUGH ITS NOT THE CASE. TODAYS EVENTS AND WHAT OCCURED SPREAD LIKE WILDFIRE THROUGH THIS PLACE. IF I WAS LOOKING

(18)

FOR RESPECT TO BOOST MY EGO I GUESS I WOULD BE HAPPY ABOUT IT ALL. FORTUANATELY I AM MORE MATURE THEN NEEDING HAPPENINGS LIKE THAT TO FEEL "COOL" NOR DO I WANT RESPECT GIVEN TO ME FOR THOSE KINDS OF ACTIVITIES AND LIFESTYLE CHOICES. I DONT NEED TO LOOK "TOUGH" OR BE SEEN AS A "BOSS" TYPE. I WANT RESPECT FOR THE RIGHT REASONS ANGEL HONESTY, DETERMINATION, LOVE, PERSERVERANCE, MORALS, VALUES, LOYALTY, BEING A LOVING COMPASSIONAT FATHER, FRIEND, PARTNER, OR JUST BEING A GOOD EXAMPLE TO THOSE who WANT POSITIVE CHANGE. I TOOK YOUR PHOTO OFF OF THE STAND I HAD MADE (AN UPSIDE DOWN COFFEE CUP) AND TAPED IT INSIDE YOUR CARD. ITS IN THE CENTER OF MY SHELF RIGHT ABOVE MY DESK. MAKES ME FEEL MORE AT HOME IN HERE. GOODNIGHT SWEET GIRL AND I SENDING LOVE AND HOPE THAT HEADACHE PASSES ♡

Z Z Z Z Z Z

2022-02-06

IT WAS SO GREAT TO SEE YOU. I FEEL BAD FOR CRACKING AGE JOKES AND HOPEFULLY YOU KNEW I WAS KIDDING. YOU ARE SO STUNNING AND LOOKED SO ADORABLE I WAS BESIDE MYSELF THAT SOME--ONE AS WONDERFUL AS YOU TAKES THE TIME TO TALK TO ME MOST NIGHTS, SEND ME BEAUTIFUL PHOTOS, AND FILL OUT DOCUMENTS TO BE ABLE TO VIDEO CHAT W/ ME. I 100% ADORE YOU ANGEL. I WAS IN AWE OF HOW BEAUTIFUL YOU ARE AND THINK YOU ARE SO DOPE DUDE. HOPEFULLY I LOOKED OK. I HAD TRIMMED MY FACE AND RE-CUT MY HAIR A FEW DAYS AGO FOR YOUR CALL LOL. I EVEN WORE MY BEST CLOTHES FOR YOU ☺ LOL.

(19)

MAYBE ITS BECAUSE I AM IN HERE AND HAVENT SEEN YOU FOR MONTHS BUT EVEN NOW AT 10:30 PM I STILL FEEL A BIT STARSTRUCK LIKE, WHICH IS A NEW FEELING FOR ME. I AM OVERLY GRATEFUL YOU TOOK THE CALL WHILE HAVE HAD BEEN IN PAIN FOR OVER A WEEK NOW. IM DROPPING THIS LETTER IN THE MAIL TOMORROW AM BECAUSE IF I GET MOVED I DO NOT WANT IT TO GET LOST IN TRASITION. I DO WISH I COULD HAVE SCREENSHOTED YOU TODAY AS I WILL ALWAYS CHERISH AND REMEMBER THAT MOMENT. TBH YOU HAVE BEEN THE BEST MOST AMAZING FRIEND TO ME ANGEL. IM HOPING TONIGHT IS MY LAST <u>NIGHT HERE</u>. WHO KNOWS. I TALKED TO SOMEONE WHO HAS BEEN TO MISSION MIN TODAY AND HE SAID I AM GOING TO BE SO HAPPY THERE. HE SAID TIME FLIES AND IT DOESNT EVEN FEEL LIKE PRISON. TONIGHT I FEEL LIKE MY LIFE IS SURREAL AND WHEN I REFLECT BACK ON THE TIME IVE BEEN ALIVE IT ALL WENT BY SO FAST. IVE LIVED A "MOVIE-LIKE" LIFE IN EVERY GENRE. WHATS NEXT? I AM GOING TO BUY ANOTHER HOUSE IN THE NEXT 5 YEARS AND WANT TO BE MARRIED ONE DAY. FINANCIAL SUCCESS HAS NEVER BEEN DIFICULT FOR ME SO I WILL FOCUS ON MY NEW VIEWS OF TRUE HAPPINESS AND LOVE WHICH TO ME IS what SUCCESS is. I AM GOING TO SLOW RIGHT DOWN AND ENJOY THE STUFF THAT THE WORLD TRIES TO DISTRACT US FROM.

20

I LOVE YOU DUDE!!

MORE THAN YOU KNOW
COULD EVER

[redacted] → [redacted]

3

Promises Made

"Love means showing up, even from in here."

I made a lot of promises in my life. Some I kept, most I didn't. But the ones I wrote from that cell came from a different place. Not from pride or guilt, but from wanting to do right by the people who still believed in me. I wasn't writing to fix the past anymore. I was writing to build the man I wanted to be when I got out.

She made me feel alive again, not in the loud, movie kind of way, but in the quiet way that reminds you you're still worth something. I told her I'd be better. I'd stay honest. I'd carry myself like the man she saw when she looked at me, even if I wasn't him yet. When I did my workouts, when I walked the yard, when I turned down old habits that used to control me, I felt closer to that promise. Every small act became proof that I meant it.

I also thought about my girls every time I sat down to write. They didn't ask for this story, but they were in every line of it. I wanted them to know their dad fought to become better inside those walls. Their mom held it down on the outside, and I'll always be thankful for that. She gave them stability when I couldn't.

Those pages stopped being love letters a long time ago. They became blueprints. Every word was a step toward something real, something solid, something I could build with my own hands when I finally walked free.

HELLO ANGEL 2022-02-08

TODAY WAS MY FIRST FULL DAY AT MISSION MIN. I AM IN QUARANTEEN W/ ~~ONE~~ OTHER DUDE FROM RRAC. ITS AN 8 BEDROOM HOUSE W/ A FULL LIVING ROOM & KITCHEN. THERE ARE 2 BATHROOM AND 2 SEPERATE SHOWER ROOMS. THE FOOD HERE IS AWESOME. SPAG FOR DINNER LAST NIGHT. EGGS & SAUSAGES FOR BREAKFAST TODAY. CHICKEN BURGERS W LETTUCE, TOMATO, PICKLES, SAUTEED ONIONS FOR DINNER TODAY. WE ARE NOT ALLOWED OUTSIDE UNTIL THE 18TH BUT ITS LIKE A GATED RETIREMENT COMMUNITY AROUND HERE. ITS DEF. A STEP FORWARD BUT I STILL MISS MY NORMAL LIFE, KIDS, YOU, A.A/N.A ETC. I HAVE 2 MILK JUGS W/ SAND IN THEM TO WORK OUT W/ AND STEPPED OUT THE BACKDOOR TODAY AND FOUND GREEN ONIONS GROWING IN AN OLD UNKEPT GARDEN BED. I DUG THEM UP AND AM GROWING THEM ON THE WINDOW SILL LIKE I ALWAYS DID AT HOME. THE SHOWER HERE IS AMAZING AND I HAVE HAD 4 ALREADY TODAY AND PROBS 1 BEFORE BED. I HAVE YOUR PHOTO IN MY ROOM WHERE I CAN SEE IT WHEN I WRITE AND GO TO BED. ITS NICE HAVING DRYWALL INSTEAD OF ICE COLD CINDER BLOCKS. THERES NO FENCES OR BARBED WIRE HERE EITHER. VIDEO CALLS WILL BE MORE REGULAR AS WELL. ATM I CAN ONLY HAVE 1 CALL FOR 30 MINS A DAY, IT KINDA SUCKS BUT ITS ONLY UNTIL THE 18TH. ITS REALLY QUIET HERE. I HOPE YOUR HEADACHE IS GONE (DAMN ZELDA). THE BED IS VERY COMFORTABLE HERE AND THE SPACE IS WELL HEATED. I HAD AN AWESOME SLEEP LAST NIGHT AND A 3 HOUR NAP TODAY. ITS WEIRD MAKING MY OWN SCHEDULE. I LIKE IT :) I CANT TO GET OUTSIDE AND WALKS THE DUCKPOND AND GO TO THE GYM. I GET TO WEAR NORMAL CLOTHING IN HERE

②

AS WELL WHICH WILL BE NICE. MOSTL LOOKING FORWARD TO NOT HAVING TO WEAR TIGHTY WHITEYS ALTHOUGH I MUST SAY I LOOK FANTASTIC AND DAPPER IN THEM LOL. I HOPE I CAN TALK TO YOU SOON AS OUR NIGHTLY CHATS MAKE THE DAY AND ARE SOMETHING I LOOK FORWARD TO. IM STILL KICKING MYSELF FOR MAKING AGE JOKES WHICH SUCKS A BIT. I WAS A BIT NERVOUS ON OUR VIDEO CHAT TO BE COMPLETELY HONEST. IM NOT EXACTLY SURE WHY BUT FOR SOME REASON I WAS AND IM NOT USUALLY LIKE THAT. WELL GOODNIGHT Z Z Z Z Z

MORNING ☺ 2022-02-09

~~WE HAD~~ TODAY WE HAD THE USUAL SAUSAGE N EGGER W/ ONIONS & TOMATO. ITS WAS GOOD. QUARANTINE IS FAIRLY BORING SO FAR AND NOT BEING ABLE TO USE THE PHONE FOR MORE THAN ONE CALL A DAY KINDA SUX. MOST OF THE DAY IS JUST SITTING AROUND AS WE ARE NOT REALLY ALLOWED OUTSIDE EXEPT ONE HOUR A DAY ON THE BACK PATIO. WE PLAY SCRABBLE AND WATCH T.V.. I DO SOME WORKOUTS TO KEEP MY MUSCLES HARD UNTIL I CAN USE THE GYM AFTER THE 18TH. I MISS MY GIRLS ALOT. I HAVENT SEEN DAUGHTER IN A LONGTIME AND AM SURE SHE HAS GROWN A LOT AND IS SUPER CUTE. I SAW MY DAUGHTERS APPROX 3-4 WKS AGO ON VIDEO CALL AND THAT WAS ADORABLE AND SUPER EMOTIONAL. TODAY IS A BIT BLAH. WE HAD PEROGIES FOR LUNCH AND CHICKEN, RICE, AND CORN FOR DINNER. IM IN MY FINAL INSTITUTION AND ALTHOUGH IT IS NICE I JUST WANT TO BE HOME WHEREVER THAT MAY BE. I NEED A HUG SO INCREDIBLY BADLY RIGHT NOW. BEING IN PRISON AWAY FROM EVERYONE I CARE ABOUT IS A NIGHTMARE THAT I CANNOT WAIT TO WAKE UP FROM. WHAT A WAKE-UP CALL. I GUESS I NEEDED THIS TO

(3)

REALIZE WHAT WAS IMPORTANT IN MY LIFE. GOODNIGHT
Z Z Z Z Z

2022-02-10

GOOD MORNING SWEET GIRL. TODAY IS LIKE GROUND HOG DAY. IM FEELING A BIT IN DESPAIR AND THATS TO BE EXP-ECTED I GUESS. THIS TO SHALL PASS. IM EXCITED TO CALL YOU TONIGHT AND I HOPE YOU ANSWER. TIME IS GOING BY SLOW AND I STILL HOPE I DIDNT OFFEND YOU DURING OUR VIDEO CALL. PRISON HAS A WAY OF REMINDING YOU OF UNRESOLVED PERSONAL ISSUES AND IF SOMETHING IS ON YOUR MIND IT LINGERS AND IS HARD TO GET PAST W/ OUT COMMUNICATION. YOUR PHOTO IS THE ONLY FAMILIAR FACE I GET TO SEE IN HERE AND IM LUCKY TO HAVE YOU HERE W/ ME. THE PEOPLE I SEE WALKING THE COMMUNE ROAD LOOK WORN DOWN. I HOPE I DONT END UP LIKE THAT. I REALIZE NOW HOW MUCH I NEED PHYSICAL TOUCH AND WORDS OF AFFIRMATION WHICH THERE IS NONE OF IN HERE. TODAY I AM/FEEL VERY LONELY IN THE WORLD. I EXPECTED THIS A BIT AND IT CAN ONLY MAKE ME MORE INDEPENDANT AND STRONGER. I DO MISS BEING IN A RELA-TIONSHIP AS I ENJOY SPENDING TIME AND SHARING MYSELF W/ ANOTHER PERSON. I MISS GOING TO BED AND WAKING UP BESIDE SOMEONE SPECIAL AND HEARING HOW THAT PERSONS DAY WAS. I MISS WATCHING MOVIES AND CUDDLING AND ESPECIALLY MISS HOLDING HANDS, KISSING, AND HUGGING. I MISS HEARING I LOVE YOU FROM MY KIDS AND HEARING THEM LAUGH AND WANT TO GET MY ATTENTION. I AM SO PROUD OF THEM IT MAKES ME SAD TO BE AWAY FROM THEM ALL. EVEN THOUGH WE TALKED SUNDAY I DEFINATELY MISS HEARING YOUR VOICE. ITS SOFT AND COMFORTING AND I CAN ALWAYS TELL WHEN YOURE EXCITED OR UPSET. YOU ARE SO INCREDIBLY CUTE & STUNNINGLY BEATIFUL →

(4)

INSIDE AND OUT (EVEN ON A MESSY HAIR DAY ☺)
YOU ARE ATTRACTIVE IN EVERY WAY POSSIBLE AND
WHOEVER IS LUCKY ENOUGH TO GET A CHANCE TO BE
YOUR PERSON WILL BE AND SHOULD BE EXTREMELY
HAPPY & GRATEFUL TO BE THAT PERSON. (HOPEFULLY
ME TELLING YOU THAT YOU ARE ATTRACTIVE DOES NOT
OVER STEP OUR FRIENDSHIP AS I WOULDNT JEOPARDIZE
THAT FOR ANYTHING. I LOVE YOU DUDE. SUBTLE 2 8)
I AM WAY TOO DENSE TO KNOW WHAT/WHERE OUR LINE
IS DRAWN AND HOPE THIS FRIENDSHIP NEVER ENDS.
I FEEL I CAN BE VULNERABLE W/ YOU AND YOU WOULD
NEVER USE IT AGAINST ME WHICH IM OBVIOUSLY NOT
USE TO. I BELIEVE YOU WHEN YOU SAY YOU LOVE ME
AND THAT IM A GOOD PERSON (EVEN THOUGH I KNOW I AM)
WHICH HAS BEEN A STRUGGLE DUE TO EMOTIONAL/VER-
-BAL ABUSE FROM MY PAS . TOD IS A SELF REFLEC-
-TIVE DAY. I FEEL A BIT DOWN PROBABLY BECAUSE QU-
-ARANTINE TIME IS SLOW AND LONELY. IM IN HERE W/
THE DUDE WHO ARSONED THE MASONIC HALLS WHICH IS
LAUGHABLY IRONIC AND HAVE STORIES THAT CANT EVEN
BE MADE UP. HE IS ACTUALLY REALLY NICE AND WE
GET ALONG GREAT. I DO WISH I GOT TO SPEND MORE TIME
W/ YOU BEFORE COMING HERE BUT AM ALSO SUPER
APPRECIATIVE FOR HOW THINGS HAPPENED EITHER WAY.
I 100% ADORE YOU. EVERYTHING ABOUT YOU IS
BEAUTIFUL. NIGHT Z Z Z Z Z Z Z

2022-02-11

GOOD MORNING SUNSHINE. I HOPE YOU SLEPT WELL ANGEL.
I HAD AN AWESOME SLEEP. THIS NEW BED IS THE MOST COMFY
BED IVE HAD IN 3 MONTHS. IT IS WARM IN MY ROOM AND
I HAVE A HUGE WINDOW THAT LOOKS OUT ONTO A BIG GRASS &
TREED AREA. I WOKE UP THINKING ABOUT YOU, OPENED MY

(5)

MY EYES AND THERE YOU WERE ALL DRESSED IN YOUR JEAN DRESS LOOKING HOT ♡☺!! I CANT SEE WHERE YOU SAID YOU HAD NO BUM BUT I AM 10000000% SURE THAT IT IS AMAZING. I MIGHT EVEN BITE OFF MY OWN ARM JUST TO SEE IT ☺. WE MET W/ THE WARDEN TODAY. HE SEEMED ALRIGHT BUT ASSURED US TO NOT BREAK ANY RULES OR ELSE WE GET MOVED TO MEDIUM. UMMMM... NO THANKS. MY VIEW IS NICE, ABOVE THE TREES I CAN SEE MOUNTAINS W/ SNOW COVERED PEAKS, WHAT A DIFFERENCE TO RRAC. I WISH I COULD HUG YOU RIGHT NOW. THE WARDEN SAID VIDEO VISITS OCCUR OFTEN HERE AND IN THE NEAR FUTURE IN PERSON VISITS MAY BE AVAILABLE. SOON I WILL BE WEARING NORMAL CLOTHES AND SOME MORE COMFORTABLE SHOES AND UNDERWEAR. I COULD NEVER HAVE ENOUGH PHOTOS OF YOUR GORGEOUS FACE AND LOOK FORWARD TO MAKING YOU LAUGH AND SMILE IN PERSON. IM SO HAPPY WHEN YOU ARE ON MY MIND AND IN MY THOUGHTS ANGEL. YOUVE BEEN THE ONLY CONSTANT IN MY LIFE WHILE IM AWAY. HOW DID I BECOME SO LUCKY? WHY ARE YOU SO AMAZING TO ME? SOMETIMES I WONDER HOW I HAVE YOU ALWAYS HERE FOR ME. I WILL NEVER TAKE YOU FORGRANTED (3)(8) ← SUPER SUBTLE I KNOW

⟹ WELL ITS 1PM AND IM ROASTING CHICKEN TO MAKE CHICKEN SALAD SANDWICHES FOR LUNCH. WE WERE ALLOWED 45 MINS ON THE BACK LAWN SO WE SAT IN THE SUNSHINE AND ENJOYED THE FRESH MOUNTAIN AIR. IT WAS VERY NICE. WHEN IM OUT OF HERE I WILL ALWAYS MAKE SURE TO FIND THE TIME TO ENJOY NATURE, LOVED ONE, AND SIMPLICITY. LIFE IS COMPLICATED ENOUGH AND IN A WAY MADE TO DISTRACT US FROM ONE ANOTHER. COUNTING DAYS IS SO STRANGE LET ALONE COUNTING HOURS UNTIL BED THEN RESTART. I CAN SEE WHERE SOME PEOPLES MENTAL HEALTH COULD DETERIORATE SO QUICKLY IN PLACES LIKE THIS. IT CAN BE A STRUGGLE THATS FOR

(6)

SURE. I USED TO THINK HOPE WAS ONLY FOR DYING PEOPLE OR PEOPLE PLAYING THE LOTTERY OR SOMETHING BUT NOW IT HAS TAKEN ON NEW MEANINGS. KEEPING FAITH & HOPE IS SURE ALOT MORE PROMISING THAN HOPELESSNESS & DESPAIR. I TRULY HOPE FOR A POSITIVE FUTURE IN LIFE AND WILL KEEP FAITH THAT IF I WORK FOR IT IT WILL MATERIALIZE. YOU ANGEL HELP ME TREMENDOUSLY IN KEEPING MY MIND IN SUCH A PLACE. YOU HAVE KEPT ME FROM BEING LOST IN HERE MULTIPLE TIMES AND JUST KNOWING YOU HAS MADE ME A BETTER PERSON.

⟹ I JUST TRIED TO HAVE A NAP TO HELP PASS SOME TIME BUT COULDN'T FALL ASLEEP UNFORTUNATELY. I WAS JUST TOLD I COULD VERY WELL BE IN HERE TIL JULY MAYBE AUGUST. KIND OF DISHEARTENING, BUT I CANT BE TOO MAD OR UPSET AS I AM THE REASON WHY I AM IN HERE. MORE TIME TO GET IN SHAPE I GUESS. ILL BE SO GLAD WHEN THIS IS ALL DONE. HOPEFULLY YOU WILL STILL FIND TIME TO TALK W/ ME WHEN THE WEATHER IS NICE AND HOT. ILL BE SAD IF I CANT SEE YOU IN YOUR NEW BATHING SUIT THAT YOU BOUGHT. MY SUMMER BODY IS GOING TO BE ON POINT THIS YEAR TOO. ID BE REALLY HAPPY TO GO TO THE BEACH W/ YOU OR WALK TO CHAPMAN FALLS TO JUMP IN THE ICE WATER TOGETHER. MAYBE EVEN GO TO EAGLE RIVER FALLS IN POWELL RIVER FOR A DAY OR AN EVENING. THAT WOULD BE AMAZING. WHO KNOWS. YOU MIGHT HAVE A BF BY THEN AS WELL. SUCH IS LIFE. TIME REALLY DOES STOP IN HERE WHILE OTHERS SLOWLY DRIFT AWAY AS THIER LIVES CONTINUE TO MOVE FORWARD. I CAN SEE TIME LOST IN OTHER INMATES AND REALLY WILL TRY HARD TO NOT SINK NTO THAT MINDSET. TODAY IS A GREAT DAY FOR A WALK. ILL SEND WELL WISHES THAT YOUR HEADACHE IS GONE NOW.

(7)

⇒ TONIGHT THE SKY IS BEAUTIFUL. THE SUNSET IS IN A DIRECTION I CANNOT SEE. ITS GOT TO BE LOW ON THE HORIZON AS I IS MAKING THE SNOW CAPPED MOUNTAINS PEAKS A HAZY PINK HUE. THE SKY ABOVE IT IS A FAINT PURPLE W/ THIN BLANKETS OF CLOUDS DISAPPEARING INTO THE DISTANCE. THE FORFRONT IS BLUE SKIES SLOWLY DARKENING AS TODAY TIME ROLLS INTO NIGHT. THE FALL TREES CLOSE BY HAVE YET TO GROW LEAVES AS THEY AWAIT SPRING SEASON TO ARRIVE. THE GRASS IS A PATCHY YELLOW-GREEN COLOR THAT TIES THE SCENERY ALL TOGETHER. IT IS SO VERY REAL AND CLOSE HOWEVER OUT OF MY REACH AS I SIT AT A DESK FIXED TO THE WALL NEAR A WINDOW THAT OPENS ONLY ENOUGH TO SMELL THE FRESH AIR, FEEL THE BRISK REFRESHING BREEZE, AND HEAR VEHICLES TRAVEL PAST IN THE DISTANCE NOT ALL THAT FAR AWAY. THERE ARE FENCES KEEP-ING ME AWAY FROM WHATS OUT THERE OR LOCKS HOLDING ME BACK FROM IT ALL. FOR NOW I MUST SIT HERE AND REFLECT ON WHY I AM HERE AS THIS TOO SHALL PASS. AS THE DAY TURNS TO EVE AND COLORS FADE TO DARKNESS I WILL KEEP LIGHT INSIDE MYSELF AS I MAY NOT KNOW WHAT THE FUTURE HOLDS BUT I KNOW WHO HOLDS MY FUTURE. LIFE IS A CHOICE FOR BETTER OR WORSE AND KEEPING MIND TO DO THE NEXT RIGHT THING IS A LESSON I WAS ALWAYS TOLD BUT NEVER SHOWN. SO QUICKLY LIKE A FLASH OR BLINK OF AN EYE LIFE CAN STAND STILL AND THE BUTTERFLY EFFECT HOLDS POWER LIKE AN ATOMIC BOMB PULVERIZING EVERYTHING WONDERFUL IN ITS PATH. THINGS COULD BE SO MUCH WORSE. I COULD BE DEAD OR EVEN ALIVE →

(8)

LIVING A LIFE I WAS NEVER MEANT TO LIVE. AT LEAST THESE EYES HAVE BEEN LIFTED AND IVE MANAGED TO RELEASE MYSELF FROM THE BURDEN OF MY CHILDHOODS WEIGHT OFF OF MY SOUL. NOW EVERYTHING I COME INTO CONTACT W/ CAN SEE ME FOR WHO I ALWAYS WAS AND AM MEANT TO BE. FOREVER FORWARD AS I GO FORTH. MY HIGHER PO-WER WILL GUIDE ME AND STEER ME IN THE PROPER DIRECTION. FOR WHATEVER REASON IT HAS PUT YOU ON THIS PATH AND IM NOT SURE OR FULLY UNDERSTAND HOW COME, BUT W/OUT QUESTION I AM IN LOVE.

⇒ DINNER IS ALL DONE. WE HAD BURGERS N FRIES. FRIDAY NIGHT TV HAS GOOD MOVIES, GHOST SHOWS, AND ALIEN DOCUMENTARIES (MY FAVORITE). I AM FAIRLY FULL ATM AND WILL CONTINUE ON MY DIET THIS TUES. I WALKED BACK & FORTH IN THE HOUSE FOR 30 MINS TO-DAY. I'M LOOKING FORWARD TO BED AND AM GOING TO ASK THE DESK TO CALL YOU TONIGHT. THE WARDEN SAID WE CAN MAKE MORE THAN ONE CALL IF WE ARE NOT RIDICULOUS ABOUT IT. DOESNT HURT TO ASK. MY HOUSEMATE (KOHLMAN) IS TALKING TO HIS SISTER SO I DECIDED TO GIVE HIM SOME PRIVACY AND CONTINUE TO WRITE TO MY FAVORITE GIRL (YOU). ILL BE STOKED ONCE MY TV SHOWS UP BECAUSE ID JUST GO TO BED AFTER A SHOWER AND WATCH T.V. I WOULD PROBABLY FALL ASLEEP VERY FAST. IF I WERE ALLOWED OUTSIDE I WOULD GO WALKING TO SHED SOME OF OUR DINNER. ILL BE STOKED WHEN WE CAN HANGOUT ONCE IM DONE HERE. ON A GOOD NOT MY GREEN ONIONS ARE THRIVING EVEN MY HOUSEMATE IS SURPRISED BY IT. PROBABLY BECAUSE TO HIM I DONT SEEM LIKE THE KIND OF DUDE WHO KNOWS ABOUT GARDENING LOL. SHOCKER... I KNOW A WEE THING OR TWO.

(9)

ITS BEDTIME NOW. JUST AFTER 10PM. IM YAWNING AND THIS NEW BED IS CALLING MY NAME ☺ GOODNIGHT. DUDE

Z Z Z Z Z Z Z

♡ ♡ ♡ ♡ ♡ 2022-02-12 ♡ ♡

GOOOOOOD MORNING SUNSHINE. AND WHAT A SUNSHINEY CLEAR BLUE SKY DAY IT IS. IT LOOKS SO INCREDIBLY NICE OUT. MY WINDOW IS OPEN AS MUCH AS IT CAN BE AND THE AIR SMELLS FRESH AND SO CLEAN CLEAN. I HAD THE SAME BREAKFASTASALWAYS AND LAYED IN BED UNTIL 10AM. ONLY 12 MORE HOURS UNTIL BEDTIME. WHICH MEANS QUARANTINE IS 1 DAY CLOSER TO FINISHED. THIS TIME OF YEAR IS MY FAVORITE. THE AIR IS COOL AND THE TREES, BUSHES, GRASS ETC BEGINS TO COME ALIVE ONCE AGAIN. ITS WARM ENOUGH TO BE IN A TEE SHIRT BUT STILL COLD ENOUGH FOR THICKER HEAVIER CLOTHES THAT I LIKE. TODAY YOU ARE GOING SHOE SHOPPING AND FOR A SLEEPOVER AT YOUR FRIENDS HOUSE. THATS EXCITING AND IM SURE YOULL HAVE A GREAT TIME. ILL PRAY FOR YOUR HEADACHE TO BE GONE. WELL LOVELY GIRL... ITS 11:15 AND IM GOING OUTSIDE FOR 45MINS WHICH IS MY TIME FOR THE DAY.

⟹ TODAY HAS BEEN A GOOD DAY. I FOUND YET ANOTHER GREEN ONION OUTSIDE AND RE PLANTED IT IN MY INSIDE POT. WE PLAYED SCRABBLE A COUPLE OF TIMES. THE MOON IS HIGH IN THE SKY ABOVE MY BEDROOM WINDOW. THE SUNLIGHT IS CASTING RAYS DOWN NEAR THE TREES AND ONTO THE MOUNTAINS. OUR HOME IS IN THE SHADE. I AM PREPARING SPAGHETTI AGAIN AS WE ARE ON A TIGHT MEAL PLAN UNTIL TUES SO OUR RATIONS DO NOT RUN DRY. THIS PLACE IS BEAUTIFUL BUT ITS NOTHING LIKE HOME. IM EXCITED TO GO TO BED TONIGHT BECAUSE I GET TO TALK TO YOU TOMORROW EVENING. I SHAVED MY

(10)

HEAD AGAIN TODAY. I AM GETTING WAY BETTER AT IT NOW. I ALSO GROOMED MY FACE AND NECK SO I LOOK/FEEL GREAT. MY LEGS ARE A BIT SORE FROM WALKING LUNGES YESTERDAY. I DONT MIND EXCERSIZE HOWEVER ~~[illegible]~~ SEXCERSIZIING IS WAY MORE FUN LOL. TOO BAD THIS PLACE DESTROYS ANY THOUGHT OF THAT FULLY HAHAHAHA. ⟹ MAN 'O' MAN I AM FILLED TO THE BRIM. THE DAY IS ALMOST OVER. I FOUND OUT TONIGHT THAT MY BABIES MIGHT BE MOVING TO ALBERTA. WOW HOW LIFE CAN CHANGE IN SUCH A HURRY. WHAT TO DO. I CANT MOVE THERE AND WOULDNT REALLY WANT TO IF I HAD THE CHANCE AND THAT PUTS MY KIDS SO FAR APART FROM EACH I AM UNSURE ABOUT MY PRIORITIES AS A DAD. ALBERTA WOULD BE A GREAT NEW START FOR THEIR MOM AND CREATE AN AWE-SOME NEW LIFE FOR MY BABIES. THEY HAVE LOTS OF FAMILY OUT THERE ON BOTH SIDES HOWEVER IT WOULD LIMIT MY REGULAR ACCESS TO THEM. I COULD GO AND TRY TO BE CLOSER TO DAUGHTER BUT IN MY HEART KNOW THAT BEING NEAR HER MOM IS ONLY GOING TO MAKE LIFE MORE DIFFICULT. I COULD COME BACK TO THE COAST BUT W/ THE RECENT NEWS I COULD ALSO BE ANYWHERE. ITS CONFUSING BECAUSE ALL I EVER WANTED WAS KIDS, A WIFE, AND A LOVING HOME. OBVIOUSLY A HIGHER POWER HAS A DIFFERENT PLAN IN MIND AND ILL HAVE TO JUST TRUST IN THAT AND BE OPEN TO CHANGE. ITS UP TO THAT NOW AND ITS WILL CAN BE MY GUIDE. WHAT AN EYE OPENING JOURNEY THIS HAS BEEN. IM NOT EXACTLY SURE HOW I SHOULD FEEL RIGHT NOW AND THERES NOT MUCH I CAN DO. I LIVE IN A DREAM PRISON HOWEVER IT IS STILL A PRISON AS REAL AS IT GETS. EITHER WAY I AM LEARNING ALOT ABOUT MYSELF AND LIFE.

(11)

GOODNIGHT Z Z Z Z Z Z Z Z

2022-02-13

ITS MIDNIGHT AND I JUST SAT DOWN TO WRITE FOR TODAY. I FOUND A HEART ROCK OUTSIDE TODAY AND THOUGHT ABOUT YOU. ITS ON MY DESK BESIDE YOUR PHOTO. I WAS SO HAPPY TO HEAR YOUR VOICE AND BLESSED TO HAVE YOU BE VULNERABLE AND OPEN UP ABOUT HOW YOU WERE FEEL-ING. I CAN SOMETIMES TELL BY YOUR VOICE IF YOU ARE DOING OK OR NOT. I WILL ALWAYS BE HERE TO LISTEN IF/WHEN YOU NEED ME. TOMORROW IS VALENTINES DAY AND YOU ARE MY VALENTINE ANGEL ♡. EVEN THOUGH WE TALK QUITE A BIT TOMORROW NIGHTS CALL IS DATE #1 ☺. IVE GROWN TO LOVE YOU W/ ALL MY HEART. YOU MENTIONED YOULL BE WEARING YOUR BESTSWEATPANTS AND IF I WERE BESIDE YOU ID BE WEARING MY BEST ONES AS WELL LOL. IM 100% SURE YOU LOOK UNREAL IS SWEATS. I WAS SO STOKED THAT YOUR MOM WANTS TO VISIT ME. ILL BE THRILLED TO HAVE MORE PHOTOS OF YOU IN MY ROOM HOPEFULLY SOON. YOUR MOM SOUNDS SO AMAZING THAT TOMORROW NIGHT IM GOING TO ASK FOR HER # JUST SO I CAN CALL HER SOMETIMES. YOUVE BECOME THE PERSON I THINK ABOUT MOST AND LOOK FORWARD TO TALKING TO. TONIGHT WHEN YOU SOUNDED UPSET I JUST WANTED TO GIVE YOU THE BIGGEST/WARMEST HUG FOR AS LONG AS I COULD. YOU ARE SO INCREDIBLE AND GREAT ANGEL AND NOW THAT WE HAVE MET I COULD NOT IMAGINE LIFE W/OUT YOU IN IT♡. IM OFF TO BED NOW FILLED W/ HAPPINESS AND THINKING GOOD THOUGHTS. CHAT TOMORROW

GOODNIGHT SWEET GIRL Z Z Z Z Z Z Z

2022-02-14

HELLO AND GOOD MORNING. I JUST LOOKED AT THE CLOCK AND IT WAS 11:11 WHICH I ALWAYS THOUGHT

12

THAT TIME WAS LETTING ME KNOW THAT I AM RIGHT WHERE IM SUPPOSED TO BE. I WOKE UP AND YOU WERE THE FIRST PERSON I SAW WHICH MADE MY DAY. TODAY IS VALENTINES DAY AND YOU ANGEL ARE MY VALENTINE. IM GOING TO ASK YOU FOR A KISS AT THE END OF OUR PHONE DATE TONIGHT. I FELL ASLEEP THINKING ABOUT HOW CUTE YOU MUST LOOK IN SWEATPANTS. AND WOKE UP WISHING YOU AN AMAZING DAY. FOR SOME REASON I REALLY WANT TO HOLD YOUR HAND TODAY. (NOT SURE IF THAT CROSSES OUR FRIEND BOUNDARIES BUT ITS WHAT I FEEL INSIDE). I AM GRATEFUL AND INSPIRED TO CONTINUE ALWAYS DOING THE NEXT RIGHT THING. JUST KNOWING YOU MAKES ME A BETTER PERSON. YOU SHOWED ME SO MUCH LOVE WHEN I WASNT FEELING LOVABLE AND ALWAYS REASSURE ME WHEN I NEED IT MOST ⟹ ITS MIDAFTERNOON NOW AND IVE MOPPED THE ENTIRE HOUSE TWICE, WON A GAME OF SCRABBLE, STARTED WASHING WALLS, DONE ALL THE DISHES, WORKED OUT A BIT, AND WRITTEN YOU. IM JUST PLUGGING ALONG TO KEEP MYSELF BUSY SO MORE AND MORE TIME WILL PASS. THERES NOT ALL THAT MUCH ON T.V. ATM. CANT WAIT TO WATCH BASKETBALL DIARIES W/YOU. OUR HOME SPACE SMELLS LIKE PINESOL AND NATIVE SMUDGE HERB SMOKE. ITS HERE FOR RELIGEOUS REASONS BUT I USE IT AS INSENCE (AND TO WARD OFF EVIL SPIRITS OF COURSE) ⟵ I HOPE THAT MADE YOU LAUGH IF NOT SMILE AT LEAST. IM CLEANING AS IF YOU WERE COMING OVER FOR DINNER AND SOME MOVIES. YOUD BE IMPRESSED IM SURE IF YOU SAW BEFORE AND AFTER PHOTOS. ILL BE STOKED TO MEET YOUR MOM AND HERE STORIES ABOUT YOU AND MAYBE ONE DAY SEE PHOTOS OF YOU GROWING UP. I BET WE WERE SIMILAR AS KIDS. YOU MUSTVE TALKED ABOUT

(13)

ME TO YOUR MOM. IT SURE DOES MAKE ME HAPPY KNO-
-WING YOU THINK ABOUT ME ANGEL B☺ ⇒
⇒ PEROGIES FOR DINNER. W/ A
MIXTURE OF ITALIAN SEASONING, DRIED
GARLIC, HOMEGROW GREEN ONION AND
PORK SAUSAGE I GROUND UP THEN SAUTEED
IN BUTTER AND MAYONAISE WHICH I THEN FRIED
WHILE I DID ALL THE DISHES. THE WHOLE PROCESS
IS QUITE ENJOYABLE. NORMALLY DOING DISHES
WAS SOMETHING THAT WAS DREADED. NOW IT ALLOWS
TIME TO REFLECT ON MY DAILY THOUGHTS AND
WIND DOWN THE DAY TO RELAX. ONCE THAT WAS ALL
DONE I CAME INTO MY ROOM TO TELL YOU ABOUT IT.
ALTHOUGH ITLL PROBS GET MENTIONED ON OUR PHONE
DATE TONIGHT. IM VERY HAPPY AND LOOKING FORWARD
TO TALKING AND LISTENING TO YOU. I TALKED TO THE
GIRLS TODAY TO SAY HAPPY VALENTINES AND TELL THEM
I LOVE THEM. THEY ARE SO SMART AND KIND, THEY
SURE DO LOVE THER DAD. THEY MELT MY HEART.
I LOVE MY KIDS SO MUCH ID TOTALLY HAVE MORE.
PRACTICING MAKING THEM IS ALWAYS FUN TOO LOL.
KIDS ALWAYS SAY THE FUNNIEST STUFF AND ITS
ALWAYS AMAZING TO SEE WHO THEY BECOME AS
THEY GROW. (THEIR). TODAY WENT BY SUPER FAST
AND MY SHOWER HASNT EVEN BEEN USED ONCE YET.
DEFINATELY HITTING THAT UP BEFORE BED TO-
-NIGHT. IT WAS NICE TALKING FOR THAT LONG AGAIN.
I WAS TOO NERVOUS TO STRAIGHT UP ASK IF YOU WOULD
KISS ME ON VALENTINES DAY... HOWEVER,.. I TOLD YOU
HOW I WOULD GET ONE AND YOU DID NOT EVEN SEEM
PHAZED. ACTUALLY SAID IT WAS ADORABLE. SOUNDS
PERFECT TO ME. TIME FOR BED GORGEOUS GIRL. NIGHT ZZZ
B

(14)

2022-02-15

WAKING UP NEXT TO YOU IS SUCH A BEAUTIFUL EXPERIENCE IN LIFE. ALTHOUGH ITS ONLY A PHOTO IT CONTINUES TO BEGIN THE DAYS W/ HAPPINESS, LOVE, AND JOY. MOMENT BY MOMENT, DAY BY DAY, AND CONVERS--ATION BY CONVERSATION YOU BECOME MORE AND MORE BEAUTIFUL IN EVERY WAY. IN YOUR DREAM YOU MENTIONED YOU HAD TO FIND ME, AND WHEN YOU DID YOU RAN INTO MY ARMS AND I PICKED YOU UP OFF OF THE GROUND. WHEN AT LAST WE FINALLY SEE EACHOTHER IN PERSON IN ALL OF MY HEART I TRULY HOPE THAT HAPPENS ANGEL. IF IT DOES I AM NEVER LETTING YOU GO. IF AT THAT MOMENT YOULL LET ME KISS YOU ITL BE THE MOST SPECIAL KISS FOR US BOTH. I MIGHT CRY IN JOY TO BE HONEST. I LOVE YOU SO MUCH MORE THAN I THOUGHT POSSIBLE. ANGEL I AM IN LOVE WITH EVERY PART OF YOU.

⇒ WOW I RE READ THIS PAGE. YEP I WROTE THAT DOWN AND I DONT REWRITE THESE LETTERS OR THROW THEM AWAY. EVERY WORD IS TRUE AND REAL. I DO LOVE YOU AND AM VERY MUCH IN LOVE WITH YOU. IVE HONESTLY KNOWN FOR AWHILE THAT IVE FELT THAT WAY ABOUT YOU, ONLY NOW MY FEELINGS ARE GROWING. I CANNOT EXPLAIN IT, THEY JUST ARE. EVERYTHING ABOUT YOU IS ADORABLE, CUTE, AND INTERESTING. IVE FOUND LEARNING ALL ABOUT YOU INTRIGUING AND IT LEAVES ME WANTING TO LEARN MORE OF WHAT INTERESTS YOU, & ON SO MANY LEVELS. ILL BE SO STOKED TO HAVE PHOTOS OF YOU TO LOOK AT AND SOME OF US TOGETHER WHEN IM RELEASED. I HOPE YOU FEEL THE SAME BUT IF NOT THATS OK. I WOULD NEVER DO ANYTHING TO CHANGE OUR FRIENDSHIP AS YOU ARE SO VERY IMPORTANT TO ME ANGEL!!!

[redacted]

TO ANGEL (15) 2022-02-17

TODAY IS A DIFFERENT DAY. ALTHOUGH IT IS DRAB AND BDREARY OUTSIDE BECAUSE OF THE CLOUDS AND RAIN, THE WAY IT LOOKS AND FEELS IS COMPLETELY DIFFERENT. YESTERDAYS LETTER WAS MISSED AS THE DAY WAS SIMILAR TO THE OTHERS EXEPT THE FEELING THAT WAS COMING TO SURFACE. IT HAD BEEN THERE AWHILE NOW AND EVEN MILDLY EXPRESSED THROUGHOUT PREVIOUS LETTERS. IN A DREAM LAST NIGHT THERE WAS A CONNECTION UNLIKE ANY OTHER AND WORDS CAN HARDLY DESCRIBE. IT PROB-ABLY BEGAN THE OTHER DAY WHEN YOU WERE UPSET AND I COULD TELL IMMEDIATELY SOMETHING WAS BOTH-ERING YOU. I HAD ASKED WHAT WAS UPSETTING YOU AND YOU OPENED YOUR HEART, BECAME VULNERABLE, AND TOLD ME. AT THAT POINT I COULD FEEL YOUR FEELINGS AND FELT WHAT YOU FELT. THE HONOR AND GRATITUDE I WAS FEELING AFTERWARDS FOR BEING ABLE TO BE A PERSON YOU TRUSTED TO DO THAT WITH FILLED MY HEART WITH COMPASSION AND I KNEW HOW MUCH I TRULY CARE ABOUT YOU. THE NEXT DAY (I CHECKED THE DATES!) I WROTE YOU A LOVE LETTER ON VALENTINES DAY AND WE HAD OUR FIRST DATE (AND MAYBE FIRST KISS ☺♡). THEN YOU HAD A DREAM ABOUT SEARCHING FOR ME AND DID UNTIL YOU FOUND ME ♡. THE LAST TWO DAYS WE HAVENT BEEN ABLE TO TALK AND YOUVE BEEN IN MY HEART AND ON MY MIND CONSTANTLY. LAST NIGHT I HAD A DREAM ABOUT YOU UNLIKE ANY OTHER DREAM IVE HAD BEFORE. MY DREAM STARTED OUT AT MY FRIENDS HOUSE. HE SHOWED ME FOOTAGE OF HIS DEER/TRAIL CAM AND TOLD ME THAT THE TRAIL SEEMED TO LEAD PEOPLE TO ANY PLACE THEY WERE SUPPOSED TO BE IN TIME & SPACE. AFTER THAT I WAS AT MY NEW FRIEND DAVES RANDOM CABIN

(16)

THAT I NEVER KNEW HE HAD WAY OUT IN THE WILDERNESS. I WAS TELLING DAVE ABOUT THIS TRAIL/PATHWAY I HEARD ABOUT AND W/OUT FLINCHING DAVE SAID WHILE POINTING TO A NARROW GAP IN THE TREES THATS IT RIGHT THERE. I JOKED IN DIS-BELIEF TO WHICH HE REPLIED TO GO LOOK FOR MYSELF. WHEN I WALKED THROUGH THE TREES I WAS BESIDE YOU IN YOUR LIVING ROOM. YOU WERE STANDING THERE IN A LONG BLACK JACKET W/ DOUBLE BUTTONS AND GUMBOOTS. YOU WERE NOT SURPRISED AT ALL WHICH SURPRISED ME THEN YOU SAID YOU WERE ALL SET AND READY TO GO AS IF YOU ALREADY KNEW WHERE WE WERE OFF TO. NOT EVEN I KNEW THE ANSWER TO THAT. YOU HELD MY HAND A WE LEFT THE HOUSE. NOW WE ARRIVED ON A LONG FORRESTED COUNTRY RD. WE COULD SEE A GAP IN THE TREES SO WE WALKED TOWARDS IT. I CANT REMEMBER WHAT I WAS SAYING TO YOU BUT IT WAS MAKING YOUR FACE LIGHT UP W/ A HUGE SMILE AND SOME GIGGLES. (I ALWAYS LOVE MAKING YOU DO BOTH THOSE THINGS) WHEN WE ARRIVED AT THE OPENING AND LOOKED THROUGH THE TREES THE SUN WAS RADIANT ON THE MEADOW-LIKE TALL GRASS. THE MEADOW WAS NARROW AND SEEMED TO GO AS FAR INTO THE DISTANCE AS THE EYES COULD SEE. WE BEGAN TO RUN W/OUR HANDS BRUSHING THE FLOWERS AND BLADES OF GRASS AND LAUGHING. YOU LOOKED GORGEOUS. SOON WE CAME ACROSS TWO PEOPLE. I FELT THAT I KNEW THEM BUT HADNT RECOGNIZED EITHER THE MALE OR FEMALE WHATSOEVER. HOWEVER WE WERE COMFORTABLE AND SAT DOWN. I SAT W/ MY LEGS OPEN AND YOU SAT BETWEEN THEM W/ YOUR BACK AGAINST MY CHEST.

(17)

THE PEOPLE SURE DID KNOW ME AS IF THEY WERE PARTS OF MY SUBCONSCIOUS. THEY KNEW EVERY DETAILS OF MY ENTIRE LIFE. EVERY PART OF MY BEING WAS SHARED LIKE A DMT TRIP. IM NOT SURE IF IT WAS WORDS OR IMAGES OR BOTH BUT IT WAS ALL OUT IN FRONT OF US. I FELT AT PEACE SHARING THESE THINGS WITH YOU BECAUSE DEEP DOWN I KNEW IT WAS ALL OK AND I COULD AT THAT POINT BE COMPLETELY VULNERABLE FOR JUST THAT MOMENT WITH ANOTHER PERSON, THEN I WOKE UP AND THERE YOU WERE AND I WAS IN AWE THAT THAT HAPPENED EVEN IF IT WAS JUST A DREAM. IT HAS NEVER HAPPENED BEFORE. WHY YOU? IM HONESTLY UNSURE BUT I KNOW THERE SOMETHING VERY SPECIAL ABOUT YOU THAT WORDS ARE NOT ENOUGH TO EXPLAIN. ⟹ WELL IT IS BEDTIME. I HOPE I AM NOT BECOMING TOO MUCH FOR YOU DUDE. I BASICALLY WROTE A LOVE LETTER TO YOU THE OTHER DAY. ITS HOW I FEEL THOUGH. THE DREAM WAS SOMETHING ELSE AND I AM STILL BESIDE MYSELF ABOUT IT. IT IS STILL EXTREMELY VIVID. IVE BEEN THINKING ABOUT IT AND YOU ALL DAY. TOMORROW IS QUARANTINE COMPLETE. IM EXCITED. ANOTHER STEP TOWARDS SEEING YOU IN PERSON. WHAT A JOURNEY. IVE SEEN A DEATH, AN O.D., FIGHTS, LOCKDOWN FREAK OUTS, WEEK LONG STINTS IN A 6X10 CELL ALONE, FREEZING COLD UP AT NIGHTS LISTENING TO PEOPLE SCREAMING, EXCRUTIATING LONELINESS, AND MENTAL AGONY. THROUGHOUT IT ALL, YOUVE BEEN THERE AND HELPED ME MAINTAIN MY POSITIVE OUTLOOK. YOU ARE AND ALWAYS WILL BE FOREVER ONE OF A KIND ANGEL. NIGHT. I LOVE YOU. I HOPE YOU SAW ME IN YOUR DREAM AGAIN ♡♡♡ZZZ

(18) 2022-02-18

TODAY IS FRIDAY, DAY ONE, FREE FROM QUARANTINE. SO FAR IT HAS BEEN GOOD. THE COMPOUND IS DECENT. THERE ~~IS A POTTERY AND~~ ARE BOTH POTTERY AND WOODWORKING SHOPS HERE. THE GYM IS BIGGER THAN I HAD IMAGINED AND IN A SEPARATE AREA A CARDIO ROOM W/ A PING PONG TABLE. THE WALKING PATH AROUND THE DUCK POND IS APPROX A 15 MIN WALK WHICH IS NICE TO HAVE THAT MUCH SPACE. IM IN GROUP ONE, MY NEW HOUSE IS NICE AND CLEAN WITH ART ON THE WALLS AND PLANTS. THE GUYS SEEM SUPER NICE. THERE ARE FOUR OF US LIVING IN THIS HOUSE AND ITS FAIRLY SPACIOUS AND COMFORTABLE. IN THE BACK YARD THERE IS A HUGE GARDEN WHICH I WILL START TILLING AND WEEDING FAIRLY SOON. IVE PLANTED MORE GREEN ONIONS (I GAVE THE LAST ONE TO BEN) AND MY ROOM NOW HAS A HOUSE PLANT. IM GOING TO TRY AND DRAW IT TONIGHT USING SOME TECHNIQUES FROM THE BOOK I SIGNED OUT FROM THE LIBRARY. EARLIER I BOOKED A DR APT. AND REGISTERED MORE PHONE NUMBERS. IN A WAY I FEEL TOO NORMAL FOR THIS PLACE BUT MY ALCOHOLIC ACTIONS WERENT WHO I AM AND HELPED PUT ME HERE. THIS EXPERIENCE IS CHANGING ME FOR THE BETTER I BELIEVE. ITS CRAZY TO THINK ABOUT HOW MUCH YOU HAVE BEEN APART OF THIS ALL. YOUVE BEEN HERE EVERY STEP OF THE WAY☺. I KNOW I TELL YOU I LOVE AND MISS YOU BUT I FEEL THERE ARE NO ACTUAL WORDS TO DESCRIBE HOW AMAZING YOU ARE. I FEEL CALM AND AT PEACE TODAY AND READY TO DO WHATEVER IT TAKES TO SHED THIS INTO THE PAST AND PROGRESS INTO THE FUTURE. ⇒ I JUST WENT FOR A NIGHT WALK IN THE AREA IM ALLOWED IN, IT IS NOT MY GROUPS TIM IN THE COMPOUND SO THE AREA IS SMALL, HUGE COMPARED TO THE PREVIOUS THREE

(19)

MONTHS. ITS LIKE A NORMAL NEIGHBORHOOD FILLED W/ ROWS OF SMALL DORM STYLE HOUSES. THE OTHER INMATES WERE ALL LOOKING OUT AT ME MOST LIKELY BECAUSE I AM NEW AND LOOK THE WAY I DO. MY HOUSEMATES AND I HAD A GOOD LAUGH WHEN I POINTED OUT THE "DOOR KNOB CLEANER" JOB. THEY HADNT REALIZED IT A PRISON KNOB POLISHER HAHAHA. SOMEONE DEFINATELY DIED W/ HYSTERICAL BELLY LAUGHS MAKING UP THAT POSITION AND SENDING OUT. EMPLOYEES NEEDED ASAP THE SHEET SAID LOL "KNOB POLISHER" NEEDED ASAP 😄 HAHAHAHA. PEOPLE NATURALLY MAKE ASSUMPTIONS ABOUT ME UPON FIRST APPEARANCE WHICH I AM FULLY USED TO. IN SOME WAYS THERES POSITIVES & NEGATIVES TO THE WAY I LOOK AND CARRY MYSELF. ESPECIALLY IF YOU DONT KNOW ME. I ORDERED AN N64 AND HOPEFULLY IT COMES WITH GOLDEN EYE, ZELDA, AND 1080 SNOWBOARDING. ILL BE HAPPY NO MATTER WHAT COMES. I HAVE MY OWN MAIL BOX AND KEY JUST LIKE THE POST OFFICE. ILL BE SO EX--CITED TO OPEN IT AND HAVE MAIL FROM PEOPLE 🙂. THE GUYS IN THIS HOUSE ENJOY CHESS, SCRABBLE, AND CRIB WHICH PASSES THE TIME. I CANNOT WAIT TO HAVE A T.V. IN MY ROOM BUT FOR NOW ILL CHILL IN THE LIVING ROOM. I WISH YOU WERE HERE W/ ME OR I WAS WITH YOU. ITS GOING TO BE SO AMAZING TO WATCH MOVIES W/ YOU AND HANGOUT, TALK, WATCH YOUTUBE, LAUGH, OR DO PRETTY MUCH WHATEVER. I FEEL TIME WILL GO BY QUICKLY IN HERE NOW. ⇒ GOODNIGHT ♡♡

2022-02-19

HELLO LOVELY ANGEL. IT IS 11:30 PM AND IM JUST SITTING TO WRITE YOU. TODAY WAS AN EXCELLENT DAY. TALKING W/ TJ & CALLUM WAS GREAT ♡. GOING TO A REAL GYM JUST UPPED MY PHYSICAL DEVELOPEMENT GAME HUGE WHICH IS SO

(20)

EXCITING AND ENCOURAGING. MY SPIRITS ARE EXTREMELY HIGH AND TALKING TO YOU (ON TOP OF AN ALREADY AMAZING DAY) WAS THE HIGHLIGHT OF IT ALL. I SCORED YOU A DENTAL DAM AS A KEEP SAKE LOL... TONIGHT YOU SAVED SOME PICS OF RYAN ASHLEY AND SAID YOU WOULD MAIL THEM TO ME WHICH IS SO INCREDIBLY DOPE.. HOWEVER AWESOME THAT MAY BE, PHOTOS OF YOU WOULD BE SO MUCH BETTER. YOU ARE SO GORGEOUS ITS UNREAL, AND COOL/DOPE AF!. TONIGHT WE CHATTED ABOUT YOUR DAY IN THE HOSPITAL. THE FACT THAT YOU TOLD ME EVERYTHING ON SUCH A PERSONAL LEVEL MEANS ALOT. I KNOW YOURE AN OPEN BOOK BUT IM SURE YOU WOULDNT SHARE THAT W/ JUST ANYONE. I MADE SOME JOKES WHICH WERE APPROPRIATELY INAPPROPRIATE. AT LEAST I DIDNT SAY ILL/ID KISS THAT BETTER FOR YOU LOL (ALTHOUGH HILARIOUS). LUCKY DOCTORS THO 😜 I MADE TOMATO, GREEN ONIONS, AND EGGS ON MULTIGRAIN TOAST FOR DINNER AFTER WE TALKED. IT WAS TERRIFIC, ESPECIALLY AFTER 3 MONTHS OF SLOP-LIKE MEALS. WHY ARE YOU SO GOOD TO ME ANGEL? IVE NEVER ONCE MET ANOTHER PERSON LIKE YOU. I MUSTVE DONE SOME-THING RIGHT AT SOME POINT FOR A HIGHER POWER TO HAVE PUT YOU IN MY PATH AT A POINT LIKE THIS IN LIFE. TODAY I HAD AN ATTITUDE OF GRATITUDE. ILL BE SO STOKED WHEN WE CAN VIDEO CHAT AGAIN. LAST TIME I WAS SO BLOWN AWAY BY THE BEAUTY THAT IS EVERYTHING YOU. (BAD HAIR DAY OR NOT ☺) WELL ITS BEDTIME NOW. I HOPE I SEE YOU IN MY DREAMS AND WE HAVE ANOTHER ADVENTURE. GOODNIGHT SWEET GIRL. XOXO CHEEK KISS ♡. Z Z Z Z Z Z Z Z

2022-02-20

GOOOOOOOD MORNING, ALMOST AFTERNOON. I CALLED TO WISH YOU A HAPPY SUNDAY ☺. SO FAR TODAY IVE HAD A GREAT BREAKFAST (SAME AS DINNER LAST NIGHT), A MONSTER WORK-OUT INCLUDING CARDIO, AND A PROTEIN SHAKE. I ALSO HAD

(21)

A NICE LONG HOT SHOWER AND GOT READY SO I LOOK DAPPER FOR THE DAY. I MOISTURIZED AS EVERYTHING HERE DRIES YOU OUT AND THEN I COMBED MY FACE. I DREW MY GREEN ONIONS FOR YOU LAST NIGHT AND TRIED SOME SHAD-ING TECHNIQUES FROM MY BOOK, CALLED "WHIP SHADING". I AM TRYING TO LEARN ABOUT SHADES AND LIGHT SOURCES/DIREC-TIONS. FOR LUNCH I WILL HAVE PLAIN YOGURT, P. BUTTER, AND BANANA AGAIN, IT IS SO GOOD. I MEET MY P.O. THIS WEEK AND WE WILL MAKE A PLAN FOR MY FUTURE. HOW EXCIT-ING. IM NOT SURE WHAT TO DO EXACTLY BUT I HAVE SOLID IDEAS OF THE DIRECTION I WOULD LIKE TO GO IN. WHAT DO YOU THINK I SHOULD DO? WHERE SHOULD I GO IF IT WAS YOUR CHOICE? HOW DO YOU FEEL ABOUT ME? ⟹ I JUST GOT BACK FROM A WALK. IT IS 3:45 AND MY GROUP (GROUP 1) IS IN FOR THE EVENING, WELL IN OUR AREA ANYHOW. ON MY WALK I WATCHED TWO CROWS INTERACTING, THEY MUST BE 'TOGETHER' BECAUSE IVE NEVER SEEN CROWS LAY ON THEIR SIDE FOR EACHOTHER, IT WAS CUTE. I ALSO MAILED MY RRAC WORKOUT/MEAL SHARE BUDDY DEVAN AND TOLD HIM ABOUT MY CURRENT LIVING AND ASKED ABOUT HIS. HE IS MY FAVORITE PERSON IVE MET SO FAR BESIDES COOPER THE CLEANER. ⟹ FOR DINNER WAS SPICY CHILI PUT ON TOP OF RICE WHILE THE RICE COOKED SO IT ABSORBED ALL THE FLAVOURS AND THEN FRIED. IT WAS VERY GOOD W/ LOTS OF LEFTOVERS. I THINK ILL GO TO BED EARLY TONIGHT AS THERE IS NOT THAT MUCH TO DO. WE PLAYED SCRABBLE & CRIB BUT THAT GETS OLD FAST ALTH-OUGH IT IS ALOT OF FUN. MY ROOM IS RIDICULOUSLY ORGANIZED ITS IN ORDER EXACTLY THE WAY I LIKE IT. JUST NEEDS SOME PHOTOS (MORE PHOTOS). MY HOUSE MATE ASKED ME IF ID LIKE TO DO A WORKOUT PROGRAM W/ HIM AND HE DESIGNED IT TO TARGET EXACTLY WHAT IM AFTER. WE START →

(22)

TUES @ NOONISH. IM STOKED, AND. EVEN MORE STOKED FOR WHEN YOU CAN SEE THE CHANGE IN PERSON. IM GOING FOR SHOCKING TRANSFORMATION. GOOD NIGHT SWEET GIRL. I LOVE YOU & MISS YOU ♥ Z Z Z Z Z Z

2022-02-21

HAPPY FAMILY DAY ♥. I HOPE YOU HAD AN AMAZING SLEEP. I DID, I WOKE UP A BIT SORE FROM THE GYM YESTERDAY. AS I WAS WAKING UP I LOOKED UP AND IN THE CENTER OF MY PHOTO BOARD WAS YOU. WHAT A GREAT WAY TO START OFF THE DAY (☺). IM NOT SURE EXACTLY WHAT ILL DO TODAY BUT IM SURE ILL WRITE ABOUT IT. ⟹ I HAVE A FEELING TO DAY WILL BE ALOT OF WRITING. I WROTE TO MY FRIEND COOPER I MET IN RRAC (THE GUY I SHARED PROTIEN POWDER W/) TO SEE HOW HE IS DOING. I ASKED WHAT HIS PLACE IS LIKE WHERE HE WAS SENT ~~AND~~ AND IF HE WAS DOING WELL. I TOLD HIM A BIT ABOUT WHERE I AM AT, AND THAT I MISS HIM. TODAY I AM MISSING MY FRIENDS, KIDS, FAMILY, AND ESPECIALLY YOU. IM STILL BOGGLED ABOUT HOW MUCH OF A CONNECTION OUR FRIENDSHIP HAS IMPACTED ON ME. I AM (AS MENTIONED MANY OF TIMES) SO GRATEFUL TO HAVE YOU IN MY LIFE. ID DO ANYTHING FOR YOU!! I WAS GOING TO SEND THIS SET OF LETTERS BUT AM AFRAID AS IVE EXPRESSED HOW IF FEEL ABOUT YOU, AND THAT SCARES ME IN SO MANY WAYS. ~~I~~ IVE WANTED TO TELL YOU BUT REAL-IZED IM SCARED OF REJECTION AND WOULDNT WANT YOU TO THINK OR ACT DIFFERENTLY TOWARDS ME. IM STOKED CHAT TO YOUR MOM AND GET TO KNOW HER AND MORE ABOUT YOU ♥ COFFEE TIME (☺) ⟹ I HAD TO SPRINT HOME AFTER OUR CALL LOL. I ABSOLUTELY ADORE YOU. IT IS FREEZING COLD OUT AND WINDY AF. WHAT A DAY. IT IS EVERYTHING TO ME THAT YOUVE SPENT SO MUCH OF

(23)

YOUR TIME WITH ME. WE JOKED ABOUT IF WE WERE ROOMATES DOING EACH OTHERS FACE MASKS, PIGTAIL BRAIDS NAILS ETC... UMMM SOUNDS LIKE WE NEED TO HAVE A MOVIE NIGHT SLASH GIRLS NIGHT ANGEL (I MEAN THAT). ALSO I WANTED TO ASK IF YOU WOULD BE MY GUEST/DATE TO MY FAMILIES WELCOME HOME DINNER? OR ANY OTHER DINNER UPON MY RELEASE? OR JUST ME BUYING YOU DINNER OR TAKE OUT FOR GIRLS NIGHT? ALSO ID BE AN AWESOME ROOMATE LOL (SERIOUSLY THO ☺) EITHER WAY LIFE IS SO BEAUTIFUL IN SO MANY WAYS. HEARING YOU SAY BYE BITCH TO YOUR SHOW REMINDED ME SO MUCH OF MY SISTERS ITS LEGIT UNREAL. YOUD LOVE THEM ALL. AND THEYD LOVE YOU TOO. I KNOW I SURE DO!! ITS HARD TO EXPLAIN HOW MUCH I ENJOY YOUR COMPANY BUT OBVIOUSLY MY SISTER CAN TELL IF SHES SENDING YOU PHOTOS. ANYWAYS GOODNIGHT BEAUTIFUL ANGEL

I HOPE MY LETTERS ARENT TOO MUCH FOR YOU. IF SO PLEASE DO LET ME KNOW.

4

Lockdown

"Finding rhythm in the noise."

By now the shock had worn off, but the routine carried its own kind of weight. The same doors, the same sounds, the same smell of steel and bleach—it all blended together until the days felt copied and pasted. You either fought it or learned to move with it, and I figured out quick that fighting it only burned you out. So, I built a rhythm. I'd wake up early, make the bed tight, do push-ups, write, think, repeat. It was the only way to stay sane when time refused to move.

Writing ended up saving me more than anything. When the range got loud or the lockdown dragged on for days, I'd go quiet and pick up the pen. I wrote to her—told her about the light coming through the window, about the thoughts I couldn't say out loud. It's strange how a voice can live in your head so clearly that it cuts through concrete. Sometimes I swore I could still hear her laughing, like the sound alone kept me breathing.

There were hard days too. Missing her. Missing my girls. Missing the kind of touch that reminds you you're still human. But even in that ache, I tried to stay grateful. I thanked God for the few things that place couldn't take—hope, memory, love that refused to die easy. Every word I wrote back then was me refusing to go numb. That place could take my time, but it never got my heart.

DEAREST ANGEL 2022-04-10

LOL IM NOT SURE WHY I STARTED THIS LETTER OFF W/ DEAREST ANGEL BUT I FIGURED I HADN'T DONE IT BEFORE AND "WOULD" SOUND NICE. WELL... TODAY I SLEPT IN A BIT AND WHEN I WENT TO THE KITCHEN TO GET A COFFEE, LOW AND BEHOLD RIGHT ON THE FRONT LAWN 2 CROWS HAVING SEX DOGGYSTYLE LMAO. HIGH FIVE CROW AT LEAST SOMEONE IS GETTING LAID LOL. (HOPE THAT MADE YOU LAUGH. ITS A TRUE STORY). ITS ALMOST 1PM AND I JUST SHAVED MY HEAD. IT IS SO INCREDIBLY SMOOTH I DO WISH YOU COULD RUN YOUR HANDS OVER IT. I TRULY HOPE YOURE HAVING AN AWESOME DAY TODAY. WHEN I THINK ABOUT YOU SMILING, LAUGHING, AND HAPPY IT REALLY DOES MAKE ME HAPPY. I DONT HAVE MUCH TO SAY AS IM LIVING GROUND HOGS DAY. DAYS LIKE TODAY I WISH I COULD GIVE YOU A HUG OR BE HUGGED BY YOU. SOME--TIMES THE THOUGHT POPS INTO MY MIND OF HOW BEAUTIFUL YOU MUST LOOK RIGHT NOW (AS YOU ALWAYS DO). I ALSO THINK ABOUT HOW WE MET AT ONE OF MY LOWEST POINTS AND THAT YOUVE STUCK WITH ME THROUGHOUT ALL OF THIS. WAIT UNTIL YOU SEE ME AT MY BEST AND CONQUERING LIFE DUDE BECAUSE IM LEAVING THIS PLACE AND HITTING THE WORLD IN OVERDRIVE. NEVER TAKES ME LONG TO GET TO WHERE I WANT TO BE. I AM OVERLY GRATEFUL TO HAVE YOU IN MY LIFE AND WILL ALWAYS BE HERE FOR YOU NO MATTER WHAT♥. WELL ITS TIME TO READ A CHAPTER OF MY COMMUNICATION BOOK ⇒ GOODNIGHT ANGEL. ILL BE LOOKING FOR YOU IN MY DREAMS TONIGHT. I MISS YOU AND LOVE YOU Z Z Z Z

2022-04-11

HAPPY MONDAY. ONE DAY AWAY FROM OUR VIDEO CALL, SUPER STOKED TO SEE YOUR FACE. HOPEFULLY YOUR DAY

(2)

HAS BEEN GOOD SO FAR. I HOPE YOU WORE THE RIGHT SHOES
SO YOUR FEET ARE NOT SORE LATER. IT IS VERY NICE OUT
TODAY SO THE BOYS AND I ARE GOING TO GO ON A WALK
THEN PROBABLY PLAY 21 AT THE B-BALL HOOPS. I THINK
ILL DRESS IN MY NICE OUTFIT TODAY (TO LOOK DAPPER/HANDSOME LOL)
IM LOOKING AT THE PHOTO YOU SENT ME. I ABSOLUTELY ADORE
YOU DUDE (JUST SAYIN). ⇒ ITS 1:07 PM AND IM THE ONLY
ONE HOME. IVE SWEPT, MOPPED, AND WIPED ALL THE
SURFACES IN THE HOUSE. I JUST POPPED A PIECE OF
NICORETTE GUM AND SAT IN MY ROOM ON MY CHAIR.
WHEN I GLANCED FORWARD THERE YOU WERE, SO I DECIDED
TO WRITE YOU. IVE OPENED ALL THE DOORS AND THE
FRESH AIR BLOWING THROUGH THE HOUSE IS MOUNTAIN
FRESH. THE BIRDS ARE CHIRPING AND I AM VERY HAPPY ⇒
WE PLAYED SOME TENNIS JUST NOW. IT WAS A LOT OF FUN.
TOMORROW OUR NEW WEEK WORTH OF FOOD WILL BE IN WHICH
IS ALWAYS EXCITING. WE WILL TRY SOME NEW RECIPES THIS
WEEK AND PORTIONING OUR MEALS. THE REST OF THE DAY WILL
BE MOSTLY CHILLING OUT AS WE ARE IN OUR RESTRICTED ZONE
FOR THE EVENING. WELL ANGEL IM GOING TO GO WATER
THE PATCHY SPOTS OF OUR LAWN THAT I SEEDED LAST WEEK.
⇒ LOL SAGE BURNING W/ SOME AMERICAN IDOL ON T.V. IN
A DIMLY LIT ROOM (MY BEDROOM). HOW SENSUAL I KNOW, ITS
LIKE IM ON A DATE W/ MYSELF. IM SO INCREDIBLY RELAXED
RIGHT NOW. IM PRETTY MUCH JUST WAITING TO PASS THE
10:00 PM STANDING COUNT THEN FALL ASLEEP. I JUST
HEARD AN AWESOME VERSION OF DOLLY PARTONS "JOLEEN".
I HAVE AN AWESOME STORY OF ME AND ALL THE WOMAN
AT A DOLLY PARTONS CONCERT AND THAT SONG.. ASK ME
ABOUT IT AND ILL TELL YOU YOULL LAUGH. ALSO... IVE
BEEN KEEPING THESE PAPER SLIPS OF ALL OUR VIDEO CALLS
AS A MEMORY IN THE FUTURE AND AS A FOREVER ⟶

(3)

REMINDER THAT A WONDERFUL LIGHT IN MY LIFE STUCK
W/ ME DURING THE TIME SPENT INCARCERATED. PLENTY
OF PEOPLE COULD HAVE DONE WHAT YOU DID BUT IT WAS
YOU THAT DID IT. FOR THIS IM GRATEFUL (I KNOW IVE SAID
IT BEFORE). MY SISTER HAS ALWAYS BEEN W/ ME AND
EX-WIFE HELD DOWN THE PARENTING WHICH I WILL
ALSO ALWAYS BE GRATEFUL FOR THOSE TWO. IT TOOK/
TAKES A REAL FRIEND TO DO WHAT YOUVE DONE ESPE-
-CIALLY ONLY HAVE HAD KNOWN EACHOTHER FOR WHAT
SEEMS LIKE MOMENTS AND NOW SEEMING LIKE A LIFE-
-TIME. AS ALWAYS I AM VERY EXCITED TO LEARN SO
MUCH MORE ABOUT YOU DUDE. YOUVE BEEN AND SEEN
ME GO THROUGH SO MUCH PAIN (SOME OF MY WORST EVEN
THOUGH I MOSTLY HIDEIT). WAIT UNTIL IM OUT AND
SHINING ONCE AGAIN. IVE GOT MY PASSION BACK AND
DRIVE LIKE NEVER BEFORE. I ASPIRE TO BE HUMBLY
GREAT AND HELP MAKE THIS WORLD A BRIGHTER
PLACE HOWEVER AND WHENEVER I CAN. I STILL DO
HOPE THAT YOU ARE THE FIRST FACE I SEE WHEN I
WALK OUT THESE DOORS. THEN SURPRISE MY GIRLS
ON THE WAY TO MY NEXT STOP, ST. LEONARDS.
THAT DAY SEEMS FAR BUT IS ACTUALLY VERY CLOSE.
ITL' BE A DREAM COME TRUE. I HAVE SO MANY STORIES
OF TRIUMPH, PERSERVERANCE, LOVE, FAITH, HOPE, LEAR-
-NING, OVERCOMING OBSTACLES, AND FINDING OUT SO
MUCH ABOUT MYSELF. I ALSO HAVE STORIES OF ALL THE
OPPOSITE AND SO MUCH STRUGGLE. TO HELL AND BACK
OVER AND OVER. ALSO YOU HAVE HELPED GET MY FAITH
IN HUMANITY BACK. YOU ARE 100% ONE OF A KIND AND
I HONEST TO MY HIGHER POWER BELIEVE THAT ABOUT
YOU. YOUVE BEEN AN ANGEL IN THIS LIFE. SOMETIMES
I WISH YOU COULD COME CHILL HERE W/ ME FOR A DAY

4

OR NIGHT TO SEE WHAT IT IS LIKE. IM SURE YOUD GET A KICK OF THE HOUSE DYNAMIC, THE VIBE, THE SPACE, THE FOOD, THE MENTALITY, AND THE ODDLY CALMING DEMEANOR ABOUT THE WING OF THE HOUSE I LIVE IN. MOU, GEORGE, AND I HAVE A LOT OF LAUGHS TOGETHER, WE EAT AMAZINGLY, AND WORKOUT EXTREMELY HARD. SOMETIMES I WORK OUT CRAZY THINKING ABOUT THE LOOK ON YOUR FACE WHEN YOU SEE THIS TRANSFORMATION IN PERSON. JUST THAT THOUGHT MAKES ME WORK HARD. I ALREADY KNOW WHAT MY DAUGHTERS WILL SAY LOL. "DADDY WHERES YOUR BELLY!" "LOOK MY DAD HAS MUSCLES NOW" HAHAHAHA LMAO. IM ALSO WORKING VERY HARD ON MY COMMUNICATION SKILLS. FINDING NEW WAYS TO USE WORDS AND DEVELOP TECHNIQUES TO EXPRESS MY FEELINGS W/ CONFIDENCE. BEING A MAN IS TOTALLY DIFFERENT TO ME NOW. COMPASSION, EMPATHY, LOYALTY, HONESTY, OPENMINDEDNESS, HUMILITY, KINDNESS, WILLIN-GNESS, AND HEALTHY LIVING AMONG SO MANY OTHER QUALITIES MAKES US BETTER (I GUESS ITS NOT ONLY ABOUT BEING A "MAN". ITS ABOUT JUST BEING THE BEST PERSON) I KNOW I HAD THOSE QUALITIES ITS JUST THAT I WOULD TEND TO LET THE WRONG PEOPLE IN MY LIFE BEAT DOWN MY SPIRITS UNTIL I WOULD LOSE WHO I WAS. NEVER AGAIN WILL THAT HAPPEN. HONESTLY IM NOT SURE WHY I WROTE SO MUCH TONIGHT, IT JUST HAPPENED. ITS 9:07 RIGHT NOW. IM SURE YOURE LOOKING ADORABLE IN YOUR PAJAMAS SNUGGLED ON THE COUCH WATCHING A SHOW. I WISH I COULD SEE YOU IN PERSON. THAT THOUGHT MAKES ME SO HAPPY. I GUESS IN MY OWN WAY WHEN I AM WRITING TO YOU I FEEL A BIT CONNECTED TO YOU IN THIS MOMENT. →

(5)

TALKING OR WRITING YOU MAKES ME FEEL SAFE AND AT HOME. HEARING YOUR VOICE AND LOOKING AT YOUR PHOTO MAKES THIS PLACE SEEM OK FOR THE TIME BEING. YOU MAKE LONLINESS GO AWAY AND BRING SO MUCH JOY, LOVE, FAITH, AND POSITIVITY TO A SITUATION THAT COULD EASILY TAKE THOSE CRUCIAL ELEMENTS AWAY FROM A PERSON. YOUVE BROUGHT WARMTH WHEN THERE WAS COLD AND LIGHT WHEN IT WAS DARKNESS. WHEN IM LIVING IN NORTH VAN WILL YOU COME VISIT ME AND/OR COME TO A MEETING W/ ME? OR MAYBE WE COULD MEET FOR LUNCH IN HORSESHOE BAY AND SPEND AN AFTERNOON TOGETHER WALKING AROUND AND TALKING. I NEVER ACTUALLY KNOW IF YOU WANT TO SPEND TIME CHILLING W/ ME OR NOT, BUT ID SURE LIKE TO CHILL OUT W/ YOU WHENEVER POSSIBLE. MAYBE WE COULD GO TO A MEETING THEN GO TO THE REC CENTER FOR SAUNA, STEAM ROOM, HOT TUB, ETC. OR GRAB LUNCH FROM THE FORMER "HURRICANE". ID BE DOWN FOR PRETTY MUCH WHATEVER. ILL BE GLAD TO BE OUT OF HERE AND SEE YOU IN PERSON. ILL BE OVER THE FENCE W/ JOY IF YOU MAKE TO MISSION TO SEE ME AS WELL. ITD BE A TRIP TO HAVE YOU COME HERE. HAVE YOU EVER BEEN IN AN INSTITUTION? I WOULDNT EXACTLY CALL IT PRISON EVEN THO-UGH TECHNICALLY IT IS ONE. I CANT EVEN IMAGINE WHAT IT WOULD FEEL LIKE WALKING INTO THE VISITS AREA AND SEE YOU THERE. I TRY TO IMAGINE IT BUT IM SURE IT WILL BE POSITIVE, EMOTIONAL, AND OVERWHELMING (IN THE BEST WAY POSSIBLE). ILL LEAVE THAT UP TO YOU. LIKE I ALWAYS SAY, NO PRESSURE OR EXPECT-ATIONS FROM ME. I AM GRATEFUL EITHER WAY NO MATTER WHAT. GOODNIGHT SWEET GIRL. I LOVE YOU ZZZ

(6)

2022-04-12

GOOD MORNING SUNSHINE. ITS ACTUALLY RAINING VERY HARD OUTSIDE BUT I GET TO SEE YOUR GORGEOUS FACE TONIGHT WHICH IN TURN MAKES TODAY FULL OF SUNSHINE TO ME. TODAY I HAVE MY JOB MEETING, TO GO OVER WHAT TASKS ILL BE DOING AND WHATS EXPECTED OF ME. I ALREADY HAVE THE JOB SO IT IS NOT AN INTERVIEW. IM STOKED ITS JUST ANOTHER ACTIVITY TO PASS THE TIME QUICKER. I WOKE UP WONDERING IF YOUR FEET WERE SORE (I HOPE THEY ARENT) AND IF YOU SLEPT SOUNDLY (I HOPE YOU DID). ILL MOST LIKELY THINK ABOUT YOU A LOT TODAY AS I AM GOING TO HAVE THE CHANCE TO SEE YOU. WE ARE CONFINED UNTIL 4PM SO ILL PROBS JUST READ A BIT AND WATCH T.V. UNTIL THAT TIME. WELL ANGEL IT IS TIME FOR ME TO BE WEARING MORE THAN BOXERS AND GET DRESSED. IM FEELING SUPER LEAN THIS MORNING AND SEXY AF. THESE WORKOUTS ARE PAYING OFF REALLY WELL. I DO HOPE YOU LIKE IT. I SURE DO. ⟹ IT IS ALMOST NOON AND SO FAR IVE WENT TO THAT MEETING AND IT SEEMS LIKE A FAIRLY EASY UNION FACED WORKPLACE. ILL LEARN SOME NEW SKILLS AS WELL WHICH WILL BE A DECENT CHANGE OF PACE. IVE BEEN PLAYING LOTS OF GUITAR PIECING A BUNCH OF RIFFS & CHORD PROGRESSIONS TOGETHER INTO A BASE FOR A SONG I AM WRITING ABOUT BEING IN HERE AND A GIRL THAT GAVE ME HOPE. THE SONG IS GOING TO BE CALLED "WAITING TO CALL HER". OBVIOUSLY ITS A SONG ABOUT YOU (I HOPE YOU DO NOT MIND). IT IS ALSO CHEST AND TRICEP DAY TODAY STARTING AT 5:30PM-7:00PM SO IM GOING TO GO CRAZY ON THAT THEN COME HOME TO SHOWER AND DRESS NICE FOR OUR VIDEO. FOR SOME REASON I HAVE BUTTERFLIES AGAIN. IM NOT SURE WHY EXACTLY. MAYBE ITS ½ EXCITEMENT AND ½ BUTTERFLIES. PROBABLY BECAUSE YOU ARE SO SPECIAL TO ME AND BECAUSE I ABSOLUTELY ADORE YOU. ⟹ THIS NON-VIOLENT COMMUNICATION

(7)

BOOK IS ABSOLUTELY 100% INCREDIBLE. I FEEL IT IS A LIFE CHANGER FOR ME. VIOLENT COMMUNICATION ISNT JUST BEING AGGRESSIVE OR MEAN AT ALL. IT CAN BE SO SUBTLE THAT PRETTY MUCH MOST PEOPLE (INCLUDING MYSELF) HAVE NO IDEA ABOUT EVEN THE SMALLEST OF WORDS WE USE DAILY. IM REALLY GRATEFUL I GOT MY HANDS ON THIS BOOK. I WILL DEFINATELY PUT INTO AFFECT ITS TEACHINGS IMMEDIATELY. WHAT A PERSPECTIVE SHIFT ABOUT HOW I WAS RAISED AND TALKED TO MY ENTIRE LIFE. AND ALSO HOW I SPEAK TO OTHERS. THIS WILL BE A HUGE STEP FORWARD TO ACHIEVE ~~SELF~~ SELF AWARENESS AND SELF HELP. IT GIVES ME A LOT TO REFLECT ON THATS FOR SURE. ⟹ ONE HOUR UNTIL I SEE YOU. I JUST WORKED OUT SO HARD SO I LOOK GOOD FOR OUR CALL LOL. NOW I WILL PRACTICE THE PARTS OF ~~THE~~ THE SONG IM TRYING TO WRITE SO ITS SEMI ON POINT FOR WHEN I SHOW YOU. WELL ITS TIME TO GET READY, DRESS NICE, AND PRACTICE A LIL BIT. ⟹ SO NICE TO TALK DUDE. AFTER OUR CALL I WENT BACK TO THE GYM FOR ANOTHER 20 MINS. NOW IM AT HOME. GEORGE AND I ARE BAKING A PIZZA (ZZAA BRAH). TRY NOT TO LET INMATES COMMENT BOTHER YOU TOO MUCH DUDE. CRC WOULDNT HAVE DONE NEARLY WHAT WAS DONE W/OUT YOU. YOU DID SO MUCH HARD WORK AND SHOULD BE SO PROUD OF WHAT HAS BEEN ACCOMPLISHED. IM GOING TO TRY AND SIT A STATION #2 NEXT WEEK FOR OUR VIDEO CALL SO I CAN SHOW YOU MY TWO WEEK PHYSICAL PROGRESSION. ALSO I HOPE ITS NOT CHEESY THAT I NAMED MY SONG THAT BUT HONESTLY I THINK ABOUT YOU AND BESIDES MY NORMAL ROUTINES I AM ALWAYS EXCITED AND WAITING FOR ~~YOUR~~ THE NEXT TIME I GET TO CALL YOU. ~~HARD~~ OUT OF ALL MY FRIENDS YOUVE BECOME THE PERSON I CALL MOST. IVE BEEN ONLY CALLING PEOPLE ONCE A WEEK. TALKING TO EVERYBODY ALL THE TIME SLOWS THE TIME HERE RIGHT DOWN. THE GIRLS, BRITTANY, AND YOU ARE REALLY WHO

(8)

I WANT TO SPEND MY SPARE TIME W/. IM LOOKING FORWARD TO CALLING MY DAD AGAIN ONCE MY CARD IS TOPPED UP AGAIN. ⇒ IT IS FINALLY BEDTIME. GEORGE, MOU, AND I JUST HUNG OUT FOR THE LAST 2 HOURS TELLING STORIES ABOUT WHEN WE WERE ALL KIDS. WE ALL LAUGHED SO HARD THAT NOW MY STOMACH HURTS. TIME FOR ME TO CLIMB INTO BED. I HAVE SO MANY BLANKETS NOW AND THEY ARE SO HEAVY I HAVE BEEN HAVING THE MOST COMFORTABLE SLEEPS (STILL NOT A CALI. KING W/ KING PILLOW A DUVET BUT I AM STILL GRATEFUL FOR THEM). ILL DO THE USUAL, FINISH WRITING, HAVE SOME WATERED DOWN CRANBERRY JUICE, LIGHT SOME SAGE, AND WATCH SOME T.V.

AS ALWAYS.. GOODNIGHT SWEET GIRL AND I LOVE YOU MORE THAN YOU KNOW, AND ALSO... I FORGOT TO TELL YOU HOW STUNNINGLY BEAUTIFUL YOU WERE TONIGHT

Z Z Z Z Z Z

2022-04-13

HAPPY WEDNESDAY [redacted]. TODAY HAS BEEN A BUSY DAY THUS FAR. IT IS STILL A BIT CHILLY OUT HOWEVER SUPER SUNNY NONE THE LESS AND THERFOR I AM GRATEFUL. 10:37AM IS THE TIME AND SO FAR IVE BEEN TO THE INDIGENOUS CLEANSING CEREMONY, WENT AND SAW THE PASTOR ABOUT A COMMUNICATIONS WORKBOOK (→ →WHICH I RECIEVED AND GOT PERMISSION TO HIGHLIGHT BOTH THE NOVEL & WORKBOOK ☺), SAW THE CONSTRUCTION SUPERVISOR TO SIGN PAPERWORK, PICKED UP RAINGEAR, AND TALKED TO THE SOCIAL PROGRAMS LADY ABOUT MORE PHOTOS. IT HAS ALWAYS BEEN IN MY NATURE TO GET LOTS DONE BUT THE DIFFERENCE NOW IS I DO NOT PROCRASTINATE (FOR THE MOST PART LOL). THE NEW PHONE CARD RENEW DATES JUST WENT UP SO NOW I KNOW WHAT DAY THATL BE DONE BY WHICH MAKES ME SUPER HAPPY. ILL WORKOUT MY BACK & BICEPS & ABS TODAY (SUPER EXCITING). LIFERING IS AT 2:15 AND THEN A WALK SHORTLY AFTER THAT.

(9)

WOW... WHAT A GORGEOUS DAY OUTSIDE. RIGHT NOW IM MISSING ALL MY BABIES AND LOVED ONES INCLLUDING YOU. BUT THAT FEELING WILL PASS ONCE IM DISTRACTED AGAIN. ← THE FEELINGS WILL STAY. THIS TIME AWAY REALLY SET IN WHAT IT MEANS TO CARE ABOUT PEOPLE AND HOW FAST THAT CAN BE LOST OR TAKEN. LIFE FOR ME NOW HAS SO MUCH MORE MEANING AND DIRECTION AND I CANNOT WAIT TO GET BACK OUT THERE AND MAKE A DIFFERENCE IN A POSITIVE WAY. LIFE IS MEANT TO BE CHERISHED NOT TAKEN FOR GRANTED. EACH MOMENT THAT PASSES IS EITHER GONE OR THERE FOREVER. I WILL MAKE EACH SECOND COUNT THIS TIME AROUND. IM FEEL HUMBLE, HAPPY, GRATEFUL, JOY, ETC. AS THE TIME ROLLS BY I STAND STILL AND PONDER THE THOUGHTS OF ALL THE TIME THAT I WASTED AND WHY. THE CONCLUSION IS THAT NOTHING IS A REAL WASTE IF A LESSON IS LEARNT AND A CHANGE/DIFFERENCE BECOMES THE NEXT MOTION. MAYBE MY FIRST BOOK WILL BE ALL THESE LETTERS I WRITE/WROTE/HAVE WRITTEN YOU SWEET GIRL TO SHOW THE UPS AND DOWNS OF BEING AWAY AND BUILDING A REAL FRIENDSHIP THROUGH PHONE CALLS AND LETTERS. I LOOK FORWARD TO READ-ING ALL THE LETTERS W/ YOU AS I NEVER RE-READ WHAT IVE WRITTEN TO YOU. THEYLL MOST LIKELY (100% WILL) NEED SPELL/GRAMMAR CHECKS. I SPIRITUALLY CLEANSE MY ROOM MULTIPLE TIME DAILY TO WARD OFF NEGATIVITY AS SOMETIMES IT INFECTS THE SPACES WE ARE SURROUNDED BY AND ARENT ALWAYS BROUGHT ON BY OURSELVES. I FIND IT PROTECTS ME AND ALLOWS CLARITY OF MIND BODY AND SOUL. IVE BEEN THINKING THAT IF IT IS OK W/ YOU I COULD CONTINUE TO WRITE YOU LETTERS WHEN I LEAVE HERE. ESPECIALLY THROUGHOUT THE NEXT PHASE IN NORTH VAN AND POSSIBLY EVEN INTO THE FUTURE BEYOND THAT. NOT MAKING A PLAN BUT AS OF RIGHT NOW THE THOUGHT OF IT WOULD BE SAWEEEET. ITD BE AWESOME TO READ THEM ALL OUT LOUD TOGETHER FOR SOMETHING TO DO.

(10)

I REMEMBER ONE TIME YOU TOLD ME THAT YOU WERE HAVING A BAD DAY AND READ THEM AND IT MADE YOU HAPPY. THAT WAS AN AMAZING FEELING FOR AS MAKING YOU SMILE, LAUGH, AND HAPPY MAKE ME FILL W/ HAPPINESS. IVE FELT SPECIAL BEING ABLE TO BE A PERSON YOU HAVE CONFIDED IN ABOUT HOW YOU FEEL, TELLING ME YOUR THOUGHTS, AND EVEN FEELING COMFORTABLE ENOUGH TO TALK ABOUT HAVING TO GO TO THE EMERGENCY ROOM. ILL ALWAYS BE A SAFE SPACE FOR YOU WHEN/IF YOU NEED ME.

AS A FIRE HAS BEEN LIT
WRITTING TO THE WALL.
PACING, STANDING, SITTING
WAITING TO MAKE A CALL.
IN A SPACE W/OUT WINDOWS
SHADOWS OF A ~~ANOTHER~~ FORMER SELF.
VOICES ~~WHEN~~ AS THE WINDS BLOWS
WORDS THAT WILL ALWAYS HELP.
PENS, PAPER, ~~AND~~ W/ TIME ~~TO~~ FOR THINKING
EXPRESSIONS THAT ALWAYS WERE.
TWENTY-EIGHTS MADE W/ IN INK → AS I WAIT...
→ ~~AS I WAIT~~
IM ALWAYS WAITING...
TO CALL HER.

AS I REVISE AND FIGURE OUT WORD PLACEMENT, RYTHYM AND VOCAL CARRY OVER A CHORUS WILL FIND ITS WAY INTO A SONG ⟹ VIDEO CHAT BOOKED AGAIN ☺. I HAVE AN APPT ~~W/~~ ~~THE~~ FOR MY CASE MANAGEMENT W/ THE PAROLE OFFICER NEXT WEEK. BOTH GROUPS ARE OUT FULL TIME AND THIS PLACE IS NOW FINALLY OPEN UP MORE AND MORE. MAYBE WE WILL BE ABLE TO HAVE A TOUCH VISIT (WHICH MEANS HUGS) BY THE TIME YOURE ABLE TO MEET ME. I GOT RESPECT FROM A LIFER IN LIFE RING TODAY BECAUSE OF THE WAY I THINK AND HANDLE MYSELF WHICH

(11)

WAS NICE. THE WHOLE INSTITUTION IS IN HIGH SPIRITS TODAY BECAUSE OF THE GROUPS MERGING. GEORGE AND I MADE SHEPHARDS PIE FOR DINNER. THIS PLACE SEEMS A WHOLE LOT BIGGER NOT BEING CONFINED TO AREAS 24hrs ON AND 24hrs OFF. I WIPED MY HEATER VENT W/ LEFTOVER DEODORANT I HAD AND NOW THIS ROOM SMELLS ABSOLUTELY AMAZING. THE DAY IS ONLY HALF OVER AND IT SEEMS LIKE SO MUCH HAS HAPPENED ALREADY. TIME JUST SPED UP AGAIN. ⟹

IT IS FINALLY FINAL COUNT (10:00PM). TONIGHT WAS REALLY COOL TO SEE ALL THE PEOPLE FROM BOTH AREAS MINGLING OUT ON ALL THE PATIOS. THE BBQS ARE COMING OUT AND EVERYONE INCLUDING THE C.O.S ARE HAPPY. IM EXCITED TO CLIMB BACK INTO BED FOR ANOTHER EVENING AND ONE MORE DAY IS COMPLETE. I CAN ALREADY TELL THAT EASTER LONG WEEKEND WILL BE STOKED. APPARENTLY THIS IS THE MOST THIS INSTITUTION HAS BEEN OPEN IN TWO YEARS. LAUGHTER WAS IN THE AIR EVERYWHERE TONIGHT. I HOPE I DREAM ABOUT YOU. ILL BE WISHING YOU WELLNESS AND HAPPINESS UNTIL WE CHAT NEXT. SWEET DREAM GORGEOUS GIRL. I MISS YOU AND LOVE YOU Z Z Z Z Z

2022-04-14

GOOOOD MORNING SUNSHINE. THE SUN IS OUT AND ALL THE DIFFERENT SPECIES OF BIRDS ARE OUT MAKING NOISE. THE GRASS IS LUSH GREEN IN COLOR. I JUST GOT BACK FROM A CLEANSING CEREMONY AT THE SWEAT GROUNDS. NOW I AM SITTING DOWN TO SAY GOODMORNING TO YOU AND LET YOU ONCE AGAIN KNOW HOW BEAUTIFUL YOU ARE AND HOW MUCH YOU MEAN TO ME. THIS MORNING IM GOING TO CLEAN THE BBQ AND MOVE IT TO THE FRONT PATIO SO WE CAN SOCIALIZE W/ ALL THE PASSERBYS AS WE COOK. I HAD SOME BAD DREAMS WHICH WOKE ME UP EARLY BUT THEY WERE QUICKLY SHAKIN OFF AND UP I GOT AND LEFT THE HOUSE. I AM GRATEFUL THAT

(12)

WEEKS ARE PASSING BY FAIRLY QUICKLY AND THAT I AM OVER HALFWAY DONE MY SENTENCE. OUR ORGANIC GARDEN CHIVES ARE ABUNDANT AND PLENTY. WHAT A GREAT THING TO GROW FOR FOOD. EASY AND SELF MAINTAINED. TODAY IS LEG & SHOULDER DAY WHICH IS VERY EXCITING AS THE RESULTS ARE STARTING TO BE VERY NOTICEABLE TO MYSELF AND OTHERS. MAN I MISS YOU ANGEL. EVERYTHING IVE WRITTEN IS HONEST AND REAL. I WRITE FROM MY HEART MINUTE BY MINUTE. AS I GROW PROGRESS, AND LEARN ABOUT MYSELF HOPEFULLY THE LETTERS GET BETTER AND MAKE YOU SMILE WHEN YOU READ THEM. ALL THE BIRDS HERE ARE NESTING. THE GEESE CHASE US AND HISS AT US AS WE WALK PASS THEM. APPARENTLY IT HURTS WHEN THEY BITE YOU LOL. TO BE COMPLETELY HONEST DUDE I FIND YOU SO SO SEXY IN EVERY WAY POSSIBLE INSIDE AND OUT. HOPEFULLY IM NOT OUT OF LINE WHEN I TELL YOU THAT. I WISH WE SPENT MORE TIME TOGETHER BEFORE I LEFT AND ITS TOO BAD I WAS W/ SOMEONE BECAUSE WHEN IM W/ SOMEONE THEN I AM LOYAL TO ONLY THAT PERSON EVEN THOUGH IT WAS SO TOXIC. I THINK ABOUT YOU ALL THE TIME IN HERE AS YOUVE BEEN THE PERSON BESIDE ME THE ENTIRE TIME NO MATTER WHAT. IN ESSENCE YOU ARE A DREAMGIRL IN MY WORLD AND THAT HONESTLY INTIMIDATES THE FUCK OUT OF ME. I HAVE LITERALLY NEVER BEEN INTIMADATED BY A GIRL BEFORE AND IT MAKES ME TIMID AND SHY SOMETIMES. I HOPE YOU SLEPT WELL AND YOUR FEET FEEL GOOD FOR THE DAY. => I WAS JUST THINKING THAT MAYBE IF YOURE NOT DATING ANYONE IN AUGUST WE COULD GO ON AN ADVENTURE WHEN IM LIVING IN N.V. I WAS THINKING OF WALKING THESE TUNNELS OUT IN HOPE OR RESEARCH A GHOST HUNTING LOCATION SOMEWHERE W/IN DRIVING

(13)

DISTANCE. OR SQUAMISH BUNGEE JUMPING OR WHISTLER ZIPLINE OR SOMETHING. SOMETHING EXCITING, ADVEN-TUROUS AND FUN. OR MAYBE GO SEE FRIEND & FRIEND OR DRIVE OUT AND VISIT FRIEND. ID LOVE TO GO SEE ALL OF THEM TOGETHER LIKE A DOUBLE BLAST FROM THE PAST. THE ONLY REASON I MENTION ABOUT SEEING SOMEONE AS IT SHOULDNT MATTER IS THAT I WOULDNT WANT TO BE ANY CAUSE OF NEGATIVITY IN YOUR PERSONAL LIFE. ITS A RESPECT THING. EITHER WAY IM DOWN FOR WHATEVER REALLY. ID JUST REALLY ENJOY SPENDING A FULL DAY W/ YOU ~~AND~~ TO SHOW YOU THE APPRECIATION YOU DESERVE FOR BEING MY HOMIE. ⇒ IT IS NOW 3:18PM AND SO FAR SINCE I WROTE EARLIER ANOTHER FRIEND I HAD SPENT TIME W/ IN R-RAC ~~SHOWED~~ HAS SHOWN UP. 5 OF US SAT ON THE PATIO AND TALKED ABOUT OUR TIME THERE AND JOKED AND LAUGHED ABOUT THE DIFFERENCE BETWEEN THERE AND HERE. WE FOUND OUT THAT THE QUARANTINES ARE OVER NOW AND THINGS ARE OPENING UP EVEN MORE. THE SWEAT LODGE IS HAPPENING IN A COUPLE WEEKS TIME AND VISITS SHOULD OPEN UP EVEN MORE WHICH IS THE MOST EXCITING. VISITS ARE THE REASON I CAME TO MISSION MIN. MY MOOD HAS BEEN ON AND OFF FOR NO REASON AND IM WOND-ERING IF ANYONE OUT THERE THAT IS EMOTIONALLY CONNECTED TO ME IS HAVING A HARD TIME. I PRAY THAT MY KIDS ARE WELL AND SAFE AND SAME FOR YOU. IM SURE IT IS ALL FINE (HOPEFULLY). ⇒ AND ANOTHER DAY DOWN ☺ TIME FOR 10PM COUNT AND BEDTIME. I WORKED OUT HARD TODAY AND AGAIN TONIGHT FOR A LITTLE BIT. HOPEFULLY THERE ARE SOME GOOD SHOWS ON TONIGHT. AT THIS MOMENT ANGEL YOU ARE ON MY MIND. I ALWAYS HOPE YOUR DAY WAS BRIGHT AND YOUR NIGHT IS COZY. HAVE LOVELY DREAMS SWEET SWEET GIRL. I TRULY DO LOVE YOU MORE THAN YOU KNOW Z Z Z Z Z Z Z Z

(14)

2022-04-15

GOOD AFTERNOON. WHAT A GORGEOUS DAY OUTSIDE. THE INSTITUTION OPENING IS MOVING FORWARD WHICH IS SO INCREDIBLE. IF YOU COME SEE ME WE MAY ACTUALLY BE ABLE TO HUG EACHOTHER. WHAT A TRIP THATLL BE. SO FAR IVE GONE FOR A WALK AND TO THE GYM. ILL DO CARDIO AT 1PM FOR AN HOUR AS WELL. WE ARE HAVING SALMON FOR DINNER TONIGHT AS IT IS GOOD FRIDAY. I GO TO CHURCH AT 2:30 FOR AN HOUR AS WELL. THE WHOLE ENVIRONMENT HERE IS GREAT VIBES AGAIN. IVE BEEN THINKING ABOUT YOU THIS MORNING AND AS ALWAYS WISHING YOU WELL. I FUCKING LOVE AND ADORE YOU WHOLE HEARTEDLY. THERE IS A LOT MORE GOING ON NOW AND PHONES ARE OPEN AT ALL TIMES YET YOURE THE ONLY ONE (BESIDES THE KIDDOS) THAT I LOOK FORWARD TO CONNECTING W/... TIME TO CHECK THE MAIL. HOPEFULLY THERE IS SOMETHING IN THERE LOL. ⟹

IT IS 333PM AND IM BACK FROM EASTER CHURCH. I RECIEVED PALMS AND ANOTHER ROSARY. IT WAS GOOD. I GOT TO PRAY FOR EVERYONE I CARE ABOUT AND REFLECT ON WHY I AM HERE AND EVERYONE IT HAS AFFECTED. I TALKED THE GIRLS AND ALL MY SISTERS. AFTER 4PM COUNT I WILL WALK OUT AND CALL YOU QUICKLY TO TELL YOU HAPPY EASTER AND WILL LEAVE A MSSG IF YOU DONT ANSWER. I TALKED TO EX-WIFE S MOM WHO IS W/ THE GIRLS AND EVERY--ONE WAS HAPPY AND WELL. SHE SAID SHE WILL SEND ME ANOTHER BUNCH OF PHOTOS OF THEM WHICH MAKES MY HEART FILLED W/ LOVE. THERES NOT ALL THAT MUCH GOING ON THIS EVENING SO ILL PROBS JUST CHILL OUT, RELAX, AND HAVE A NICE SALMON DINNER W/ DIRTY RICE AND MAYBE SOME VEGGIES. ⟹ JUST IN FOR 7PM COUNT. IT WAS JUST HACKY-SACK CENTRAL IN FRONT OF MY HOUSE. DUDE SHOWING ~~OFF THIER~~ THEIR PATTERN & STITCHING AND TALKING ABOUT MATERIALS AND FILLERS LOL. ITS THE LITTLE THINGS IN HERE. IT WAS FUN TO PLAY. THE SKY

(15)

IS DOING STRANGE THINGS. ITS BLUE IN SOME SPOTS W/ WHITE CLOUDS. THE SIDE OF THE SKY IS LIKE A DARK GREY WALL TRYING TO TAKE CONTROL AND RAIN. EITHER WAY ILL BE HAPPY. I GOT TO CHILL W/ MY QUARATINE BUDDY BENJAMIN WHICH WAS NICE. I REALLY ENJOY THAT DUDE. HE HASNT BEEN OUT N ABOUT THE LAST COUPLE DAYS AND SAID HES BEEN BINGE READING "REACHER" BOOKS BACK TO BACK 10 HOURS AT A TIME UNTIL HE IS CROSS EYED LOL. I COULD NOT KEEP CONCENTRATION OR INTEREST FOR EVEN CLOSE TO THAT LONG. THE INSTITUTION IS HAVING AN INMATE BBQ FOR MAY LONG WEEKEND WHICH SHOULD BE HALF DECENT I THINK. I GOT SOME NEW MAGAZINES TODAY WHICH IS 100% ABSOLUTELY AWESOME. ILL BE MORE THAN STOKED WHEN ITS THE REAL THING AGAIN. HOLY DOES THIS PLACE STRIP THAT TO THE CORE. I WAS DEFINATELY NOT USED TO ZERO FEMALE CONTACT. I DONT KNOW WHY I TOLD YOU ALL THAT BUT WHATEVS.. ITS TRUE AND A FACT AND ALSO MY CURRENT REALITY. IM SURE YOU WONT BE PHASED. NOTHING HAS PHASED YOU THUS FAR. ⇒♥⇒ THE NIGHT IS FINALLY AT AN END. WE PLAYED MORE HACKI-SACK AND SAT ON THE PATIO AND SOCIALIZED W/ ALL THE PEOPLE WALKING. FOR A COUPLE MOMENTS I ALMOST FORGOT WHERE I WAS AS IT FELT SO CHILL AND NORMAL. IM EXCITED TO FINALLY LAYDOWN, TURN OUT THE LIGHTS, LIGHT SOME SAGE, AND WATCH T.V/MOVIE. I AM GRATEFUL FOR ANOTHER WONDERFUL DAY. AS OF NOW I HAVE NO PLANS FOR TOMORROW BUT AM STOKED FOR YET ANOTHER DAY. IF ITS SUNNY ILL PLAY SPORTS AND GO FOR A WALK. AND IF IT IS ~~SUN~~ RAINING ILL RELAX IN MY ROOM WATCH T.V., READ MY BOOKS, AND AS ALWAYS WRITE TO YOU AND SOME FRIENDS IN OTHER INSTITUTIONS. ONCE AGAIN I HOPE YOU SMILED

(16)

LOTS TODAY, LAUGHED, AND WERE HAPPY. HAVE A GREAT SLEEP AND IF YOU DREAM ABOUT ME TELL ME A SECRET. GOODNIGHT BEAUTIFUL ANGEL AND I LOVE YOU AND MISS YOU. Z Z Z Z Z Z

2022-04-16

ITS THE 16TH PAGE OF THE 16TH DAY, WHAT A COINCEDENCE LOL. TODAY IS A LIGHTLY OVERCAST DAY AT 11:09AM. I BOILED SOME EGGS FOR GEORGE (GEO) AND I, AT NOON IM GOING ON A RUN IN THE BACK ROAD BEHIND THE DUCK POND. I HAD AN AWESOME DREAM LAST NIGHT AND EVERY TIME I WOKE UP I RUSHED TO FALL ASLEEP BACK INTO IT. I SLEPT IN UNTIL JUST AFTER 10am BECAUSE OF IT. I WILL WRITE A STORY ABOUT IT INSIDE OUR "DREAM PASS" WHICH WILL BE FUN. I HAD COMPANY BRIEFLY WHILE I SAT ON THE DECK FOR A ½ HOUR THIS MORNIN. MY ENTIRE BODY IS VERY SORE FROM ALL THE PHYSICAL ACT--IVITIES IVE BEEN DOING TO GET MY BODY WHERE ID LIKE IT TO BE BEFORE MY RELEASE. IT SEEMS FAR FROM NOW BUT YET SO VERY CLOSE AS WELL. DAUGHTER WAS FINALLY ABLE TO GET A FRENCH BRAID IN HER HAIR AFTER 4 YEARS W/ NO HAIRCUT. GRA-NDMA TOLD ME SHE WAS SO EXCITED, PROUD, AND OBVIOUSLY CUTE AS HELL. THEY ARE MAILING MORE PHOTOS NEXT WED-THURS WHICH MELTS MY HEART. I SURE DO MISS THEM AND DAUGHTER. PRETTY PLEASE ANGEL CAN YOU SEND ME MORE PHOTOS OF YOURSELF? I TRY MY HARDEST NOT TO ASK BUT WOULD LOVE TO SEE MORE OF YOU. I COULD LOOK AT YOU EVERY DAY AND HEAR YOUR VOICE ALL DAY EVERYDAY AS YOU KNOW HOW I FEEL ABOUT YOU. THAT HASNT STOPPED FOR ONE SECOND. IM NOT AFRAID TO TELL YOU AS I ALREADY HAVE AND YOU HAVENT PUSHED ME AWAY OR STOPPED BEING AMAZING TO ME WHICH I DO BELIEVE WOULD HAVE HAPPENED BY NOW. IT JUST SUCKS THAT IM IN HERE FOR NOW. THE POSITIVE SIDE OF ME BEING AWAY IS THAT I AM GROWING AS A PERSON IN EVERY SINGLE WAY POSSIBLE

(17)

AND OUR FRIENDSHIP HAS BEEN ABLE TO GROW IN A WAY THAT IS SO MUCH DIFFERENT THAN MOST PEOPLE THESE DAYS GET TO EXPERIENCE. I CHERISH THE FACT IT HAS BEEN THROUGH COMMUNICATION AND LEARNING ABOUT ONE ANOTHER. MY FRIENDSHIP W/ YOU ANGEL HAS BECOME OF SUCH IMPORTANCE THAT I WOULD NOT TRADE WHAT IT IS RIGHT NOW FOR ANYTHING. AS IM READING THIS BOOK & LEARNING I CAN SEE ALL THE LOVE I FEEL AND UNDER--STAND WHY IM FEELING IT WHERE IN THE PAST IVE GOTTEN CONFUSED AND/OR WITHDRAWN BY FEAR OF REJECTION OR FEAR OF VULNERABILITY. IVE REALIZED THAT REAL FRIENDSHIPS MEAN SO MUCH MORE IN LIFE THAN I EVER THOUGHT POSSIBLE. ONCE I OPENED MY HEART TO ALLOW MYSELF TO LOVE MYSELF THAN I COULD LOVE OTHERS FOR WHO THEY ARE. I COULD SEE BEAUTY RADIATE OUT LIKE GLOWING IN THE DARK AND FEEL OTHER PEOPLES EMOTIONS. I HAVE ALWAYS BEEN AN EMPATH THAT FELT THE WEIGHT OF OTHERS AND FELT IT HAD BEEN A CURSE. SLOWLY ITS FLIPPED AROUND TO THE POINT ITS BEEN A FOCAL POINT OF GRATITUDE. THE MAIN DIFFERENCE IS THE UNDERSTANDING OF IT ALL AND NOT BEARING THE HEAVINESS LIKE A TON OF BRICKS ANYMORE. NOW I FILTER IT ALL AND PROCESS WHY I ATTACH TO IT OR IT ATTACHES TO ME. AS FRIENDS I ALWAYS WANT TO LET YOU KNOW HOW I FEEL ABOUT YOU BECAUSE IF SOMETHING WERE TO HAPPEN TO EITHER OF US AT LEAST POSITIVE & LOVING WORDS WOULD HAVE BEEN SPOKEN. I KNOW THAT YOU KNOW HOW AMAZING, AWESOME, AND UNBELIEVABLY BEAUTIFUL YOU ARE AND IF YOU DONT KNOW IT YOU SHOULD KNOW IT. I HOLD YOU UP ONE THE HIGHEST PEDASTAL THERE IS AND FEEL UNCONDITIONAL LOVE FOR WHO YOU ARE IN EVERY WAY IMAGINABLE/POSSIBLE. YOUVE BECOME LIKE AN ANGEL TO ME. I WILL ALWAYS BE HERE WHEN YOU

(18)

NEED ME. WELL SWEET GIRL. I AM GOING TO GET READY FOR MY RUN. IM AGGRESSIVELY WORKING TOWARDS THE SEXIEST BODY IVE EVER HAD. AND IN TURN ITS HELPED FOR A BETTER MINDSET AND HEALTHIER, MORE APPRECIATIVE, AND TRUE CONFIDENCE W/ OUT EGO ATTACHED. ⇒ I AM BACK FROM A 5K RUN AND USING THE PHONE. I TALKED TO MY SISTERS AND INMATE WHICH WAS NICE. FOR SOME REASON I AM HEAVY-HEARTED. I KNOW THAT ITS BECAUSE I AM IN HERE AND WORRIED ABOUT MY CHILDREN AS ~~TH~~ BOTH MOMS ARE STRUGGLING. IVE LEARNED THAT GIVING SOLUTIONS DOES NOT HELP ANYONE AS ALL PEOPLE NEED TO SORT THEMSELVES OUT. THE ONLY REASON I AM AFFECTED IS BECAUSE IF I WERE OUT THERE AT LEAST I COULD HAVE THE KIDS AND GIVE THEM ALL THE LOVE THEY ARE NEEDING FROM THEIR PARENTS, ESPECIALLY THE LOVE FROM A DAD WHICH DAUGHTERS NEED. I WILL EXCERSIZE AND READ TO HELP THE FEELINGS PASS BY. I HOPE YOU ARE HAVING A GREAT DAY. IM THINKING ABOUT YOU A LOT AS WELL I JUST LIT SOME SAGE. ITS FUNNY HOW RELAXING IT IS. WRITTING IS DEFINATELY A CALMING ASPECT OF LIFE IN HERE. GEO IS MAKING HAND MADE TORTILLAS FOR OUR BURRITOES TONIGHT. MAYBE ILL HAVE A HOT SHOWER FOR 30+ MINS SO I AM ALL SMOOTH EVERYWHERE. I CAN SEE WHY WOMAN DO IT LOL. I LOVE EVERY PART OF SHAVING AND THE FEELING OF IT ALL. 100% DEFINATELY NOT SOMETHING I EVER IMAGINED ID DO, SAY, OR EVEN WRITE. ANOTHER THING I AM MISSING TODAY I JUST REALIZED IS PHYSICAL CONTACT/CONNECTION OF SOMEONE I AM IN LOVE WITH AND NOT JUST IN AN INTIMATE WAY. JUST BEING IN MY PERSONS COMPANY WOULD BE A DREAM COME TRUE TODAY. UNFORTUNATELY IT IS NOT IN MY REALITY ATM SO I WONT DWELL ON THIS EMOTION, ILL JUST FEEL AND OBSORB IT

19

AND LET IT PASS THROUGH W/ LOVE. ⟹ I JUST WENT FOR A WALK AND SOCIALIZED W/ SOME OTHER INMATES WHICH WAS NICE AND DISTRACTING ALSO TOTALLY NEEDED. NOW I JUST CUT & PREPPED VEGETABLES FOR DINNER. AFTER 5ISH ILL USE THE PHONE FOR A MINUTE THEN LATER ON CRUSH SOME WEIGHTS AT THE GYM FROM 8PM UNTIL 10PM. ILL BE WORKING ON BACK & BICEPS AND THEN THROW IN SOME CENTER & UPPER CHEST. IM TRYING TO DEVELOP MY CHEST AS MUCH AS I CAN, ESPECIALLY NOW THAT RESULTS ARE BECOMING NOTICEABLE MORE & MORE WEEK TO WEEK W/ THIS NEW CRAZY PROGRAM I AM ON. ALL IN ALL MY GOALS ARE TO BE ALL AROUND EXTREMELY STRONG BUT MAINTAIN GREAT CARDIO AND FLEXIBILITY FOR A MORE ACTIVE, HEALTHY, AND SOBER LIFESTYLE. ⟹ ITS 10:42PM AND ANOTHER DAY DOWN. TIME FOR BED. HOPE YOU HAD AN AWESOME DAY DUDE. HAPPY EASTER ANGEL. ILL MEET YOU IN DREAMLAND MY FRIEND Z Z Z Z Z Z Z Z

2022-04-17

DEAR ANGEL. I MISS YOU. ITS YET ANOTHER BEAUTIFUL DAY OUT AND IT REMINDS ME OF YOU. WE ARE INSIDE FOR 11AM COUNT SO I FIGURED ID COME WRITE TO YOU FOR A MOMENT AND LOOK AT THE GORGEOUS PHOTO YOU GAVE ME OF YOURSELF. HAPPY SUNDAY AND I WISH YOU AN ASTONISHING AFTERNOON. I AM NOT SURE EXACTLY WHAT TO WRITE OR SAY BUT JUST WANTED YOU TO KNOW THAT I LOVE YOU DUDE. ⟹ 2:46PM AND SO FAR THE DAY HAS BEEN SUPER DECENT. I WENT TO THE PROT-ESTANT CHURCH AND IT WAS SWEET. PASTOR DAN REALLY DELIVERS HIS MESSAGE WELL AND ALWAYS HITS HOME A COUPLE TIMES. THEN I WENT FOR A WALK W/ A DUDE ILL BE WORKING W/ AND SHOT THE SHIT ABOUT BIKES, TIME INSIDE, AND LIFE IN GENERAL. IT IS FOR SURE A GREAT DAY TO WALK THE GHETTO (LOWER HOUSES) THE HAMPTONS (UPPER HOUSES WHERE I LIVE) AND THE BACK RD →

(20)

OUT BEHIND THE POND AND AROUND THE BACK OF THE SPORTS FIELDS. THE LOCAL MOUNTAIN RANGE IN OUR VIEW IS MAJESTIC AND GIVES ME HOPE FOR THE DAY I AM RELEASED. NOW I AM GOING TO GO CALL MY FRIEND DOUGY AND THE GIRLS AND TRY YOU AGAIN LATER ON. ⟹ COFFEES, BADMINTON, HACKY-SACK, AND SHORTSLEEVE SHIRTS IN THE BACKYARD SUN JUST BEFORE THE 7PM COUNT. WHILE WE WAIT IVE RETREATED TO MY ROOM FOR SOME SPACE AND SOLITUDE FOR A BIT. THIS DAY HAS PASSED BY FAIRLY QUICKLY IT SEEMS. HONESTLY IM LOOKING FORWARD FOR THIS DAY TO WRAP UP SO I CAN CLIMB INTO MY WARM BED AND WATCH T.V. I THINK ITS BECAUSE IVE BEEN MISSING HOME LATELY. I DONT MIND MEETING NEW PEOPLE AND BEING INDEPENDANT BUT HOME IS HOME AND FAMILIAR FACES WOULD BE A NICE CHANGE AFTER SO MUCH TIME AWAY. IM TRYING TO NOT SUCCUMB TO LONELINESS AND SOMETIMES IT CREEPS IN FOR A MOMENT OR TWO SO I TRY MY HARDEST TO FIND HEALTHY DISTRACTIONS AND OUTLETS FOR THIS ENERGY WHEN I FEEL ALONE. IN HERE EITHER YOURE MADE OR BROKEN AND IT CAN BE A VERY FINE LINE THAT I TRY MY HARDEST TO STAY AWAY FROM. SELF AWARENESS AND SELF SABOTAGE ARE VERY REAL. INSIDE THIS PLACE IT DOES NOT ALLOW FOR "BAD" OR "OFF" DAYS BECAUSE THE WRONG WORDS CAN LEAD INTO ANY NUMBER OF DIRECTIONS. I FOCUS ON KEEPING A FORWARD AND POSITIVE HEADING. IT CAN BE TOUGH TO MAINTAIN IN HERE WHEN THERE IS NO ONE TO TALK TO. I TRY NOT TO LET OUT MY EMOTIONS IN HERE OR ON THE PHONE MOST OF THE TIME BECAUSE THE WRONG SEED PLANTED CAN GROW INTO A MONSTER SO FAST. IVE SEEN MANY PEOPLE "BREAK" AND COME CLOSE A COUPLE OF TIMES MYSELF. CRYING IS NOT OPTIONAL WHATSOEVER IN THIS PLACE. AS IM HERE

(21)

AND TIME PASSES IVE LEARNED SOME THINGS ABOUT HUMAN BEINGS THAT LIFE OUTSIDE KEEPS US IGNORANT FROM/TO. I USED TO WATCH A SERIES/SHOW CALLED "ALONE" AND WOULD MAKE FUN OF PEOPLE FOR MISSING THEIR FAMILIES AFTER 60 DAYS W/ 500K ON THE LINE. NOW I CAN UNDERSTAND WHY. I KNOW I COULD LAST LONGER ESPECIALLY W/ A PRIZE LOL ESPECIALLY AFTER ALL OF THIS BUT I GET IT NOW AND WONT MAKE FUN ANYMORE. ISOLATION IS A WHOLE DIFFERENT LEVEL BEAST THAN IVE EVER REALIZED OR EXPERIENCED. LATELY ITS BEEN LOVE, HOPE, AND FAITH THAT GETS ME THROUGH IT ALL. ITS REALLY ALL I HAVE THAT IS KEEPING MY SANITY IN AMONGST INSANITY. I CANNOT WAIT TO HUG OR HOLD HANDS AGAIN. THE THOUGHT OF PHYSICAL CONNECTION AGAIN FILLS MY HEART. JUST THOSE TWO ACTS MEAN SO MUCH MORE TO ME NOW THEN EVER BEFORE. THOSE TWO SIMPLE THINGS ARE SO TAKEN FOR GRANTED IN SOCIETY THESE DAYS THAT I WILL FOREVER BE GRATEFUL TO HAVE HAD MY EYES RE-OPENED TO HOW SPECIAL SHARING THOSE LITTLE EMOTIONS ARE. I AIM TO CREATE MORE MEANINGFUL CONNECTIONS TO PEOPLE I LOVE ONCE THIS TIME IS COMPLETE. TO LAY DOWN, WATCH A MOVIE, AND CUDDLE IS LITERALLY I WANT TO DO RIGHT NOW. TO BE UP AGAINST ANOTHER PERSON, RELAXED, AND WARM IS WHAT I AM MISSING MOST. NOT JUST ANYONE THOUGH. SOMEONE SPECIAL OR SNUGGLING MY KIDDOS. ⇒ I... LOVE...... AMERICAN IDOL (NOT WORDS I THOUGHT ID EVER SAY LOL). I JUST LEFT THE LIVING ROOM BECAUSE PEOPLE WERE TALKING TO WATCH IT ON MY T.V. ALONE ZERO DISTRACTIONS HAHAHA. I LITERALLY CALLED YOU.. LEFT A MESSAGE AND WALKED HOME SO I ~~WA~~ WOULDNT MISS OUT. ~~AN~~ AAAAANND THATS WHAT I DO ON SUNDAY EVENINGS. IM HAPPY

(22)

THAT TODAY IS ALL WRAPPED UP AND OVER. SOON ILL FINISH WRITTING TO YOU AND GET READY FOR BED. MY BED IS LOOKING SO INCREDIBLY COMFY RIGHT NOW. TONIGHT I CONNECTED W/ SOME FRIENDS I HADNT TALKED TO IN AWHILE AND WAS ON THE PHONE FOR ALMOST TWO HOURS TODAY. THE FUNNY THING IS THAT I REALLY ONLY WANTED TO TALK TO YOU AND ~~HERE~~ HEAR YOUR VOICE. IM REALLY MISSING YOU THE LAST COUPLE DAYS AS YOUVE BECOME SUCH AN IMPORTANT PERSON TO ME AND I HOPE THAT IM NOT OVERWHE--LMING YOU IN ANY WAY. JEEEEESUS THIS SHOW IS GIVING ME GOOSEBUMPS AND CHILLS. NONSTOP CHILLS. SOMETIMES I WONDER ABOUT YOU AND WHY YOUVE BEEN ABLE TO AFFECT ME SO MUCH (BECAUSE YOURE AWESOME OBV.) AND HAVE YOU IN MY THOUGHTS ON A DAILY BASIS. HOWEVER IT HAPPENED [redacted] IM AMAZED BY IT EITHER WAY. OBVIOUSLY I TALK ABOUT YOU TO MY FAMILY AND I KNOW YOU TELL YOUR FAMILY ABOUT ME AS WELL... IM NOT SURE WHAT ANY OF IT MEANS BUT IM HAPPY TO HAVE SOMEONE AS GREAT AS YOU ARE LOVING AND SUPPORTING ME AT MY TURN--ING POINT. THIS SCRIPT HAS BEEN FLIPPED RIGHT SIDE UP SO KEEP YOUR EYES & ARMS OPEN AND WATCH FOR WHAT IS COMING NEXT. [redacted] I CAN FEEL SOMETHING GREATER THAN EVER BUILDING UP INSIDE AS I EXPERIENCE EVERYTHING THAT IS GOING ON DEEP DOWN. THIS HIGHER POWER KEEPS RE-ASSURING ME IN OBVIOUS WAYS. LIKE SMALL GLITCHES IN THE MATRIX. ALL I NEED TO KNOW IS THAT TO GET THROUGH THIS I NEED TO KEEP PUTTING IN DAYS ONE DAY AT A TIME. MY GOAL THIS WEEK IS TO PUSH HARDER THAN EVER AT THE GYM AND JUST EXPLODE. ANYHOW IT IS TIME FOR BED (11:00PM). AMERICAN IDOL IS ENDING SO ILL GET

23

INTO MY SLEEPWEAR (BOXERS LOL) AND CLIMB INTO BED
AS ALWAYS AND LIKE EVERY NIGHT ILL EXPRESS THAT
I REALLY MISS YOU AND UNCONDITIONALLY LOVE YOU
GOOD NIGHT SWEET GIRL & SWEET DREAMS XOXO
Z Z Z Z Z Z

2022-04-18

A NEW DAY HAS ARRIVED. ALTHOUGH IT IS POURING OUT I CAN STILL SEE THE BEAUTY IN NATURES GIFT FULLY. YESTERDAYS SUN HELPED ALL THE VEGETATION GROW AND DRINK. TODAY IT WILL BE FED AND NOURISHED. AS THE SURROUNDING TREES, SHRUBS, AND FLOWERS ETC BEGIN TO GAIN VIBRANT COLORS I AM MORE THAN GRATEFUL TO BE ALIVE. TODAY (MONDAY) IVE DECIDED TO FAST FOR 24hrs. IM NOT 100% SURE WHY BUT FOR SOME REASON I AM PROPELLED TO DO SO. MAYBE ITS BECAUSE IVE BEEN COMING TO AN UNDERTANDING OF MY CONSTANTLY PASSING EMOTIONS. AS I LEARN TO HARNESS THEM AND CHANNEL THEM, TODAY I WILL FAST I THINK TO GIVE MYSELF THE DAY TO RECONSILE MY THOUGHTS AND PRAYERS SO TOMORROW I CAN START FRESH W/ A HIGHER APPRECIATION FOR ~~A~~ ALL ASPECTS OF LIVING. JUST SO YOU KNOW (WHICH IM SURE YOU DO) YOU ARE SO BEAUTIFUL. I HAD AN AMAZING ADVENTURE IN DREAMLAND LAST NIGHT AND WOKE UP IN SUCH A GREAT MINDSET. THE MSSG IN THE DREAM WAS TO STAY ON THE PATH I AM ON AND ALL DOORS WILL OPEN. I EVEN GOT KISSED IN THE DREAM AND IT FELT SO REAL IT WAS UNREAL. I CANNOT WAIT TO KISS AGAIN. IT WAS JUST A NORMAL GOODBYE KISS BUT ITS BEEN ON MY MIND ALL DAY (MORNING AS ITS ONLY 1040) EARLIER I WAS AWOKEN BY THE MORNING BIRDS CHIRPING, A SINGLE FROG CROAKING BENEATH MY WINDOW, AND THE WIND MOVING THE BRANCHES OF THE TREES MAKING A LIGHT RUSTLING SOUND. MY ROOM WAS NICELY WARM THIS A.M. —

(24)

AND MY HEART WAS FULL (PROBS FROM THE DREAMKISS). ANOTHER THOUGHT THAT I HAD RECENTLY WAS ABOUT MY LETTERS TO YOU. [redacted] ID LIKE TO READ THEM W/ YOU AND FILL IN SOME OF IT AFTER THE FACT AS I RECALL HOW I FEEL REREADING THEM ALL W/ YOU. I CAN TELL/WRITE YOU THE STORIES I COULDNT PUT INTO THE LETTERS AND EDIT ALL THE GRAMMAR AND PUNCTUATION PROPERLY. ID REALLY LIKE TO TURN IT INTO A BOOK EVEN IF ONLY ONE COPY IS EVER PRINTED WHICH ID GIVE TO YOU. IT HAS ALWAYS BEEN A LIFE GOAL OF MINE TO PRINT A BOOK I WROTE AND MY LETTERS TO YOU IS SECOND TO SECOND ABOUT MY DAILY PROGRESSES, STRUGGLES, PERSEVERANCE, AND LOVE FOR A GIRL. SEEMS LIKE A GOOD BOOK TO ME. ⟹ SO FAR I HAVE SLEPT THE MIDDLE OF THE DAY AWAY TO PASS TIME, READ A CHAPTER IN THIS NOVEL, DID SOME ABS & CARDIO, AND TALKED TO MY DAD FOR APPROX 30 MINS. IM NOT FEELING ALL TO SOCIAL TODAY AND ENJOYING SOME ALONE TIME. ONE OF THE DUDES IN MY HOUSE TALKS SO LOUD ITS A BIT MUCH. HE IS A GOOD GUY AND ITS NOT THE LOUDNESS IT IS JUST ME AND TODAY WHICH IS OK. ALL I DO IS RETREAT INTO MY PERSONAL SPACE, LIGHT SAGE AND FOCUS ON A POSITIVE WAY OF THINKING AND TRY TO HAVE AN ATTITUDE OF GRATITUDE. CURRENTLY I AM JUST WAITING TO CALL YOU. IF YOU HAVE TIME THATS AWESOME. IF NOT I SEND WELL WISHES AND WILL HEAD BACK TO THE GYM. WHEN I TALKED TO INMATE, HE TOLD ME PEOPLE ARE LIVING AT CRC NOW. I SIT AND WONDER ABOUT YOUR THOUGHTS AND FEELINGS ABOUT IT ALL. IM SURE WE WILL TALK ABOUT IT ONCE YOU HAVE SOME FREE TIME. TOMORROW I GET TO GO

(25)

CHILL W/ THE PASTOR (PASTOR DAN) FOR A BIT WHICH I'D NEVER HAVE THOUGHT IN A MILLION YEARS WOULD BE THE CASE. I HAVE A DR. APPT. @ 9:55am THAT IVE BEEN AWAITING FOR MONTHS AND I AM INCREDIBLY STOKED ABOUT IT. THE DOC IS GOING TO MAKE ME EVEN MORE HANDSOME THAN I ALREADY WAS. (I KNOW, HARD TO BELIEVE RIGHT LOL). IT IS 6:37am, AFTER THE 7am COUNT THEN ILL HAVE A SUPER HOT LONG SHOWER. SOMETIMES AFTER I AM FINISHED SHAVING, WASHING, EXFOLIATING, AND BRUSHING/FLOSSING MY TEETH ILL DO STRETCHES OR JUST SIT ON THE SHOWER BENCH AND CRANK THE HOT WATER WAY UP. WHEN IM RELEASED THE FIRST TUB I SEE I AM HAVING A BUBBLE BATH. ONCE I CAN GO TO THE REC CENTER ILL BE USING A HOT TUB, STEAM ROOM, OR SAUNA EVERY DAY I CAN, NO MORE TAKING THOSE THINGS FOR-GRANTED. TONIGHT I WILL ASK IF YOULL VISIT ME FOR MY ONE YEAR (AND YOUR 11 MNTH) SOBER DAY. ITS A SATURDAY THAT DAY SO YOU PROBS WONT BE ABLE TO, BUT ILL ASK EITHER WAY (ZERO EXPECTATIONS). I CANNOT BELIEVE ITLL BE ONE FULL YEAR SOBER NEXT MONTH. THAT WENT BY SO FAST, LIKE A BLINK OF AN EYE AND ON TOP OF IT, IT HAS BEEN THE HARDEST YEAR IVE EVER ENDURED. THANK FUCK IT WAS SOBER. I CAN ROLL THE TAPE OUT TO SEE WHAT IT WOULDVE BEEN LIKE "TRASHED" AND WHAT A BLESSING SOBRIETY IS. SHOWER TIME ⟹ ITS 8:43am, I CALLED TWICE SO I WONT CALL AGAIN TONIGHT. IT IS DUMPING ~~BU~~ BUCKETS OUT AND I AM THOROUGHLY SOAKED LOL. I HOPE EVERY-THING IS OK. FOR SOME WEIRD REASON I FEEL LIKE YOU ARE UPSET. I HOPE ALL IS WELL W/ YOU DUDE. SWEET DREAM SWEET GIRL. LOVE & MISS YOU

Z Z Z Z Z Z Z

(26)

2022-04-19

ANOTHER MORNING IS UPON US. AND TO THAT I SAY/WISH YOU A GOODMORNING. THE WEATHER SEEMS TO BE VERY UNSURE OF EXACTLY WHICH WAY IT IS DECIDING ON. EITHER WAY IS GOOD W/ ME. I WOKE UP IN DEEP THOUGHT AND LAYED IN BED FOR AWHILE THINKING ABOUT LIFE PAST, PRESENT, AND FUTURE. AS MY THOUGHTS SETTLED IN I GOT UP AND THE MORNING ROUTINE SUCH AS BRUSH TEETH, GET DRESSED, PUT ON COFFEE, MAKE THE BED AND WRITE TO YOU. I SAT ON THE PATIO BRIEFLY WHILE I DRANK CUP#1 OF COFFEE AND WATCHED THE CROWS PICK AT THE GRASS IN SEARCH OF THEIR DAILY FOOD. THEY MUST BE ALMOST READY TO HATCH EGGS AS THE DUO THAT IS MOST COMMONLY IN OUR FRONT YARD WAS W/OUT ITS FEMALE. THE TWO REASONS I COULD ~~TH~~ TELL IT WAS A FEMALE WAS THAT SHE HAD A FEATHER THAT HUNG OUT OF PLACE AND THAT SPECIFIC CROW IS NOTICABLY DIFFERENT FROM THE OTHERS AND ALSO I SAW THE BOY SENDING IT TO HER DOGGYSTYLE ON THE LAWN NOT TOO LONG AGO LOL (I HOPE THAT MADE YOU CHUCKLE). I FOUND OUT THE CROWS MATE FOR LIFE. I DONT HAVE GOOGLE SO I COULDNT FACT CHECK IT BUT BY THE WAY THESE CROWS ACT IT SEEMS LEGIT. RIGHT AT THIS MOMENT I AM WAITING FOR 9:55am FOR THIS DR. APPT. I AM NERVOUS AND EXCITED AT THE SAME TIME. I HOPE IT GOES WELL, IM SURE IT WILL. IVE BEEN AWAY NOW FOR 6 MONTHS AND 3 MORE TO GO. THE TIME IS PASSING BOTH QUICKLY AND SLOWLY AND ~~AND~~ A NEW LIFE IS MATERIALIZING AS I WORK INCREDIBLY HARD FOR IT.

⇒ THIS AFTERNOON I AM GOING TO PHOTOCOPY A PHOTO MY BUDDY BEN DREW OF OUR BACKYARD AND SEND IT WHEN I SEND THIS LETTER TO YOU LATER. THIS PAGE IS ALMOST DONE SO ILL FINISH THE BOTTOM LINE W/ LOVE + HEARTS

♡ ♡

5

Mail Call

"Hope in an envelope."

There was a sound every man in there listened for—the officer's boots echoing down the range, letters in hand. Mail call. That word could shift the air in an instant. No matter how much time you'd done, when they started reading names, everyone froze. It wasn't about weakness; it was about proof that you still existed to somebody on the outside.

Some days my name got called, some days it didn't. When it did, I'd hold that envelope like it was breath itself. The cards she sent me, her photos—they pulled me out of that place for a few minutes and reminded me why I was fighting to stay human. But when it didn't come, the silence hit harder than any noise in there. You'd tell yourself maybe tomorrow, but deep down you felt the ache settle in.

Still, I kept writing. Every letter I sent out was a small act of faith, a way of saying, I'm still here. I wrote to her about the little things—the smell of the rain through the vents, the thoughts that never made it past my head—and to my girls, to remind them their dad hadn't given up. Those letters were my heartbeat leaving the cell. Even now, when I think back on that sound—the shuffle of paper, the pause before my name—it reminds me what hope really sounds like. Quiet, steady, and worth waiting for.

(1)

2022-04-19

GOOD AFTERNOON ANGEL. THIS IS A CONTINUATION OF THE SAME DAY AS MY LAST PAGE INSIDE THE PREVIOUS LETTER. EARLIER I WAS AT THE DR AND THAT WAS MEH. AFTER THAT I WENT TO THE GYM AND LIFTED HEAVIER ON MY CHEST THAN EVER (FLAT-BENCH DUMBELLS @ 100 LBS PER ARM), WHICH IS SUPER STOKING!!! NEXT I WENT TO PROTESTANT CHURCH AGAIN, THE GROUPS ARE GROWING BIGGER & MORE OFTEN. AS THINGS OPEN THIS PLACE GETS BETTER & BETTER. I WENT USE THE PHONE ON MY WALK HOME AFTER CHURCH BUT FINANCE APPARENTLY MADE SOME MISTAKES & HALF THE POPULATION HERE WERE AFFECTED BY IT AND ARE W/OUT PHONE CARD BALANCES. AH WELL, IT IS WHAT IT IS I GUESS. I'VE LOST SOME MORE WEIGHT (YAY!!!), FOUND OUT WHEN I CHECKED THIS MORN @ THE GYM (SUPER PUMPED). ITS CRAZY THAT AS I BEGIN TO LOOK AND FEEL BETTER THAT IT WAS NEVER A MATTER OF HOW I ACTUALLY LOOKED BUT MORE ABOUT HOW I FELT ABOUT MYSELF INSIDE WHICH PROJECTED OUTWARD ONTO MY PHYSICAL BODY AS I HID MY PAIN FROM THE SURFACE. IT IS TRUE THAT CHANGE COMES FROM W/IN. BOY OH BOY HAVE I CHANGED (STILL STRUGGLE). CHANGE STILL TAKES A SHITLOAD OF RELENTLESS DEDICATION AND DRIVE BECAUSE IF I SETTLE FOR ONE SECOND AND SLIP, A SLIP COULD BE THE FALL, OR FINAL FALL FOR THAT MATTER. AND A SMALL PERK OF ALL THIS FOCUS AND CHANGED IS GETTING A BODY THATS SEXY AF (HUBBA HUBBA LOL) ← I HOPE YOURE SMILING RIGHT NOW ☺ BIGGER, STRONGER, FASTER PAIRED W/ NICER, HUMBLE, LOVING, FUNNY, SMART, AND MORE LOVING & CARING ♡

→ TODAY THE WEATHER HAS BEEN EXTREMELY BI-POLAR, ATM IT IS BEAUTIFUL OUT W/ CLOUDS OF ALL SORTS (CUMULUS & NIMBUS) W BRIGHT BLUE SKY IN SOME AREAS AND

(2)

DARK GREY CLOUDS LURKING IN THE DISTANCES IN ALMOST EVERY DIRECTION. ON ONE SIDE OF ALL THE BIG MOUNTANOUS BUBBLY CLOUDS THE SUN RADIATES AGAINST THEM SHOWING A HEAVEN-LIKE SHADE OF WHITE HOWEVER ON THE OTHER SIDE IT IS VERY DARK AND ~~SHOW~~ SHADOWY LIKE A YIN & YANG SYMBOL. AS WE SAT OUT ON THE PATIO SOME OF THE INDIGINOUS DUDES POP--PED OVER AND SHARED SOME BUFFALO JERKY AND IT WAS SOME OF THE BEST JERKY IVE EVER EATEN. AS WE SAT AROUND THERE IS A SLIGHT BREEZE COMING DOWN OFF OF THE SNOW CAPPED MOUNTAINS AND ALTHOUGH IT WAS FRESH IT WAS SUPER COLD AS WELL. EARLIER THE YARD GUY MOWED OUT BACK AND IT LOOK FRESH AND SO CLEAN-CLEAN. IT IS NOW NICE AND SHORT AND READY FOR LAWN GAMES. TONIGHT ILL PROBABLY RELAX BECAUSE TOMORROW IS MY FIRST DAY AT WORK SO ILL SLEEP EARLY TO WAKE EARLY AND EAT SOME BOILED EGGS PRIOR TO WORK. IM SURE WORK WILL BE WAY EASIER THEN MY NORMAL WORK PACE BUT WORK IS WORK SO I MIGHT AS WELL BE PREPARED. LATER ON ILL THROW ON SOME LAUNDRY SO MY CLOTHES ARE FRESH AND CLEAN FOR OUR VIDEO CALL TOMORROW EVENING?. NOT THAT YOUD EVER NOTICE BUT I FEEL THAT OUR VID CHATS ARE SPECIAL SO I LIKE TO FEEL LIKE I MADE AN EFFORT TO SEE YOU PLUS IT IS WHAT I LOOK FORWARD TO ALL WEEK AS SOON AS WE LEAVE THE PREVIOUS VIDCHAT. ITS LIKE DATE NIGHT WHEN YOURE INCARCERATED THATS FOR SURE. ⇒ TIME FOR BED (11:24PM) BEAUTIFUL BEAUTIFUL GIRL!! GOODNIGHT ANGEL

Z Z Z Z Z

2022-04-20 (420 FOR ALL THE STONERS OUT THERE LOL)

HELLO MY FRIEND. I HEARD YOU ARE SICK TODAY. THAT SUX DUDE. I WISH/HOPE THAT YOU HAVE SOMEONE THERE TO TAKE

(3)

GOOD CARE OF YOU. SOMEONE TO BRING YOU SOUP, TEA, OR MEDICINE... FOR THAT MATTER... JUST SOMEONE ON 24hr CALL TO HELP YOU IF YOU'RE IN NEED. TODAY WAS MY 1ST DAY OF WORK AND IT WENT BY FAST & SMOOTHLY. UNFORTU-NATELY THE PHONE SERVICE (BELL) STILL HAS A NUMBER OF ACCOUNTS DOWN AND I AM UNABLE TO MAKE ANY CALLS OUT. IT TOO BAD I COULD NOT SEE YOU TODAY BUT I UNDERSTAND FULLY. IM MISSING YOU TODAY. IN HERE CAN MAKE A PERSON OVERTHINK. AHWELL I JUST HAVE TO REMIND MYSELF THAT THERE IS NOTHING I CAN DO AND TO LET GO OF WORRYSOME THINKING FOR THE TIME BEING. I JUST WISH I COULD CALL AND SEE IF YOU WERE OK THATS ALL. IT IS CRAZY THAT IVE BEEN AWAY NOW FOR 20 WEEKS. ONLY 12-14 MORE WEEKS TO GO AND HONESTLY IT IS PASSING FAIRLY FAST MOST DAYS. TODAY IT IS A SNAILS PACE AS I AM TRYING TO NOT WORRY ABOUT YOU ALL TOO MUCH. ITS VERY DIFFICULT TO NOT WORRY ABOUT THE ONES YOU TRULY DO CARE ABOUT. IM ALSO FEELING LIKE MAYBE I HAVE BECOME TOO MUCH FOR YOU OR OVERWHELMING YOU WHICH IN TURN MAKES ME WANT TO GIVE YOU YOUR SPACE. I DO HOPE THAT YOU WOULD TELL ME OR LET ME KNOW IMM-EDIATELY IF THATS WHAT YOU WERE FEELING, AS THE LAST THING ID EVER WANT, IS TO SEEM LIKE I AM BEING TOO MUCH. AS FAR AS TOMORROW I WILL PUMP UP AS MUCH AS I CAN AT THE GYM THEN HOPEFULLY ITS NICE ENOUGH OUTSIDE TO HAVE ANOTHER PHOTOSHOOT IN DIF. OUTFITS TIME W/ DIF. BACKGROUNDS. TONIGHT BESIDES USING THE GYM ILL MOST LIKELY READ A COUPLE CHAPTERS OF MY BOOK TO TRY AND MAKE THIS DAY PASS BY FASTER SO I CAN FALL ASLEEP. ⟹ GOODNIGHT. I HOPE YOU ARE OK B

2022-04-21

HOLY COW IT IS DUMPING BUCKETS OUT RIGHT NOW. I WALKED

(4)

TO MY NEIGHBORS HOWS TO GET SOME MILK AND WAS ABSOLUTELY SOAKED. ITS 5pm NOW AND THE DAY HAS BEEN A TAD BIT BLAH. THE BOOK I AM READING IS AFFE-CTING ME SO I HAVE TO TAKE A BREAK FROM IT FOR A DAY OR TWO.

2022-04-22

TODAY HAS BEEN VERY DIFFICULT FOR ME. IM NOT SURE WHO TO TALK TO ABOUT WHATS GOING ON BUT IM HURTING INSIDE VERY MUCH SO. I FEEL LIKE ANGEL IS BEING STRIPPED FROM ME COMPLETELY THROUGH EXTREMELY ONE SIDED MANIPULATION WHICH IS BREAKING MY HEART TO A POINT I TOOK DOWN THE PHOTOS I HAD OF HER BECAUSE WHEN I LOOK AT HER I JUST WANT TO BREAK OUT IN TEARS. IM HAVING A DIFFICULT TIME EVEN MUTTERING OUT WORDS W/ OUT CHOKING UP. I FEEL ALL ALONE IN THE WORLD RIGHT NOW AS I TRY AND PROCESS WHAT I AM FEELING THE BEST I CAN. I AM SO HURT. I LOVE MY BABIES SO MUCH AND AT THIS VERY POINT IN TIME THAT LOVE IS BREAKING ME DOWN. THIS TOO SHALL PASS. I KEEP TELL-ING MYSELF THIS OVER AND OVER AND OVER. I KNOW THERE IS NO WAY AROUND THIS BUT TO GO RIGHT THROUGH IT BUT FUCK IS THE PAIN I AM IN EXCRUCIATING. IVE BEEN HERE MORE THAN ONCE IN MY LIFETIME AND THE ONLY THING I CAN DO IS LET IT GO AND TRY TO KEEP LOVE IN MY HEART ALTHOUGH I AM CURRENTLY HEARTBROKEN. KIDS ARE SUPPOSED TO BE BLESSINGS NOT USED AS WEAPONS TO HURT SOMEONE. I NEED TO CRY SO BADLY RIGHT NOW AND AM HOLDING IT IN. I FEEL LIKE IM LOST BECAUSE OF DAUGHTER. IM A GOOD DAD AND A GOOD PERSON IN MY HEART. ⇒ JUST GOT BACK FROM A.A... THERE IS/WAS A FORSURE REASON THIS DAY HAS BEEN ON A DAY W/ A MEETING. I AM STILL IN PAIN BUT HAVE FAITH IN GODS PLAN FOR ME

5

ILL GIVE MY THOUGHTS OVER TO MY HIGHER POWER AND TRY TO LET GO WHAT I CANNOT CHANGE. ONE THING I CAN CHANGE IS TO KEEP BUSY AND LET TIME PASS. I WAS FEELING HOPE-LESSNESS EARLIER TODAY AND AM STRUGGLING W/ LONE-LINESS. WITH THAT BEING SAID I NEED TO STAY FOCUSED AND POSITIVE ONE DAY AT A TIME. BEING IN HERE IS ONE OF THE MOST CHALLENGING THINGS IVE EVER BEEN FACED W/. FOR THE NEXT 6 DAYS I WILL FOCUS ON OUR UPCOMING SOBER DAY, ALSO I WAS TOLD THAT THE GUYS IN HERE GOT ME A ONE YEAR COIN FOR NEXT MONTH WHICH IS SO SPECIAL. WHEN I GET OUT WE CAN WATCH A DOCUMENTARY ABOUT THE PERSON WHO GOT IT FOR ME. THIS SOBER JOURNEY HAS BEEN ONE FOR THE AGES THAT IS FOR SURE!! TODAY WE RECIEVED A NOTICE THAT PFV & TOUCH VISITS ARE OPEN NOW. HOPEFULLY I CAN HAVE SOME VISITS FROM YOU OR THE GIRLS AS I COULD REALLY USE A LONG HUG OR TO HOLD HANDS EVEN IF FOR ONLY A MOMENT OR TWO. IT WOULD MEAN THE ABSOLUTE WORLD TO ME HONESTLY. I WISH I COULD EXPRESS THE IMPORTANCE OF PHYSICAL CONN-ECTION AND WHAT IS LIKE WHEN JUST THAT ONE THING HAS BEEN TAKEN AWAY. JUST THAT ALONE HAS MADE ME A BETTER PERSON AS I 100% WILL NEVER IN THE REST OF MY LIFE TAKE THAT FORGRANTED. THROUGHOUT THE REST OF THE EVENING I WILL JUST TAKE IN THE EPIC MOUNTAIN VIEWS AND THEN DOUBLE DOWN AT THE GYM FOR A COUPLE OF HOURS. ITS 10:21pm AND BEDTIME. AFTER TALKING TO YOU I STOPPED BY HOUSE #7 AND WAS GIVEN SOME HOMEMADE BLUEBERRIES CHEESE CAKE. IT WAS DELICIOUS. IM GLAD THAT YOU FELT COMFORT-ABLE TALKING/VENTING TO MY DUDE. I AM ALWAYS GOING TO BE HERE FOR YOU. I UNDERSTAND FULLY HOW YOU ARE FEELING ABOUT EVERYTHING. ILL

6

SEND OUT WELL WISHES THAT IT PASSES AND WORKS OUT THE WAY IT WAS ALL ORIGINALLY MEANT TO. I KNOW HOW MUCH YOU PUT INTO IT W/ YOUR WHOLE HEART AND SOUL. YOU DEFINATELY HAVE EVERY RIGHT TO HAVE THOSE FEELINGS. JUST KNOW THAT MY HEART WILL ALWAYS BE OPEN TO YOU WHEN YOU NEED ANYTHING AT ANY TIME. ILL ALWAYS BE HERE FOR YOU ANGEL I PROMISE YOU THAT. ILL LEAVE AT THAT FOR THE NIGHT. YOU ARE SO BEAUTIFUL AND SPECIAL
GOODNIGHT SWEETGIRL Z Z Z Z Z Z

2022-04-23

GOOD MORNING. I HOPE YOU SLEPT WELL LAST NIGHT. YOUVE BEEN ON MY MIND CONSTANTLY SINCE WE SPOKE. I WAS/HAVE BEEN THINKING ABOUT HOW YOU ARE FEELING AS IT AFFECTS ME BECAUSE I CARE ABOUT YOU SO MUCH. I WISH I COULD HELP BUT ALL I CAN DO IS LISTEN AND BE SUPPORT FOR YOU & ALSO A SAFE PERSON FOR YOU TO BE ABLE TO SHARE FEELINGS W/ IN ABSOLUTE CONFIDENCE. I DO KNOW HOW DIFFICULT THOSE FEELINGS ARE AS I HAVE BEEN IN YOUR POSITION MORE TIMES THAN I WOULD HAVE LIKED. I HEARD EVERY SINGLE WORD YOU SPOKE & FULLY SEE THE HUGE HEART THAT YOU HAVE. YOU ARE ONE OF THE MOST AMAZING PEOPLE IVE EVER MET AND THAT IS 100% TRUTH/FACT. I PERSONALLY FEEL BLESSED & HONOURED TO BE A PERSON WHO YOU TALK TO. 3 MORE MONTHS AND WE CAN FINALLY HANGOUT IN PERSON. I HOPE THAT WE CONTINUE TO TALK ALL THE TIME STILL AND FIND TIME TO SEE ONE ANOTHER IN PERSON OUTSIDE OF THE ROOMS AND GO ON SOME ADVENTURES. TODAY IM GOING TO DO SOME CARDIO/ABS AT THE GYM, RELAX, WRITE, MAYBE READ MY BOOK WHICH IS HARD AT TIMES BECAUSE OF THE SELF REFLECTION ON THE PAST IT CREATES,

(7)

, WATCH THE NEW BATMAN @ 8PM, AND HOPEFULLY THE DAY PASSES FAIRLY FAST. WELL [redacted] IM HEADING OUT. ILL MOST LIKELY WRITE LATER. LOVE YOU DUDE AND ILL BE WISHING YOU WELL & THINKING ABOUT YOU ALL DAY IM SURE. ⇒ IT IS 6:02PM AND WE JUST ATE PIZZA ON THE DECK W/ SOME COKE ZEROS. PEOPLE PASSING BY POP IN TO SAY HELLO WHICH IS NICE. SOME OF THEM STOP TO SIT W/ US AND OTHERS KEEP WALKING. THE NEW BATMAN IS ON AT 8PM SO ALOT OF PEOPLE HERE WILL BE WATCHING IT AND BEING 3 HOURS LONG, ITLL TAKE THE NIGHT RIGHT TO THE END AND ANOTHER DAY WILL BE BEHIND US. IVE THOUGHT ABOUT YOU MORE THAN USUAL TODAY. I DO WISH SOMETIMES I HAD MORE PHOTOS OF YOU OR ID OPEN MY MAILBOX AND THERED BE SOME THERE AS A SURPRIZE. THEY WOULD MAKE ME SO HAPPY. EITHER WAY I AM GRAT-EFUL JUST TO HAVE THE TIME YOU ALREADY MAKE FOR ME. ABOUT 20 MINS AGO I WAS OUT WATERING THE FRONT YARD AT THE PATCHES I RE-SEADED ARE BEGINNING TO SPROUT NICELY. I AM TRYING TO HAVE THE NICEST GRASS ON THE STREET. THE OLD KODGER ACROSS THE STREET IS A LAWN NAZI SO I HAVE MY WORK CUT OUT FOR ME LOL. MY HOUSEMATES GET A KICK OUT OF ME LITERALLY HAND WATERING GRASS FOR FUN BUT FOR SOME REASON I FIND IT EXTREMELY RELAXING. EARLIER TODAY WE WORKED OUT ON THE FIELD FLIPPING TIRES, PLATES, AND BACK & FORTH ABS PUNCHES. THEN CHARLIE & I WENT ON A 2K WALK AROUND THE WHOLE INSTITUTION. LOL THERE IS DRAMA IN THE HOUSE HAPPENING RIGHT NOW HAHAHA. OUR WING IS SO LAX & CHILL. THE DUDES WING IS DEBATING ABOUT LOUD DOORS AND HAIR IN THE SINK, SO ME BEING ME LIT MY CLEANSING SMUDGE AND TOLD THEM TO KEEP THEIR BAD OMEN AWAY FROM

(8)

OUR AREA/WING. GEO IS LAUGHING AT ME QUOTING COMMUNICATION TECHNIQUES TO THEM LOL. THIER TOILET IS GROSS AND NO ONE IS OWNING UP TO NOT BRUSHING IT. GROWN ADULTS CAN BE SO CHILDISH AT TIMES. SOMETIMES I HONESTLY WONDER WHAT IT WILL BE LIKE TO HANGOUT W/ YOU AFTER GETTING TO REALLY BOND FOR THIS LONG OVER THE PHONE. NEVER HAVE I EVER BECOME FRIENDS LIKE THIS BEFORE. THAT BEING SAID IVE NEVER BEEN IN PRISON BEFORE. IF IN THE END OF MY "BIT" (BIT IS SLANG HERE FOR JAIL TIME) HAVING YOU AS A FRIEND LIKE YOUVE SHOWN TO BE IS SOMETHING THAT HAS HAPPENED IT WILL HAVE BEEN WORTH IT. ALSO BECAUSE OF THIS "BIT" I GET MY BODY BACK AND A HEALTHY HAPPY LIFE TO APPRE-CIATE. SUBTLE 2828 (ONE FOR YOU AND ONE FOR ME)

⇒ WELL HELLO AGAIN. IT WAS NICE TO BRIEFLY HEAR YOUR VOICE BEFORE YOU LEFT. ILL PRAY FOR YOU AND YOUR FAMILY WHILE YOU ARE AWAY AND SEND LOVE DURING THIS TOUGH TIME. IT IS ALMOST 7PM AND THE SUN IS GOING DOWN FAST. AS IT DECENDS ITS LIGHT SHINE DIRECTLY UPON THE SNOW CAPPED MOUNTAINS IN THE DISTANCE BEHIND MISSION MEDIUM. DINNER WAS ANOTHER AMAZING PORK ROAST, RICE, AND VEGGIE COOKED BY MOU WHO IS AN AMAZING COOK. GEO & I WASH, DRIED, AND PUT AWAY THE DISHES. PRIOR TO DINNER WE WORKED OUT IN THE BACKYARD W/ BOXING GLOVES AND HAND PADS, IT WAS INSANE TO SAY THE LEAST. TONIGHT AT 8PM CHARLIE & I WILL WORKOUT BACK & BICEPS AT THE GYM FOR AN HOUR THEN THE KARATE SENSIE IS POPPING IN AT 9PM TO TRAIN US ON ABS FOR A BIT. IM FEELING HAPPY AND AM MOTIVATED TO FOCUS ON EVE-RYTHING THAT IS GOOD IN LIFE RIGHT NOW. ⟶

9

THROUGHOUT THE DAYS I STILL GET GUT SHOTS OF EMOTIONAL PAIN BUT HAVE FOUND THAT JUST BY TELLING MYSELF TO LET IT ALL GO A COUPLE OF TIMES MAKE MY FEELING SUBSIDE. ALL I CAN DO IS PUSH THROUGH THESE NEXT 3 MONTHS, KEEP BUSY, AND TIME WILL GO FASTER. OUR HIGHER POWER WILL ALWAYS SHOW US WHAT WE NEED IT TO AND WHEN WE NEED IT TO BE SHOWN. ONE STEP AT A TIME IS THE ONLY WAY TO GO. UNFORTUNATELY BEING HERE HAS BEEN THE HARD LESSON I WAS SUPPOSED TO GO THROUGH BUT I TRUST THE PATH THAT LIES AHEAD. WELL [redacted] I AM GOING TO GO RE WATER THE LAWN EVEN THOUGH THE SKY APPEARS TO BE SENDING US RAIN THIS EVENING. ⟹ IT IS 10:10pm AND THIS DAY IS ALMOST ALL WRAPPED UP. TONIGHTS WORKOUT WAS GREAT AS USUAL AND WHEN CHARLIE & I LEFT THE GYM ON CAME THE RAIN. I PICKED ALL THE DANDELIONS IN OUR YARD AND WENT AND ASKED FOR MORE GRASS SEED. FOR THE REST OF THE NIGHT ILL FOLD MY CLEAN LAUNDRY AND PUT IT INTO THE DRAWERS I MADE FOR MY BEDROOM SHELVING. I FOUND SOME NEW BOXES OUTSIDE ONE OF THE BUILD-ING THAT WERE PERFECT TO USE FOR IT. THIS ROOM IS SO ORGANIZED LOL, EVERYTHING IN IT HAS BEEN CATAGORIZED AND COMPARTMENTALIZED TO DAMN NEAR PERFECTION. SOMETIMES A PERSON NEEDS TO CREATE SOMETHING OUT OF NOTHING TO FIND JOY IN THE SMALL CREATIVE SOLUTIONS IN ANY SCENARIO THATS FOR SURE. I TRY TO NOT CALL THIS MY HOME EVEN THOUGH IVE MANAGED TO CREATE A HOMELIKE FEEL TO THIS VERY SMALL SPACE, IT COULD BE WORSE. & VERY SOON ILL HAVE MY OWN PLACE AGAIN, I CANNOT WAIT TO GO FURNITURE & KITCHEN & BEDROOM SET SHOPPING.

(10)

I SURE DO LOVE SETTING UP PLACES TO LIVE. A KING SIZE BED, PILLOWS, AND KING DUVET IS LIKE A DREAM TO ME RIGHT NOW. → IT IS 11:11PM AND LIFE IS EXACTLY WHERE IT IS EXACTLY WHERE IT IS SUPPOSED TO BE. W/ THAT BEING SAID ILL LEAVE THIS DAYS LETTER COMPLETE. ROOM IS SPOTLESS AND IMPECABLY ORGA-NIZED TO A LEVEL EVEN GEO WAS LIKE "WTF BRO HOW ORGANIZED DOES IT REALLY NEED TO BE LOL" WELL I LIKE TO LIVE NICE & COMFY IN ANY SPACE I AM IN. ANYHOW... I HOPE YOURE COMFORTABLE, RELAXED, AND SETTLED IN WHEREVER YOU MAY BE. GOODNIGHT SWEET GIRL, I LOVE YOU UNCONDITIONALLY AND HOPE YOU COME VISIT ME ONCE YOU GET BACK. ♡

Z Z Z Z Z Z Z

2022-04-25

HELLO, IT IS 10:47pm AND ALREADY BEDTIME. I HOPE YOUR TRAVEL WENT SAFE & SMOOTH FOR YOU. I THOUGHT ABOUT YOU TODAY AS USUAL BUT DID NOT SIT DOWN TO WRITE BECAUSE I DECIDE TO HAVE A NOTHING DAY AFTER A 5K JOG THIS MORNIN. I HOPE YOU DREAM OF ME & VISA-VERSA B.. SLEEP WELL BEAUTIFUL ANGEL AND GOODNIGHT

Z Z Z Z Z Z

2022-04-26
-27

HELLO THERE... I DIDNT WRITE YESTERDAY AS I WAS WAY TOO TIRED AND DID NOT HAVE ALL TOO MUCH TO SAY. LAST NIGHT I WORKED OUT HARDER THAN I EVER HAVE BEFORE IN MY WHOLE LIFE. I HAVE BEEN WORKING ALL WEEK AND BOY DOES IT KICK THE SHIT OUT OF ME ON TOP OF EVERYTHING ELSE IM DOING PHYSICALLY. I AM HAPPY AND GRATEFUL FOR WHAT THIS IS DOING

(11)

TO MY BODY AND MIND. ALL OF IT ALSO HELPS PASS
THE TIME AND DISTRACT ME. TODAY IM THINKING
ABOUT YOU AND YOUR MOM AND SENDING A TON OF
LOVE TO YOU BOTH. ITS A FUNNY THING IN HERE
~~AB~~ WHAT A PERSON THINKS ABOUT AND DOES W/ ~~TEHER~~
THE TIME THEY HAVE. ALTHOUGH I HAVE A LOT OF
PEOPLE TO CALL APPROVED ON MY LIST I HARDLY
EVER CALL ANYONE. I CALL THE GIRLS, MY SISTER,
MY DAD, AND YOU. SOMETIMES RANDOMLY ILL CALL
MY FRIENDS ROB, DAVE, AND DOUG BUT HONESTLY
HARDLY EVER. ~~FM~~ IM NOT SURE WHY BUT I ONLY
FEEL LIKE CALLING FAMILY AND YOU. YOU GUYS ARE
THE ONES WHO REALLY STAYED W/ ME THROUGHOUT
THIS ALL AND PUT IN THE EFFORT AND FOR THAT
I AM FOREVER APPRECIATIVE. WHEN I AM ALL DONE
HERE I WILL SHOW HOW EXACTLY APPRECIATIVE I AM.
I JUST REALIZED THAT TOMORROW IS OUR DAY (28) AND
I AM STOKED ON 11 & 10 MONTHS FOR US BOTH.
THIS YEAR HAS BEEN SO UNBELIEVABLY ROUGH AND IT
IS A MIRACLE I AM STILL SOBER. I AM 100% DETERM-
-INED TO NOT HAVE RELAPSE IN MY STORY THATS
FOR SURE. NO MATTER THE OBSTACLES THE TRUE
DEDICATION I HAVE TO THIS IS ABOVE EVERYTHING...
ALSO F.Y.I. YOU ARE DROP DEAD GORGEOUS DUDE AND
I LOVE YOU & MISS YOU ALL DAY EVERYDAY (JUST
SAYIN) ⟹ TONIGHT SO FAR IVE PONDERED LIFE,
WATCHED FORGED IN FIRE, AND NAPPED. I DIDNT MAKE ANY
CALLS OR HANGOUT WHATSOEVER, JUST CHILLED IN MY ROOM
PRETTY MUCH SINCE ABOUT 3:30PM, IT WAS A VERY NICE
CHANGE OF PACE. IT IS NOW 9:25Pm AND IM GOING TO LAY
DOWN FOR THE EVENING. I WISH YOU WELL SWEET GIRL
GOODNIGHT Z Z Z Z Z Z

(12) 2022-04-28

SERENITY, COURAGE, WISDOM. TODAY IS ANOTHER ONE OF OUR DAYS. I SURE AM GRATEFUL TO SHARE IT W/ YOU DUDE. IT IS 7:05pm AND I AM READY FOR BED. I BUSTED ASS AT WORK THEN WORKED HARD AT THE GYM. I DONT HAVE ALL TOO MUCH TO WRITE BUT FINGERS CROSSED THAT WHAT I AM APPLYING TO DO GOES THROUGH. IF IT DOES ILL WRITE ABOUT IT. I ONCE AGAIN SEND YOU, YOUR MOM, AND THE REST OF YOUR FAMILY TONS OF LOVE. ♡ I SURE DO MISS HEARING YOUR VOICE MY FRIEND (A BEST FRIEND A GUY COULD EVER ASK FOR)... GOOD NIGHT SWEET GIRL Z Z Z Z Z

2022-04-29

ANOTHER DAY ANOTHER DOLLAR AN HOUR LOL. WORK FOR THE LAST FEW DAYS HAS BEEN SUPER HARD. JACK HAMM-ERING AND DIGGING FOR 5 HOURS IS NOT FUN BUT GOOD CARDIO I GUESS. LUCKY THE WEEK IS OVER. TODAY MUST BE DIFFICULT FOR YOU GUYS. SENDING LOVE & PRAYERS TO YOUR FAMILY ♡. MY THOUGHTS ARE W/ YOU AND YOUR MOM ALL DAY. ⇒ IM FEELING A TAD BIT ANTI-SOCIAL THESE DAYS.. IM NOT SURE WHY EXACTLY BUT I FEEL A BIT DIS-CONNECTED FROM MY SURROUNDINGS HERE. MAYBE IT IS THE THOUGHT OF JUST GETTING OUT OF HERE BEING JUST AROUND THE CORNER AND MISSING EVERYONE PLUS THE WEATHER IS A LOT NICER. LIFE IS GOING BY OUTSIDE AND THE TIME HAS BEEN OFF AND ON FAST TO SLOW. I AM LACKING DISTRACTIONS AND RUNNING OUT OF THINGS TO DO ON A DAILY BASIS. MY DAUGHTERS WERE EXCITED THAT THEYLL SEE ME AT THE END OF THE SUMMER. I MISS THEM SO MUCH, DAUGHTER TOO. ⇒ AAAAND WORK IS ALL DONE FOR THE DAY & WEEKEND. NOW I WILL CHILL UNTIL 7pm THEN DO 140 BURPEES THEN RELAX FOR THE REST OF TONIGHT. HALLOWEEN KILLS

(13)

IS ON AT 9:50pm SO ILL PROBABLY LAY IN BED AND WATCH IT UNTIL I FALL ASLEEP. I WATCHED THE NEW BATMAN MOVIE LAST WEEK. AND IT WAS ABSOLUTE GARBAGE WHICH WAS DISAPPOINTING. THE GIRLS ARE W/ THEIR MOM FOR THE WEEKEND SO ILL HAVE TO WAIT UNTIL MONDAY TO TALK TO THEM. THEY ARE LIVING W/ THEIR MOM'S MOM UNTIL SHE FIGURES OUT HER SITUATION. I AM HAPPY THEY ARE THERE AS IT IS A SAFER, HAPPIER, AND MORE STABLE ENVIRONMENT FOR THEM UNTIL I AM DONE HERE. ⟹ AAAND I JUST WOKE UP FROM A NAP FROM 7pm - 10pm NOW IT IS TIME FOR BED ☺ ANOTHER DAY PASSED. ON T.V ARE ALL MY FAVORITE SHOWS SUCH A ALIEN, BIGFOOT, UFO, GHOST, AND UNEXPLAINED STUFF. ANYHOW... GOODNIGHT LOVELY ANGEL Z Z Z Z Z Z ♡

2022-04-30

HELLO GORGEOUS GIRL... TODAY HAS BEEN AN ENJOYABLE LAZY DAY. THUS FAR IVE DONE ABSOLUTELY ZERO. WELL... I SHOWERED AND SHAVED ER'THANG AND WATCHED THE SHOW "ALASKA TRIANGLE" LITERALLY ALL DAY. THIS MORNING I SAW THE TIME 11:11 AND ONCE AGAIN IT GAVE COMFORT THAT I AM WHERE IM SUPPOSED TO BE. AT 5PM (ITS 4:40PM NOW) ILL GO DO 20-30MINS OF CARDIO AND A SHORT MUSCLE PUMP UP THEN COME HOME TO CHILL UNTIL N.A AT 7:30. WE HAVE 2 NEW VOLUNTEERS FROM THE COMMUNITY COMING TONIGHT WHICH BRINGS A LITTLE BIT OF NORMALITY TO THIS PLACE. LAST I SLEPT A TON, I THINK ITS FROM MY ENTIRE BODY BEING SORE FROM WORK AND AGGRESIVE WORKING OUT. IM NOTICING CHANGES DAILY NOW AND ALSO GET TOLD SEMI REGULARLY HOW MUCH BIGGER I LOOK. I CANNOT WAIT FOR A HUG FROM YOU SO YOU CAN FEEL THE DIFFERENCE FROM OUR LAST HUG AT THE DOOR OF CRC (THE SHOP)

(14)

I KNOW THAT IT PROBABLY DOES NOT MEAN AS MUCH TO YOU AS IT DOES TO ME BUT SINCE YOUVE BEEN MY MOST CONSISTENT SUPPORT (+ MY SISTER) AND BIGGEST SUPPORT, I LOOK TO IMPRESS YOU AND ALWAYS HAVE YOU IN MY MIND WHEN I PUSH HARD. I FIND SO MUCH COMFORT IN YOU AND TRUST YOU 100%. I REALLY AM TRYING TO MAKE EVERYONE WHO BELIEVES IN ME PROUD. I TRULY AM HUMBLY PROUD OF MY EFFORTS TO CHANGE AND STRIVE TO BECOME THE PERSON THAT I KNOW I AM AND ALWAYS HAVE BEEN. SOMEWHERE ALONG THE WAY I GOT LOST AND SURROUNDED MYSELF W/ NEGATIVE INFLUENCES AND ALLOWED MY BEING TO TAKE A PATH THAT WAS NEVER MEANT FOR ME. IVE FOUND MYSELF AND KNOW/TRUST A PATH THAT MY HIGHER POWER HAS SET OUT FOR ME. SOMEDAYS I STRUGGLE WHICH IS ABSOLUTELY OK. OTHER DAYS I HAVE STRENGTH. EITHER WAY WE ARE HUMAN AND EMOTIONAL BEINGS. LEARNING TO COMMUNICATE + EXPRESS OUR NEEDS IS SO VERY IMPORTANT. ⇒

IT IS NOW 10:18 PM AND THIS DAY IS FINITÕ ☺...

I WENT TO N.A AND IT WAS GREAT. THE 2 VOLUNTEERS WERE REALLY NICE PEOPLE AND I GOT THE CHANCE TO STAY BEHIND AND CHAT FOR SOME TIME AFTERWARDS. AFTER THAT I WENT TO THE GYM FOR 1½ HOURS AND WORKED ON CHEST & TRICEPS. IM PRETTY HAPPY TODAY AS I THINK IVE SETTLED IN TO THIS REALITY MAYBE A BIT MORE THAN I SHOULD BUT TOMORROW IS A BRAND NEW DAY SO ILL GET THROUGH THAT AS IT COMES AT ME. TOMORROW WILL BE 7 DAYS SINCE WE SPOKE LAST... I HOPE YOU ARE DOING OK. IVE THOUGHT ABOUT YOU TONS AND AS ALWAYS

(15)

SENT YOU LOVE & WELL WISHES. WELL ANGEL W/ THAT BEING SAID ILL SAY GOODNIGHT LIKE I DO EVERYNIGHT TELL YOU THAT I LOVE & MISS YOU AND TELL YOU THAT I CANT WAIT TO SEE YOUR STUNNING BEAUTY AND HEAR YOUR BEAUTIFUL VOICE ON OUR NEXT VIDEO CALL. I LOVE & APPRE-CIATE YOU MORE THAN I THINK YOU KNOW AND SLEEP WELL GORGEOUS GIRL XOXXOOX ♡

Z Z Z Z Z Z

2022-05-01

HAPPY MAY 1ST ANGEL I HOPE YOURE HAVING AN ABS-OLUTE WONDERFUL SUNDAY AFTERNOON. IT IS 3:44PM NOW AND I AM CURRENTLY WAITING FOR COUNT THE PRO-TESTANT CHURCH FROM 4-5PM. SO FAR TODAY IVE MOSTLY CHILLED OUT. I HIT THE GYM EARLIER FOR A BIT THEN PLAYED A COUPLE SHORT GAMES OF PICKLE-BALL W/ THE BOYS. IM MISSING YOU TODAY A BIT AS IT HAS BEEN A WEEK SINCE WE LAST SPOKE TO ONE ANOTHER. ITLL MOST LIKELY BE ANOTHER WEEK UNTIL WE CHAT. TIME WENT BY SWIFTLY THIS PAST WEEK. HOPEFULLY NEXT WEEK PASSES AT THE SAME RATE. 3 MORE MONTHS TO GO UNLESS WHAT IM WORKING ON CURRENTLY MIRACULOUSLY WORKS OUT, FINGERS CROSSED. CAN YOU PRETTY PLEASE SEND ME ANOTHER SET OF PHOTOS I MISS SEEING YOUR FACE EVERYDAY. I STILL HAVE THE ONE YOU SENT ME IN THE SAME EXACT SPOT AND FYI YOU ARE ASTONISHINGLY BEAUTIFUL IN THAT JEAN OUTFIT 😍 ⇒ HELLO, IT IS 7PM NOW AND IVE GONE TO CHURCH... IT WAS DECENT, THERE IS ALWAYS SOME-THING THAT MAKES ME CHOKE UP A BIT WHEN I THINK ABOUT WHAT LIFE WAS LIKE, WHAT ITS LIKE NOW, AND THE PATH THAT IS AWAITING ME IN THE SHORT

(16)

AND CLOSE FUTURE. I SPOKE TO MY SISTERS AND DAD TODAY AS WELL WHICH IS ALWAYS GOOD BECAUSE THEY KNOW ME TO A TEE AND SUPPORT ME SO MUCH IT MELTS MY HEART. IT IS HARD SOMETIMES TO TALK TO THEM DO TO BEING WHERE I AM (UNDERSTANDABLY) IS VERY HARD FOR PEOPLE TO RELATE TO UNLESS IT HAS BEEN EXPERIENCED FIRST HAND. I DO NOT WISH THIS ON ANYONE EVEN THOUGH I AM MENTALLY STRONG, THESE PLACES ARE 100% MEANT TO BREAK DOWN YOUR WILL. LUCKY FOR ME IVE BEEN THROUGH SO MUCH DIFFICULTY & PAIN IN MY LIFE SO FAR AND IM STILL HERE SMILING SAYING BRING IT THE FUCK ON. NO MATTER THE DEPTH ILL FIND LIGHT AND MAKE MYSELF GLOW IN IT FULLY. SEAN LIZÉE IS MADE TO GLOW IN THE DARK!!! FOR THE REST OF THE EVENING I WILL ENJOY AMERICAN IDOL, CLEANSING SAGE, AND A COMFORTABLE BED TO LAY IN AND JUST ENJOY SOME ME TIME... AND MAYBE LATER SOME HOMEMADE NEW YORK CHEESECAKE THAT GEC MADE FROM SOME OF THE INGREDIENTS WE BOUGHT. IM PRETTY SURE ITS BLUEBERRY MMMMMMM. ILL LEAVE THIS LETTER RIGHT HERE TONIGHT AND SAY LOVE YOU/MISS YOU AND GOODNIGHT. ALSO.. I WISH YOU WERE SITTING NEXT TO ME WATCHING SHOWS TOGETHER ♡ Z Z Z Z Z

2022-05-02

HAPPY MONDAY DUDE. TODAY WAS A DECENT DAY. WORK WAS WORK AND WE ARE NOW FRAMING CEMENT FORMS FOR THE FOUNDATION. IT DOES MAKE DAYS/WEEKS PASS BY. AFTER WORK I MADE A CALL TO MY SISTER BRITTANY THEN LAYED DOWN AND WAITED FOR DINNER WHICH WAS AMAZING (GEO MADE IT). SINCE APPROX

(17)

7-9PM WE WERE IN THE GYM AND THIS WEEK IS WEEK 2 OF EXTREME BEAST MODE FOR ME. I HAVE IT SET IN MY BRAIN NOW AFTER 3 MONTHS OF HARD WORKING WORKOUTS TO STEP MY MINDSET TO A LEVEL OF INTENSITY THATS MENTALLY & PHYSICALLY CRAZY. TONIGHT THE OTHER DUDES WERE STANDING AROUND ME CHEERING ME ON AND I ~~WAS~~ AM SO HAPPY BECAUSE OF IT. I CANT WAIT FOR YOU TO SEE ME IN PERSON DUDE!!!.. FOR THE REST OF THE NIGHT I AM GOING TO RELAX IN MY ROOM, HAVE A COFEEE, WATCH T.V., AND ENJOY HOW PUMPED MY BODY FEELS RIGHT NOW. WELL SWEET GIRL ITS TIME FOR ME TO END THIS DAY W/ AN I LOVE YOU AND IMMISSING YOU TONS... GOODNIGHT XOXOOXXO ♡ Z Z Z Z Z Z

2022-05-03

GOODMORNING, GOOD AFTERNOON, AND GOODNIGHT. I WISH YOU WELL SWEETGIRL. TODAY IS OVER AND WENT BY QUICKLY. LOVE YOU DUDE XO Z Z Z Z Z Z.

MAY THE 4TH BE W/ YOU (2022-05-04)

AAAAAND ANOTHER WORK DAY COMPLETED. IM ALL SHOWERED N SHAVED READY FOR A NIGHT AT THE GYM (BACK N BICEPS) I BOOKED SOME VIDEO VISITS OVER THE WEEKEND AND AM SUPER EXCITED FOR THEM. MY WORK BOSSES ARE EXTRE-MELY HAPPY W/ MY PRODUCTION AND POSITIVE ATTITUDE WHICH MAKES FOR EASY DAYS, ALTHOUGH IM SURE THEIR EXPECTATIONS ARENT TOO HIGH LOL. I STILL WORK LIKE IM MAKING AS MUCH AS I NORMALLY DO. THE LAST TWO WEEKS WENT BY PRETTY FAST AND SMOOTHLY. I AM AWAITING ON WORD FROM MY P.O. STILL REGARDING MY REQUEST WHICH ILL WRITE ABOUT WHEN I GET A YAY OR NAY FROM HIM. FINGERS CROSSED. I WILL BE SUPER EXCITED TO HEAR FROM YOU WHEN YOURE HOME AND SETTLED. IVE DECIDED

(18)

TO GIVE YOU SPACE AND WAIT UNTIL YOU MSSG MY SISTER. I HEARD CRC IS GETTING RECOGNITION, FROM THE GIRLS' GRANDMA, AND DONT WANT TO OVERWHELM YOU AS I AM SURE YOU ARE VERY BUSY W/ THAT. I HOPE THE VIBES W/ CRC ARE GOOD AND POSITIVE FOR YOU. ~~B~~, EITHER WAY IM ALWAYS HERE FOR YOU. (UNCONDITIONAL). I AM TRYING TO NOT WONDER ABOUT HOW YOU FEEL BECAUSE WHEN I FEEL THAT YOURE UPSET IF FEEL UPSET AS WELL. IM NOT SURE WHY BUT I DO. ⟹ IM FINALLY BACK INTO MY BEDROOM SITTING DOWN TO WRITE YOU. I GOT AN AWESOME LETTER TODAY FROM AN OLD FRIEND AND SOME NEW PHOTOS FOR MY WALL. I AM SO GRATEFUL AND HAPPY, IT MADE MY WHOLE DAY AS IT WAS COMPLETELY OUT OF THE BLUE AND CAUGHT ME OFF GUARD. I JUST FINISHED HANGING THE ALL ☺. I HAVE VIDEO VISITS W/ THE GIRLS THIS WEEKEND AND ANOTHER ON TUESDAY W/ MY BABY SISTER COURTNEY. ALSO SHE IS COMING TO SEE ME ON THE 15TH OF THIS MONTH WHICH IS A SUNDAY. I AM FILLED W/ SO MUCH LOVE AND JOY. MY WORKOUT TODAY WAS GOOD, TOMORROW I GET YET ANOTHER CANTEEN WHICH IS ALWAYS EXCITING AND I GET SOME NICORETTE GUM AGAIN LOL (ITS MY GUILTY PLEASURE IN HERE). NOW ILL GET READY FOR BED, LIGHT THE SAGE NEXT TO MY BED, PUT ON THE HISTORY CHANNEL, AND REST. TODAY I AM IN LOVE AND HAPPY, TODAY I AM GRATEFUL, AND TODAY I AM CONTENT. THE FUTURE LOOKS VERY BRIGHT [redacted]. WITH THAT BEING SAID ILL SAY GOODNIGHT SWEET GIRL... I LOVE & MISS YOU MORE THAN YOU KNOW XOOXXO Z Z Z Z Z Z

CINCO DE MAYO (2022-05-05)

HELLO LOVELY [redacted]. I JUST WENT AND GOT CANTEEN

(19)

AND THAT MEANS ONLY 5 MORE CANTEENS TO GO (MAYBE 6 AND ~~THERE~~ THEY ARE EVERY TWO WEEKS) NOW I HAVE TO HEAD BACK TO WORK UNTIL 10:30AM IN THE RAIN UNFORTUNATELY ⟹ GOOD EVENING IT IS 6:38PM AND SO FAR IVE MET W/ PASTOR DAN WHICH WAS AWESOME. WE TALKED ABOUT FAITH, HAPPINESS, SELF LOVE, A RIGHTEOUS PATH, AND WHAT DIFFERENCES I WANT TO MAKE IN THE WORLD W/ MY STORY. AFTER THAT I CAME HOME AND CLEANED THE ENTIRE HOUSE AS IT IS MY DAY, NOW I DO NOT HAVE TO CLEAN FOR ANOTHER 12 DAYS. I WAS SOAKED TO THE BONE ALL DAY AT WORK WIRING REBAR INSIDE THE FOOTING WE BUILT FOR THE NEW MEDICAL WING. I THEN REARRANGED THE REST OF MY PHOTOS AND REDECORATED MY ROOM LOL, IM FEELING HAPPY AND CONTENT AGAIN TODAY AND AM JUST LOOKING IN A FORWARD DIRECTION. IVE BEEN MISSING YOU A LOT LATELY. TWO WEEKS NOT HEARING YOUR VOICE IS ONE OF THE LONGEST GAPS WEVE HAD IN QUITE SOME TIME. I STILL LOOK AT YOUR PHOTO MULTIPLE TIMES DAILY AND WISH I HAD MORE OF THEM TO LOOK AT. YOU ARE SO RADIANT, ~~AND~~ BRIGHT EYED, AND BEAUTIFUL... YET TO MENTION KIND HEARTED, BOLD, AND CLASSY AF!!! ....ALSO ELEGANT. AS FOR THE REST OF THE EVENING I WILL JUST CHILL IN MY ROOM AND RELAX, IM NOT USING THE PHONE AS MUCH THESE DAYS, ZERO PHONE CALLS TODAY. IM FINDING DAYS PASS BY RAPIDLY WHEN I CALL PEOPLE LESS. BESIDES THE OBVIOUS & MY SISTER & THE GIRLS, THE ONLY PERSON I REALLY ENJOY TALKING TO IS YOU. I REALLY DO ENJOY OUR TIMES AND APPRECIATE THE TIME YOU MAKE FOR ME IN YOUR BUSY SCHEDULE WHEN YOU CAN. TBH IT DOES MEAN THE ABSOLUTE WORLD TO ME. BEING IN HERE REALLY DOES SHOW A PERSON EXACTLY WHO THEY ARE AND WHO EVERY ONE

(20)

ELSE IS AS WELL. I DONT CARE MUCH THAT PEOPLE HAVE
NOT WRITTEN OR REACHED OUT, I UNDERSTAND LIFE IS
VERY BUSY OUT THERE. IN TURN I JUST APPRECIATE ALL
THE PEOPLE WHO DID ALL THAT MUCH MORE, ESPECIALLY
THE ABSOLUTE UNEXPECTED ONES. ILL NEVER EVER
IN MY WHOLE LIFE TAKE FORGRANTED THE FEW THAT
WENT ABOVE AND BEYOND. I HONESTLY NEVER THOUGHT
THAT YOU WOULD HAVE BEEN THE MOST PROMINENT
PERSON IN MY LIFE DURING THIS TIME. YOUVE BEEN A
FUCKING ANGEL FOR ME ANGEL!! ANGEL IS ONE
OF THE MOST WONDERFUL PEOPLE THERE IS. I TRULY
THINK YOU ARE PERFECT AS YOU ARE. SO SOFT SPOKEN
WHEN YOURE HAPPY AND SUPER FAST TALKING WHEN YOURE
UPSET. ADMIRABLE AND PASSIONATE... PERFECT... ALSO...
SUPER QUIRKLY, CUTE, AND FUNNY AF TOO ☺ ⟹
WELL THE END OF THE NIGHT IS NEAR. I HOPE FOR NO RAIN
TOMORROW BUT IF IT DOES RAIN ILL STILL BE HAPPY THAT
ANOTHER WEEK HAS GONE BY SMOOTH & FAST. T.G.I.F.. AT
THIS MOMENT I AWAIT THE 10PM STANDING COUNT WHICH
IS IN 10 MINS, ONCE ITS DONE ILL HAVE A LONG SUPER HOT
SHOWER AND DO SOME STRETCHES. I THINK I MAY HAVE
STRETCHED/PULLED A MUSCLE SLIGHTLY IN MY LEFT UPPER
LAT & BACK TRICEP. IT IS VERY TENDER LIKE SOMEONE
GAVE ME A CHARLIE HORSE OR SOMETHING. TONIGHT I FEEL
CONTENT AND HUMBLE, THESE SURROUNDING CIRCUMSTANCES
OF THIS REALITY HAVE BECOME NORMALIZED FOR ME. IT
IS HUMBLING & ENCOURAGING AT THE SAME TIME, I THINK BE-
CAUSE IF A PERSON CAN SURVIVE THE YEAR THAT WILL BE
IN THE PAST SOON ENOUGH, A PERSON CAN/COULD SURVIVE
ANYTHING CURVEBALL LIFE WANTS TO THROW IN THEIR
DIRECTION. THANK YOU FOR THE PART YOU PLAY IN MY
SOBRIETY DUDE. I DONT THINK I COULDVE HAVE DONE

(21)

THIS ANY OTHER WAY BUT SOBER. 28-28. WELL... GOOD-
-NIGHT DUDE. I WISH YOU WELL AND YOU'RE WARM AND HAPPY.
BIG HUGS AND A CHEEK KISS. SWEET DREAM GORGEOUS GIRL.
♡♡XO Z Z Z Z Z Z Z♡

2022-05-06

FRIDAY NIGHT HAS ARRIVED. TODAYS WORK WENT BY SO FAST IT WAS AWESOME. THE BOSSES ARE MORE THAN STOKED ON THE PRODUCTION, AND GOOD VIBES THAT WE MADE THE EFFORT TO BRING TO THE TEAM. I LIKE TO BE LOUD AND EXCITED AT WORK TO BRING UP THE MORALE IN THE GROUP. I SPOKE W/ MY P.O. AND GET TO SEE HIM ON MONDAY MORNING AT 9AM ABOUT THE PLAN IVE BEEN WORKING. I PRAY THAT IT HAPPENS AS IT IS VERY POSITIVE AND LIFE CHANGING. WE DECIDED TO SKIP THE GYM TONIGHT AND JUST RELAX IN MY ROOM. AFTER A.A WE ATE HUGE BOWLS OF PHO, SO BEING THIS FILLED UP MAKES FOR A GREAT TIME FOR R&R. EARLIER I CHECKED THE MAIL AND MY FRIEND WHO RANDOMLY SENT ME A LETTERS NAME WAS APPROVED, SO WE SPOKE FOR 30 MINS OR SO WHICH WAS ENCOURAGING AND VERY SPECIAL. TOMORROW AT 12:30PM I GET TO SEE MY GIRLS FOR THE FIRST TIME IN 4 MONTHS. I HAVE BUTTERFLIES AND WILL PROBABLY GET EMOTIONAL. I LOVE THEM W/ ALL MY HEART & SOUL. THEY TELL ME HOW PROUD THEY ARE AND MY LOVE TANK FILLS UP SO MUCH IT SOMETIMES MAKES ME CRY. IVE BEEN THINKING ABOUT YOU ALOT AND WANT TO CALL YOU BUT WILL WAIT UNTIL YOU REACH OUT. I DONT WANT TO BUG OR OVERWHELM YOU RIGHT NOW AS YOU ARE PROBABLY BUSY & DEALING W/ A LOT. ⟹ BED TIME. GOODNIGHT XOXOOO♡
Z Z Z Z Z Z

2022-05-07

LAZY SATURDAY ☺ RELAX RELAX RELAX... I WENT TO THE GYM AT 9am TO WORK OUT/OFF THE LATE NIGHT CHEESE

(22)

CAKE THAT HAD BEEN DELIVERED BY ANOTHER HOUSE 2MINS BEFORE LOCKUP LAST NIGHT. BY FAR THE BEST ONE YET. AFTER LUNCH I WENT FOR A ~~BREIF~~ BRIEF CHEST PUMP BEFORE MY VIDEO CALL, UNFORTUNETLY THE INSTITUTIONS SYSTEM HAD BEEN DOWN. AH WELL I HAVE ANOTHER ONE TOMORROW. AFTERWARDS I CAME HOME AND JUST HAVE BEEN WATCHING A DOCUMENTARY ABOUT CAMAN CROCODILES ON NATIONAL GEOGRAPHIC. I OFTEN WONDER HOW YOU ARE DOING AND IF YOU OCCASSIONALLY THINK ABOUT ME AT ALL. I THINK ABOUT YOU LOTS. HOW COULD I NOT. ⇒ 7PM COUNT TIME. I AM SO RELAXED TODAY. I HAD A VERY HOT 30 MIN SHOWER THEN A NAP. GEO WOKE ME UP FOR SOME DINNER AND AN AFTER DINNER COCA-COLA AND THEN I CAME STRAIGHT BACK TO MY ROOM. THERE ARE ALL MY FAVORITE SHOWS ON THE HISTORY CHANNEL TONIGHT. THE ONLY WAY IM LEAVING THIS SPACE IS IF SOMEONE STOPS BY TO SAY HI. OTHER THAN THAT IM CHILLIN FOR THE NIGHT IN MY WARM BED ALL SNUGGLED UP AND WARM ☺ ⇒ WELL I AM GOING TO WALK OUT TO CHECK THE MAIL, DROP A VID APPLICATION FOR MY DAD AND MAIL THIS TO YOURS TRULY. GOODNIGHT SWEET GIRL AND I LOVE & MISS YOU VERY VERY MUCH

♡ ♡ ♡ ♡ ♡

6

Daydreams

"Freedom starts in the mind."

Back then my thoughts didn't always stay locked in that cell. They drifted. Out past the fences, over the hills, into her arms. Some nights I could almost feel her there, hear her laugh, see the way sunlight might fall across her face. I'd close my eyes and let the world rebuild itself, one detail at a time—the smell of rain, the sound of traffic in the distance, the simple peace of standing in fresh air.

Those dreams weren't just escape. They were practice. Each one was me remembering what it meant to live again. I pictured walking out, hearing my name called without fear, breathing air that didn't taste recycled. I could see her waiting, the look in her eyes when she realized I'm finally out. I imagined the weight of the first hug, the quiet of a night without locks or alarms. Holding on to those moments in my head made the walls feel smaller.

But I never let the dreaming carry me too far. I still heard the count, still felt the steel, still felt the weight of my mistakes. That balance mattered—between where I was and where I was going, between the truth that held me down and the hope that lifted me back up. So I wrote it all down. Every image, every promise, every small piece of faith. And I told myself, if I could see it clearly enough on paper, maybe one day I'd step into it for real.

(1)

2022-05-07

DEAREST [redacted]... IT IS ANOTHER DAYS END. I SPENT THE LAST TWO HOURS OR SO DRINKING COFFEE W/ MY GOOD FRIEND CHARLIE ON OUR PATIO AND TALKING ABOUT LIFE, FAMILY, LOVE, RELATIONSHIP, AND LIFE GOALS. HE LEAVES HERE IN JULY AND IS SOMEONE ILL KEEP IN CONTACT W/ AFTER MY TIME HERE IS FINALLY COMPLETE. I HOPE YOU ARE HAPPY AND WELL. IVE BEEN KEEPING YOU IN MY NIGHTLY PRAYERS. HOPEFULLY THE SYSTEMS HERE ARE BACK ONLINE TOMORROW SO I CAN SEE THE GIRLS AT 4:30PM AS IT HAS BEEN 4 MONTHS SINCE IVE SEEN THEIR ANGELIC LITTLE FACES. I LOVE ALL MY BABIES SO MUCH AND WISH TO HAVE MORE ONE DAY IF LIFE, LOVE, AND A HAPPY HEALTHY RELATIONSHIP PERMITS IT. IF NOT THAT IS OK AS WELL. HAVING A LOVING FAMILY WOULD BE A DREAM COME TRUE. BEING HERE HAS CEMENTED THE PATH I WILL BE LEAVING TO GO ACHIEVE. I AM HAPPY AND CONTENT AND ONCE AGAIN IN LOVE ON SO MANY LEVELS. LIFE IS BEAUTIFUL EVEN IN TRYING TIMES AS THOSE/ THESE TIMES GIVE OPPORTUNITIES TO GAIN PERSPECTIVE, LEARN, AND GET SOME OFTEN NEEDED WISDOM THROUGH EXPERIENCE. ON ANOTHER NOTE THERE IS A SHOW ON JACK THE RIPPER ON THE HISTORY CHANNEL (SUBTLE MUDDLERS LOL) AND IT MAKES ME THINK OF A MOVIE, NAILS, BRAIDS, AND FACE MASK NIGHT W/ YOU IF YOURE STILL DOWN WHEN THE TIME COMES. EITHER WAY THE THOUGHT PUTS A SMILE ON MY FACE. GOODNIGHT SWEET GIRL AND BIG HUGS TO YOU B ZZZ

2022-05-08 (MOTHERS DAY)

HAPPY MOTHERS DAY DUDE.. EVEN THOUGH YOURE NOT A MOM YET, WHEN YOU ARE I KNOW YOULL BE THE BEST MOM A CHILD COULD EVER ASK FOR. TODAY I SLEPT IN UNTIL 11am AFTER A REALLY NICE LONG SLEEP. MY DREAMS WERE GOOD ALL NIGHT AS WELL. I HOPE YOUR MOM HAS A GOOD DAY EVEN →

(2)

THOUGH I KNOW IT WILL PROBABLY BE A TOUGH ONE. SHE IS IN MY THOUGHTS AND PRAYERS AND IM SENDING YOUR MOM ALL MY LOVE ♡. TODAY I DONT HAVE MUCH PLANNED, NOW THAT I WROTE THAT I REALIZED THAT I HAVE A FEW THINGS PLANNED LOL. FIRST A VID CALL W/ THE GIRLS AT 4:30, THEN A HOUSE TURKEY DINNER, AND FINALLY MY NEW FAVORITE SHOW IN JAIL... AMERICAN IDOL... I WROTE THAT LARGE TO SHOW MY EXCITEMENT AND ENTHUSIASM. I HOPE YOURE SMILING!! SOMETIMES I LAUGH WHEN I THINK ABOUT THE TIME WE WERE TALKING AND YOU ASKED ME TO HOLD ON FOR A MOMENT TO WATCH THE END OF YOUR SHOW, WHEN THE PERSON WAS ELIMINATED YOU WERE LIKE "BYE BIIITCH" HAHA HAHAHA. I ABSOLUTELY ADORED THAT BECAUSE YOU SOUNDED LITERALLY THE EXACT SAME AS MY YOUNGER SISTERS BRITTANY & COURTNEY TO A TEE. YOUD LOVE THEM SO MUCH (THEY ARE THE BEST OBVIOUSLY LOL) IT HAS BEEN EXACTLY 2 WEEKS SINCE LAST SPOKE AND IM MISSING YOU TONS. THE WEATHER TODAY IS REALLY BEA-UTIFUL, BLUE SKIES W/ ALL SORTS OF DIFFERENT KINDS OF CLOUDS. ITS A BIT WINDY AND THERE IS A TON OF BIRDS OF ALL SPECIES FLYING IN EVERY DIRECTION. WHEN I LOOK OUTSIDE I IMAGINE BEING IN AN AIRPLANE OR HELICOPTER PASSING THROUGH THE CLOUDS AND OVER TOP OF MOUNTAIN RANGES LIKE IN OUR DREAM STORIES. ANYWHERE BUT HERE. I FEEL CONTENT IN MY ROOM TALKING/WRITING TO YOU. I KNOW I SAY IT A LOT BUT I APPRECIATE YOU SO MUCH. I TRULY AM IN LOVE W/ YOU. IN LOVE IN A WAY THAT I WISH YOU THE BEST IN YOUR LIFE NO MATTER WHAT I BELIEVE YOU DESERVE EVERYTHING GREAT IN LIFE ♡. KNOWING YOU HAS TAUGHT ME EXACTLY WHAT UNCONDITIONAL LOVE IS, UNCONDITIONAL IS THAT

(3)

NO MATTER THE CIRCUMSTANCES ARE I WILL ALWAYS BE HERE FOR YOU IF YOU NEED ME AND I WOULD STOP LIFE TO BE THERE FOR YOU AT ALL COSTS. I WOULD DROP WHAT I WAS DOING AND SAIL THE WORLD TO FIND YOU IF YOU WERE LOST. I WOULD TRAVEL TO HELL AND BACK FOR YOU ANGEL [redacted]!!! RECENTLY I HAVE BEEN PRAYING EVERY EVENING FOR EVERYONE I CARE ABOUT AND SENDING LOVE OUTWARDS NO MATTER THE PAIN IVE BEEN THROUGH. POSITIVITY AND LOVE ARE SO IMPORTANT TO ME SO IM PUTTING FORTH ONLY GOOD INTENTIONS SELFLESS AND SELFISH AND HAVE FELT AT PEACE IN LIFE MORE AND MORE LATELY. I AM CHANGING INTERNALLY AS IF SOMETHING HAS BEEN CALLING ME. MY WHOLE BEING HAS SO MUCH EMPATHY, COMPASSION, AND AN EXTREME AMOUNT OF DRIVE TO STRIVE TOWARDS EVER-YTHING POSITIVE AND UPLIFTING. THE HIGHER POWER HAS SOMETHING IN STORE FOR ME AND I CAN FEEL IT BUILDING UP INSIDE MY HEART & SOUL. OBVIOUSLY DAY BY DAY THERE CAN BE HIGHS & LOWS AND THAT IS DEFINATELY A.OK.. AS THEY COME TRY TO MAINTAIN CALM, THINK RATIONALLY, AND FIND LOVE IN EVEN DARK SPACES. I TRY TO LET GO OF THE NEGATIVE THOUGHTS THE BEST I CAN AND WORK HARD AT LETTING GO COMPLETELY W/ OUT REELING IT BACK IN DUE TO FEAR OF CHANGE. CHANGE CAN BE SCARY HOWEVER IT IS 100% NESSESSARY (← SPELL CHECK LOL) ⟹ IM BACK TO MY ROOM (3:21 PM) CHARLIE AND I WENT FOR A WALK TO WHATS BEEN NAMED "THE GHETTO" WHICH ARE THE HOUSES DOWN BELOW. ONCE AGAIN WAS GIVEN YET ANOTHER PIECE OF CHEESECAKE / ICE CREAM CAKE. THAT MEANS 4 HOUSES ARE NOW IN THIS CHEESECAKE COMPETITION LOL. I BROUGHT IT HOME TO SHARE W/ THE BOYS... THEY LAUGHED AT THE FACT THAT EVERY TIME I LEAVE THE HOUSE SOMEONE GIVES ME A TREAT OR PEOPLE KNOCKING ON OUR DOOR TO BRING ME TREATS

(4)

LOL. CHARLIE AND I SAT IN THE SUN FOR A BIT JUST TALKING. I REALLY LIKE HIM. HIS CASE IS LIKE MINE IN THE FACT THAT WE MADE MISTAKES AND ARE PAYING FOR IT BY BEING HERE. I'VE BEEN ENJOYING NICORETTE GUM IN MY ROOM WATCHING A SHOW ON BIGFOOT AND TAKING SOME TIME TO TALK (WRITE) TO YOU. ⟹ ANOTHER NIGHT HAS PASSED US BY DELIGHTFULLY. I SKIPPED AMERICAN IDOL TO CHAT TO A BUDDY FOR AWHILE. HE HAS BEEN HAVING A DIFFICULT TIME LATELY AND WAS VERY HAPPY TO HEAR MY VOICE HE SAID. THEN I WENT HOME BUT GEO WASNT HERE, I FOUND HIM AT THE GYM SO I WORKED FOR 20 MINS AND THEN WE WALKED THE GHETTO R AROUND THE COMPOUND. IT IS A VERY CALM AND SERENE EVENING OUTSIDE. I DID NOT TALK TO MY MOM TODAY AS MY EMOTIONS TOWARDS HER ARE VERY CONFLICTED LATELY. IM HAVING DIFFICULTIES PROCESSING WHAT WE HAVE BEEN THROUGH AND ALL THE THINGS THAT HAVE BEEN DONE. ON ONE HAND I FEEL BAD FOR NOT CALLING BECAUSE I LOVE MY MOM BUT ON THE OTHER I AM IN HERE AND THAT CALL WOULD HURT ME TO A POINT IT WILL SLOW DOWN TIME FOR ME. I DEFINATELY NEED TIME TO HEAL SOME OBVIOUSLY DEEP WOUNDS. OTHER THAN THAT TODAY WAS GOOD, THE BOYS AND I MADE TURKEY, STUFFING, GRAVY, VEGGIES, AND MASHED POTATOES... AAAAAND IT WAS INCREDIBLE. I THINK THIS WEEK SOME OF THE OTHER HOUSE GUYS AND I WILL BE STARTING A NON-VIOLENT COMMUNICATION STUDY GROUP. SUPER EXCITING!!! IM A TAD BIT ANXIOUS ABOUT MY MEETING TOMORROW AM W/ MY P.O. AS WHAT I AM PROPOSING IS AND WILL BE A MIRACLE IF IT HAPPENS. I REALLY DO HOPE IT DOES. AND IF IT DOES THEN SOME-ONE IS DEFINATELY WATCHING OUT FOR ME THATS

(5)

FOR SURE. IF FOR SOME REASON IT DOES NOT GO THROUGH THEN I GUESS GOD HAS A DIFFERENT PLAN IN MIND FOR ME. EITHER WAY ILL SHOW/HAVE GRATITUDE. ONCE AGAIN FINGERS ARE CROSSED. I CANT WAIT TO TELL YOU ABOUT IT (IF IT HAPPENS). PROGRESS NOT PERFECTION. I DIDNT GET TO TALK TO THE GIRLS TODAY BECAUSE THEIR MOM MIXED UP THE TIMES, HOWEVER I DID TALK TO THEIR MOM FOR 35 MINS. I HAVENT SPOKEN TO HER IN OVER A MONTH AND HAVENT SEEN HER IN ALMOST 5 MONTHS OR SO. IT WAS NICE TO SEE A FAMILIAR FACE. SHE SNAPPED SOME SCREENSHOTS OF MY PHYSICAL CHANGE. SHE SEEMED VERY PROUD AND SUPRIZED AT ALL THE WORK I PUT INTO THIS TRANSFORMATION. IT HASNT BEEN EASY WHATSOEVER. DEDICATION AND HARD WORK ARE ALWAYS WORTH IT IN THE LONG-RUN. SLOW IS SMOOTH AND SMOOTH IS FAST. WELL DUDE TIME FOR ME TO REST FOR THE NIGHT. ILL DREAM ABOUT YOU, I MISS AND LOVE YOU VERY VERY MUCH LOVE ANGEL

♡ Z ♡ Z ♡ Z ♡ Z ♡ Z ♡ Z ♡ Z

2022-05-09

WELL TODAY HAS BEEN A TOUGH ONE TO SAY THE LEAST. THIS DAY TOO SHALL PASS. I STILL HAVE LOTS OF LOVE IN MY HEART AND MY HIGHER POWER IS TESTING ME THROUGH PAIN ONCE AGAIN. THATS OK IM CERTAIN HIS REASONING IS GOOD. THE DIFFERENCE THIS TIME IS THAT I REMAIN CALM AND ACCEPT THESE FEELING. SOBRIETY HAS TAUGHT ME TO NOT REACT AND TO ALLOW FOR TIME TO SHOW ITS PURPOSE. I HOPE ALL IS WELL W/ YOU DUDE. I MISS YOU TONS DAILY. ⟹ THIS MORNING AT WORK I WAS SOAKED TO THE BONE BY 9am AND WORKED UNTIL NOON STRAIGHT TO GET THE REBAR COMPLETED FOR INSPECTION... IT PASSED. W/ FLYING COLORS (OBV. LOL) MY BOSSES WERE VERY

(6)

HAPPY. I HAVE BEEN LOSING TOUCH W/ THE OUTSIDE WORLD LATELY AS THE OUTSIDE WORLD IS MOVING ON W/OUT ME. ITS UNDERSTANDABLE AND I FIGURED AT SOME POINT IT WOULD HAPPEN, IM JUST HAPPY THAT IT LASTED AS LONG AS IT DID. ITS A FUNNY THING BEING INCARCERATED. ITS A CULTURE SHOCK TO SOME EXTENTS AND A WORLD OF ITS OWN. BEING DETACHED FROM ALL WORLDLY THINGS I.E. LOVED ONES, PHONES/TEXTING, SURROUNDING COMFORTS, AND CHOICE ETC. IS A REALITY OF ITS OWN 100%. NOT MUCH LONGER NOW. I AM 2/3 DONE THIS PHASE. I DEFINATELY THRIVE WHEN I FEEL LOVED OR BEING TOLD IM LOVED. MY LOVE LANGUAGES FROM THE BOOK 5 LANGUAGES OF LOVE ARE PHYSICAL TOUCH AND WORDS OF AFFIR--MATION, BEING IN HERE COULDNT MAKE THAT MORE APPARENT. I AM STRONG ENOUGH TO MAKE MY WAY THROUGH BUT AM FOR SURE LACKING THOSE TWO THINGS IN MY LIFE. ILL BE SO HAPPY TO CUDDLE AGAIN ONE DAY, HOLD SOMEONE SPECIALS HAND, HUG, AND KISS,... I TRULY DO LOVE, LOVE. FOR NOW ILL SEND ALL MY LOVE OUTWARD AND HOPEFULLY SOME WILL BE SENT BACK IN ONE FORM OR ANOTHER. ⟹ I JUST RETURNED HOME FROM MY CHAT W/ YOU... I AM SO GLAD I CALLED TONIGHT. THERE SURE WAS A REASON FOR ME TO MAKE THAT CALL. AS SOON AS I HEARD YOUR VOICE I COULD FEEL EXACTLY HOW MUCH I HAD BEEN MISSING YOU DUDE. I LOVE YOU SO MUCH ANGEL. TALKING TO YOU MADE MY WEEK. I LOOK FORWARD TO CALLING ON WEDNESDAY AND KNOWING YOU MIGHT VISIT AT THE END OF THIS MONTH FILLS MY HEART. I AM GOING TO HUG YOU FOR AS LONG AS YOU WILL LET ME IF THAT HAPPENS, IF NOT THATS OK AS WELL I WILL PRAY THAT IT DOES EVERY NIGHT ♡. I CHERISH EVERY

7

PART OF OUR FRIENDSHIP. I HOPE I DREAM I GET TO DREAM ABOUT YOU TONIGHT. FOR THE REST OF TONIGHT I AM GOING TO WATCH SHOWS, BURN SAGE, AND POP A PIECE OF NICORETTE GUM THEN LAY DOWN AND WRAP MYSELF IN THE BLANKET I HAVE FOR YOU (IF THEY LET ME LEAVE W/ IT THAT IS). OH HELL YEAH DUDE AMERICAN IDOL IS ON AGAIN. I GET TO WATCH WHAT I MISSED LAST NIGHT :) GOODNIGHT SWEET GIRL. I LOVE YOU MORE THAN YOU COULD EVER KNOW AND CANNOT WAIT TO HUG YOU

Z Z Z Z Z Z Z

2022-05-10

HELLO BEAUTIFUL GIRL. I HOPE YOURE DAY WAS GREAT AND THAT YOU HAVE A FUN & SAFE TIME AT KARAOKE THIS EVENING. YOU DESERVE IT DUDE. MY DAY HAS BEEN OK SO FAR. THIS MORNING I WENT TO CEREMONIAL CIRCLE OF HEALING UNTIL NOON. I SPOKE W/ THE ELDER AND GOT SOME ADVICE ON WHAT TO DO ABOUT DAUGHTER. FOR NOW I WILL VUST LET HER GO AND BETTER MYSELF. IT BREAKS MY HEART BUT I AM AT PEACE W/ THIS CHOICE. I CANNOT FIGHT W/ HER MOTHER... THE IS ZERO PEACE IN WAR. ALL I CAN DO IS SEND LOVE AND CARRY ON MY PATH FORWARD. AFTER THAT I WENT TO WORK THEN CHECKED MY MAIL W/ LEO... HIM AND I STROLLED DOWN TO THE GHETTO TO HANGOUT. AN HOUR PASSED US BY VERY QUICKLY. IT IS 3:58 NOW. AT 5:15 I HAVE A VIDEO CALL AND HOPEFULLY EX-WIFE IS W/ THE GIRLS THIS TIME. I THOUGHT ABOUT YOU A LOT TODAY AS ALWAYS. I WISH I COULD HUG YOU RIGHT NOW, ⟹ AAAND SHE WAS NOT W/ THE GIRLS. ALL I CAN DO IS SUPPORT HER THE BEST I CAN AND SEND LOVE. I CALLED MY BABIES AT 6:40 AND THEY ARE SO AMAZING. I LOVE THEM SO MUCH I STARTED TO CRY AND HAD TO HANGUP AFTER TELLING THEM HOW PROUD DADDY IS AND HE LOVES & MISSES THEM. TALKING W/ THEM

(8)

MAKES ME SO HAPPY AND EQUALLY SAD. THEY DESERVE THE WORLD. RIGHT NOW I AM WAITING THE 7PM COUNT AND THEN ILL CALL MY DAD AND HIT THE GYM. I KEEP ALL MY FAITH IN MY HIGHER POWERS HANDS BECAUSE HE MUST HAVE A PLAN FOR ME. I AM HAPPY & GRATEFUL FOR THIS EYE OPENING EXPERIENCE BECAUSE ALL THIS TIME AND PAIN HAS HELPED ME BECOME THE BEST PERSON I CAN BE. IM POSITIVE THAT REINTEGRATING BACK INTO SOCIETY IS GOING TO BE FROM A VERY DIFFERENT PERSPECTIVE/OUTLOOK. FOR NOW THE NEXT MILESTONE WILL BE OUR 11 & 12 MONTH COINS. IF ONLY I WAS THERE TO CELEBRATE MY ONE YEAR FOLLOWED BY YOUR ON THE NEXT MONTH. I CAN ALREADY TELL THAT I WILL HAVE TEARS OF JOY WHEN I FINALLY SEE YOU AND HUG FOR THE FIRST TIME SINCE I LAST SAW YOU 6 MONTHS AGO. IT SEEMS LIKE JUST YESTERDAY BUT ALSO LIKE A WHOLE OTHER LIFETIME AWAY. JUST LIKE I AM SO CLOSE YET SO VERY FAR AWAY. SOMETIMES I WONDER IF ILL EVER BE ABLE TO GET MANI-PEDIS W/ YOU AND ACTUALLY BRAID YOUR HAIR, ESPECIALLY SINCE HAS GROWN SO GORGEOUSLY LONG. ⇒

GREAT HEAVY LIFT WORKOUT AFTER COUNT (7PM) EARLIER. ANOTHER DAY HAS FALLEN TO NIGHT AND IS ALL WRAPPED UP. ONE MORE DAY CLOSER ☺. I HOPE YOUR EVENING WAS/IS FUN AND YOU GOT HOME HAPPY AND SAFELY. IM SENDING LOTS OF LOVE & WARMTH AS YOU SNUGGLE UP INTO YOUR BED. ONCE AGAIN I SAY TO YOU GOODNIGHT PRECIOUS ANGEL AND I WISH FOR YOU THE SWEETEST OF DREAMS AND THE VERY BEST OF SLEEPS ♡ Z Z Z Z

2022-05-11

GOOD MORNING & GOOD AFTERNOON. ANOTHER BEAUTIFUL WEATHER DAY. TODAY WAS A DAY OF REFLECTION FOR ME

(9)

I HAD TO FIND CALMNESS AND SERENITY THE FEEL ALL THE EMOTIONS AS THEY PASSED THROUGH ME. I TRY TO IDENTIFY THEM AND UNDERSTAND THEM THE VERY BEST I KNOW HOW. SOME ARE MORE DIFFICULT THAN OTHERS BUT THAT IS ABSOLUTELY O.K. I MANAGED TO MAINTAIN A LOVING AND PEACEFUL ATTITUDE AND TO BE VERY GRATEFUL FOR MY SOBRIETY. I FIND MYSELF EMPATHETIC FOR THE ALCOHOLICS & ADDICTS STILL SUFFERING AS I ONCE WAS. I STILL STRUGGLE AND SUFFER EVEN THOUGH I AM A DIFFERENT MAN NOW. A LEVEL HEAD HELPS TO KEEP AWAY FROM IRRATIONAL THINKING AS THOUGHTS ARE EVERYTHING THAT WE WILL BECOME. CLEAN THO-UGHTS, CLEAN WORDS, CLEAN HEART. I AM GRATEFUL THAT MY BABY SISTER COURTNEY WILL BE HERE TO SEE ME ON SUNDAY AFTERNOON. MY SISTER BRITTANY HAS BEEN AN ALL-STAR DEALING W/ LAWYERS AND THE TREATMENT CENTER. WE WILL SEE WHAT IS IN STORE FOR ME ON THE HORIZON. ITS IN GODS HANDS NOW ♡. I HAVE TO KEEP ON REMINDING MYSELF THAT THIS WORLD IS GODS WILL NOT OUR OWN. AS I SIT HERE I LOOK UP AT MY WALL AND THERE YOU ARE SMILING. OBVIOUSLY LOOKING FLY AF LIKE A ANGEL (← PUN OBVIOUSLY INTENDED LOL). WELL IM GOING TO WALK TO THE PHONE TO CALL YOU. YOU ARE PROBS AT YOUR FRIENDS PLACE BUT ILL TRY ONCE MORE BEFORE I LAY DOWN UNTIL BEDTIME. ⇒ I AM GLAD I GOT TO SAY A QUICK HI TONIGHT WHILE YOU WERE OUT A [redacted] PLACE. I CAME BACK TO THE HOUSE AND PLAYED TONY HAWK ON GEOS PS1 (THE ORIGINAL PLAYSTATION) I HAVENT PLAYED IT IN LIKE 25 YEARS. 100% A BLAST FROM THE PAST. NOW ILL WATCH FORGED IN FIRE FOR A LIL BIT. ⇒ AAAND ONE DAY CLOSER YAY... TONIGHT WAS GOOD AND I HOPE YOURS WAS AS WELL. GEO AND I WENT FOR A

(10)

NIGHTTIME STROLL AROUND THE COMPOUND AND THROUGH THE GHETTO. THEN WE WENT AND KNOCKED ON CHARLIES WINDOW AND WE ALL CAME BACK TO OUR HOME PATIO FOR COFFEE. AS THE CHATTED I STOOD ON THE ROAD AND HAD A GREAT CONVO W/ THE LIFERS NEXT DOOR, WELL ACROSS THE SINGLE LANE RD FROM US (ALSO A HAMPTON NEIGHBORHOOD HOUSE). MORE NEW GUYS ARE SHOWING UP DAILY NOW AND THING ARE OPENING UP FOR US HERE. THERE HAS BEEN A BEAR WARNING TODAY AND HE HAS BEEN HANGING OUT IN OUR AREA. NOW ITS TIME FOR FINAL COUNT ONCE AGAIN. TIME TO GET INTO MY PJS (BOXERS... THANK GOD I DO NOT HAVE TO WEAR TIGHTY WHITEYS ANYMORE) AND FIND ANOTHER SHOW TO FALL ASLEEP TO AND REST THESE EYES UNTIL MORNING. ILL LOOK FOR YOU IN MY DREAMS I HOPE TO SEE YOU IN THERE TONIGHT. GOODNIGHT SWEET GIRL, I DO MISS YOU A LOT AND LOVE YOU W/ ALL MY HEART B Z Z Z Z Z

2022-05-12

HELLO BEAUTIFUL ANGEL. (4:51PM) I AM LOOKING FORWARD TO CHATTING W/ YOU LATER IF YOU HAVE TIME. TODAY HAS BEEN GOOD SO FAR. WORK WENT FAST, NOW IM OFF TO LIFE RING, THEN DINNER AT 6PM AND THEN THE GYM. ONCE AGAIN MY FINGERS ARE CROSSED AT POTENTIAL NEW DEVELOPMENTS W/ TREATMENT. I CANNOT WAIT TO TELL YOU ALL ABOUT IT. ⟹ WELL BEDTIME IS HERE YAAY. A SCOOP OF PEANUT BUTTER WHILE I WRITE TO YOU ☺. KINDA SAD WE COULDN'T TALK TONIGHT AH WELL. I JUST WENT BACK TO THE GYM UNTIL 9:50 THEN CAME HOME AND PLAYED A GAME OF RUMI W/ THE BOYS (I WON) IT IS ABSOLUTELY POURING OUT SO I GUESS ILL SLEEP W/ THE WINDOW OPEN, THE SOUND IS EXTREMELY CAL-MING. I DO HOPE IT STOPS FOR WORK TOMORROW

EITHER WAY ILL BE HAPPY AS IT FRIDAY THE 13TH EVEN THOUGH THERE HAS BEEN SOME STRUGGLES LATELY ALL IN ALL I FIND MYSELF STILL HAPPY & GRATEFUL. I JUST CHOOSE TO REFLECT LOVE INTO THE ATMOSPHERE AND IVE BEEN RECIEVING IT BACK FROM THE UNIVERSE. I FEEL GOD OF MY UNDERSTANDING HEARING ME + SEEING MY PRAYERS IN MY DAILY ACTIONS. WHAT A BLESSING SOME REALIZATIONS CAN BE EVEN THROUGHOUT TEMPORARY PAIN. "THIS TOO SHALL PASS". GOODNIGHT SWEET GIRL. I LOVE YOU

Z Z Z Z Z Z Z

2022-05-13 FRIDAY THE 13TH MUAHAHA

GOOD DAY TO YOU DUDE. IM HOME NOW FOR LUNCH THE & TWO MORE HOURS OF WORK AND ANOTHER HOUR OR SO AT THE NVC COURSE (NON VIOLENT COMMUNICATION) A COUPLE OF US STARTED. BASICALLY WE MEET ON FRIDAYS TO WORK ON THE COURSE BOOK + READ THE BOOK AND DISCUSS IT. ITS NOT MANDA--TORY BUT WHY NOT FURTHER OUR EDUCATION TOWARDS HEALTHIER COMMUNICATION W/ THE TIME WE HAVE HERE. MY MOOD IS CONTENT AND HAPPY. IM ALSO STOKE THAT YET ANOTHER WEEK HAS FASTLY PASSED US BY BRINGING ME CLOSER TO THE NEXT STEP TO HAVING ALL OF THIS BEHIND ME.. IT HAS BEEN A LONG TIME COMING AND MY FEELINGS OF RELIEF ARE SLOWLY SETTING IN. I PRAY FOR EVERYONE NIGHTLY BEFORE BED THEN FIND THAT I HAVE BEEN HAVING MUCH BETTER SLEEPS. I FORGOT HOW PRAYER HAD HELPED ME DURING THE BEGINNING OF SOBRIETY ONLY TO REALIZE HOW MUCH I NEED TO BE CONSISTENT W/ IT. IT REALLY DOES HELP.. A... LOT. IM MISSING YOU TODAY BECAUSE WE DID GET THE CHANCE TO TALK LAST NIGHT AND I FIND MYSELF WONDERING IF YOU ARE DOING OK. IM NOT

(12)

ENTIRELY SURE WHEN WE WILL CHAT NEXT HOWEVER I LOOK FORWARD TO HEARING YOUR VOICE IN THE HOPEFULLY NEAR FUTURE. THE WEATHER IS PATCHY W/ BLUE SKIES BUT MOSTLY CLOUDS... AT LEAST IT IS NOT RAINING WHILE WE WORK & THE WEEKEND IS ONLY HOURS AWAY. → THE WEEKEND IS FINALLY HERE YAAAAAAAAAAAAAAY!! WEELLLL. THE END OF THE WORKDAY WAS GREAT. I WENT TO LIFERING (NVC) WHICH WAS VERY EASY TO CONNECT TO. WE READ SOME OF CHAPTER ONE THEN DISCUSSED OUR EXPERIENCES W/ WHAT WAS READ I FOUND IT EASIER TO REFLECT ON MY LIFE IN A GROUP OF LIKE MINDED DUDES RATHER THAN ON MY OWN. I FIND DOING IT ALONE VERY DIFFICULT DUE TO REGRETS IN MY PAST BASED ON LETTING MY EMOTIONS GET THE BEST OF ME TO A POINT OF FIXATION, REACTION, AND NOT WALKING AWAY OR LETTING THINGS GO. ITS VERY GOOD TO BE WORKING ON IT FINALLY. THIS WILL HELP DEFINE WAY MORE HEALTHY AND POSITIVE INTERACTION W/ THE PEOPLE IN LIFE AND THOSE WHO I MEET IN THE FUTURE. AFTER LIFERING (NVC) I CALLED ADMIN FROM HALFWAY-HOUSE AND SPOKE W/ HIM FOR APPROX 20-30 MINS. HIS NUMBER PASSED THROUGH THE SYSTEM HERE AT A RECORD PACE. ALMOST AN UNHEARD OF RATE. HE WAS CALLED AFTER 8:30PM LAST NIGHT AND THE APPROVAL WAS IN THE MAILBOX BY NOON. I WAS 100% SHOCKED. I AM TRULY AND HONESTLY AMAZED AND EXTREMELY GRATEFUL. IT GIVES ME FAITH & HOPE AND SOLIDIFIES TO ME ME THAT OPEN ONES HEART TO PRAYER IS GOOD FOR THE MIND, HEART, & SOUL. THINGS DO HAPPEN AS

(13)

THEY SHOULD SOMETIMES. SOMETIMES QUICKLY SOMETIMES SLOWLY (DID YOU IMMEDIATELY IN YOUR HEAD FINISH THE NEXT PART LOL)... THEY ALWAYS MATERIALIZE IF YOU WORK FOR THEM. I FUCKING MISS YOU DUDE AND ABSOLUTELY ADORE YOU!!! AT THE INSTITUTION THE VIBES ARE OVERALL DECENT. PEOPLE GET ALONG AND ARE FOR THE MOST PART HAPPY. IN HERE THE STRUGGLES ARE REAL BUT YOU LEARN THROUGH HELPLESSNESS AND BEING POWERLESS TO UNDERSTAND AND WORK PAST IT. SOMETIMES ITS EVEN EASIER THEN OUT THERE BECAUSE OF THOSE TWO REASONS. THOSE SAME TWO REASONS CAN ALSO BE A HARSH REALITY AS WELL AND I COULD SEE WHERE A PERSON COULD BE "MADE" OR "BROKEN" BY IT. I PERSONALLY HAVE SAT ON THE EDGE OF THE FENCE A FEW TIME ONLY TO COME OUT STRONGER W/ A BETTER OUTLOOK AND MORE RESOURCEFUL AS TO WHERE I USE MY THOUGHTS & ENERGY. IT HAS BEEN TOUGH THATS FOR SURE!!! SOMEDAYS I THINK OF WHAT IT WOULD HAVE BEEN W/ OUT YOU OR IF I DIDNT JOURNAL/WRITE TO YOU EVERYDAY. IT DEFINATELY WOULD HAVE GONE A LOT DIFFERENT AND MOST LIKELY WAY TOUGHER ON ME. I WILL ALWAYS LOVE YOU FOR BEING THE PERSON YOU ARE AND HAVE CONSISTANTLY BEEN... LIKE MY ANGEL SOME DAYS.

⟹ IT WAS SO NICE TO TALK TO EVERYONE AND YOUR MOM TOO.. THAT MADE MY NIGHT. WHAT A TREAT. AFTER WE TALKED GEO AND I WALKED OUT TO THE DUTY DESK SO I COULD SUBMIT MY NUMBER LIST W/ YOUR MOM'S CONTACT ON IT. THEN A WALK THROUGH THE GHETTO. AS WE

(14)

SAUNTERED SLOWLY THROUGH THE HOOD WE STOPPED TO CHILL ON THE STOOP OF ONE OF THE HOUSES. WE WERE MET W/ COFFEE AND ANOTHER CAKE LOL. WE BROUGHT THE CAKE HOME TO SHARE W/ MOU... HE LAUGHED AND SAID "WTF ALWAYS GETTING TREATS LOL". AFTER THAT THE 3 OF US PLAYED RUMI FOR OVER AN HOUR AND NOW IVE FINALLY RETREATED TO MY ROOM. IT IS 11:18PM AND IM READY TO SNUGGLE IN BED TO WATCH THE HISTORY CHANNEL. THANX FOR ALL THAT TONIGHT DUDE... I FUCKING LOVE AND ADORE YOU 100%. YOU ARE SO AMAZING.. IM STOKED TO CHAT W/ YOU TOMORROW EVE AFTER THE GYM. HAVE AN AMAZING TIME W/ YOUR MOM.. I LOVE YOU BOTH!!! GOODNIGHT TO YOU THE MOST AMAZING PERSON (SWEETGIRL) THERE IS IN THIS WORLD. I LOVE YOU SO MUCH ♡ Z Z
Z Z Z Z Z Z Z

2022-05-14

GOOD AFTERNOON ☺, I WOKE UP W/ YOU AND YOUR MOM ON MY MIND THIS MORNING.. IM NOT SURE EXACTLY WHY BUT I WOKE UP VERY HAPPY BECAUSE OF IT. ⇒ WOW THAT DAY HAS BREEZED BY, IT IS 4PM AND THE REST OF THE AFTERNOON IS BOOKED. GYM AT 5ISH, N.A. AT 730, THEN I GET TO CALL YOU.. HOPEFULLY YOU ARE FREE AND ABLE TO CHAT FOR A LITTLE WHILE ♡. I JUST GOT HOME FROM A WALK W/ CHARLIE. WE WALKED THE BACK AREA BEHIND THE DUCK POND AND PAST THE GHETTO. WE SAT AT THE BENCH IN FRONT OF THE PROGRAMS BUILDING FOR A BIT AND AS ALWAYS SPOKE ABOUT LIFE. WE TALKED ABOUT OUR KIDS AND THINGS WE LOOK FORWARD TO DOING WHEN OUR TIME IS UP. I TOLD HIM ABOUT YOU AND WHAT ITS BEEN LIKE HAVING YOU IN MY CORNER AND HOW SPECIAL YOUVE BECOME TO ME BEING IN MY LIFE. HE TALKED

(15)

ABOUT HIS RELATIONSHIP W/ HIS WIFE AND HOW HIS VIEWS ON LIFE, LOVE, AND TIME HAS CHANGED TREMEN--DOUSLY WHILE BEING HERE. WE JOKED ABOUT OUR FIRST TIME MEETING. HE DIDN'T KNOW HOW TO OPEN HIS DOOR IN R RAC LOL. I WALKED UP TO HIS WINDOW AND TOLD HIM HOW. I WAS THE FIRST PERSON HE MET IN THERE. HE SAID AT FIRST HE WAS INTIMIDATED BY ME BECAUSE OF HOW I LOOK ONLY TO REALIZE IT WAS A MISCONCEPTION. WE LAUGHED. HE THOUGHT I RAN THE UNIT BECAUSE OF MY PULL W/ THE GUYS AND THE GUARDS. I REALLY LIKE HIM AS HE ALSO MADE A MISTAKE AND IS LEARNING FROM IT. HES LEAVING A MONTH BEFORE ME AND IS HEADED TO KAMLOOPS BUT LIVES IN REVELSTOKE. ILL DEFINATELY KEEP CONTACT W/ HIM AND ROAD TRIP OUT THERE TO SEE HIM AND MEET HIS FAMILY. SPEAKING ABOUT FAMILY IM STOKED ONCE AGAIN I CHATTED W/ MOMMA ANGEL. IM HAPPY THAT YOU ARE COOL AND SUPPORTIVE OF ME GETTING TO KNOW YOUR FAMILY. IT MEANS SO MUCH TO ME. RIGHT AT THIS MOMENT OUR HOUSE SMELLS OF FINE ASIAN CUISINE MADE BY MY FRIEND WHO GAVE ME YOUR BLANKET. HONESTLY HE IS ONE OF THE MOST GENUINE PEOPLE IVE MET IN HERE AND ILL NEVER FORGET HIM. GEO AND I DID OUR FOOD ORDER AND NEXT WEEK I AM MAKING PEANUT BUTTER BANANA CHEESE CAKE W/ GRAHAM CRACKER CRUST TOPPED W/ CRUMBLED PBCUPS AND CHOCOLATE SNOWDROPS ANGEL!!! ⇒ HELLO AGAIN TO YOU THE MOST AMAZING AND BEAUTIFUL ~~THE~~ GIRL IVE EVER MET. I VERY MUCH ENJOYED OUR CONVERSATION TONIGHT. TALKING ABOUT FEELINGS USED TO HONESTLY TERIFY ME, I MUST BE CHANGING BECAUSE NOW I FIND

(16)

IT SO INCREDIBLY CRUCIAL AND IMPORTANT FOR PEOPLE TO DO. I TRULY ENJOY LISTENING TO YOU INTENTLY AND KNOW EXACTLY HOW YOU FEEL AS I WOULD FEEL THE EXACT SAME WAY.. AND HAVE MANY OF TIMES IN MY EXISTENCE. IVE FOUND COMMUNICATING W/ YOU VERY COMFORTABLE AND ITS EASY TO OPEN MYSELF AND LISTEN WHEN YOU SPEAK... ALSO THANKS YOU FOR THE EXFOLIATION TIPS BRO. NOW ILL BE SO SOFT AND SMOOTH AF LOL (I HOPE THAT MADE YOU CHUCKLE A BIT). I REALLY MEANT IT WHEN I SAID THE WORLD NEEDS MORE OF YOU AND THAT YOU CONSTANTLY RESTORE MY FAITH IN HUMANITY WHEN I THINK ABOUT YOU. I ALSO MEAN IT WHEN I TELL YOU I ADORE YOU AND LOVE YOU I REALLY HOPE YOU BELIEVE IT AND KNOW IT TOO. YOU ~~ARE~~ ARE AN ANGEL IN MY LIFE AND IM SURE IM NOT THE ONLY ONE WHO THINKS THAT WAY ABOUT YOU. I HOPE ~~TO~~ TO SEE YOU SOON AND EVEN DREAM ABOUT YOU TONIGHT. THE DAY IS FINALLY AT AN END AND TIME TO STRIP DOWN INTO MY BOXERS AND SNUGGLE UP INTO BED TO WAIT FOR MATRIX 4 TO BE ON. GOODNIGHT SWEET SWEET GIRL I MISS YOU AND DO LOVE YOU SO MUCH. YOU MEAN THE WORLD TO ME ANGEL

Z Z Z Z Z Z

2022-05-15

DEAR MY BEST FRIEND. I JUST GOT BACK FROM A VID CALL W/ THE GIRLS AT 10 AND BOY I HAD A HARD TIME HOLD-ING BACK TEARS. DAUGHTER GOT UPSET AND SHY WHICH MADE ME FEEL SADNESS AND COMPLETELY HELPLESS. DAUGHTER IS SO STRONG AND SMART. MY GIRLS ARE SUCH BEAUTIFUL LITTLE PEOPLE I MISS THEM SO MUCH. THEY MAKE ME SO PROUD. ALL THEY WANT IN LIFE IS FOR DADDY TO BE

(17)

HOME W/ THEM AGAIN. THIER MOM IS VERY INCONSISTENT ATM AND THAT HURTS ME AS WELL. I AM CRYING WHILE WRITING THIS AND FEEL HELPLESS AND ALONE. THIS TOO SHALL PASS, THIS TOO SHALL PASS. I AM GRATEFUL THAT I GOT TO SEE THEM THIS MORNING AND AM EXCITED TO SPEND AN HOUR W/ COURTNEY THIS AFTERNOON AS WELL. SEEING THEM BRINGS UP EMOTIONS THINKING ABOUT DAUGHTER AND HOW SHE DOESNT EVEN KNOW ME YET AND I MISS HER SO SO VERY MUCH. AS MUCH AS IM FILLED W/ LOVE IT EQUALLY IS PAIN. ALL I CAN DO IS GROW AND LEARN TO ACCEPT THINGS FOR THE WAY THEY ARE WHICH IS DIFFI--CULT, MY HIGHER POWER MUST BE TEACHING ME A LESSON BY FORCING ME TO PRACTICE ACCEPTANCE & HUMILITY OVER AND OVER AGAIN. AS I BEGIN TO CALM DOWN MY THOUGHTS ALL I CAN DO IS SHOW GRATITUDE AND LOVE. I SURE COULD USE A HUG AND A SHOULDER TO CRY ON BUT THIS PLACE FORCES ME TO SET FEELINGS ASIDE AND SHOW NEXT TO NO UPSETTING EMOTIONS. GOD GRANT ME SERENITY, COURAGE, AND WISDOM WHILE I NAVIGATE THROUGH THIS MESS IVE CREATED DURING MY ACTIVE ADDICTION AND ALLOW ME THE STRENGTH TO SHINE LIGHT THROUGH DARKNESS FOR THE REST OF MY LIFE. I AM A GOOD PERSON THAT WENT DOWN THE WRONG PATH AND IS SUFFERING TREMENDOUS--LY DUE TO IT. I AM NOT THAT PERSON. I AM GRATEFUL W/ ALL MY HEART FOR MY SOBRIETY AND ALL THE PEOPLE THAT ARE HERE W/ ME ON MY NEW PATH FORWARD. EVEN THOUGH I AM SAD ATM I AM ALSO HAPPY TO KNOW IVE GOTTEN MYSELF OUT OF ADDICTION HELL, AND AM SOBER AND READY TO SERVE THE COMMUNITY THAT HELPED TO SAVE MY LIFE AND SEE THE LIGHT SHINE EVER SO BRIGHTLY. THANK YOU ANGEL FOR BEING HERE FOR ME DURING ALL THIS, EVEN THOUGH I TELL

(18)

YOU CONSTANTLY HOW MUCH YOU MEAN TO ME, I HONESTLY FEEL THAT THERE ARE NO ACTUAL WORDS TO DESCRIBE HOW UNBELIEVABLY GRATEFUL THAT GOD HAS PUT YOU IN MY LIFE. I WILL FOREVER LOVE YOU AND WILL 100% ALWAYS BE HERE FOR YOU NO MATTER WHAT. WRITING TO YOU ANGEL HAS CHANGED MY LIFE AND IF IT IS COOL W/ YOU, CAN I CONTINUE TO WRITE YOU ONCE I AM OUT? SITTING HERE FOR THE LAST 30 ~~HRS~~ MINS TALKING TO YOU AND OCCASSIONALLY LOOKING AT YOUR PHOTO HAS CALMED ME DOWN QUITE A BIT. GEO CAME IN MY ROOM AND ASKED HOW IT WENT, SAW I WAS UPSET, AND GAVE ME A HUG. HE ALSO HAS BEEN A BLESSING IN DISGUISE IN HERE, I AM GRATEFUL HE IS HERE W/ ME. JUST SO YOU KNOW ANGEL I WILL ALWAYS BE IN LOVE W/ YOU AND AS LONG AS MY SOUL EXISTS IT WILL SHINE LOVE IN YOUR DIRECTION. YOU ARE MY BEST FRIEND AND MEAN EVERYTHING TO ME IN THIS WORLD. ⟹ OMG MY VISIT W/ COURTNEY WAS ASTONISHING. WHAT AN INCREDIBLE FEE-LING IT WAS TO HUG AND HOLD HAND W/ A LOVED ONE AGAIN. WE TALKED AND LAUGHED AS I TOLD HER STORIES ABOUT MY STAY IN RRAC AND MISSION. MY SISTERS ARE ALL SO BEAUTIFUL AND SPECIAL TO ME. THAT WAS A MOMENT I WILL CHERISH FOR THE REST OF MY LIFE. SHE MADE COMMENTS ON HOW I SHADE IVE GOTTEN AND HOW BIG MY ARMS LOOKED. THAT MADE ME HAPPY INSIDE AS I VE BEEN WORKING SO HARD ON MY BODY PHYSICALLY LET ALONG MY MIND AND SOUL. THERE ARE ZERO WORDS TO EXPRESS MY GRATITUDE RIGHT NOW. ~~FOR~~ NOW I AM WAITING FOR 7PM COUNT THEN MAYBE A ~~FEEL~~ SHOWER AND FULL BODY EXF-CLIATION (NOW THAT I KNOW I CAN ☺) IM NOT SURE EXACTLY WHAT THE REST OF THIS EVENING HOLDS BUT ILL SAY GOODNIGHT BEFORE BED AS ALWAYS. ⟶

(19)

WELL ANGEL IT IS NOW BEDTIME. THE MATRIX 4 IS ON AGAIN SO I'LL LAY DOWN AND WATCH WHAT I FELL ASLEEP TO LAST NIGHT. I HOPE YOUR DAY WAS GREAT AND FILLED W/ HAPPINESS. IM SENDING WARM HUGS TO YOU. I LOVE AND MISS YOU MORE THAN YOU KNOW. GOODNIGHT SWEET GIRL 2 ♡ 2 ♡ 2♡2♡ 2♡2♡2

2022-05-16

(10:45) GOOD MORNING MY SWEET FRIEND. TODAY IS AN OK/ MODERATELY GOOD DAY. THIS MORNING I WAS AT CIRCLE CEREMONY AND THE ELDER TALKED TO ME ABOUT MY COURT CASE ON THURSDAY AM. HE SPOKE ABOUT DIFFICULT CHOICES THAT SOMETIMES WE ARE FORCED TO MAKE IN ORDER TO BETTER OUR OWN LIVES AND ENRICH OUR POSITIVE STATE OF MIND DURING THIS DIFFICULT TIME. I FIND MYSELF CALM AND READY TO LET GO OF MY BABY GIRL DAUGHTER FOR THE TIME BEING. I FEEL AT PEACE W/ MY DECISION AND AM HAPPY TO FINALLY BE ABLE TO REST AGAIN. IT WILL CAUSE TEMPORARY PAIN FOR ME BUT THIS TOO SHALL PASS. ALL I TRULY WANT IN LIFE IS TO MOVE FORWARD AND GET PASSED THE PAST. THINKING ABOUT HER ONLY MAKES/CREATES A MORE DIFFICULT STAY AS I TRY TO NAVIGATE THROUGH THE MESS I HAD MADE DURING MY ACTIVE ADDICTION. ALTHOUGH I CAN ONLY SPECULATE THAT HER MOTHER IS STILL ACTIVE BECAUSE OF HER ACTIONS BEING THE SAME AS ALWAYS WHEN SHE USED BEFORE, SHE IS IN GODS HANDS NOW AND THAT IS FOR THEM TO DEAL W/ NOT ME. I AM A GOOD PERSON AND FEEL I DO NOT DESERVE TO HAVE DAUGHTER TAKEN AS A RESULT ~~OF~~ BEING STRICTLY TO CAUSE ME PAIN, HOWEVER, MY HIGHER POWER HAS A PLAN FOR ME AND I'LL PUT ALL MY LOVE, FAITH, AND WILL INTO HIS HANDS AS HE HELPS TO GUIDE ME BACK TO MY TRUE CALLING. I FOREVER AM

20

IN DEPT TO HIM AND HELP CARRY OUT HIS MESSAGE
AND TRY TO USE THIS STORY IVE BEEN GIVEN
TO HELP PEOPLE FIND SOBRIETY. LIKE IVE MENTIONED
BEFORE THAT THE WORLD NEED MORE OF YOU, I
WILL TRY TO BE A PERSON LIKE YOU THAT THIS
WORLD NEEDS MORE OF. LATELY IVE VERY MUCH
SO FELT HIS CALLING WHEN I PRAY AT NIGHT AND
KNOW DEEP DOWN MY LIFE FINALLY HAS PURPOSE
AND MEANING. IVE BECOME A BETTER MAN, DAD,
PARTNER, BROTHER, SON, AND FRIEND. I CANNOT
WAIT TO GET THE FUCK OUT OF HERE & SHOW IT TO
THE WORLD. LIFE IS SUCH A BEAUTIFUL EXPERIENCE,
FOREVER FROM HERE FORWARD I WILL HAVE SO MUCH
LOVE IN MY HEART AND ~~LIFE~~ LIVE ALL OF THE EXPERIENCES
OF THIS LIFE. THIS TOO SHALL PASS. THIS TOO SHALL PASS.
TODAY I KEEP THINKING ABOUT MY HUG AND HOLDING
HANDS W/ MY SISTER AND WHAT IT MIGHT FEEL LIKE
TO BE ABLE TO HUG YOU AND HOLD YOUR HANDS IF
YOU ARE ABLE TO VISIT ME. (IF YOULL LET ME HOLD YOUR
HANDS) COURTNEY AND HELD HANDS ALMOST THE ENTIRE
TIME SHE WAS HERE, IT WAS SO SPECIAL. TALKING TO
THE GIRLS FILLED MY HEART AS WELL BUT ALSO
MADE ME SAD KNOWING HOW MUCH THEY MISS ME
AS I DO THEM. ALL THEY WANTED WAS TO BE ABLE
TO TOUCH ME AND COULDNT. THEY ARE SUCH STRONG
LITTLE GIRLS, SUCH ANGELS TO ME. I HAVE A WHOLE
NEW APPRECIATION OF WHAT BEING A FATHER IS.
I ALSO LOOKFORWARD TO THE DAY I CAN SURPRISE
EVERYONE. I 100% KNOW THAT ILL HAVE TEARS OF JOY
THE ENTIRE TIME. IT FRIGHTENS AND EXCITES ME
KNOWING THAT I AM NOW UNAFRAID TO SHARE MY TRUE
FEELINGS W/ OTHERS BECAUSE OF ALL THIS

(21)

AND HOPE I CAN INSPIRE OTHERS TO SHED THE EGO THAT CREATES AN EMOTIONAL BLOCKAGE. I KNOW NOW THAT EMOTIONS ARE NOT TO BE BLOCKED AND ARE MEANT TO BE ACCEPTED, COMMUNICATED, AND FELT. I EVEN FIND MYSELF (MY PREVIOUS SELF) FEELING REST-RAINT EVEN WRITING IT DOWN AND SHARING IT W/ YOU. I KNOW THAT YOU ARE A PERSON I CAN DO THAT W/ BECAUSE I TRUST LOVE & TRUST YOU COMPLETELY. I KNEW IT FULLY WHEN MY ~~SUBCONSCIOUS SUBCONSCIO~~ SUBCONSCIOUS OPENED ALL DOORS TO YOU IN THAT DREAM I HAD OF US THAT I TOLD YOU ABOUT. ANGEL [redacted], YOU ARE ABSOLUTELY ONE OF A KIND AND IVE NEVER MET ANYONE ELSE LIKE YOU BEFORE. IN SOME WAYS YOU DEFINATELY INTIMIDATE THE FUCK OUT OF ME. ⟹ HOLEY MOLEY ANGEL SOMETHING IS HAPPENING. EITHER WAY ILL BE GRATEFUL AND EITHER WAY MY PLANS WONT CHANGE. THINGS WILL CONTINUE MOVING FORWARD. I FINALLY NOW AT 5:25PM AM HOME AFTER WORK, RUNN-ING AROUND, AND MAKING SOME IMPORTANT CALLS. I SAT DOWN AT MY DESK, TURNED ON MY T.V., LOOKED AT THE PHOTO OF YOU AND DECIDED TO WRITE TO YOU BEFORE A LONG SUPER HOT SHOWER. MY HANDS ARE COVERED IN DIRT AND RUST FROM DIGGING AND TOU-CHING REBAR. ~~HONESTLY~~ I GOT CALLED INTO THE DUTY DESK AND WAS TOLD I HAVE A PSYCHOLOGY ASSESSMENT TOMORROW FOR MY PAROLE. I KNEW IT WAS COMING BUT IT WASNT SUPPOSED TO BE FOR AWHILE YET. HONESTLY I THOUGHT ID BE NERVOUS BUT I AM ACTUALLY EXCITED BECAUSE IT MEAN PROGRESSION. JUST ANOTHER STEP TOWARDS THE GOAL. ⟹ (7am) AND IT AIS TIME TO PUMP UP AT THE GYM THEN CALL YOU. IM STOKED FOR BOTH. HOPEFULLY YOU HAVE TIME

(22)

IN YOUR HECTIC SCHEDULE TO CHAT FOR A BIT. I HAVE SOME EXCITING THINGS TO TELL YOU. ANYHOW, CHAT SOON. EITHER WAY ILL WRITE MY USUAL GOODNIGHT BEFORE BED. IF PERHAPS YOU ARE UNABLE TO CHAT I WILL DOUBLE DOWN AT THE GYM UNTIL 10PM ♡.

BEDTIME ONCE AGAIN FRIEND ☺ TONIGHT WAS A GREAT NIGHT. IT WAS CHARLIE AND I AT THE GYM THE MY HOUSE WING BROS ATE STEAK'N' ONIONS W/ BROCOLLI THE PLAYED SOME RUMI AGAIN. RUMI HAS BECOME A NIGHTLY OCCORANCE FOR US THREE. WE HAD SOME GOOD LAUGHS TONIGHT. ANYHOW... GOODNIGHT SWEET GIRL. HAVE AN AMAZING SLEEP DUDE XOXOXO B

Z Z Z Z Z Z Z

2022-05-17

(11:04AM) IM HOME AWAITING 11 O'CLOCK COUNT SO I CAN GO HAVE A SHOWER BEFORE MY PSYCHOLOGICAL ASSESSMENT. I AM HAPPY AND GRATEFUL TO HAVE THAT BEHIND ME. NOW I JUST HAVE TO GET THROUGH COURT ON THURS AND I CAN GET BACK TO MY REGULAR LIFE PATTERNS. WORK TODAY WENT WELL AS USUAL. WE HAD A LATE START DUE TO THE BOSSES HAVING APPOINTMENTS. I JUST CLEANED AND PRESSURE WASHED THE PARKING LOT UNTIL 10:30AM. I OVERALL FEEL GOOD TODAY. I HAD A DREAM WHERE I WAS DRINKING W/ A FRIEND ONLY TO WAKE UP FEELING LIKE I HAD A HANGOVER. I SHOOK IT OFF QUICKLY AND WAS ENTHRALLED THAT I NO LONGER HAVE THAT FEELING IN MY LIFE. ONCE AGAIN TODAY I FEEL CALM, CLEAR, CONTENT, AND COLLECTED. IM FINDING THAT MY EMOTIONS ARE STABLE EVEN THOUGH THEY HAVE BEEN TESTED A LOT LATELY. I CAN HONESTLY TELL THAT I AM GROWING INSIDE AND HAVE BEEN PUTTING IN THE WORK ON A DAILY BASIS. ⟶

(23)

I CONTINUE TO PERSERVERE FORWARDS TOWARDS THE GOAL I HAVE SET FOR MY LIFE, I MAINTAIN MY FOOTING TO NEVER BACKSLIDE BY CHOICE OR THE CHOICE I MAKE. LIFE IS WAY TOO SHORT TO LIVE IN TURMOIL WHEN A PERSON CAN LIVE IN ACCEPTANCE, HUMILITY, AND A LOVING NATURE. ⟹ (5:15) MY TURN TO CLEAN THE HOUSE AND I AM ALL DONE. PSYCH ASSESSMENT IS ALSO COMPLETE, I HOPE YOU ANSWER MY CALL TONIGHT SO I CAN TELL YOU ABOUT IT. I AM STOKED. GEO HAS A BEEF ROAST IN THE OVEN FOR DINNER AND SMELLS GREAT. IVE OPENED ALL THE DOORS TO AIR OUR COZY LIL HOME OUT LOL. TODAY HAS TURNED OUT TO BE EVER SO BEAUTIFUL OUTSIDE. ITS CANTEEN ON THURS WHICH MEANS YET ANOTHER TWO WEEKS HAS PASSED US BY. HOW EXCELLENT IS THAT ☺♡. ⟹ NICE SHORT CHAT GOODNIGHT DUDE Z Z Z Z Z Z

2022-05-18

~~THE~~ (11:15am) ANOTHER IS HERE AND THE WORK DAY IS HALF DONE. BESIDES THIS RAIN WORK HAS BEEN DECENT. I FIND MYSELF INCREASINGLY HAPPY W/ A POSITIVE AND MOTIVATED MINDSET. I HAVE BEEN IMPROVING IN MY ACCEPTANCE TOWARDS ALL THINGS I CANNOT CHANGE. PRAYER HAS HELPED TO [redacted] LET THINGS PASS BY. & THROUGH PRAYER I AM GETTIN COURAGE THE CHANGE THE THINGS I CAN, LIKE HOW I DEAL W/ EMOTIONS AT THE TIME CERTAIN FEELING ARRISE. I CONSISTENTLY ASK FOR THE WISDOM TO KNOW THE DIFFERENCE BETWEEN THE TWO. FINALLY AFTER 1 YEAR (ALMOST) OF BEING SOBER I ONLY BEGINNING TO GET THE WHOLE MEANING OF THE SERENITY PRAYER. MAYBE JUST MAYBE THATS WHY MY JOURNEY HAS LEAD ME ~~TO~~ THROUGH ALL OF THIS, THE WAY IT HAS. HOPEFULLY MY PATH

(24)

AND STORY WILL HELP/INSPIRE OTHERS TO ACHIEVE SOBRIETY W/OUT HAVING TO BE PUT IN SUCH PLACES AS JAILS, INSTITUTIONS, AND DEATH. I SEE NOW THAT THOSE 3 THINGS ARE VERY VERY REAL, AND I AM TRULY GRATEFUL IT WAS NOT DEATH AND WAS ONLY DEATH OF EGO!!! ⟹ (4pm) TIME TO GO CHECK MY MAIL. WORK WENT WELL THIS AFTERNOON. I AM FAIRLY TIRED RIGHT NOW AND STILL HAVE SHOWER, HIT THE GYM, GO TO LIFE RING, AND REST SO IM CALM FOR WORK TOMORROW MORNING. I CANNOT WAIT FOR THIS LONG WEEKEND BBQ AND CHEESECAKE CONTEST GOING BETWEEN HOUSES. WHO WOULDVE THOUGHT OF CHEESECAKE COMPETITIONS IN JAIL LOL. ... SOME OF THE BEST IVE EVER HAD TBH. I LOOK FORWARD TO FINALLY HAVING TOMORROW IN THE REARVIEW MIRROR AS IT IS YET ANOTHER PART OF FORWARD MOVEMENT IN LIFE ☺ THE ACTUAL ONLY THING I LOOK FORWARD TO BEING IN MY MAILBOX BESIDES A SURPRIZE PHOTO OF YOU IS HAVING YOUR MOMS # APPROVED AND VIDEO APPROVAL OF MY DAD & SISTER COURTNEY. FINGERS CROSSED FOR ONE OF THE THREE. ⟹ AAAAND YOUR MOMMA IS APPROVED YAAAAAY!!! I CALLED AND LEFT A MSSG SO SHE WOULD KNOW WHAT WILL SHOW UP ON CALLER I.D. HOW STOKING. I HOPE YOUR EVE-NING HAS BEEN GOOD. I WENT TO THE GYM AND TRIED CALLING YOU TWICE THEN BACK TO THE GYM THEN HOME. CHARLIE MIGHT POP BY BEFORE THE 10PM COUNT TO ENJOY SOME McCAKE AND A NICORETTE GUM LOL. A.K.A JAIL COFFEE N SHMOKE. MY DAILY VICE ATM. IM LOOKING FORWARD TO THIS WEEKEND TO GET HERE AS I COULDNT COME

(25)

ANY FASTER. WELL ANGEL IM ALL SHOWERED AND READY FOR BED. GOODNIGHT SWEET GIRL ♥ Z Z ZZZ

2022-05-19

(8:04AM) MORNIN SUNSHINE. TODAY IS COURT ABOUT MY BEAUTIFUL BABY DAUGHTER. I FEEL CONTENT W/ WHATEVER THE OUTCOME IS AS I ACCEPT THAT IT IS TEMPORARY AND THERE IS NOT ALL THAT MUCH I CAN DO AT THIS TIME. I AM STRONGLY FOCUSED TOWARDS THE FUTURE AND KNOW I AM HEADED IN THE RIGHT DIRECTION. EITHER WAY I AM GRATEFUL FOR ALL THE LESSONS LEARNED WHETHER PAINFUL OR JOYOUS. EVEN THOUGH IT IS A PHONE CALL I WILL DRESS NICELY AND FEEL GOOD IN MY HEART & SOUL. I KNOW WHAT IS RIGHT IN THE END AND DOING WHAT NEGATIVE OR WRONG JUST LEAVES A PERSON HOLLOW INSIDE. I DO NOT WANT A HOLLOW EXISTENCE EVER AGAIN. ⟹ (11:04) FINALLY BACK HOME COURT WAS TO MOVE THE CASE MANAGEM- TO KAMLOOPS WHICH I AGREED ON, SO WE WILL SEE WHATS NEXT. I GOT MY CORRECTIONAL PLAN REVIEW WHICH SEEMS GOOD. TODAY WAS CANTEEN AND ALL IS WELL. I FEEL CONTENT FOR THE MOST PART BUT STILL FEEL SOME SADNESS. I TRY TO SEE THE GOOD IN THIS LESSON ALTHOUGH THERE IS SOME PAIN INSIDE ME. IM GLAD TO BE SOBER AND THIS TOO SHALL PASS. AFTER 12PM I AM BACK TO WORK SO HOPEFULLY THESE OFF AND ON DOWNPOURS SUBSIDE FROM NOON - 12:30 UNTIL I AM HOME ONCE AGAIN. AFTER WORK I AM GOING TO CHILL (BACK IS SORE). TONIGHT ALSO RELAX AND WAIT TO CALL YOU. ONLY 1.5 MORE DAYS OF WORK THEN A LONG WEEKEND...WAAHHOOOOO.!!! ⟹ (6:53) BBBBRRRR IT IS CHILLY OUTSIDE. I JUST WALKED THE GHETTO TO CHILL ON A STOOP AND SHOOT THE SHIT W/ A COUPLE DUDES. NOW IM HOME FOR DINNER WHICH IS SOME CURRY CHICKEN N RICE. THE HOUSE SMELLS

(26)

AMAZING. WE GOT OUR MEAT ORDER OF MAY LONG EXTRAS FOR OUR BBQ ON SATURDAY. ⟹ (10:04) LMAO SOOO I CAME HOME AND DRANK COFFEE W/ CHARLIE THEN SHAVED IN MY "CULDESAC" HAIR CUT AND WENT IN GEO'S ROOM UNTIL HE NOTICED WHAT I HAD DONE. WHEN HE FINALLY DID BOY DID WE LAUGH, LIKE CRY LAUGH HYSTERICALLY LOL. I WAS SO HAPPY TO HEAR YOUR VOICE TONIGHT ♡. YOU ARE UNDENIABLY THE MOST BEAUTIFUL GIRL IVE EVER MET IN EVERY WAY POSSIBLE. ILL LOVE AND ADORE YOU FOREVER. GOODNIGHT SWEAT GIRL. I LOVE YOU SO MUCH!!! Z Z Z Z Z Z

2022-05-20

(7:03pm) WELL HELLO LOVELY LADY. I KNOW YOU ARE AT YOUR WOMANS ANGER MANAGEMENT COURSE ATM, [redacted] I BET YOULL DO SO AMAZING DUDE. I AM SO PROUD OF YOU AND PROUD TO KNOW YOU. ALSO IM STOKED TO HEAR ABOUT IT WHEN WE TALK NEXT. TODAY I WENT TO WORK FOR A HALF DAY THEN CAME HOME, CUT A HOUSEMATES HAIR, AND WENT AND CALLED YOUR MOM. WE TALKED FOR APPROX AN HOUR OR SO AND I AM SO GRATEFUL WE DID. I REALLY REALLY LIKE HER AND FELT SO COMFORTABLE AND HAD A GREAT CONNECTION. THANK YOU FOR THAT. I CANNOT WAIT TO CALL HER NEXT WEEK. AFTER THE 7PM COUNT IM GOING TO FIND CHARLIE AND GET HIS CHEESECAKE RECIPE, HIT THE GYM, CALL YOU AT 9:30, THEN COME HOME AND BAKE THAT CAKE. I THOUGHT ABOUT YOU QUITE A BIT TODAY. CAN YOU SEND ANOTHER PHOTO OF YOURSELF FOR ME TO LOOK AT? I COULD LOOK AT YOU EVERY DAY NO MATTER WHERE I AM. EITHER IN HERE OR OUT THERE LOOKING AT YOU AND HEARING YOU FILLS MY HEART W/ ⟶

(27)

HAPPINESS. FOR DINNER MOU MADE A TRADITIONAL VIETNEMESE ROLL W/ PEANUT SAUCE AND IT WAS SO GOOOOOD.!!.! I AM SO GRATEFUL TO HAVE ~~BEEN~~ PUT IN THIS HOUSE W/ HIM. HE'S BY FAR ONE OF THE MOST INTELLIGENT PEOPLE IVE EVER MET. TONIGHT WAS ANOTHER A.A NIGHT AND ONCE AGAIN IT WAS AMAZING. THE TOPIC WAS GRATITUDE AND ONE DAY AT A TIME. AFTER MY SHARE ~~AND~~ I MENT-IONED HOW GRATEFUL I WAS FOR THE MOST SPECIAL FRIEND IVE EVER MADE AND HOW I GOT A CHANCE TO TALK TO HER MOST LOVELY MOM. MY HEART IS SO FULL ♡ XOXOOXXO ⟹ WELL SWEET GIRL ITS SHOWER AND BEDTIME (11:00PM). IM SHAVING THE REST OF MY HAIR, I COULDNT TAKE MYSELF SERIOUSLY AT THE GYM TONIGHT W/ A CUL DE SAC LMAO. I HOPE YOU HAVE A WARM AND AMAZING SLEEP TONIGHT. IM MISSING YOU A LOT ♡.. NIGHT Z Z Z Z Z Z

2022-05-21

TODAY IS AWESOME ⟹ (8:07PM) I AM STOKED I WILL BE GOING TO THE PHONES TO SEE IF YOURE ABLE TO TALK SOON. TODAY WAS GREAT. GREAT WEATHER, FOOD VIBES, DESSERTS, CONVOS, LAUGHS, AND GAMES. I HAD A LONG NAP (FROM 4-7) AND IT WAS 100% NEEDED. GEO AND HIT THE GYM HARD TODAY AS WELL. THE ONLY THING THAT COULD MAKE A DAY THIS GREAT EVEN BETTER WOULD BE TO HEAR YOUR VOICE ⟹ NIGHT NIGHT SWEET SWEET ANGEL ♡XO Z Z Z Z Z Z Z

2022-05-22

GOOD AFTERNOON SWEET GIRL. IT IS SO AMAZINGLY GORGEOUS OUTSIDE THAT WHEN I LOOK OUT THERE I THINK OF YOU. ANOTHER DAY HAS PASSED IS ANOTHER DAY

(28)

CLOSER TO FREEDOM. THE ATMOSPHERE AROUND THIS PLACE IS FAIRLY JOYFUL AND LIGHT, ALTHOUGH THE ELEPHANT IN EVERY ROOM HERE IS THAT ITS STILL PRISON. WE WOULD ALL RATHER BE OTHER PLACES. ID RATHER BE W/ FRIENDS & FAMILY. FOR NOW I WILL BE GRATEFUL TO HAVE GEO, MOU, AND CHARLIE TO GET ME THROUGH ALL OF THIS IN HERE. I DREAM OF THE DAY I CAN GIVE YOU, THE GIRLS, AND MY SISTERS HUGS & KISSES, WHAT A DREAM THAT TRULY SEEMS TO BE. IM NEVER LETTING GO AGAIN!!! ESPECIALLY OF MYSELF. ♡ ⟹ IM SENDING THIS TO YOU NOW.

JUST SO YOU KNOW ANGEL

I FUCKING LOVE YOU DUDE !!!

♡ xoxo ♡

7
The Wait

"Patience is a kind of faith."

The hardest part was never the noise. It was the waiting. Waiting for mail, for count, for food, for the next sunrise that looked just like the last. Time in there didn't move in a straight line; it circled. You learned quick that patience wasn't peace. It was endurance. It was surviving the space between what you hoped for and what you had.

When I didn't hear from her, I talked to her in my head anyway. I told her about my day, about the guys arguing on the range, about the guard who always looked at me a certain way. Small things, but they kept me grounded. Some nights I'd lay there staring at the ceiling, counting the cracks, letting the silence stretch until it became its own kind of conversation. It wasn't much, but it was something.

I'd think about everything I couldn't control—my case, my past, the distance between us—but I always came back to one thing: I could still control who I was that day. I could choose how I spoke, how I carried myself, how I treated the inmates around me. The waiting taught me discipline, but more than that, it taught me faith.

Because waiting isn't empty. It's a kind of prayer. Every quiet moment, every unanswered letter, every sunrise that felt the same as the one before—it all built something in me I didn't know I was missing. Strength that doesn't shout. Peace that doesn't depend on change. And the belief that some things are worth the wait.

(1)

2022-05-22

HELLO... THIS IS A CONTINUATION TO THE END OF MY
LAST LETTER. WELL I GUESS THEY ALL ARE. EARLIER
I WENT AND PRACTICED W/ THE NEW CHURCH BAND. IT
WAS LIVELY AND FUN. I AM PLAYING THE DRUMS. I HOPE
IT GOES OVER WELL AT SERVICE TONIGHT AT 4:15PM.
AFTERWARDS I CALLED MY DAUGHTERS THEN PLAYED 21
AT THE B-BALL COURTS W/ THE BOYS. THERE IS A LOT
GOING ON IN HERE TODAY DUE THIS AMAZING WEATHER
HOWEVER I JUST FEEL LIKE RETREATING TO MY ROOM
TO WRITE TO MY FAVORITE INDIVIDUAL (YOU) ← OBVIOUSLY.
I CLEANED MY ROOM EARLIER AND JUST NEED TO FOLD
LAUNDRY AND PUT IT IN THE DRAWERS I MADE OUT OF
CARDBOARD BOXES A COUPLE WEEKS AGO. TODAY IVE
BEEN FEELING A LIL BIT LONELY. PROBS BECAUSE
IT IS SO NICE OUT AND IM MISSING ALL THE PEOPLE THAT
I CARE ABOUT. IM NOT SAD AT ALL, JUST REFLECTING ON
MY TIME AWAY. A HUG WOULD FEEL AMAZING RIGHT
NOW... NOT GOING TO LIE... HUGS MEAN SO MUCH MORE
TO ME NOW. MORE THAN EVER BEFORE IN THIS LIFE.
I FEEL A HIGHTENED SENSE OF EMOTION & CONNECTION
BECAUSE OF ALL OF THIS FOR WHICH I AM OVERLY GRATEFUL
FOR. I WILL FOCUS ON KEEPING IT W/ ME AS LONG AS
I LIVE. EVERYTHING IS GREATER IN FEELING RATHER
THAN NUMBNESS. I LOVE TO LOVE AND AM IN LOVE.
⟹ OFF TO PLAY DRUMS AT CHURCH I GO.
I QUICKLY CAME TO MY ROOM BEFOREHAND TO LOOK
AT YOUR PHOTO AND THE GIRLS TO FILL MY HEART
W/ LOVE & HAPPINESS. B⟹ ALL DONE AT THE GYM
AND SO HAPPY WE TALKED. YOU HAVE BECOME SUCH A
BLESSING MY LIFE DUDE. SOMEDAY TALKING TO YOU
IS THE HIGHLIGHT OF MY DAY (LETS BE HONEST...

(2)

YOU ARE ALWAYS THE HIGHLIGHT DUH... OBVIOUSLAAAY LOL)(I HOPE THAT MADE YOU SMILE ☺). NOW I AM WAITING FOR CHARLIE TO POP BY. THEN SHOWER AND BED.. OR MAYBE SHOWER IN A.M. WE WILL SEE. IM PRAYING THAT YOU'RE ABLE TO COME SEE ME THIS WEEK. THAT WOULD MEAN THE ABSOLUTE WORLD TO ME... WHATEVER HAPPENS HAPPENS I GUESS. WELL I HOPE YOU SLEEP EVER SO SOUNDLY THIS EVENING [redacted] A.K.A MY ANGEL. GOODNIGHT SWEET GIRL. I MISS & LOVE YOU VERY MUCH

Z Z Z Z Z Z Z

2022-05-23

TODAY IS ANOTHER DAY. SO FAR IT HAS BEEN DECENT. (10:56am) AT 9:30AM CHARLIE TAPPED ON MY WINDOW AND WE WENT TO THE GYM. I DID MY FULL BODY MAIN--TENANCE TO KEEP MY MUSCLES HARD. THIS WEEK MOU AND I BEGIN ANOTHER PHASE OF HEAVY LIFTING, CARDIO, AND DIET/MEAL RATIONS. I SAID MY MORNING PRAYERS WHICH MADE THE DAY BEGIN WELL. I PRAYED FOR ALL THOSE SUFFERING THAT GOD MAY HELP THEM FIND THEIR WAY. I PRAYED FOR MY LOVED ONES TO BE SAFE AND SERENE. ALSO FOR ALL MY GIRLS THAT THEY KNOW IN THEIR HEARTS HOW MUCH DADDY LOVES THEM, AND FOR YOU THAT YOU RECIEVE EVERYTHING YOUR HEART DESIRES AS YOU DESERVE ALL THAT YOU DESIRE OUT OF LIFE. I ALSO SENT YOU A HUGE HUG. FOR THE REST OF THE DAY ILL STAY AROUND THE HOUSE UNTIL ITS TIME TO MAKE CALLS AT 5:00-5:30 (YOU, THE GIRLS, MY SISTERS) ⟹ AMERICAN IDOL LIVE FINALLY IM STOKED. I HOPE YOU HAVE A BLAST AT YOUR FRIEND [redacted] TONIGHT. IM JUST GOING TO TAKE IT EASY FOR A BIT AND SEE WHERE THIS

(3)

NIGHT GOES. PROBABLY THE EXACT SAME AS USUAL BUT YOU NEVER KNOW. ILL WRITE IN A BIT AND SAY GOODNIGHT. IM PRAYING THAT THEY WILL LET YOU IN HERE TO SEE ME. IT WOULD MEAN THE ABSOLUTE WORLD TO ME. IF ONLY YOU KNEW B ⟹ GOODNIGHT ANGEL I JUST TOOK A LONG SHOWER AND AM READY FOR BED. HAVE A WARM SLEEP SWEET GIRL. XOXOXOO

Z Z Z Z Z Z

2022-05-24

GOOD MORNING BEAUTIFUL GIRL. I HOPE YOUR SLEEP WAS PEACEFUL AND COMFORTABLE AND OF COURSE SNUGGLY & WARM. MINE WAS GOOD, I DIDNT WANT TO GET OUT OF BED☺. AFTER PULLING MYSELF UP FROM BED I WENT TO THE CEREMONIAL CIRCLE THEN TO WORK. BOTH WERE POSITIVE & GOOD. WHEN I WAS RETURNING HOME AT 10:30am I STOPPED BY THE PHONES TO CALL ADMIN FROM HALFWAY HOUSE AND HE WANTED ME TO CALL BACK AT 2:30PM. I AM LOOKING FORWARD TO TOUCHING BASE W/ HIM AND CHAT A BIT. I AM ALSO LOOKING FORWARD TO CALLING YOURS TRULY LATER ON. YOUR VOICE BRINGS JOY TO MY LIFE IN HERE. THIS WEEK I GET BACK TO MY HEAVY LIFTING ROUTINE PLUS MEAL RATIONING. RESULTS RESULTS RESULTS DURING THIS NEXT PHASE FOR ME. WELL... THE GUARDS JUST WALKED THROUGH FOR 11am COUNT SO I AM GOING TO LAY DOWN UNTIL I HAVE TO BE BACK AT WORK AT NOON... B ⟹ AND WORK IS COMPLETE (2:30) IM THINKING ABOUT YOU A LOT TODAY AND REALLY HOPING I GET TO SEE YOUR GORGEOUS FACE IN PERSON THIS WEEK SOMETIME. FOR NOW I AM PRE--TTY MUCH JUST WAITING TO CALL YOU. B ⟹ GYM TIME. ILL CALL YOU TOMORROW. YOU SOUNDED RUSHED

(4)

AND A BIT STRESSED. PROBABLY DUE TO WORK, RUSH HOME TO GET READY, FERRY SCHEDULES, 8% PHONE CHARGE, AND HIGHWAY DRIVING AT NIGHT ONLY TO ARRIVE AT MOMMAS LATE TONIGHT (AM I RIGHT?) ILL SEND YOU SOME CALMING VIBES/THOUGHTS. ILL WRITE TO YOU BEFORE BED. ILL PROBABLY LAY DOWN RIGHT AFTER SHOWER AFTER THE GYM. I HONESTLY CANNOT WAIT TO CLOSE MY EYES AND PUSH FORWARD ONTO YET ANOTHER DAY CLOSER TO THE END OF ALL OF THIS. I HAVE A FEELING I MAY NOT SEE YOU THIS TRIP AND THATS OK. I STILL HOPE I DO BUT SOMETIMES ITS THE WAY THE WORLD WORKS AND I AM JUST GRATEFUL TO HAVE YOU IN THIS AWE-SOME WORLD!!! ⟹ FINALLY BEDTIME. I JUST SLAUGHTERED THE BOYS AT RUMI LOL. THE GYM WAS INSANE THIS EVENING. I AM BEAT AND READY FOR A WARM BED. I HOPE YOU GOT TO YOUR MOMS SAFELY. GOODNIGHT ONCE AGAIN SWEET GIRL XOXOOB

Z Z Z Z Z Z

2022-05-25

WORK WORK WORK. MAN I WAS TIRED THIS MORNING. I HAD A GOOD SLEEP W/ CRAZY DREAMS THE LAST FEW NIGHTS. AFTER WORK ILL CHECK MY MAIL, CALL YOU, SHOWER, THEN TRY AND NAP AS MUCH OF THIS DAY AWAY AS I CAN. ANYTHING TO PASS ANOTHER DAY QUICKLY. OH... I ALSO HAVE LIFERING RIGHT AFTER WORK TOO.. BUSY BUSY. LATELY IVE BEEN FEELING MORE AND MORE ANSY AND WANTING TO BE AWAY FROM HERE. I AM 100% NEVER COMING BACK TO AN INSTITUTION AGAIN. I AM MISSING MY LIFE AND ALL THE PEOPLE IN IT (LOVED ONES). I MISS A.A/N.A GROUPS AND ALSO JUST BEING ABLE TO WATCH A

(5)

MOVIE W/ ANOTHER PERSON INSTEAD OF ALWAYS BEING/FEELING ALONE. EVEN THOUGH I AM GRATEFUL FOR THIS LIFES JOURNEY, ILL BE VERY HAPPY TO HAVE THIS ALL IN THE REAR-VIEW MIRROR FINALLY. TODAY IS ANOTHER DAY I COULD USE A HUG OR HAVE SOMEONE TELL ME THAT THEY LOVE ME. THIS PLACE HAS STRIPPED THAT AWAY. ⟹ (3:42pm) I AM SO INCREDIBLY HAPPY THAT I FINALLY GET TO SEE YOUR BEAUTIFUL FACE TOMORROW. THERE ARE NO WORDS TO DESCRIBE THE FEELING I HAVE INSIDE ME RIGHT NOW. THANK YOU SO MUCH FOR BEING SUCH AN EXTRA-ORIDINARY HUMAN BEING, ANGEL. MY LOVE TANK IS OVER FLOWING ♡!!! I ALSO JUST READ MY PSYCH REVIEW AND IT LOOKS REALLY GOOD AS WELL. I AM BESIDE MYSELF THAT I GET TO FINALLY HAVE YOU IN MY ARMS FOR A MOMENT. YOU ARE TRULY AMAZING ANGEL!!! ♡ TO HAVE YOU AS MY FRIEND IS THE BIGGEST BLESSING IN MY LIFE ([redacted] AND MY KIDS OF COURSE). YAAAAAAAAAAAY!!! ⟹ TOMORROW COULD NOT GET HERE SOON ENOUGH. I WENT FOR A WALK W/ CHARLIE FOR A BIT AND WE ENDED UP HAVING COFFEE IN THE GHETTO FOR AN HOUR OR SO. I JUST RE READ MY PSYCH REPORT FOR SOME REASON AND I AM SURE GLAD THAT IT IS DONE AND BEHIND ME. GUESS WHATS IN FRONT OF ME...... A VISIT W/ YOU ☺ ♡. I AM ON CLOUD 9 RIGHT NOW!!! ⟹ IT IS FINALLY 10PM COUNT AND I COULD NOT BE HAPPIER. I FEEL LIKE ITS CHRISTMAS EVE AND WANT TO BE ASLEEP. SINCE WE TALKED ALL I CAN THINK ABOUT IS TOMORROWS VISIT. SWEET DREAMS BEAUTIFUL GIRL ♡ Z Z Z Z Z Z Z Z Z

26

2022-05-26

TODAY IS THE MOST EXCELLENT DAY. I HAD A GOOD SLEEP AND GOT UP EARLY. ITS 7:45am RIGHT NOW AND I AM FEELING HAPPINESS AT AN UNDESCRIBABLE LEVEL KNO-WING THAT I GET TO HUG YOU AND ABLE TO SEE THE MOST GORGEOUS & BEAUTIFUL GIRL IVE EVER KNOWN LATER TODAY. I CANNOT WAIT. I FUCKING LOVE YOU DUDE!!!!! ⇒ WORK WENT WELL THIS MORNIN IT WENT BY SUPER FAST WHICH IS AWESOME. I JUST GOT HOME FOR LUNCH UNTIL NOON THEN BACK UNTIL 2:30pm. ONCE WORK IS DONE I WILL COME HOME AND SORT OUT MY OUTFIT FOR OUR VISIT, GO TO THE GYM FOR 45MINS OR SO, SHOWER, AND WAIT PATIENTLY/EXCITEDLY UNTIL THEY CALL MY NAME TO VISITS. ☺♡♡. SEEING YOU IS A DREAM COME TRUE. ⇒ (4:00pm) TIME FOR THE GYM TO HELP PASS THE NEXT HOUR QUICKLY. IVE HAD THIS EXCITED/NERVOUS/BUTTERFLY FEEL-ING ALL DAY. EXTREMELY HAPPY ALL DAY AS WELL. AS I WALKED IN THE DOOR FOR COUNT THE BOYS HAD MADE A SAVOURY GARLIC SOUFLÉ WHICH WAS SO DELICIOUS. I AM VERY LUCKY TO LIVE W/ GEO & MOU. I COULD NOT IMAGINE A BETTER HOUSE LET ALONE US ALL BEING IN THE SAME WING TOO. I HOPE THAT YOURE AS EXCITED TO SEE ME AS I AM YOU. I FIND MYSELF PLAYING OVER IN MY HEAD WHAT IT WILL BE LIKE HAVING YOU HERE IN PERSON. WORK WAS GREAT TODAY AND WE GOT TO LEAVE EARLY. REBAR IS COMPLETE AND WE GET TO WRAP UP THEN POUR CONCRETE THIS COMING WEDNESDAY. AFTER THAT WORKDAY WILL BE TIRING AND FULL W/ A LOT LESS THINKING. ⇒ (10:54pm) THIS WONDERFUL DAY IS DONE. OUR MEETING TODAY FELT MAGICAL

(7)

YOU ARE SO BEAUTIFUL IN EVERY WAY IMAGINABLE. MY HEART IS FULL OF GRATITUDE. YOUR HUGS WERE AMAZING, I HONESTLY DIDNT WANT TO LET GO. AFTER YOU DROVE AWAY I WISHED WE HUGGED ONCE MORE. I WILL FOREVER CHERISH HOLDING HANDS TODAY. ITS DIFFICULT TO DESCRIBE THAT FEELING AFTER BEING PHYSICALLY DISCONNECTED FROM THE OUT-SIDE WORLD FOR 7 MONTHS. I ABSOLUTELY ADORE YOU ANGEL. YOU TRULY DO MEAN THE WORLD TO ME !!! THAT WAS SO MUCH MORE THAN I COULDVE IMAGINED. I HOPE YOU FELT THE SAME WAY WHEN YOU SAW ME TOO. I ABSOLUTELY LOVED HAVING YOU IN MY ARMS AND WISH WE COULD DO THAT EVERY DAY... WELL SWEET GIRL IT IS NOW TIME FOR BED. I WISH YOU THE BEST DREAMS AND AS ALWAYS SENDING LOVE TO YOU AND YOUR FAMILY XOXOO Z

Z Z Z Z Z

2022-05-27

(7:32am) THIS MORNING I WOKE UP SO HAPPY AND HAD THE BEST SLEEP. YESTERDAY SEEMS LIKE A DREAM AND YOU A DREAM GIRL. ALTHOUGH IT IS POURING RAIN OUTSIDE AND ILL BE SOAKED AT WORK, THE JOY & LOVE I FEEL IS OVERFLOWING THROUGH ME. TODAY I AM EVER SO GRATEFUL. ⇒ (3:42pm) ALL DONE WORK AND JUST GOT BACK FROM NON-VIOLENT COMMUNI-CATION COURSE WHICH WENT WELL. I AM LEARNING SO MANY LIFE ALTERING SKILLS ABOUT LISTENING FROM THE HEART WHEN OTHER SHOW THEIR VULN-ERABLE SIDE... ALSO ABOUT HOW TO SHARE & EXPRESS MY EMOTIONS IN HEALTHY WAYS SO THAT WHAT I FEEL IS CORRECTLY COMMUNICATED. IM FINDING THIS TYPE OF LEARNING TO BE ESSENTIAL AND

8

CRUCIAL FOR A POSITIVE WAY OF LIVING. I CANNOT WAIT TO BE OUT OF HERE AND LIVE A MUCH MORE MEANINGFUL LIFE LET ALONE HAVE MORE MEAN-INGFUL RELATIONSHIPS/CONNECTIONS/INTERAC-TIONS. IVE THOUGHT A LOT TODAY ABOUT OUR TIME TO TOGETHER AND AMAZING I FELT/FEEL BEFORE/DURING/AFTERWARDS. LIKE IVE SAID BEFORE THAT I WILL FOREVER REMEMBER & CHERISH THAT VERY MOMENT FOR THE REST OF MY LIFE. IT TRULY FELT AS IF THAT WAS THE FIRST TIME I WAS VULNERABLE TO ANOTHER PERSON. BEING CONFINED HERE HAS BROUGHT SO MUCH MEANING TO EXPERIENCES SUCH AS THOSE. I WISH THAT MEETING WE HAD WAS FOREVER AND NEVER ENDED. IN THAT SPACE & TIME FOR ONE HOUR NOTHING ELSE MATTERED OR EXISTED, ONLY THE VERY MOMENT. EVEN THOUGH IT WENT FAST THE TIME STOOD STILL. TO BE ABLE TO HOLD HANDS, LOOK INTO YOUR STUNNINGLY BEAUTIFUL EYES, AND HERE/SEE YOU SPEAK I FELT LIKE I COULD TRULY SEE YOU AND YOUR HEART. YOU ARE MY BEST FRIEND ANGEL AND ILL LOVE YOU FOREVER UNCONDITIONALLY!!!

⇒ (7AM) THE SUN HAS POKED ITS HEAD OUT AND CLEARED UP THE SKIES. IN FRONT OF OUR HOUSE A RAINBOW ARCHED UP OVER THE MOUNTAINS. WE SAT ON OUR PATIO FOR THE LAST HOUR OR SO LAUGHING AND JOKING W/ EVERYONE WHO PAST BY. GEO IS MAKING PEANUT BUTTER COOKIES AND THE HOUSE SMELLS AMAZING BECAUSE OF IT. ITS NICE THAT YET ONE MORE WEEK HAS GONE BY AND WORK IS FINISHED FOR THE WEEKEND.

(9)

JUNE IS RIGHT AROUND THE CORNER. SUNDAY I HAVE A VIDEO VISIT BOOKED W/ THE GIRLS. THEIR G-MA TOLD ME TODAY THAT DAUGHTER TEACHER TOLD HER THAT SHE WAS ONE OF THE NICEST, CARING, AND POLITE KIDS SHES EVER MET ♡... OBV. LOL... AND OTHER DAUGHTER HAD HER KINDERGARTEN ORIENTATION, SHE WAS SO PROUD OF HERSELF BECAUSE SHE IS A BIG GIRL NOW ♡. JUST ANOTHER REASON THAT MY HEART IS SO FULL. I HAVE SO MUCH TO BE GRA-TEFUL FOR AND TO LOOK FORWARD TO. AS I SIT HERE WRITING TO YOU THE VIEW OUT MY WINDOW IS LUSH GREEN GRASS ON ROLLIN HILLS, TREES FULL OF LEAVES, A GROWING GARDEN, A TWO SEPERATE FAMILIES OF GEESE W/ SUPER CUTE GOSLINGS ALWAYS CLOSE BY. THE GRASS HAS THOUSAND OF YELLOW BUTTER CUP FLOWERS EVERY-WHERE. I HONESTLY WISH YOU WERE HERE FOR A DAY TO SEE IT ALL AND TO WATCH SOME MOVIES AT NIGHT. WHAT I WOULD GIVE TO SPEND MORE TIME W/ YOU. I CANNOT WAIT TO BE FREE FROM ALL OF THIS BUT WOULDNT CHANGE THE JOURNEY IT HAS BEEN. IVE GROWN INTO A BETTER HUMAN BECAUSE OF IT ALL. ⟹ (10:58am) WELL ANGEL IT WAS NICE TO HEAR YOUR VOICE BRIEFLY WHILE YOU VAPED AT YOUR ~~FRIE FREN~~ FRIENDS ENGAGEMENT PARTY EARLIER TOMORROW IS OUR 11 MNTH 7 YR... YAAAY FOR US. I AM SO GLAD AND PROUD TO SHARE THIS DAY W/ YOU DUDE. I HOPE YOURE HAVING FUN AND STAY SAFE TONIGHT. I CAN FEEL THAT YOURE UPSET ABOUT CRC AND I WILL ALWAYS BE A SAFE SPACE FOR YOU TO OPEN UP TO W/ 100% CONFIDENCE. I KNOW HOW YOU ARE FEELING AS I CAN FEEL IT W/

10

YOU. WHEN YOUR HEART HURTS SO DOES MINE. I WILL PRAY ABOUT IT ALL. EVERY WORD I WRITE AND SAY I 100% MEAN IT. YOUVE BECOME A VERY VERY IMPORTANT PERSON TO ME, I WILL ALWAYS BE HERE FOR YOU IN ANY WAY YOU NEED ME. JUST REMEMBER TO BE BLUNT AS I DONT PICK UP ON SUBTLETY (ALTH-OUGH I AM LEARNING TO). HAVE A GOOD SLEEP & GREAT DREAMS. GOODNIGHT SWEETGIRL. I LOVE YOU AND MISS YOU ALWAYS XOXO Z Z Z Z Z Z Z Z Z

2022-05-28

ONE YEAR SOBER 24 HOURS AT A TIME. I FEEL ACCOMPLISHED AND FULFILLED TO HAVE RE-ACHED THIS MILESTONE. HAPPY 11 MONTHS TO YOU. I HONESTLY CANNOT EXPLAIN HOW SPECIAL YOU ARE TO ME AND HAVING YOU BESIDE ME THROUGHOUT THIS YEAR HAS BEEN PHENOMENAL I FIND MYSELF ALONE BUT FEELING LOVED AND FULL OF COMPASSION. I HAD A DREAM ABOUT YOU ALL LAST NIGHT. WE WERE JUST SITTING ON A COUCH TOGETHER. THE WHOLE DREAM WAS BLURRY BUT EVERY ONCE IN A WHILE YOUR FACE CAME TO FOCUS. AS I WOKE UP A BIT DISORIENTED I FELT YOUR BODY AGAINST MINE AND YOUR HANDS IN MINE. WHEN I REALIZED IT WAS A DREAM I COULD STILL FEEL YOU. MOST LIKELY BECAUSE WE JUST SAW EACHOTHER, HUGGED, & HELD HANDS TWO DAYS AGO. EITHER WAY THE DREAM WAS LIKE ANOTHER GIFT FROM YOU FOR TODAY... OUR DAY ☺ MM. SO FAR IVE JUST RELAXED, PLAYED A GAME BASKETBALL, AND TALKED TO FAMILY.

(11)

I GET MY N.A TAG TONIGHT. THEN HEAD TO THE GYM FOR A MAINTENANCE WORKOUT. AFTERWARDS IM BASICALLY JUST WAITING TO CALL YOU. I KNOW I TELL YOU THIS A LOT BUT I FUCKING LOVE YOU DUDE. EVERYTHING ABOUT YOU IS SO BEAUTIFUL. ON TOP OF EVERYTHING INTERNALLY BEAUTIFUL ABOUT YOU, YOU ARE DROP-DEAD GORGEOUS AND SEXY BEYOND BELIEF. ⟹ (6:40) EARLIER I SENT A FRIENDS FAMILY SOME MONEY TO HELP THEM SURVIVE WHILE HE GETS THROUGH HIS TIME HERE W/ ME. LIKE ME HE MADE A MISTAKE ALTHOUGH HE WAS NOT AN ADDICT. HIS WAS TO PROTECT HIS WIFE AND KIDS FROM A STALKER. HE IS A GUY I WILL 100% KEEP IN CONTACT W/ ONCE THIS IS ALL DONE. RIGHT NOW I AM WAITING FOR N.A. THEN CALL YOU AFTER. I HOPE YOUR NIGHT IS GOOD. EITHER WAY I AM HERE FOR YOU ALWAYS. IF YOU END UP BEING BUSY I WILL HEAD TO THE GYM UNTIL BEDTIME. ALL IN ALL THE DAY HAS OVERALL BEEN GOOD. ⟹ AAAAAND ANOTHER DAY HAS GONE BY. I TRIED CALLING AFTER N.A... IT WENT WELL... I REALLY DO HOPE YOU ARE O.K AND NOT UPSET. I CAN FEEL YOU RIGHT NOW AND HOPE I AM OVERTHINKING HOW YOU'RE DOING AND THAT YOUR EVENING IS ACTUALLY AMAZING MY FRIEND. EITHER WAY IM SENDING LOVE, THOUGHTS, HUGS, AND A KISS. GOODNIGHT SWEET GIRL (THE SWEETEST OF GIRLS IVE EVER KNOWN) I LOVE YOU VERY MUCH ♡ Z Z Z Z Z Z Z

2022-05-29

♡ MY HEART IS/WAS BROKEN THIS MORNING. I FOUND OUT THAT THE GIRLS GET ANXIETY WHEN THEY VIDEO CALL ME BECAUSE THEY ARE MISSING ME SO MUCH

(2)

IT GIVES THEM ANXIETY TO SEE ME AND NOT BE ABLE TO TOUCH ME. I FULLY UNDERSTAND AND AS A DAD WOULD NEVER WANT THEM TO FEEL THIS WAY BUT THAT UNFORTUNATELY HAS BECOME OUR REALITY. I AM VERY SAD BECAUSE OF IT. HEARING THAT THEY FEEL THAT WAY IS TRULY THE PUNISHMENT GIVEN TO ME WHILE I AM HERE. I LOVE THEM W/ EVERY PART OF MY HEART & SOUL. THIS TOO SHALL PASS. GOD GRANT ME THE SERENITY, COURAGE, & WISDOM TO GET THROUGH THIS. ALTHOUGH THIS TIME AWAY IS HELPING ME BECOME A BETTER PERSON, TIMES LIKE THIS ARE LONELY & TOUGH BEING BY MYSELF. I TRULY AM A VERY LOVING PERSON, BY HAVING HAD BEEN AWAY FOR THIS LONG IF FEEL EMPATHY ON A HIGHER [redacted] LEVEL TO A POINT I CAN ACTUALLY FEEL OTHER PEOPLES EMOTIONS INSIDE ME AS IF THEY WERE MY OWN FEELINGS. MY HEART MY BE BREAKING OVER AND OVER ATM IT IS STILL FULL OF LOVE. I CAN STILL [redacted] SEE THE POSITIVE OUTCOMES IN SITUATIONS. LIKE THESE. IM JUST MISSING YOU ALL SO MUCH. IT IS HARD TO DESCRIBE WHAT THE FEELINGS ACTUALLY ARE BUT FOR NOW I WILL CALM MYSELF BY WRITING TO MY BEST FRIEND (YOU). ILL TRY TO IDENTIFY WHAT IS HAPPENING INTERNALLY FOR A BETTER UNDERSTANDING. THIS IS THE MOST IVE CRIED SINCE I LEFT. I AM SO THANKFUL TO BE ABLE TO WRITE THIS TO YOU ANGEL. WHEN I WRITE TO YOU I FEEL AS I AM W/ YOU. THANK YOU SO MUCH FOR ALL-OWING ME TO HAVE YOU IN MY LIFE. LIFE WOULD NOT BE THE SAME W/ OUT YOU. I FEEL SO LUCKY TO KNOW YOU AND HOPE OUR FRIENDSHIP IS LIFE LONG. YOU ARE AN ANGEL!!! ♡♡♡ YOUVE HELPED CHANGE MY

(13)

LIFE. IF ONLY YOU KNEW EXACTLY HOW MUCH. ⟹
(3:43) THIS DAY HAS GOTTEN BRIGHTER. I HIT THE
GYM FOR A BIT THEN CALLED EVERYONE ON MY LIST.
SOME OF THEM I WILL NOT CALL AGAIN, SOME OF
THEM ILL CALL ONCE A WEEK. BUT FOR THE MOST PART
I REALLY LIKE MY PHONE SCHEDULE OF CALLING
MY DAUGHTERS, SISTERS, AND YOU. TODAY WAS MY
DAY TO CLEAN THE HOUSE WHICH PASSED AN HOUR.
IVE MANAGED TO COMPARTMENTALIZE MY EMOTIONS
FROM THIS MORNING AND FULLY ACCEPT THEM AS
THEY ARE. WRITING YOU ABOUT THEM DEFINATELY
MAKES IT EASIER. THANK-YOU FOR THAT ♡. FOR THE REST
OF TODAY I WILL SHOWER THEN RELAX & REFLECT ON
MY LIFE, MYSELF, AND WHAT IS TRULY IMPORTANT TO
ME. LATER ON I WILL WALK OVER TO THE PHONE TO
CALL YOU AROUND 8:30-45 AFTER YOUR WOMANS MEET-
-ING. IF YOURE BUSY ILL MOST LIKELY EITHER CHILL
ON THE DECK W/ CHARLES OR WATCH T.V. ILL ABSO-
-LUTELY WRITE TO SAY GOODNIGHT ♡ ⟹ WELL [redacted]
ANGEL IT IS THAT TIME (10:45). I WAS SO GLAD TO
TALK TO YOU AND MAYBE AGAIN TOMORROW. I DID
NOT TELL YOU THE WHOLE STORY ABOUT THE C.O.
ASKING ABOUT THE VISIT W/ MY GF. I ACTUALLY
SAID THAT WE WERE JUST FRIENDS BUT WISHED
YOU WERE. SOMEONE WOULD BE EXTREMELY LUCKY
TO BE THE PERSON YOU CHOSE TO BE W/ AS YOU ARE
AN ABSOLUTE DIAMOND. IM NOT SURE WHY I HADNT
MENTIONE THAT PART BUT FOR SOME REASON YOU
MAKE ME SHY ABOUT THINGS LIKE THAT WHEN I
WAS NEVER SHY BEFORE. ITS BECAUSE YOU ARE VERY
SPECIAL TO ME. NORMALLY I CAN READ PEOPLE
BUT W/ YOU I CANT BUT ALSO DONT TRY TO READ

(14)

DEEPER THAN FACE VALUE. OUR FRIENDSHIP HAS BEEN SO OPEN AND UPFRONT I FIGURE IF YOU HAD MORE THAN FRIEND FEELINGS FOR ME YOUD TELL AS I DONT CATCH SUBLETY. ALL I KNOW IS THAT IF ALL WE EVER HAVE IS FRIEN-DSHIP I AM A MORE THAN LUCKY DUDE FOR IT. ALSO YOU MEAN MORE TO ME THAN ANYONE AND ID PICK FRIENDSHIP W/ YOU OVER A RELATIONSHIP W/ ANOTHER PERSON IF THEY COULDNT ACCEPT THAT YOU ARE MY VERY BEST FRIEND/FAVORITE PERSON.

ID DEFINATELY LIKE TO TAKE YOU ON SOME DATES IF YOU WOULD LET ME. IN AUGUST-SEPTEMBER. IF YOURE DOWN FOR A DINNER/MOVIE DATE IN THE CITY OR AT HOME ON THE COAST LET ME KNOW ON PHONE/COME VISIT AGAIN/OR EVEN WRITE ME A LETTER. GOODNIGHT SWEET GIRL. I LOVE YOU MORE THAN ONE PERSON COULD POSSIBLY LOVE ANOTHER PERSON. ♡XOXO (CHEEK KISS) Z Z Z Z Z Z Z Z

2022-05-30

HI!!!!!!... IT IS 2:30PM AND WORK IS ALL DONE FOR TODAY. NOW I HAVE LIFERING, NVC @ 5PM GYM @ 7PM AND AM WAITING TO CALL YOU WHICH IS WHAT I LOOK FORWARD TO MOST. TODAY WHILE I WAS THINKING ABOUT YOU I THOUGHT ABOUT HOW PERFECT AND BEAUTIFUL YOUR EYES ARE. I REALIZED THAT BEFORE OUR VISIT I HAD NEVER TOOK THE TIME TO STARE DIRECTLY INTO THEM. THEY ARE PEIRCING AND STUNNING ♡. I CANNOT WAIT TO LOOK AT YOU AGAIN. SOON I HOPE. TONIGHT WE ARE HAVING SALMON W/ FETA & FRESH TOMATO PASTA FOR DINNER. MMMMMM M IM STOKED ⇒

(15)

A SHOWER WAS JUST HAD AND NOW I AM CLEAN & SHAVED IN NICE CLOTHES. TIME TO GO FIND CHARLIE AND CHAT W/ HIM UNTIL 4PM COUNT. THEN I CHECK MY MAIL AND ONCE AGAIN HOPING FOR MAIL FROM YOU ♡ ☺ ... I FOUND CHARLES. WE WENT TO BENS HOUSE (BEN THE GUY I QUARANTINED W/) AND GOT SOME HOMEMADE SOUR DOUGH. IT WAS DELICIOUS. I HAVENT EATEN FRESH BAKERY STYLE BREAD IN OVER 7 MONTHS. I GAVE SOME TO THE DUDES IN MY WING OF THE HOUSE AND THEY WERE STOKED. IT WAS CHEDDAR GARLIC. GEO SAYS HE IS GOING TO LEARN HOW TO MAKE IT FOR US. I SURE HOPE HE DOES.!!! ILL WRITE BEFORE BED. I TRULY LOVE YOU MORE THAN WORDS CAN DESCRIBE. ⟹ (7PM) LIFERING NVC WAS GREAT. I LEARNED ALL ABOUT MY FEAR OF REJECTION, VULNERABILITIES, AND HOW WHEN I COMMUNICATED I TEND TO CONVELUTE MY NEEDS BY NOT EXPRESSING WHAT I AM ACT-UALLY WANTING OUT OF FEAR OF BEING HURT. I REALIZED THAT I HAVE BEEN HURT A LOT SINCE CHILDHOOD AND ALL THROUGHOUT ADULT-HOOD. IT IS MOST OF WHY I STRUGGLE. LEARNING AND WRITING HELPS A LOT TO UNDERSTAND IT EVEN THOUGH SOME THINGS I NEED TO EXPRESS CONTINUE TO TERIFY ME. BEFORE WHEN I WAS AN ADDICT I COVERED IT UP W/ HUMER OR ANGER. NOW BEING SOBER I FIND MYSELF HAVING STRONGER & MORE REAL FEELINGS TOWARDS OTHERS. THE FEELINGS SOMETIMES CONFUSE ME AS SOME OF THEM I THOUGHT I HAD EXPERIENCED BEFORE. NOW HAVING A CLEAR MIND THOSE FEELINGS DONT EVEN COME CLOSE TO WHAT I FEEL NOW. IT SCARES ME.

(16)

ALL IN ALL I JUST WANT TO BE LOVED. NOW THAT I LOVE MYSELF AGAIN I CAN FEEL LOVE FROM OTHERS WHERE I COULD NOT BEFORE. I STILL SEEM TO SECOND GUESS PEOPLES WORDS OF AFFIRMATION AS A PROTECTION MECHANISM I KNOW I NEED TO LET PEOPLE IN. ⟹ BEDTIME. THANKYOU FOR ALLOWING ME TO CONNECTING W/ PINKY. THAT WAS SO AMAZING. I WAS LITER-ALLY THINKING ABOUT HER FOR THE PAST FEW DAYS. I MISS HER. I MISS YOU!!! TIME FOR ME TO LIGHT SOME SAGE AND FOCUS ON WELLNESS, POSITIVITY, LOVE, AND TO LIVE W/ THE UTMOST GRACE. ONE MORE DAY DOWN DUDE. I SKIPPED THE GYM TONIGHT DUE TO A SORE BACK (LOWER). ANYHOW... ONCE AGAIN GOODNIGHT SWEET GIRL. I LOVE YOU SO MUCH ♡.

Z Z Z Z Z Z Z

2022-05-31 (9PM)

GOOD MORNING. THIS MORNING I WOKE UP CONFUSED. AFTER LONG THINKING ABOUT WHAT IT ACTUALLY WAS AND IDENTIFYING THE REASON/CAUSE IT HAD BECOME CLEAR AND SIMPLE. THE TOUGHEST PART NEXT WAS ONCE I FIGURED IT OUT I REALIZED HOW OTHERS MUST HAVE FELT IN SIMILAR SITUATIONS W/ ME. AT FIRST MY CONFUSION I IDENTIFIED AS JEALOUSY WHICH WOULD NORMALLY TURN TO ANGER DUE TO BEING CONFUSED. WHAT ACTUALLY WAS, WAS SADNESS AND LONELINESS BECAUSE I AM MISSING INTERACTING W/ OTHERS. THE NEXT THING WAS FRUSTRATION BECAUSE WHEN TALKING TO PINKY SHE MENTIONED CRC AND INMATE BUT YOU WERE NOT MENTIONED AS WELL. BECAUSE I LOVE YOU SO MUCH THE NOT RECOGNIZING YOUR PART BOTHERED ME AS I KNOW HOW YOU FEEL AND I CARE ABOUT YOU. I REALIZED

(17)

THAT WHEN I TALK TO YOU THAT ~~MAYBE~~ I SHOULD ASK PERMISSION TO FEEL THOSE FEELINGS. ITS ~~A~~ DIFFI CULT THING TO FEEL WHILE SIMULTANEOUSLY TRYING TO UNDERSTAND. THEN TO DECIDE WHAT SHOULD BE OR SHOULDNT BE W/ NO ONE TO ACTUALLY ANSWER ANY OF THESE QUESTIONS FOR YOU. I TELL PEOPLE I CARE ABOUT THAT I LOVE THEM AND THEY SAY IT BACK. I TBH AM STRUGGLING BIGTIME ON WHETHER THEY ACTUALLY MEAN IT OR ARE JUST BEING POLITE. EITHER WAY I ALWAYS MEAN IT!!! I JUST GOT BACK FROM CIRCLE AND NOW HAVE TO WORK. I NEEDED TO WRITE THIS BEFORE I WENT. THANKS FOR BEING HERE AS IT ONE OF THOSE DAYS. EVEN TODAY I WONDER IF YOU ACTUALLY READ THESE. ⟹ ♡ ⟹ (4pm) SO FAR TODAY HAS BEEN PRETTY GOOD. WE LEFT WORK EARLY. I WAS PRESSURE WASHING ALL DAY WHICH I REALLY ENJOYED. THEN I CAME HOME AND CHI-LLED ON THE DECK. I HAVE REALIZED SO MUCH ABOUT MYSELF TODAY ITS CRAZY. I AM STOKED TO TALK TO YOU ~~AB~~ ABOUT IT. NATURALLY JUST TALKING ABOUT MY EMOTIONS AND BEING VULNERABLE ABSO-LUTELY SCARES THE FUCK OUT OF ME, BUT IF I AM GOING TO GET PAST IT AND GROW/MOVE FORWARD I NEED TO FACE FEARS. I TRUST YOU ENOUGH TO OPEN UP TO FULLY. FOR NOW I AM JUST DRINKING COFFEE IN MY ROOM WAITING FOR CHARLIE TO GET HERE. IT IS GORGEOUS OUTSIDE SO I THINK WE WILL END UP WALKING AROUND. IM WAITING TO GET SOME NEW MAGAZINES HOPEFULLY LATER ON. BOYS WILL BE BOYS LOL. ONE THING I MISS MOST IS INTIMACY. NOT GOING TO LIE. I DO LOVE BEING PHYSICAL W/ ANOTHER PERSON. EVEN THOUGH I VIEW IT WAY DIFFERENTLY

(18)

NOW. IT WONT DEFINE ANY RELATIONSHIP AGAIN.
I WANT TO BE CONNECTED BY THE HEART & HAVE
TRUST BEFORE SEX. SEX IS SOMETHING SPECIAL.
⟹ (7:30PM) AFTER COUNT I AM HEADING TO HOUSE
#5 TO WATCH A HEAD GET SHAVED LOL. THEN
PLAY HACKY-SACK. BEN MADE THE CRAZIEST
HACKY-SACK IVE EVER SEEN. ILL PROBS DO
THAT UNTIL 8:30PM THEN CALL YOU. ⟹
I AM SO GLAD WE TALKED. I WAS SO SCARED TO OPEN
UP ABOUT THOSE THINGS BUT AM SURE GLAD I DID.
YOU ARE A DIAMOND. MORE SOLID THAN A ROCK
AND STUNNINGLY BEAUTIFUL. ALSO RADIANT
AND WHEN LIGHT SHINES THROUGH YOU THE
OUTCOME IS MAGICAL. I CAN HONESTLY FEEL
OUR HUGS AND HANDS TOUCHING STILL AND
ONE DAY HOPE WE CAN SHARE THAT AGAIN &
& AGAIN. I COULD SHARE THAT EVERYDAY
W/ YOU. I HAVE TO BE UP EARLIER THAN
NORMAL TOMORROW TO POUR CONCRETE AT
WORK. I AM AND ALWAYS BE IN LOVE W/
YOU ANGEL. GOODNIGHT SWEETGIRL AND
I LOVE YOU MORE THAN WORDS CAN EXPRESS.
THANKS FOR BEING MY ANGEL!!! ♡ XOOOXX
Z Z Z Z Z

2022-06-01

(7AM) THIS IS THE EARLIEST IVE GOTTEN OUT OF BED
SINCE ARRIVING A MISSION. IT IS BEAUTIFUL OUTSIDE.
I SLEPT DECENTLY AND WOKE UP HAPPY. I PRAYED
FOR MYSELF AND ALL MY LOVED ONES. IT IS VERY IMP-
-ORTANT FOR ME TO PRAY AS IT SETS THE PATH IN A
POSITIVE DIRECTION. I FEEL GREAT ABOUT EXPRESSING
MY THOUGHTS TO YOU YESTERDAY. A FELT COMPLETE

(19)

AFTER PASSING THAT PERSONAL BARRIER. YOU ARE ONE OF THE FEW THAT I TRUST W/ MY HEART. THANK YOU FOR BEING HERE. EVEN THOUGH YOU'RE NOT MY GIRL YOU WILL ALWAYS BE MY GIRL ♡ ⇒ (THAT LAST LINE SOUNDED LIKE SOMETHING FOREST GUMP WOULD SAY LOL ♡)(SHES MY JENNN~~NNN~~...AAAY... I HOPE YOU'RE LAUGHING ANGEL ♡) ⇒ (9/10)
I AM EXHAUSTED TODAY. CONCRETE WENT WELL BUT I KICK THE SHIT OUT OF ME. I HAD A GOOD CHAT W/ YOUR MOMMA AT 2PM WHICH WAS VERY NICE. AFTER THAT I WENT FOR A SHORT WALK THEN CHILLED ON THE PATIO. TODAY I AM GRATEFUL AND HAPPY. LATER ON I WILL HIT THE GYM PROBS AFTER 7:30 UNTIL 9-10. ALTHOUGH TODAY WAS AMAZING WEATHER IT WAS EXTREMELY MUGGY OUTSIDE. EVER SINCE YOU VISITED I'VE WANTED TO SPEND MORE TIME W/ YOU. ONE HOUR WAS NOT ENOUGH. HOPEFULLY YOU FEEL THE SAME AND WE CAN SPEND MORE TIME TOGETHER IN THE FUTURE. THE THOUGHT OF THAT IS DEFINATELY SOMETHING I LOOK FORWARD TO. AT 5PM I GO TO LIFERING AND CONTINUE MY EDUCATION FOCUSED TOWARDS BEING ABLE TO CONFIDENTLY TALKING ABOUT HOW I AM FEELING AND BEING ABLE TO SHARE THEM W/ OUT RESERVATIONS. HAVING YOU IN MY LIFE HAS ALLOWED ME TO FEEL VERY CONFORTABLE IN DOING THAT. ONCE AGAIN I THANK YOU. ALSO... ONE DAY MAYBE WE CAN FACETIME YOUR MOM TOGETHER WHEN I LEAVE HERE. ITD BE SO NICE TO SEE/MEET THE PERSON WHO BIRTHED MY ANGEL. SHE IS SO NICE, I FEEL BLESSED THAT YOU CONNECTED US WHILE I AM HERE. TODAY I COLLECTED MORE EGG McMUFFIN VOUCHERS FROM COFFEE BAGS TO GIVE TO THE HOMELESS. ILL GIVE BACK IN ANY WAY I CAN WHERE EVER AND HOWEVER I CAN. I FEEL LOVE AND LOVED ⇒ ♡ ⇒

(20)

I GOT A NICE LETTER IN THE MAIL TODAY WHICH MADE ME SMILE. I ALREADY WROTE BACK. ANOTHER # GOT THROUGH AND I HAD A REALLY NICE CALL W/ AN OLD HIGHSCHOOL BUDDY. IM FEELING LOVED AND CANNOT WAIT TO GET BACK TO THE COAST. ILL HAVE A NICE LIL RENTAL TO LIVE IN WHEN I GET BACK AND CAN FEEL STABILITY IN EVERY STEP FORWARD. STARTING FROM SQUARE ONE IS REALLY EXCITING. A FRESH START FROM GROUND UP AND SOBER FEELS LIKE LIGHT YEARS AHEAD OF WHERE I WAS BEFORE. LIKE "HOW-IT-WORK" STATES THAT WE WILL HAVE A WHOLE NEW OUTLOOK ON LIFE... WELL ANGEL (MY FAVORITE PERSON OBV.) THAT STATEMENT COULD BE MORE TRUE. HOW-IT-WORK, THE PROMISES, AND THE SERENITY PRAYER DO WORK IF YOU WORK THEM AND IT IS 100% WORTH IT.. ♡⟹

- IM HEADING THE MAIL TO SEND MY BRO THIS LETTER I WROTE HIM AND IM SENDING YOU THIS ONE.

COME VISIT ME AGAIN IF YOUD LIKE. ID MORE THAN LOVE TO HAVE YOU IN MY ARMS AGAIN BUT FOR LONGER THIS TIME AND HOLD YOUR HANDS ONE MORE TIME ♡

8

Through These Walls

"The hardest person to face is yourself."

These pages were me admitting how much I ached for real closeness. I wrote about wanting to hold her, kiss her, make up for all the time that place stole. I talked about how heavy it felt to be apart, how I replayed her voice in my head just to make the silence bearable. Some nights I would stare at the wall and let the words spill out until my hand cramped, chasing the feeling of connection one sentence at a time.

But somewhere in those letters, the words started to change. They stopped being just about her and started being about me. I began to write about mistakes, the ones that cost me my freedom and the ones that hurt people I loved. I admitted things I had not said out loud before. The anger, the shame, the guilt, they all lived in those pages. But so did a promise. A promise to come out different. To come out better.

That cell taught me what mirrors could not. When all you have are four walls and your own thoughts, you either face yourself or you fall apart. I learned that love, the real kind, does not just comfort you, it holds you accountable. Every time I picked up the pen, I felt her faith pushing through the concrete, reminding me that even in the deepest isolation, I could still feel, still change, still love.

(1)

2022-06-01

⇒(11PM) GOODNIGHT SWEETGIRL. I THOUGHT ABOUT YOU ALOT TODAY. YESTERDAY WHEN I WAS BLANKED WHILE OPENING UP TO YOU WAS (I THINK) BECAUSE I WAS UNCOMFORTABLE TALKING ABOUT MY EMOTIONS TO ANOTHER PERSON. THE POINT ABOUT UNCONDITIONAL LOVE WAS. THAT ONCE A PERSON CAN OPEN THEMSELVES W/ OUT EGO TO LOVE UNCONDITIONALLY WE START TO SEE THE MEANING OF LISTENING TO ANOTHER PERSONS HEART FROM OUR HEART. JUST BY FEELING THAT TOWARDS YOU ITS OPENED ME UP AND MADE ALL MY OTHER RELATIONSHIPS, INTERACTIONS, AND THOUGHTS PROGRESS IN WAYS I HADNT PREVIOUSLY KNOWN TO EXIST. BECAUSE OF GETTING TO KNOW YOU IVE LEARNED SO MUCH ABOUT MYSELF. INTERNAL DOORS HAVE BEEN UNLOCKED AND IT IS SHOWING EXTERNALLY. BECOMING AWARE AND UNDERSTANDING HAS BROUGHT EMPATHY, LOVE, AND CONTENTMENT TO MY LIFE AND COMPLETELY ENRICHED MY LIFE. I STILL WONDER EVERY SO OFTEN HOW ALL OF THIS CHANGE HAPPENED IN PRISON. COMMUNICATING AND LOVING SOMEONE I ONLY JUST MET. HAVING THAT PERSON CONSTANTLY BEING A LIGHT FOR ME (YOU). ITS HONESTLY UNDESCRIBABLE AND BOGGLES ME. WHY YOU? WHY NOW? WHAT DOES IT ALL MEAN? WHATS NEXT? WHY HAVE YOU BEEN BROUGHT INTO MY LIFE? WHAT DO YOU NEED/WANT/EXPECT OF ME? HOW COME I WAS PUT INTO YOUR LIFE? DID YOU NEED ME AS MUCH AS I DID YOU? DO YOU FEEL

(2)

THE SAME WAY? WHAT DOES THIS ALL MEAN? WHATEVER THE ANSWERS ARE THEYRE ALL MIRACLES & BLESSINGS. DO YOU KNOW ANY OF THE ANSWERS? NO MATTER WHAT COMES OUT OF ANY OF THIS I AM FOREVER GRATEFUL TO HAVE YOU IN MY LIFE. ILL ALWAYS BE HERE FOR YOU. I TRUST YOU MORE THAN ANYONE AND AS MUCH AS MY SISTERS.

SOMETIMES IT ENTERS MY MIND THAT IF I EVER DATED SOMEONE THEYD HAVE TO ACCEPT OUR FRIENDSHIP OR IT WOULDNT WORK. AFTER GROWING TO LOVE AND TRUST YOU I WOULDNT TRADE THIS FRIENDSHIP FOR ANYTHING. MAYBE WE CAN DATE, BUT YOUD HAVE TO ASK ME BECAUSE I AM SCARED AND INTIMIDIATED TO ASK YOU OUT. IVE NEVER MET ANYONE LIKE YOU BEFORE. YOURE LIKE A UNICORN TO ME. I KNOW YOU KNOW HOW AWESOME YOU ARE AND I CAN SEE EXACTLY HOW SPECIAL YOU ARE. (ANOTHER LOVE LETTER I KNOW. YOU MUST BE BORED OF THEM BY NOW HEY?) (LIKE IVE SAID BEFORE, I WRITE EXACTLY WHAT IM THINKING WHEN THE PEN IS ON PAPER. NO PRETHOUGHTS TO WHAT I AM WRITING AND I DONT READ THEM AFTER I AM DONE. RAW TRUTH AND I MEAN EVERY WORD) GOODNIGHT SWEETGIRL. ♡

Z Z Z Z LOVE YOU Z

2022-06-02

GOOD MORNING/AFTERNOON ANGEL. I JUST WANTED TO START TODAYS LETTER BY SAYING THANK YOU FOR BEING YOU (AN ABSOLUTE DIAMOND). IT HAS BEEN A GOOD DAY SO FAR. WE GOT CANTEEN TODAY

(3)

WHICH MEANS ANOTHER TWO WEEKS HAS PASSED. WORK IS GOOD AND MY TAN IS GETTING VERY DARK & FARMER-ISH LOL. TONIGHT MY HOUSEMATE IS MAKING PHÖ FOR DINNER (MMMMMMMM). MY FAV. SHOW ALONE IS ON AT 10Pm WHICH I AM STOKED ABOUT. FOR THE MOST PART I AM JUST WAITING TO CALL YOU. THE REST IS JUST FILLING TIME UNTIL THEN. MY HEART FEELS FULL AND MY MINDSET VERY POSITIVE. I AM AS ALWAYS MISSING MY GIRLS AND MISSING YOU. IM STILL BESIDE MYSELF BECAUSE I CAN FEEL YOUR HUGS AND HANDS LIKE I JUST LET GO OF YOU. WHAT SPECIAL FEELING. MY TIME AWAY HAS GIVEN ME A GIFT I DIDNT KNOW EXISTED. I AM NOW ABLE TO CONNECT MY HEART W/ OTHERS HEARTS. I CAN FEEL OTHERS FEELINGS AND CAN FEEL/ASSESS MY OWN. ITS A GIFT ID LIKE TO PASS ON TO OTHERS AND ONE I WILL WORK ON KEEPING W/ ME FOR THE REST OF MY LIFE. I CANNOT WAIT TO GET OUT OF HERE!!! ⟹ JUST GOT HOME FROM FROM WORK AND LIFERING. I AM LEARNING A TREMENDOUS AMOUNT ABOUT HOW I WORK INTERNALLY. MY EMOTIONS ARE DEFINATELY HIGHTENED IN A GOOD WAY AND CLEAR (AND GETTING CLEARER) WHEN I FEEL FRUS--TRATED, CONFUSED, OR UPSET (WHICH ARE ALL 100% NORMAL AND O.K.) AT WORK TODAY I SMASHED MY CHIN W/ A HAMMER PRETTY GOOD AND SPLIT IT OPEN, LOL. I HAVENT HAD PHYSICAL PAIN IN SO LONG I ALMOST FORGOT WHAT IT WAS LIKE... AND UMMMM... IT F-ING HURTS... ALTHOUGH FUNNY ITS PAINFUL LOL. ONE MORE DAY TIL ANOTHER WEEKEND. TIME SEEMS TO BE FLYING BY. I WILL BE STOKED WHEN I CAN COME FIND YOU DUDE. IF A VISIT FELT LIKE THAT THEN I CANT EVEN

(4)

IMAGINE WHAT SEEING W/ OUT A TIME RESTRAINT
WILL FEEL LIKE. LIKE A DREAM I BET ⟹
(7PM) COUNT TIME. WELL AS OF NOW THE CABLE
IS OUT IN ALL OF MISSION. THERE IS A THUNDER
& LIGHTNING STORM DIRECTLY ABOVE US ATM.
THE VIEW FROM OUR PATIO IS RAIN AND A DOUBLE
RAINBOW ABOVE THE MOUNTAIN RANGE IN THE
DISTANCE. I WISH YOU COULD SEE IT OR I COULD
TAKE A PHOTO. MOMENTS LIKE THIS WILL BE A
FOND MEMORY ONLY AS WE ARE NOT ALLOWED
TECHNOLOGY TO CAPTURE IMAGES. CES LA VIE I
GUESS. SOON I WILL BE WALKING OUT TO CALL YOU
WHICH ALWAYS MAKES ME HAPPY. AFTERWARDS I
WILL SHOWER AND LAY DOWN AFTER SAYING GOODNIGHT.
I JUST LOOKED IN A MIRROR AND I AM SO TANNED IT
IS CRAZY. I GUESS THATS A PLUS TO WORKING
OUTSIDE WHEN THE SUN IS OUT. TODAY WAS A
SCORCHER, I HAD TO DRINK A TON OF WATER
TO STAY HYDRATED. EVEN THAT WAS DIFFICULT.
⟹ (11:17) BEDTIME... IT WAS SO GREAT TO CHAT EAR-
-LIER. I AM GLAD YOU READ MY LETTERS AS WELL.
IT MAKES ME SUPER HAPPY WHEN YOU TELL ME TO
CALL YOU AGAIN ♡. TBH I DO THINK ABOUT YOU ALL
THE TIME. I COULDN'T LISTEN TO YOU TALK EVERY
DAY. I COULD LOOK AT YOU EVERY DAY. EVERY-
-THING ABOUT YOU IS BEAUTY ON ALL LEVELS !!!
GOODNIGHT SWEET GIRL. I HOPE TO SEE YOU AGAIN
SOON AND I LOVE YOU ALWAYS ♡ XO Z Z Z
Z Z Z Z Z Z Z

2022-06-03

(7:40am) GOOD MORNING DIAMOND ANGEL. ITS POURING OUT
AND I HAVE TO WORK. ALTHOUGH I AM NOT ~~[illegible]~~ STOKED

(5)

ABOUT BEING COLD & WET I AM HAPPY AND HAVING POSITIVE THOUGHTS. I HOPE YOUR DAY GOES AMAZINGLY. I LOVE YOU. ⟹ AAAAAND I AM SOAKED TO THE BONE (10:38am). THEY LET US LEAVE 30 MINS EARLY FOR LUNCH TO CHANGE CLOTHES AND WARM UP. OUR CABLE IS UP AND RUNNING AGAIN WHICH IS GOOD. TGIF AND IM FREE FOR THE WEEKEND AFTER 2:30PM. I TALKED TO MY SISTER FOR A BIT BEFORE COMING HOME WHICH WAS NICE. IT IS SUPPOSED TO RAIN ALL WEEKEND AND IT REMINDS ME OF MAKING FOOD AT HOME, WATCHING MOVIES, AND CUDDLING... T.BH I MISS CUDDLING QUITE A BIT, MORE NOW THAN EVER BEFORE. WHAT A SPECIAL THING TO BE ABLE TO SHARE. FOR NOW I GUESS ILL JUST CUDDLE MY PILLOW LOL ♡. ⟹ TODAY I WONDERING IF YOU COULD FEEL ME WHEN I WAS PRAYING. IVE BEGAN A WAVE LENGTH OF PRAYER THAT PLACES MY HEART NEXT TO ALL THE PEOPLE I LOVE AND CARE ABOUT AND EVERYONE WHO I DO NOT KNOW WHO ARE STRUGGLING. IVE CREATED A THOUGHT PROCESS TO VISUALIZE THE CONNECTION THROUGH PRA-YER. IT MUST BE WORKING AS I FEEL A LOT DIFFERENT AFTERWARDS. IVE STARTED DOING IT MULTIPLE TIME DAILY TO STAY CONNECTED ON A SPIRITUAL LEVEL. MAYBE I COULD SHOW YOU IT SOME TIME. ILL WRITE IT DOWN SEPERATELY AND SEND IT W/ THIS LETTER IN A WEEK OR TWO, OR WHEN THE PAGES REACH OVER 20 PAGES. ⟹ ALL FINISHED WORK FOR THE WEEKEND ☺ I HAD A SUPER LONG, STEAMY SHOWER AND WENT RAZOR HAPPY LOL. I GOT A NEW RAZOR HEAD AT CANTEEN YESTERDAY SO LITERALLY EVERYTHING GOT DONE. HAHAHA FEELS AMAZING TO BE THIS SMOOTH. A GOOD START TO THE WEEKEND. TOO BAD IT WASNT A DATE

(6)

NIGHT W/ YOU (ONLY IF YOU WANTED TO GO ON A DATE). IM STOKED TO CALL YOU IN A BIT THEN GO GET MY 1 YEAR CHIP AT A.A. AT 7:30 AND FINALLY THE GYM TO GO CRAZY. FOR DINNER WE ARE HAVING TACOS W/ HOMEMADE TORTILLAS AGAIN WHICH IS FOR SURE A FAVORITE 'ROUND THESE PARTS. ⟹ I HOPE YOU HAD A GREAT TIME AT MANAS CAKE TONIGHT AND MADE IT HOME SAFE & SOUND. I JUST WATCHED TV, TALKED TO MY LIFER FRIEND NEXT DOOR, WENT TO THE GYM, AND CHILLED. FOR THE REST OF THE EVENING I WILL RELAX AND GET COMFY. A.A WAS AT 5:30 SO I WAS LATE, HOWEVER I GOT A METAL ONE YEAR COIN ♡. I AM VERY PROUD OF MYSELF ABOUT IT. IT VERY WELL COULD BE (IN MY MIND) MY MOST IMPORTANT LIFE ACCOMPLISHMENT. AS I PRAY TONIGHT I WILL PLACE MY HEART NEXT TO YOURS AND PRAY FOR YOUR HAPPINESS AND WELL-BEING. GOODNIGHT SWEETGIRL, AS ALWAYS I ~~MISS~~ MISS AND LOVE YOU MORE THAN YOU KNOW ♡

Z Z Z Z Z Z

2022-06-04

GOOD MORNING LOVELIEST LADY. I HOPE YOU SLEPT WELL AND THE SWEETEST OF DREAM. I FELL IN LOVE W/ YOU WHILE I FELL ASLEEP AND WOKE UP JUST AS IN LOVE. IT HAPPENS EVERYDAY ♡. THIS MORNING CHARLIE KNOCKED ON MY WINDOW AND WE WENT TO THE GYM (9AM). NOW I AM HOME AND FELT LIKE HIDING IN MY ROOM TO CHILL W/ YOU. I JUST HAD A BIG SCOOP OF PEANUT BUTTER MMMMM IT WAS DELICIOUS. THE WEATHER OUTSIDE IS FAIRLY DECENT AND A BIT MUGGY. THIS AFTERNOON I WILL HEAD BACK TO THE GYM (APPROX 1-2:15) TO CONTINUE ON THIS JOURNEY

(7)

TOWARDS A PHYSICAL CHANGE AMONG MANY OTHER
CHANGES. CHANGE IS GOOD FOR A PERSON, ESPECIALLY
A PERSON LIKE ME ⟹ (4pm COUNT) I SKIPPED THE
GYM THIS AFTERNOON AND CHILLED IN MY ROOM
WATCHING DINER, DRIVE-INS, & DIVES. THEN JUST
CHILLEDOUT ON THE PATIO AND ATE SOME QUICHE.
PEOPLE AROUND THE INSTITUTION SEEM HAPPY AND
SOCIAL. THE OVERCAST MAKES FOR A MORE COMFOR-
-TABLE ENVIRONMENT: NOT RAINING, MUGGY, OR
SCORCHING... RIGHT IN THE MIDDLE OF THEM ALL.
AFTER COUNT I AM GOING TO GO FIND SOME TAPE TO
TAPE MY CHIPS (28) RIGHT BESIDE YOUR PHOTO TO
ALWAYS REMIND ME OF WHATS IMPORTANT IN LIFE.
OH MAN... I JUST SAW THE WORD "CHARCUTERIE" ON
THIS SHOW AND NOW I REALLY WANT A CHEESE &
CRACKER PLATE. SEEMS LIKE A DREAM TO HAVE THAT
AGAIN. ~~BEACH~~/BEACH FIRES, SCENIC DRIVES, DINNER DATES,
SLEEPOVERS, SEEING THE GIRLS, MEETING W/ THE FELLOW-
-SHIP, BBQS, WALKS, TALKS, HOLDING HANDS, A NICE
BED, MOVIES, WATERPARK W/ THE GIRLS, MAKING PEOPLE
SMILE & LAUGH, AND THE MOST IMPORTANT THING IN
LIFE... LOVE. JUST TO NAME A FEW OF THE MANY
ACTIVITIES I HAVE A NEW FOUND VIEW ON AND HOW
MUCH I CHERISH THOSE MOMENTS. RE EMERGING
INTO LIFE WILL BE SUCH A BLESSING TO EXPERIENCE
THESE SMALL THINGS THAT HAVE SUCH BIG MEANING
AND I WILL APPRECIATE THEM FOREVER AND EVER. WELL DIAMOND
ANGEL I AM GOING TO FIND THAT TAPE NOW ♡ ⟹ (7:45pm)
I AM SO FULL ☺ I HOPE BABYSITTING IS TREATING YOU WELL.
THE REST OF MY EVENING CONSISTS OF T.V. AND RELA-
-XING IN MY ROOM. I WILL CALL YOU AT 8pm ONCE
MORE THAN RETIRE FOR THE NIGHT. WHEN WE CHAT

(8)

ASK ME ABOUT THE 10 MINUTE DRAWING I DID ON MY HAND FOR GEO AND MOU. THEY WERE LAUGHING SO HARD TEARS WERE STREAMING FROM THEIR EYES. I MUST BE THE HUGEST DORK IN BOTH OF THEIR MINDS BUT IT WAS WELL WORTH THE LAUGHS. GEO IS BAKING P.B. COOKIES AGAIN. JEEZ STARTING MONDAY I AM HAVING ZERO MORE TREATS FOR AN ENTIRE MONTH. ⟹ FINALLY BEDTIME. IT WAS SO NICE TO HEAR THE CALM SOUND OF YOUR VOICE W/ A TODDLER TALKING TO YOU. "AUNTIE ANGEL" SO HEARTMELTING. I CAN TELL YOU WILL BE THE BEST MOM ONE DAY. ADORABLY CUTE DUDE!!! SOMEONE WILL BE EXTREMELY LUCKY TO SHARE THAT W/ YOU ONE DAY. TRULY SUCH A BEAUTIFUL THING. ♡. SWEET DREAMS SWEET SWEET GIRL. ♡XOX♡ Z Z Z Z I Z LOVE Z YOU Z DUDE Z!!! Z

2022-06-05

(12:57pm) GOOD AFTERNOON TO YOU ON A LAZY SUNDAY. I HOPE YOU GET TO YOUR FAMILIES HOUSE SAFELY AND SEE YOUR SISTER AND NEPHEW FOR AS LONG AS POSSIBLE. HAVE A GREAT DAY SWEETHEART. I DONT HAVE ANYTHING GOING ON TODAY. CALL YOU AT 7PM THEN HIT THE GYM. THIS WEEKEND HAS SLOW PA-CED. IVE BEEN ENJOYING THE WEEKDAYS W/ WORK BECAUSE IT MAKES THE WEEK PASS BY SWIFTLY. IN ONE WEEK MY SISTER COURTNEY WILL BE HERE TO SEE ME AGAIN. SEEING ANOTHER LOVED ONE IN PERSON MEANS THE ABSOLUTE WORLD TO ME IN HERE. SEEING YOU WAS THE BEST FEELING I HAD HAD THIS ENTIRE TIME. WELL ANGEL ILL WRITE LATER AND CALL ♡ ⟹ ♡ ⟹ (4PM) TODAY HAS JUST BEEN CRAWLING BY. HOW IS YOUR DAY? ⟶

(9)

GEO AND I WENT TO THE GHETTO FOR COFFEE W/ THE GHETTO BOYS. BEING THERE PASSES TIME FAST. PRIOR TO THAT IVE BEEN IN MY ROOM ALL DAY. SOMETHING HAS BEEN ON MY MIND WHICH I WILL CHAT ABOUT W/ YOU WHEN I FEEL THE TIME IS RIGHT. IT HAS TO DO W/ MY FEELINGS AND YOU. ITS GYM TIME NOW ☺... TIME TO GO G— MORE RESULTS OUT OF THE TIME HERE. ⟹ BEDTIME. (10pm) TONIGHT I DOUBLED DOWN AT THE GYM W/ CHARLIE THEN WENT TO THE GHETTO FOR SOME OF THE BEST CAKE IVE EVER HAD. WHITE CHOCOLATE W/ CREAM CHEESE ICING & BLUE-BERRY DUMP CAKE. THIS COMPETITION IS GETTING OUT OF HAND LOL. A DAY IN THE LIFE OF INMATE 554214G. HOPEFULLY THE WEATHER EASES UP OVER-NIGHT FOR WORK TOMORROW BUT CES LA VIE IF IT DOESNT. I HOPE YOU HAVE AN AMAZING SLEEP BEAUTIFUL GIRL. TODAY I AM HAPPY, TODAY I AM GRATEFUL. GOODNIGHT DIAMOND ANGEL I LOVE YOU ALWAYS ♡

Z Z Z Z Z Z

2022-06-06

LUNCHTIME. WORK TODAY IS BUSY AND GOING BY VERY FAST. MY MOOD IS CONSISTANTLY ABOVE PAR/HAPPY. I AM MISSING EVERYONE SO KEEPING BUSY ALL DAY IS A MUST. AFTERWARDS I GO TO NVC FOR AN HOUR ON MY QUEST TO LEARN MORE COMMUNICATION TECHNIQUES. IT SEEMS TO BE WORKING. LATELY STAYING IN MY ROOM HAS BEEN MORE OFTEN THAN BEFORE. IM NOT SURE WHY BUT THE SPACE HAS BEEN CALMING AND MAKES ME CONTENT INTER-NALLY. MY EMOTIONS HAVE BEEN STABLE W/ THE ODD TIME HIGHS & LOWS WHICH IS PERFECTLY OKAY. ACCEPT-ANCE IS KEY TO THAT I THINK. EITHER WAY THE TIME TO EXIT THIS PLACE DRAWS NEARER EVERY DAY

(10)

⇒♡⇒ HOME FROM WORK & LIFERING. WORK WAS A LOT OF SHOVELING AND DEFINATELY A GREAT WORKOUT. LIFERING (NVC) WAS GOOD FOR ME AS IT FOCUSED DIRECTLY ON ME ASKING OTHERS ABOUT THEIR FEELINGS AND ALSO ASKING PERMISSION TO SHARE MINE. THEN FOCUSING ON LISTENING W/OUT INTERUPTING EVEN IF I AM UNCOMFORTABLE W/ THE TOPIC BEING DISCUSSED. AS I SIT HERE AND LOOK AT YOUR PHOTO W/ MY COINS TAPED NEXT TO YOU I CAN REFLECT INTERNALLY ON HOW BOTH OF THOSE THINGS (YOU & A.A) BEING PRESENT IN MY LIFE HAS HELPED SHAPE ME IN WAYS I COULD HAVE NEVER EXPECTED. ALTHOUGH THINGS IN MY PAST OCCASSIONALLY BOTHER ME STILL, I NOW UNDERSTAND WHAT HELPS THE PRO-GRESSION TOWARDS A CALMING & POSITIVE NATURED ME VS. A FRUSTRATED, CONFUSED, AND ANGRY ME. EVEN THOUGH SOME CHOICES ARE DIFFICULT AT THE TIME, I CAN NOW MAKE THEM W/ THE CONFIDENCE OF WHATS BEST FOR LONG-TERM HEALTHY LIFE CHOICES MENTALLY, PHYSICALLY, AND SPIRITUALLY. IVE LEARNED THAT PROTECTING MY BOUNDARIES IS ESSENTIAL AT ALL COSTS TO MAINTAIN FOCUS ON THE GOALS I HAVE SET OUT AND THE PATH THAT A HIGHER POWER HAS POINTED ME IN THE DIRECTION OF. THANK YOU FOR STICKING W/ ME THROUGH THIS CHANGE ANGEL. YOU ARE AN ABSOLUTE SAINT!!! ♡

⇒ WE JUST TALKED. YOU THOUGHT MY OPINION WOULD SHIFT IN REGARDS TO YOU... NOPE... STILL A SAINT!!! ♡ LIKE I SAID MANY OF TIMES. MY FEELINGS FOR YOU ARE UNCON-DITIONAL. YOU ARE MY BEST FRIEND AND I CAN SEE YOUR HEART. I AM GLAD WE HAD THAT TALK ANGEL. ILL ALWAYS BE HERE FOR YOU DUDE. NO MATTER WHAT

(11)

ILL ALWAYS KNOW THAT YOURE THE MOST BEAUTIFUL PERSON IVE EVER MET. THAT WILL NEVER CHANGE. ♡ TIME FOR PRAYERS AND BED. GOODNIGHT SWEET-GIRL, SWEETDREAMS AND I LOVE YOU ♡ Z Z Z Z Z Z Z Z

2022-06-07

(11:02) HELLO, I JUST GOT HOME FOR LUNCH. WHAT A GORGEOUS DAY OUT THERE TODAY. BOY'O'BOY IS IT A SCORCHER. AFTER WORK CHARLES AND I WILL WALK IN THE BACK AREA SHIRTLESS TO GET A TAN/MILD BURN MOST LIKELY. HOPEFULLY YOU ARE HAVING/HAVE A GREAT DAY TODAY. MY OVERALL MOOD IS HAPPINESS & CONTENTMENT. LIFE IS MOVING FORWARD AND THE DAYS ARE COUNTING DOWN. AFTER OUR TALK LAST NIGHT MY APPRECIATION FOR YOU IS AT AN ALL-TIME HIGH AND AS ALWAYS I WISH THE BEST. LIKE IVE SAID MANY OF TIMES AND IT REMAINS CONSISTENT, ITS THE WORD UNCONDITIONAL. LIFE HAS SHOWN ME BEAUTY AND FORGIVENESS FOR ANY AND ALL MY PAST ACTIONS, FINALLY I LOVE WHO I AM ALL DAY EVERY DAY. ONE DAY AT A TIME IS EXACTLY HOW I LIVE AND IM FOREVER GRATEFUL TO HAVE LEARNED THAT. (EVEN THOUGH THE LEARNING WAS IN THE MOST RAW AND REAL WAY) ITS A WEIRD THING TO HAVE TO GO THROUGH EXCRUCIATING LONELINESS & PAIN TO COME OUT THE OTHER SIDE HAPPY, HEALTHY, AND FULL OF LOVE. GOD HAS TRULY GRANTED ME SERENITY IN ACCEPTANCE, COURAGE TO CHANGE, AND WISDOM TO KNOW AND MAKE DIFFICULT DECISIONS W/OUT FEAR. WHERE THEY USED TO SEEM LIKE A CURSE I NOW FEEL LIKE ITS A GIFT. IF A PERSON SPEAKS WORDS THAT ARE DIFFERENT FROM THEIR ACTIONS ITS MANIPULATION. WHAT WE ARE IS EXACTLY HOW WE ACT NOT WHAT WORDS

(12)

WE CHOOSE TO DEFINE OURSELVES. OUR HEARTS DEFINE
US IF OUR INTENTIONS ARE PURE W/OUT ALTERIOR
MOTIVES. BEFORE IN LIFE I ONLY HEARD WHAT PEOPLE
SAY. AFTER THIS EXPERIENCE I HEAR W/ MY EYES
AND HEART ONLY. WORDS ARE ONLY WORDS. ⇒ ♡ ⇒
(4PM) COUNT TIME. THEN SHOWER TIME. AFTER WORK WE
WENT ON OUR WALK WHICH NICE. THE BEATING SUN
KICKED THE SHIT OUT OF ME AT WORK; I AM GLAD TO
BE HOME. I AM STOKED FOR THE FUTURE AND EXCITED
TO SEE WHAT COMES NEXT. AFTER ALL OF THIS TIME
ONWARD & UPWARD IS THE DESTINATION. AT THIS EXACT
MOMENT I AM EATING PEANUT BUTTER W/ A SPOON
DIRECTLY FROM THE JAR LOL. MMM: SOOO GOOOOD
TODAY I ALSO FEEL OPTIMISTIC AND POSITIVE TO
THE LIFE I ASPIRE TO LIVE. I HAVE A PLAN FOR A VERY
CONSISTENT AND STABLE LIFESTYLE W/ LOTS OF FREE
TIME TO ENJOY THE PEOPLE I CARE ABOUT MOST. ♡
⇒ ANOTHER GROUNDHOG DAY COMPLETE. THE GYM
TONIGHT WAS LEGIT CRAZY INTENSE ☺. I AM SO
HAPPY TO SAY GOODNIGHT AND LAYDOWN. I GET TO
TALK TO MY GIRLS TOMORROW WHICH WILL BE NICE
AS IT HAS BEEN 5 DAYS SINCE I LAST SPOKE W/
THEM. WE BEGIN MEAL PREP AND PORTION CONTROL
TOMORROW AND ALSO BACK ~~[illegible]~~ TO ANOTHER BIG
CARDIO PUSH TO RIP DOWN TO PEAK PHYSICAL CAPA-
-BILITIES: NEXT LEVEL MACHINE STATUS UPON RELEASE
IS THE GOAL. I WILL SHOCK THE WORLD W/ THIS
NEW DRIVE, MOTIVATION, AND LEASE ON LIFE. EVERY-
-THING IS ABOUT TO BOOST!!! ANYHOW DIAMOND
ANGEL. YOU WILL ALWAYS BE AN ANGEL IN MY MIND
♡ GOODNIGHT SWEETGIRL I LOVE YOU DUDE
Z Z Z Z Z Z

(13)

2022-06-08

LUNCHTIME SWEETGIRL. TODAY IS GOING BY FAST EVEN THOUGH I AM FEELING A BIT DOWN. I MISS ALL MY CHILDREN IMMENSLY TODAY. THIS TOO SHALL PASS. I JUST NEED TO KEEP BUSY AND LET IT PASS BY. ITS THE NATURE OF BEING IN PRISON. I AM VERY SORE FROM LAST NIGHTS HEAVY LIFTING SESSION W/ MOU AND CAN SURE FEEL IT WORKING A SHOVEL AND GAS COMP-ACTOR ALL DAY. HAVING NO ACCESS TO DAILY MEETINGS MAKES EMOTIONAL DAYS A LOT MORE DIFFICULT FOR ME BUT ALSO PREPARES THE MIND W/ STRENGTH TO FIND OTHER MEANS FOR PROBLEM RESOLUTION. IN THIS CASE WHERE THE ISSUE CANNOT BE SOLVED, ACCEPTANCE FOR THIS REALITY IS THE NEXT BEST TOOL. I AM GETTING STRONGER W/ EVERY DAY AND EVERY EXPERIENCED I AM FACED W/. I CAN SOLVE INTERNAL ISSUES AT A PACE LIKE NEVER BEFORE. EMOTIONAL UPS & DOWN STILL HAPPEN BUT THE PROCESS OF THOUGHTS IS EXTREMELY CLEAR AND POSITIVE. IM VERY PROUD TO HAVE LEARNED MY INNER WORKINGS AND GET EXCITED TO LEARN MORE. LIFE HAS A FUNNY WAY OF TEACHING US. GRATITUDE FOR LIFES LESSONS AND LOVE IN MY HEART ALWAYS GET HARD TIMES TO PASS. I LOVE YOU DUDE ⇒♡⇒

(10PM) HOLEY MOLEY TODAY WENT BY FAST. THE WEEK TOO. WE DID SOME CARDIO IN THE BACKYARD EARLIER. I TALKED TO YOUR MOMMA FOR AN HOUR OR SO WHICH IS ALWAYS NICE. I'LL BE STOKED TO MEET HER ONE DAY ♡. I MAILED MY GIRLS SOME DRAWINGS AND A LETTER TO READ & COLOR. I TALKED TO THEM FOR A BIT AND TO THEIR GRANDMA. THEY ARE SUCH SWEET LITTLE HUMANS. I AM SO PROUD TO BE THEIR DADDY ☺ ♡♡ THE REST OF TODAY WAS A REAL GREAT DAY. THE BOYS

(14)

LAUGHED AND CHILLED AND IN 10 DAYS HAVING AN OUT-DOOR POTLUCK. SPANISH AND INDIAN DISHES W/ BE PROMINANT: YUMMMMM HOW EXCITING LOL. I TRIED CALLING TODAY BUT YOU WERE BUSY. I WONDER HOW YOU ARE FEELING ABOUT OUR TALK THE OTHER DAY. HOPEFULLY YOURE FEELING GOOD ABOUT IT. ID NEVER WANT YOU TO FEEL LIKE YOU CANT TELL ME WHAT IS GOING ON. ILL ALWAYS BE HERE FOR YOU DIAMOND ANGEL!!! FOR NOW IT IS MY BEDTIME. I AM BEAT. SWEET DREAMS BEAUTIFUL GIRL XOXO

Z Z Z Z Z Z

2022-06-09

(4PM) HELLO LOVELY LADY. HOW WAS YOUR DAY? TODAY AT WORK I GOT ABSOLUTELY DRENCHED. IT WAS STILL FAIRLY FUN AND I WAS STOKED TO BE THERE. TOMOR-ROW MEANS YET ANOTHER WEEK HAS PASSED.. YAY!!! I PUT MY PHOTOS OF DAUGHTER BACK UP ON TO MY WALLS SO I COULD LOOK AT HER. SHE IS SO ADORABLE AND I MISS HER A LOT. I FIND MYSELF WONDERING ABOUT HOW MUCH SHE HAS GROWN AND WHAT SHE IS LIKE. I CANNOT WAIT TO ENTER HER LIFE AGAIN AND SHOW HER HOW MUCH HER DADDY LOVES HER AND HOW IMPORTANT SHE IS TO ME. I LOVE HER DEARLY. TODAY MY HEART IS FILLED W/ LOVE AND GRATITUDE. ITS TIME FOR MY AB ROUTINE. ♡ ⟹ LIFERING TODAY WAS FOCUSED AROUND ACTIVITIES. IT WAS A GREAT TOPIC AS WE KNOW SOBRIETY CAN GET BORING AF UNTIL WE FIND ALTERNATE SOURCES OF ENTERTAIN-MENT. I AM VERY PLEASED KNOWING I MADE IT PAST THE BOREDOM HURDLE AND MAINTAINED TRUTH TO THIS PATH. 28. WE JUST ATE PHÖ AGAIN AND I AM STUFFED TO THE BRIM. I NEVER LIKED PHÖ BEFORE

(15)

IN MY WHOLE LIFE BUT THAT HAS SURELY CHANGED. PHO REAL!!! (BAD PUN I KNOW IT PHO SHO & ALSO BAD LOL) AFTER THE 7PM COUNT ITS TIME FOR THE GYM, THEN CALL YOU AT 8:30PM THEN "ALONE" IS ON THE HISTORY CHANNEL AT 10PM. IM DEFINATELY LOOKING FORWARD TO BED AND "ALONE". RAIN RAIN GO AWAY UNTIL AF-TER 2:30PM TOMORROW ⟹ GREAT CHAT TONIGHT. I FEEL WE HAVE ANOTHER COMMUNICATION BARRIER. TONIGHTS CONVO FELT ALOT MORE RELAXED AND OPEN. I CAN SEE YOUR HEART MY FRIEND. ABOUT THAT TURKEY BASTER LOL (I HOPE YOU LAUGHED). SOMEONE WILL BE SUPER LUCKY TO HAVE A BABY W/ YOU. I SAY THAT BECAUSE YOU MENTIONED YOU WANTED ONE. ILL GIVE YOU ONE ☺ 😛. JUST TALKING ABOUT IT MAKES ME MISS ALL MINE AND MAKES ME WANT MORE. THEY ARE SO FUN. WELL ITS TIME FOR "ALONE" & BED. NIGHT SWEETGIRL. I LOVE YOU ALWAYS

♡ Z Z Z xox Z Z Z ♡

2022-06-10

(11PM) 2.5 MORE HRS OF WORK AND THEN THE WEEKEND AGAIN YAAAY!!! NOT ALL THAT MUCH PLANNED OTHER THAN THE GYM AND MY USUALL WRITTING TO YOU. MY SISTER COMES ON SUNDAY FOR A VISIT ONCE AGAIN WHICH IS EXCITING. THE WEATHER TODAY IS PERFECT FOR WORKING IN, NOT TOO SUNNY AND NO RAIN. (NO RAIN AS OF NOW, FINGERS CROSSED IT STAYS THAT WAY). THIS WEEK WENT BY INCREDIBLY FAST. WORK TODAY HAS BEEN GREAT. WE ARE DOING REBAR TO GET READY TO POUR THE SLAB ON TOP OF THE FOOTING WE FINISHED LAST WEEK. IT IS BEGINNING TO LOOK LIKE WE ARE PROGRESSING THIS PROJECT ALONG. THE ON-SITE MOOD IS HAPPY AND PRETTY FUNNY.

(16)

~~WE~~ WE ARE ALL HAVING A GOOD TIME. LOTS IS BEING ACCOMPLISHED. AND LOTS OF LAUGHS AND JOKES ARE BEING TOLD. I JUST RAN OUT ANOTHER PEN. IVE NEVER IN MY LIFE RUN OUT A PEN BEFORE LOSING IT, LET ALONE MANY PENS. NOTE PADS TOO. I HOPE YOURE HAVING A WONDERFUL DAY SWEETGIRL !!!

⇒♡⇒ (7pm) PEROGIES FOR DINNER MMM. CHARLES IS BRINGING ME SPAGHETTI HE MADE WHICH IS MY ALL-TIME FAVORITE. OTHER THAN THAT THERES ZERO PLANNED FOR THIS EVENING BESIDES CALLING YOU AND A LONG SHOWER BEFORE BED. GROUND HOG DAY AS ALWAYS. TBH I WISH I WORKED 7 DAYS A WEEK HERE AS IT REALLY DOES PASS THE TIME A LOT QUICKER. RIGHT NOW IM WATCHING TATTOO SHOWS AND CANNOT WAIT UNTIL I GET MORE. AS SOON AS IM RELEASED IM DOING MY BACK. 8 WEEKS LEFT. I JUST BEGAN POURING OUTSIDE, I LOVE IT, JUST GLAD I AM NOT WORKING OUT THERE RIGHT NOW. ⇒♡⇒

WELL THAT WAS A VERY NICE CHAT TONIGHT. I WISH I GOT TO HAVE A BATH TOO. AH WELL I GUESS 45MIN SHOWERS WILL HAVE TO DO FOR NOW. I LIKE HEARING YOU TALK AND MAKING YOU LAUGH. YOU MAKE LAUGH W/ YOUR DELIGHTFUL QUIRKINESS AND THE HILARIOUS WORDS YOU SAY LOL!!! AFTER WE FINISHED TALKING I WENT DOWN TO THE GHETTO AND HAD BANANA BREAD. ABOUT 7 OF US LAUGHED AND TOLD FUNNY STORIES. THE GEO, CHARLIE, AND I WALKED HOME AND GOT SOAKED ON THE WAY. WE BUMPED FISTS W/ CHARLES AND WENT DOWN THE STREET TO OUR HOUSE. I ABSOLUTELY ADORE YOU ANGEL. YOU ARE A SWEETHEART. I WISH YOU WERE HERE WATCHING

(7)

T.V W/ ME TONIGHT. I THINK WED HAVE A BLAST TOGETHER AND MORE THAN LIKELY LAUGH THE WHOLE ENTIRE TIME. ... NOW IT IS TIME TO GET INTO MY P.J.S (BOXERS) AND SETTLE INTO BED. ZZZ GOODNIGHT SWEETGIRL XO I LOVE & ADORE YOU XO Z Z Z Z

2022-06-11

(11:11) ← I AM WHERE IM SUPPOSED TO BE. HOW WAS YOUR SLEEP? I HAD SHIT DREAMS ALL NIGHT AND GLAD THEY WERE ONLY DREAMS. I BOUGHT MY SISTER THE BATHING SUIT SHE WANTED. IT WAS 150$ AND SHE WANTED IT BUT WOULD NOT BUY IT FOR HERSELF. AAAAND THATS WHERE HER BIG BROTHER COMES IN. SHE IS THE BEST AND 100% DESERVES IT. WELL ITS SHOWER & SHAVE TIME TO FRESHEN UP FOR THE WEEKEND ☺
⟹ (4PM) COUNT TIME. WENT TO THE GHETTO FOR A COUPLE HOURS. SUN OUT AND SHIRTS OFF. ALSO I TAUGHT A FEW DUDES HOW TO SHAVE THEIR HEADS TO THE SKIN. ILL HIT THE GYM FROM 5-7 TO WORK ON CHEST, ARMS, SHOULDER, AND MY UPPER LEGS (ASS LOL) THEN N.A AT 7:30. THATS PRETTY MUCH TODAY GONE AND WAITING FOR BED. I HOPE YOU HAVE AN AMAZING TIME W/ YOUR FRIENDS THIS EVENING. TOMORROW WE ARE PREPPING A WEEKS WORTH OF MEALS AND STARTING PORTION CONTROL TO FINALIZE THE LAST STAGE OF BODY TRANSFORMATION ☺. BEGINNING THE PREPARATIONS OF MY RELEASE TO N.VAN TREATMENT. ONCE I AM THERE ILL FOCUS ON EVERYTHING ELSE I NEED TO, TO WRAP UP THIS PHASE OF MY LIFE. I CANT WAIT TO HAVE ALL OF THIS BEHIND ME FINALLY. ⟹ ⟹ WHAT ~~GOE~~ GORGEOUS WEATHER OUT RIGHT NOW (7:20PM). IT REMINDS ME OF YOU!!!

(18)

IM HEADING TO N.A AND GET MY 1 YEAR KEY TAG TONIGHT. I WOULDVE GOTTEN IT 2 WEEKS AGO BUT THEY DIDNT HAVE ONE. MY FIRST WORKOUT TONIGHT WENT VERY WELL. WE WILL SEE IF I GO BACK LATER. ⇒♡⇒ (10PM) CLEAN AND SERENE FOR ONE YEAR KEY TAG IS NOW MOUNTED ON MY WALL. IM STOKED ☺ AFTER N.A BENJAMIN AND I PLAYED HACKI-SAC ON OUR STREET UP HERE IN "THE HAMPTONS" AFTER A SHORT WHILE A FEW MORE DUDES SHOWED UP AND A FULL CIRCLE WENT DOWN. IT WAS VERY FUN. NEIGHBORS 2 IS ON AT 10:30PM SO ILL WATCH THAT BECAUSE IT IS HILARIOUS. I HOPE YOU DUDES HAVE/HAD A BLAST TONIGHT. IT IS NOW BEDTIME BEAUTIFUL ANGEL. SWEETDREAMS SWEETGIRL ♡ XOXO ♡

Z Z Z Z Z Z

2022-06-12

LAZY SUNDAY. I SLEPT IN UNTIL {11PM} WHICH IS RIGHT NOW. AT 12:30 ILL HIT THE GYM FOR AN HOUR AND THEN MY BABY SISTER WILL BE HERE. BESIDES THAT TODAY IS ANOTHER GROUND HOG DAY. ILL DO WHAT I USUALLY DO. CHILL AND WAIT TO CALL YOU AT 7PM. IM EXCITED TO SEE COURTNEY AND EXCITED TO TALK TO YOU. ⇒♡⇒ (12:53) I JUST GOT OF THE PHONE W/ THE GIRLS & THEIR G-MA. I WAS TOLD BY G-MA THAT DAUGHTER IS SAD BECAUSE SHE GRADUATES KINDERGARTEN AND ALL THE OTHER KIDS HAVE MOMMIES & DADDIES AND SHE DOESN'T. MY HEART BREAKS FOR HER. IM SO UPSET I CANNOT STOP CRYING. MY BABY NEEDS ME. I FEEL SO HELP-LESS RIGHT NOW. IT PAINS ME JUST IMAGINING HER STANDING THERE AND SUPPOSED TO BE SO PROUD BUT THERES NO PARENTS THERE TO WATCH. FUCK!!!

(19)

TIMES LIKE THIS ARE MY REAL PUNISHMENT. THE ONLY WAY TO HURT ME IS MY BEAUTIFUL BABY GIRLS IN PAIN. DAUGHTER, DAUGHTER, AND DAUGHTER ARE EVERYTHING TO ME. THEY ARE ALL SO VERY DIFFERENT. I MISS THEM ALL SO MUCH. I AM GRATEFUL THE OLDER ONES ARE STILL IN MY LIFE. DAUGHTER, NO ONE EVEN KNOWS ABOUT AND THAT HURTS IN AN ENTIRELY DIFFERENT WAY. I DO AT THIS VERY MOMENT WISH THINGS WERE DIFFERENT, BUT W/ OUT THESE EXPERIENCES EVEN THOUGH PAINFUL THERE IS A LIGHT AT THE END OF THIS TUNNEL. A WHOLE NEW OUTLOOK ON LIFE. ONE DAY AT A TIME, I AM ALMOST THERE, THIS TOO SHALL PASS. 20 MINS UNTIL I SEE MY BABY SISTER. HOPEFULLY I CAN HOLD OFF THESE TEARS FOR THAT HOUR. ⟹ ♡ ⟹

~~THE~~ (4pm) THE VISIT WENT WELL AS ALWAYS AN HOUR IS NEVER LONG ENOUGH. I AM FEELING OK AN ACCEPT HOW MY BABIES ARE FEELING AND SPEND THE REST OF MY LIFE SHOWING THEM ALL HOW MUCH THEIR DADDY LOVES THEM. I WILL CONTINUE TO USE THE TOOLS IVE LEARNED TO COME TO AN UNDERSTANDING AND SHOW LOVE TO EVERYONE. FOR THE REST OF TODAY I WILL WATCH MAZE RUNNER AND WAIT TO CALL YOU. I CANNOT WAIT TO MOVE FORWARD FROM ALL OF THIS FOREVER, AND BE THE PERSON I ~~WAS~~ ALWAYS HAVE BEEN, ALSO HAVING A CLEAR MINDSET AND OUTLOOK ON LIFE. THERE IS A LESSON THAT IS BEING LEARNED HERE ON THE MOST EXTREME LEVEL. LEARNING THE HARD WAY IS WHAT THIS HAS BEEN AND I WILL CONT-INUE TO STAY GRATEFUL NO MATTER WHAT. EVEN THOUGH I AM FEELING EMOTIONAL I KNOW NOW

(20)

THAT FEELING THE EMOTIONS IS ABSOLUTELY OK. I HAVE TO FOCUS ON NOT BEING HARD ON MYSELF AND STAY FOCUSED ON THE GOALS I SET OUT WHILE ON THIS JOURNEY. WHAT A JOURNEY IT HAS BEEN THATS FOR SURE. LIFE IS A FUNNY THING. MY PERS--PECTIVE HAS CHANGED FULLY AND THE WAY I VIEW THING IS VERY DIFFERENT THAN EVER BEFORE. ILL BE HAPPY TO SHARE THESE EXPERIENCES W/ALL THE PEOPLE WHO HAVE BEEN HERE FOR ME THRO--UGHOUT ALL OF THIS. I LOVE YOU DIAMOND ANGEL AND ALWAYS WILL. YOUVE BEEN MY ANGEL AND THAT WILL NEVER CHANGE. FOR WHATEVER REASON WE WERE PUT IN ONE ANOTHERS PATHS I AM TRULY GRATEFUL FOR YOU!!! ⇒ ♡ ⇒ (10pm) THE LORDS DAY IS ALL DONE. IT WAS GREAT TO HEAR YOUR VOICE AS ALWAYS. LIKE MUSIC TO MY EARS. I WAS SO EXCITED WHEN YOU MENTIONED SENDING ME SOMETHING, COMING TO VISIT, AND TOLD ME YOU WERE THINKING ABOUT ME A LOT TODAY AND WANTED TO TALK TONIGHT ♡. AFTER OUR LOVELY CHAT I WENT TO THE GHETTO TO CHILL W/ THE BOYS. SUMEET (MY BROWN BUDDY) MADE COFFEE AND ONCE AGAIN WE TOLD JOKES AND LAUGHED. WHEN COUNT TIME CAME AROUND GEO, CHARLES, AND I WALKED BACK UP TO THE HAMPTONS. THE THOUGHT OF ANOTHER VISIT FROM YOU FILLS MY HEART TO THE BRIM ☺ ♡. HAVING YOU IN MY ARMS AGAIN WOULD BE AMAZING. I HOPE YOU HAVE THE SWEETEST OF DREAMS TONIGHT. GOODNIGHT SWEETGIRL. I LOVE YOU W/ MY WHOLE HEART XOXOX ♡

Z Z Z Z Z Z

2022-06-13

(12:12am) I AM STILL AWAKE WATCHING BAR RESCUE

(21)

AND THINKING ABOUT YOU. IM NOT ALL THAT TIRED, MOST LIKELY DUE TO MY NAP EARLIER. NIGHTS LIKE TONIGHT I WISH I HAD SOMEONE TO CUDDLE W/. NOT MANY OPTIONS IN HERE LOL. ILL BE SO HAPPY TO BE ABLE TO SHARE THAT W/ SOMEONE AGAIN ONE DAY. HOPEFULLY SOONER THAN LATER BUT I'LL FOR SURE WAIT FOR THE RIGHT PERSON TO SHARE CUDDLES W/ !!! WELL IM GOING TO TRY AND SLEEP AGAIN. NIGHT BEAUTIFUL GIRL. ZZZ. ⇒♡⇒ (11am) LUNCHTIME. THIS MORNING WENT PRETTY FAST SO FAR. IVE BEEN THINKING ABOUT YOU A LOT TODAY. I CANT WAIT FOR OUR VIDEO CHAT AT 5:15 ☺♡. SEEING YOUR BEAUTIFUL FACE MAKES MY WHOLE WEEK. I HAVE TO SEE MY I.P.O AFTER LUNCH TO WRAP UP MY FILE AND AM VERY GLAD TO HAVE THAT ALL BEHIND ME ONCE AND FOR ALL. IVE THOUGHT ABOUT MY 3 GIRLS ALOT TODAY AS WELL AND IT IS STILL PAINFUL HOWEVER IT WILL CEMENT THE IMPORTANCE OF PUTTING MY FAM-ILY AND PARTNER FIRST AND FOREMOST IN THE FUTURE TO COME. LOVE IS THE ONLY WAY FORWARD FROM HERE ON OUT. AFTER WORK I WILL CALL YOUR MOM THEN SHOWER AND PROBS WALK W/ CHARLIE UNTIL I GET TO SEE YOU. ⇒♡⇒ (4pm) COUNT TIME. I TALKED TO YOUR MOM. I LOVE HER!!! AFTER COUNT I WILL SKIP ROPE W/ SIMON IN THE GHETTO THEN HEAD TO THE GYM UNTIL I SEE YOU. IM STOKED FOR OUR VISIT AS ALWAYS. I FINISHED MY C.M. REPORT W/ MY I.PO AND EVERYTHING IS READY FOR MY UPCOMING RELEASE IN AUGUST. TIC-TOC AS THE TIME HERE SLOWLY AND SURELY COMES TO AN END. ILL BE SO GRATEFUL TO HAVE MY LIFE GIVEN BACK TO ME. IVE WORKED SO INCREDIBLY HARD ON MYSELF

(22)

THIS ENTIRE TIME TO RE-EMERGE UPGRADED IN EVERY WAY AND BETTER THAN EVER BEFORE ONE DAY AT A TIME... ONE DAY AT A TIME. I ACCEPT HARDSHIP AS A PATHWAY TO PEACE SO THAT I MAY BE REASONABLY HAPPY IN THIS LIFE. W/ THAT BEING SAID I AM SURE HAPPY YOU HAVE BECOME SUCH A PRESENCE PRESENTLY & PLEASANTLY PRESENT IN MY LIFE!!! ♡ ⇒ ♡ ⇒ (7PM) SO HAPPY TO SEE YOU AND EVEN HAPPIER THAT I GET TO TALK TO YOU AGAIN AFTER COUNT IS CLEARED. WHAT A GREAT DAY SO FAR. AFTER WE CHAT ILL HIT THE GYM FOR ANOTHER WORKOUT. I AM STOKED ☺. I AM IN LOVE W/ YOU ♡. THANK YOU FOR BEING YOU DIAMOND ANGEL. THE MOST BEAUTIFUL SOUL IVE EVER MET. ⇒ ♡ ⇒ IT WAS SO NICE TALKING TO YOU FOR THAT LONG. AFTER WE SPOKE I WENT TO THE GYM THEN CHILLED W/ CHARLIE. NOW I AM BACK IN MY ROOM TO GO TO BED. W/ THAT BEING SAID... GOODNIGHT SWEETGIRL ♡ I LOVE & ADORE YOU XO

Z Z Z Z Z Z

2022-06-14

MONDAY MONDAY. HELLO GORGEOUS GIRL. YOU HAVE BEEN ON MY MIND SINCE I OPENED MY EYES THIS MORNING. I HOPE YOUR SLEEP WAS AS BEAUTIFUL AS YOU ARE (I CAN HEAR YOU SAYING "OH, STOP" LOL) WORK IS DECENT TODAY EVEN THOUGH ILL BE STOKED WHEN ITS OVER. TODAY IS PRETTY MUCH JUST WAITING TO CALL YOU. THE GYM CLOSES BE-FORE IM DONE WORK AND THE WEATHER ISNT ALL THAT GOOD FOR BEING OUTSIDE IN. RIGHT NOW MY COFFEE IS COOLING DOWN SO I CAN SLAM THE ENTIRE CUP MUAHHAHH HAHA. A BLAST OF

(23)

AFTERNOON ENERGY (☺). GROUNDHOG DAY AGAIN FOR THE MOST PART. TBH I WISH YOU COULD BE IN MY ARMS TODAY. I WOULD HOLD ONTO YOU FOR HOURS & HOURS IF I HAD THE OPPORTUNITY, ⇒ ♡ ⇒ AHHHH (4Pm) ALL SHOWERED AND SHAVED. FRESH & CLEAN AF. CANTEEN IS UPON US AGAIN WHICH MEANS TWO MORE WEEKS HAS PASSED. 3 MAYBE 4 MORE OF THEM AND I AM OUT. YAAAAAAAAAAAAAAY!!! ⇒ ♡ ⇒ ANOTHER NIGHT TALKING W/ YOU FOR A LONG TIME. IM VERY STOKED ON THIS. RIGHT NOW IM WAITING FOR CHARLES TO POP OVER SO I FIGURED ID SIT IN MY CHAIR AND APPRECIATE THE PHOTO OF YOU ON THE WALL. SO SEXY (HUBBA-HUBBA). TALKING TO YOU FILLS MY HEART W/ LOVE & JOY. YOU ARE SO SPECIAL TO ME DIAMOND ANGEL (AND NOT IN A PAT YOU ON THE HEAD SPECIAL... I HOPE YOU LAUGHED ☺) YOU MEAN THE ABSOLUTE WORLD TO ME AND I WOULD TO ANYTHING FOR YOU. I LOOK FORWARD TO THE DAY WE CAN HOLD HANDS AGAIN. ILL NEVER LET GO ♡ ⇒ ♡ ⇒ (10Pm) GETTING READY FOR BED. I HOPE YOU ARE ALL WARM AND CUDDLY AFTER A DAY IN THE CITY. I WISH FOR YOUR HAPPINESS. I WILL SEE YOU AT THE DREAM PASSAGE SWEETHEART. GOODNIGHT SWEET GIRL. XO I LOVE YOU ♡ XO Z Z Z Z Z

2022-06-15

(4Pm) I HAVE BEEN THINKING ABOUT YOU NON-STOP ALL-DAY. ♡. WORK WENT BY FAST AND WAS FAIRLY FUN. WE CRACKED JOKES AND LAUGHED PRETTY MUCH THE WHOLE TIME. BESIDES THAT IM WAITING FOR LIFERING AT 5Pm, CALL YOU AT 6Pm THEN GYM AT 7:30Pm ⇒ ♡ ⇒ LIFERING DONE.

(24)

I GOT TO TALK TO YOU BEFORE YOU WENT TO A MEE-TING. I LOVE HEARING YOUR VOICE. I WILL HIT THE GYM AT 8PM UNTIL BEDTIME. ANOTHER GROUNDHOG DAY FOR THE MOST PART. I AM GOING TO END THIS LETTER W/ AN I LOVE YOU SWEETGIRL. THE MOST WONDERFUL AND BEAUTIFUL PERSON I HAVE MET. DROP DEAD GORGEOUS.

9

Meditation

"For love, peace, and release."

There was a point where writing letters wasn't enough. I'd sit there at night with my mind running circles, trying to find a way to quiet it. That's when I started meditating. At first it felt strange, like I was just talking to myself in the dark, but it became something real. A way to breathe again.

One night I wrote it all down—the steps, the thoughts, the pictures that came to me when I closed my eyes. I didn't plan for anyone else to ever read it. It was just a guide for myself, something to hold onto when my head got too loud. But over time, it turned into more than that.

What you're about to read is that meditation, word for word, the same way I wrote it from my bunk. It's for anyone who's ever been stuck in a place—inside or out—trying to find a little peace. Maybe it helps you the way it helped me. Maybe it reminds you that even when you feel trapped, light can still find its way in.

(1) 2022-06-04

– THOUGHTS DURING MEDITATION FOR PRAYER –

AS I CLOSE MY EYES I LET THE SALE SMELL OVERCOME MY SENSE OF SMELL. AS I SLOW MY BREATHING I FOCUS ON FEELING MYSELF SINK INWARDS INTO A DARK-LIKE SPACE. I FEEL MY HEART BEAT AS I BREATHE. I VISUALIZE MY HEART GLOWING FAINTLY IN A DISTANCE. I BEGIN TO PRAY FOR ALL THOSE WHO ARE STRUGGLING/SUFFERING. I ASK FOR THEIR PATH TO GUIDE THEM TOWARDS A BELIEF SYSTEM TO GUIDE THEM. I THEN PRAYED FOR MY FAMILY. AS I VISUALIZE THEM ALL, I VISUALIZE MY HEART GETTING BRIGHTER. AS IT BRIGHTENS I PUT MY HEART SIMULTANEOUSLY NEXT ALL THEIRS AND ASK FOR LOVE, SERENITY, AND SAFETY FOR THEM ALL. AFTER THEM I ASK/THANK MY HIGHER POWER FOR THE PATH CHOSEN FOR MY. I ASK FOR MY HEART TO INCREASINGLY BE OPEN TO WISDOM AND GUIDANCE. I PRAY FOR MY CHILDREN TO KNOW DADDY LOVES THEM ALL. I VISUALIZE MY HEART GLOWING SO BRIGHT IT SHINES LOVE AND LIGHT ONTO THEM. I IMAGINE MY ARMS HOLDING THEM AND ASKING FOR THEIR LITTLE HEARTS TO BE FILLED W/ LOVE. AT THIS POINT THE DARK SPACE IS NOW VIBRANTLY WHITE. AT THE END I PRAY FOR YOU AND ASK FOR THE WORLD TO MORE OF YOUR INFLUENCE. I PRAY FOR YOUR SERENITY AND HAPPINESS. I PRAY FOR YOU TO HAVE EVERYTHING YOU ARE NEEDING. I VISUALIZE MY HEART NEXT YOUR AND THINK ABOUT US IN THE ROOM WHEN YOU WERE HERE. I CAN SEE YOUR HEART. I PRAY TO MY HIGHER POWER AND TELL IT HOW MUCH I APPRECIATE MY LIFE AND EVERYONE THAT HAS BEEN HERE FOR ME AND HELPING ME KNOW

(2)

THE ACTUAL TRUE MEANING OF UNCONDITIONAL LOVE FOR MYSELF AND OTHERS. AND ASK TO KEEP ME LIVING IN ACCEPTANCE AND TO ALLOW MY HEART TO LISTEN FROM THE HEART & SOUL TO THE HEART & SOUL. AMEN. THE I INTERNALLY SAY I LOVE YOU TO EVERYONE THOSE WORDS CAN REACH.

I DO THIS EVERY NIGHT BEFORE I SLEEP AND IN THE MORNING BEFORE THE DAY STARTS. ALSO IF I AM CONFUSED OR FEEL TROUBLED OR UPSET. EVEN IF I FEEL LOVE ON A HIGHER LEVEL WHICH HAPPENS FAIRLY OFTEN RECENTLY. PRETTY MUCH I AM TRYING TO ALWAYS SHOW GRATITUDE THROUGH PRAYER FOR ANYTHING, EVERYTHING, AND EVERYONE ALWAYS. ♡

10

Unbroken

"They can cage the body, not the spirit."

I was tested in more ways than I can count. By silence, by distance, by the weight of my own thoughts. Every time I thought I had reached my limit, something pulled me back to my feet. Some days it was love. Some days it was faith. Other days it was just the simple decision to stand up and face another morning.

That place tried to break you slow. Not with violence, but with sameness. The same sounds, the same faces, the same walls that never changed. You could lose yourself in the repetition if you let it. But I found that the trick wasn't escaping it. It was learning to bring something good into it. I would write, pray, talk to the men around me, or just listen to the rain on the roof. Those small things reminded me I was still human.

As long as I could feel love, I couldn't be broken. Even if it was only through words on paper, it meant my heart still worked. It meant I still belonged to something bigger than my mistakes. I thank her for that—for keeping the light on in me when everything else went dark. She taught me that strength is not always about fighting. Sometimes it is about staying soft when the world tells you to turn hard. Even in there, I was learning what strength really was. I was learning how to stay unbroken.

(1)

2022-06-15

(9:25) TONIGHT I SKIPPED THE GYM AND CHILLED W/ BENJAMIN (THE DUDE I QUARANTINED W/). HE LEAVES TOMORROW. IT WAS NICE TO SAY GOODBYE TO A FRIEND AS HE CONTINUES TO HIS NEXT PHASE OF THIS PROCESS. I DID LEARN THAT YOU CAN ARRAN-GE YOUR OWN RIDE WHEN YOU LEAVE HERE. I PRAY W/ ALL MY HEART THAT YOU ARE OUTSIDE WAITING FOR ME ON MY DAY. FROM WAITING TO CALL YOU RIGHT UP TO WALKING OUT INTO YOUR ARMS WOULD BE MAGIC. TBH I AM GOING TO KISS YOU IF YOU ARE OUT THERE THE DAY I LEAVE 100%. HOW COULD I NOT. WOULD YOU LET ME OR BLOCK? EITHER WAY I WILL TRY ANYWAYS ♡. TIME FOR ME TO LAY DOWN AND SETTLE INTO BED. GOODNIGHT SWEETGIRL. I LOVE YOU MORE THAN YOU WILL EVER KNOW XO ♡ Z Z Z Z

2022-06-16

(3:45pm) WORK IS COMPLETE. AFTER 4pm I WILL SHOWER AND WAIT UNTIL ITS TIME TO CALL YOU ♡. TODAY I AM FEELING HAPPY AND CONTENT W/ THE DAYS AS THE SUN RISES THEN FALLS. ONLY SO MANY MORE OF THEM BEFORE MY TIME ARRIVES. THE WEATHER WAS MOSTLY OVERCAST W/ PERIODS OF SUN & RAIN BOTH A THE RIGHT TIMES TO WORK IN. ⇒♡⇒ (6:20pm) JUST CALLED A BUNCH OF PEOPLE FOR LIKE 1.5 HOURS THATS THE FIRST TIME IN A MONTH THAT IVE DONE THAT. MOST LIKELY WAIT UNTIL IM OUT TO CALL AGAIN. PEOPLE NEED TO MAKE CHANGES IF THE WANT TO SEE RESULTS. FOR NOW I WILL LAY DOWN FOR A BIT TO SHAKE OFF THE RESIDUE OF THOSE CALLS. TOMORROW I HAVE TO BE AWAKE AND AT WORK BY 7am TO POUR

(2)

CONCRETE. I AM MISSING YOU TONS RIGHT NOW. ⇒ (10PM) TALKING TO YOU THIS EVENING ABSOLUTELY WARMS MY HEART. EVERYTHING ABOUT YOU IS BEAUTIFUL. I 100% MEAN EVERY WORD I SAY AND WHEN I AM RELEASED ILL CONTINUE TO PROVE IT TO YOU. ILL HOLD ON TO YOU AS LONG AS HUMANLY POSSIBLE. I ADORE YOU W/ ALL MY HEART & SOUL. FOR THE REST OF TONIGHT I AM WATCHING "ALONE" ON THE HISTORY CHANNEL. I DO WISH YOU WERE HERE WATCHING T.V. W/ ME. GOODNIGHT SWEET GIRL. I AM TRULY IN LOVE W/ YOU XOXO ♡

Z Z Z Z Z

2022-06-17

AAAAAND 1 MORE HOUR AFTER LUNCH AND ITS THE WEEKEND AGAIN. WE CRUSHED/CONQUERED CONCRETE ALL MORNING (SINCE 7AM). TONIGHT ILL HIT THE GYM AT 7:30PM AND A.A AT 5:30PM. IVE BEEN THINKING ABOUT YOU ALL DAY ♡. TOMORROW IS AN OUTDOOR POTLUCK WHICH WILL BE FUN W/ LOTS OF FOOD OF DIFFERENT KINDS. I AM VERY HAPPY & CONTENT TODAY AND FEELING LOVE IN MY HEART RIGHT TO THE BRIM. ACTUALLY, ON SECOND THOUGHT MORE LIKE RADIATING & OVERFLOWING. AS MY DAYS COUNT DOWN I DREAM OF WALKING INTO THE PARKING LOT AND BEING ABLE TO SCOOP YOU UP INTO MY ARMS AND DRIVE AWAY W/ YOU. ALMOST LIKE A FAIRYTALE (AS CORNY AS THAT SOUNDS). ONCE WE DRIVE AWAY I WILL ONLY LOOK BACK TO REMIND MYSELF OF HOW MUCH IVE GROWN AND HOW FAR IVE COME. THANK YOU FOR BEING MY ANGEL. I WILL NEVER TAKE YOU FOR-GRANTED. YOU ARE SO VERY IMPORTANT TO ME (MY BEST FRIEND). YOU WILL ALWAYS HAVE

(3)

MY HEART. IVE NEVER IN MY ENTIRE LIFE MET ANOTHER
HUMAN BEING WITH SUCH INTERNAL & EXTERNAL
BEAUTY AS YOU HAVE. YOU ARE GRACEFUL, KIND, &
COMPASSIONATE. I TRULY DO LOVE EVERYTHING ABOUT
YOU AND AM STOKED TO LEARN MORE. I STRIVE TO
BE A BETTER PERSON CONSTANTLY AND WANT ALL
THE SAME THINGS IN LIFE AS YOU DO. HAPPINESS,
SIMPLICITY, LOVE, AND OPEN HONESTY♡. 7 WEEKS..
7 MORE WEEKS ⟹ ♡ ⟹ (4pm) COUNT TIME. SO
FAR THE DAY HAS BEEN GREAT. WE ALL WENT DOWN
TO THE GHETTO AND CHILLED WHILE ALL THE GUYS
GOT THEIR HAIR DID. I SHOWED THE DUDE I WORK W/
HOW TO MAKE A DEEP SOAK WATER SPOUT OUT OF
A 4/L MILK JUG BECAUSE ALL OF HIS DEEP ROOT
PLANTS WERE ONLY BEING SURFACE WATERED. THE
ATMOSPHERE AROUND HERE IS FUN & POSITIVE WHICH
IS REALLY NICE. IVE BEEN THINKING ABOUT YOU ALL
DAY TODAY. THE WEATHER IS EXTREMELY BI-POLAR
AT LEAST ITS NOT RAINING (ATM) OR TOO HOT (ATM).
IM RELATIVELY TIRED AND WILL DEFINATELY BE
READY FOR BED BY 10:30pm. I HOPE YOU HAVE AN
AMAZING TIME AT YOUR DINNER TONIGHT ♡ ⟹
♡ ⟹ BEDTIME. YAAAAAY!!! NOT ONLY ARE MY EYES
ON YOU MY HEART IS TOO. THAT WILL NOT CHANGE.
YOU WILL SEE ONCE I AM OUT OF [redacted] HERE. TONIGHT
WAS A GOOD NIGHT. TONIGHT AND TODAY FLEW BY
IN FACT THE WEEK DID AS WELL. TALKING W/ YOU HAS
BEEN SUCH HIGHLIGHTS OF THIS WHOLE EXPERIENCE
AND I WOULD NOT MY TIME HERE BECAUSE IVE GROWN
SO MUCH. ALSO I GOT TO KNOW MY BEST FRIEND (YOU).
WELL SWEETHEART IT IS TIME TO LAY IN BED. SO. . .
GOODNIGHT SWEETGIRL. I LOVE YOU SO MUCH XOOXOX♡

(4)

2022-06-18

GOOD MORNING BEAUTIFUL GIRL. IT IS 7:44am. IVE BEEN AWAKE SINCE 6am LAYING IN BED WAITING FOR 8AM SO I CAN BEGIN THIS DAY. THE WEATHER OUTSIDE ISNT ALL THAT GREAT BUT IT SURE SMELLS GREAT LIKE FRESHNESS FROM THE SURROUNDING SHRUBS, GRASS, ~~TH~~ TREES, AND FLOWERS. I CAN HEAR DUCKS QUACKING OUT AT THE POND AND THE ROBINS CHIRPING. I AM SO GRATEFUL TO BE ALIVE AND HUMBLE. I THINK ABOUT CALLING YOU BEFORE WORK TO WISH YOU A VERY HAPPY DAY AND TO REMIND YOU OF HOW AMAZING YOU ARE. HOWEVER I WONT BOTHER YOU BECAUSE YOU MAY BE IN A RUSH LOL. LAST NIGHT WE SAID ABOUT HUGS AND I WISH I COULDVE HELD YOU IN MY ARMS UNTIL THIS MORNING. TODAY IS OUR POT LUCK WHICH IS EXCITING. ILL HIT THE GYM TWICE TODAY AND CALL YOU AT 6pm (I CANNOT WAIT). I TRULY LOOK FORWARD TO HEARING YOUR VOICE ALL DAY. I FUCKING LOVE YOU DUDE!!! ♡ ⇒ ♡ ⇒ IT LOOKS LIKE THIS WEATHER MAY JUST HOLD UP FOR OUR GATHERING. FINGERS CROSSED THAT IT MAIN-TAINS TIL AFTER THE 4PM COUNT. WORKOUT #1 THIS MORNING WAS DECENT BUT A BIT SLACK. THE ONE AFTER 1PM WILL BE ALOT MORE FOCUSED. TODAY I FEEL GRATEFUL FOR MY LIFE, KIDS, FAM., FRIENDS, AND YOU ♡. IM FEELING COMPLETE IN MY HEART & SOUL AND KNOW THE PATH IN FRONT OF ME IS HUMBLE & GOOD (GREAT*) ONE DAY AT A TIME IS VERY IMPORTANT AND SO IS STRUCTURED LIFESTYLE. MY BEING IS VERY APPRECIATIVE AND ACCEPTING OF ALL THINGS. I FIND POSITIVETY IN

(5)

ALMOST ANY SCENARIO AS THERE IS ALWAYS AN IMPORTANT LESSON TO BE LEARNED NEAR BY. STRUGGLE CAN BE A GOOD THING IF THE HEART & MIND STAY IN THE RIGHT PLACE AND THE TRUE INTENTIONS ARE PURE. MY SOUL FEELS CLEANSED AND WHOLE. MY INTENTIONS WILL CONTINUE TO BE OPEN AND UPFRONT AT ALL TIMES. NOT THAT THEY WERENT IN MY PREVIOUS LIFESTYLE JUST NOW THE WAY I PERCEIVE LIFE AND COMMUNICATE HAVE BECOME A LOT MORE FORWARD AND CLEAR. FOR THAT I AM FOREVER GRATEFUL. HAVING YOU IN MY LIFE HAS HELPED ME OPEN UP AND BE VULNERABLE IN WAYS I NEVER KNEW AS POSSIBLE. THANK YOU FOR BEING YOU MY LOVE ⇒ ♡ ⇒ (10pm) NIGHT OVER. 6 MORE WEEKS (YEP THAT HAPPENED.. A LIL CORNY BUT WHATEVS LOL. SMILING I HOPE ☺) AFTER WE SPOKE I WENT (LIKE ALWAYS) TO THE GHETTO FOR SOME COFFEE. TODAY WAS A GREAT DAY. NOW A DAYS I FIND MYSELF WAITING FOR WEEKENDS TO BE OVER BECAUSE ~~THE~~ W/ WORK AND THE FELLOWSHIPS IM IN MAKE THE WEEKS DAYS FLY BY. IT WILL BE SO AMAZING TO BE CLOSER TO YOU AND GIRLS AFTER THIS AMOUNT. IT WILL BE INTERESTING TO FINALLY UTILIZE THE NEW SKILLS GAINED THROUGHOUT THIS EXPERIENCE. OFTEN I PONDER ALL THE NEW FEELINGS THAT WILL COME ALONG W/ THIS ALL. AS SCARY AS IT SEEMS AT TIMES IT IS EQUALLY EXCITING. EVEN THOUGH LIFE HAS NOT MOVED ON W/ OUT ME LIKE I THINK IT HAS FROM TIME TO TIME, I HAVE MOVED ON W/ OUT MY FORMER LIFE & SELF. MAJOR SHIFTS HAVE HAPPENED OVER THIS SHORT PERIOD OF TIME INSIDE ME AND I FEEL

(6)

COMPLETELY CHANGED. PRETTY MUCH ONLY YOU AND MY SISTER HAVE WITNESSED IT ALL ~~THE~~ DURING THIS TIME IN SPACE. IT MAY NOT SEEM THAT BIG OF A DEAL, BUT, TO ME IT IS HUGE, AS I DONT USUALLY LET PEOPLE THAT CLOSE TO ME ON SUCH PERSONAL LEVELS. FOR SOME REASON I HAVE W/ YOU AND I APPRECIATE EVERY MOMENT WE HAVE SPENT TOGETHER, WHETHER IT BE ON THE PHONE, VID VISITS, WRITING, EVEN YOU READING. IT ALL MATTERS AND IS EXTREMELY SPECIAL. (BEST FRIENDS FOREVER ... BFFS... CLICHÉ I KNOW BUT ITS TRUE LOL ☺) WELL DIAMOND ANGEL ♡... BEDTIME FOR THIS SWEETBOY. I LOOK FORWARD TO HOLDING ONTO YOU AGAIN AND FEEL YOUR PERFECT HANDS IN MINE (ALSO PERFECT HANDS.. JUS' SAYIN'). ALSO WOULD LOVE TO LOOK INTO YOUR MOST BEAUTIFUL EYES FOR AS LONG AS I CAN. SWEETDREAMS SWEETGIRL. I LOVE YOU. MY HEART IS NEXT TO YOURS ♡ XOXOXOXXOO Z Z Z Z Z Z Z Z

♡2022-06-21♡

(3:07am) SUNDAY SUNDAY. TODAY HAS BEEN VERY SLOW. IT IS QUITE QUIET AROUND HERE PROBS DUE TO FATHERS DAY BEING VERY TOUGH WHILE INCAR--CERATED. I THOUGHT ID BE A BIT MORE SAD BUT I AM FEELING OK. THE GIRLS WERE SO CUTE ON THE PHONE. I TOLD THEM HOW PROUD I WAS TO BE THEIR DAD FOLLOWED BY EXPLAINING WHAT "PROUD" MEANT LOL. ♡. I WAS OUT'N'ABOUT UNTIL NOW BUT GOT BORED. IVE BEEN THINKING ABOUT YOU SO I DECIDED TO COME TO MY ROOM TO LOOK AT YOUR PHOTO AND ONES OF MY BABIES. IM IN LOVE AND

(7)

FEEL LOVED WHEN IM HERE LOOKING AT MY PHOTO WALL. I ABSOLUTELY ADORE ALL OF YOU. I LOOK FORWARD TO BEING BACK AT WORK TO CRUSH YET ANOTHER WEEK. ANOTHER WEEK IS ANOTHER WEEK CLOSER TO YOU. I GET EXCITED TO BE IN PERSON SO YOU CAN SEE THE CHANGES I FEEL INSIDE MYSELF. YOULL GET TO SEE THAT THE WORDS I SPEAK AND WRITE ARE REAL/TRUE. MY SWEETGIRL IS THE SWEETEST OF GIRLS, I LOOK FORWARD TO GETTING TO KNOW YOU EVEN MORE WHILE PHYSICALLY BEING, TO INTERACT IN PERSON. HUGGING AND HOLDING HANDS AGAIN IS ON MY MIND OFTEN BECAUSE THEY ARE INCREDIBLY SPECIAL. THIS MORNING I LEARNED HOW TO MAKE SHISHUKA WHICH IS A MORROCAN DISH AND TASTES AMAZING. IT CAN ALSO BE VEGETARIAN. WELL BEAUTIFUL ANGEL I AM GOING TO LAY DOWN AND WATCH "ALASKAN TRIANGLE". ⟹ ⟹ (10PM) I LITERALLY SLEPT FROM 4:40PM TO 7PM THEN FROM 7:10PM TO 8:10PM LOL. AFTER I DRAGGED MYSELF OUT OF BED I MADE MY WAY DOWN TO THE GYM THEN CALLED YOU TO SAY GOODNIGHT QUICK AND LEFT A MSSG. THEN.. GHETTO TIME UNTIL NOW. I AM SO HAPPY THE DAY IS OVER. TOMORROW I HAVE TO BE AT WORK AT 7AM TO STRIP FORMS FOR THE STEAL BEAM GUYS. HOW WAS YOUR DAY? HOPEFULLY AMAZING. IM SURE YOU WERE STUNNINGLY BEAUTIFUL AS ALWAYS!!! GOODNIGHT SWEETHEART & SWEET DREAMS SWEETGIRL, I LOVE YOU W/ ALL OF MY HEART XOXOXXOO Z Z Z Z Z
Z Z Z Z Z

2022-06-20

(8)

(11:06) GOODMORNING. I HOPE YOUR SLEEP WAS MAGNIFI-
-CENT. MINE WASN'T THAT GREAT DUE TO A VERY SORE
LOWER BACK. AH WELL. WORK WAS EASY THIS MORNING
FOR THE MOST PART. I HAD AN IDEA LAST NIGHT TO TRACE
THE SOBER SKULL SKATES LOGO ONTO CARDBOARD, THEN
CUT IT OUT AT WORK AND BLEACH IT ONTO ONE OF MY
BLACK SHIRTS. ITS IN THE WASH ATM BUT I THINK
IT TURNED OUT GOOD. INSTEAD OF SOBER IT SAYS
LIZÉE LOL. IM STOKED. IF IT TURNS OUT AFTER IT
DRIES I THINK ILL BE MAKING MORE OF THEM. WOULD
YOU LIKE ONE? WHEN WORK IS DONE I HAVE NVC
THEN AM ENJOYING THE LONGEST HOT SHOWER I CAN.
BESIDES A SORE BACK I AM IN A PRETTY GOOD MOOD.
TONIGHT ILL DO STRETCHES AND RELAX IN MY ROOM
UNTIL I CALL YOU. ⇒ ♡ ⇒ (4PM) THE HOUSE SMELLS
OF PHÖ, I NEVER APPRECIATED PHÖ EVER IN MY LIFE...
NOW... I ABSOLUTELY LOVE IT. LIFERING (NVC) WAS
REALLY GREAT AND GAVE ME A LOT TO THINK ABOUT.
AND GAVE SOME QUESTIONS TO ASK YOU TO GET TO KNOW
YOU ON A DEEPER LEVEL. ON ANOTHER NOTE, MY ATT-
-EMPT AND BLEACHING A DESIGN ON TO A BLACK SHIRT
WAS A FUNNY SUCCESS. ITS NOT PERFECT AND THATS
WHAT MAKES IT JUST SO. I THINK IT QUITE COMMICAL
LOL. IT MUST BE DECENT BECAUSE NO ONE HAS EVEN
NOTICED IT AS OUT OF THE ORDINARY ☺. YOU CAN
HAVE IT ONCE I AM OUT IF YOUD LIKE. THERE ONLY ONE
THING PLANNED FOR THIS EVENING BESIDES A SHOWER,
AND THAT IS TO CALL MY BEST FRIEND (YOU) ⇒ ♡ ⇒
(10:36) SHOWER TIME FINALLY. TODAY WAS A GREAT DAY.
I REALLY ENJOYED OUR TALK THEN AGAIN TO SAY GOOD-
-NIGHT. WHAT A BLESSING. THE NIGHT WENT AS USUAL
THEN I CAME HOME AND MADE YOUR SHIRT. GEO WATCHED

(9)

W/ A VERY SKEPTICAL EYE QUESTIONING MY METHOD
THE ENTIRE TIME. AT THE END HE WAS SUPER SURP-
-RIZED LOL. IT IS IN THE WASH RIGHT NOW ♡. I THINK
YOULL LIKE IT ☺. ITL MOST LIKELY BE A NIGHTY
AND I BET YOULL LOST SO BEAUTIFUL IN IT TOO (DUH!)
MY HEART FILLED WHEN YOU TOLD ME YOU HAD LIST-
-ENED TO LAST NIGHTS MESSAGE AND SAVED IT. AND
THEN FILLED EVEN MORE WHEN I COULD CALL BACK
TO SAY GOODNIGHT. ALSO... SUPER EXCITED THAT
SOME PHOTOS MIGHT GET SENT (NO PRESH OR EXPEK...
HOPEFULLY YOURE SMILING RIGHT NOW) SENDING
HUGS & KISSES XOXO SWEETDREAMS SWEETGIRL. I
LOVE & MISS YOU ALL DAY ERRR'DAY ANGEL!!!
[redacted] XOX Z Z Z Z Z
Z Z Z Z Z

2022-06-21

DEAREST ANGEL. IM NOT SURE WHY I STARTED TODAYS
WRITING W/ "DEAREST ANGEL"... I DOES SOUND NICE
THOUGH. THE SWEAT WENT AWESOME AND I AM
VERY GRATEFUL TO HAVE SHARED THAT EXPERIENCE
W/ THOSE DUDES ON INDIGINEOUS DAY. IM EXCITED
TO TELL YOU ABOUT IT LATER IF YOURE NOT BUSY.
IT WAS NICE TALKING THIS MORNING AND ASKING THOSE
QUESTIONS. LEARNING ABOUT YOU MEANS SO MUCH
AND IS VERY VERY IMPORTANT TO ME. THANK YOU
FOR ALLOWING ME TO BE CLOSE ENOUGH TO YOU
THAT THOSE THING YOU FEEL SAFE SHARING. ILL
ALWAYS BE HERE FOR YOU. ⇒ ♡ ⇒ (4PM) VIDEO
VISIT PAPER IS IN FOR MONDAY. SINCE THE SWEAT
EARLIER IVE FELT SOME RELIEF AND COMPACENCY
INTERNALLY. IVE FOUND MYSELF IN A REFLECTIVE
STATE OF SORTS. AFTER HEARING OTHERS PRAY W/

10

HONESTY AND OPENESS (MYSELF INCLUDED) A SHIFT INSIDE ME HAS BEGUN ONCE AGAIN. I FEEL A CONTENTMENT AND CONFIDENCE IN MYSELF THAT I AM A GOOD PERSON WHO DESERVES TO LOVE AND BE LOVED ON ALL LEVELS. NO LONGER WILL I SECOND GUESS THE PERSON I HAVE ALWAYS BEEN, OR SHADOW IT W/ SELF DOUBT DUE TO FEAR OF REJECTION OR ABANDONMENT. BECAUSE OF SUCH FEARS I TENDED TO REJECT ME AND ABANDON ME. INSIDE THAT DARKEST OF DARK SPACES THERE SEEMED TO BE ONLY LIGHT. A LIGHT THAT WAS SHINING IN ALL 9 OF US AS WE CONNECTED TO ONE ANOTHER, TO GOD, AND TO OURSELVES. HOW AWESOME. AN ENRICHMENT OF ONE SELF & SOUL OCCURED AS POWERFUL AS EVER FELT BEFORE. WHAT WAS TAKEN AWAY FROM THIS HAS BEEN EXTREMELY VALUABLE. WHAT WAS FELT IN THAT MOMENT WILL RESONATE FOR AGES AND PASS ON TO FUTURE INTERACTIONS OF EVERY FORM. ANOTHER FIRE HAS BEEN LIT AND NOW WHATS NEEDED IS CONSTANT & CONTINUEOUS REFLECTION TO DETERMINE THE NATURE OF THE BLESSING WHICH HAS BEEN WHILE ON THIS PATH. ITS YET ANOTHER EXPERIENCE THE HIGHER POWER HAS PRESENTED DURING THE TIME INCARCERATED IN WHICH TO BE TRULY GRATEFUL FOR. ONE THAT CAN BE SHARED W/ THE ONES WHO HAVE BEEN ALONG THIS WILD RIDE W/ ME THROUGHOUT ITS ENTIRETY. TODAY WAS THE SIGN NEEDED TO CEMENT THE TIME NEEDED FROM MAY-AUGUST. SO MUCH HAS BEEN LEARNED SINCE MAY THAT WOULD HAVE MISSED ENTIRELY HAD A MOVE TO A DIFFERENT

(11)

LOCATION BEEN MADE. WHAT A LIFE WE ARE CURRENTLY LIVING. EVEN BEING VERY EMOTIONAL AND TOUGH SOMETIMES, IT COULD NOT HAVE BEEN AT A BETTER TIME. LIFE HAS MADE A COMPLETE 180° SHIFT. TO TOP IT ALL OFF IVE HAD BEEN BLESSED W/ THE CHANCE TO GET TO KNOW THE MOST INCREDIBLE AND SWEET GIRL IMAGINABLE. (YOU). VULNERABILITY HAS BECOME EMPOWERING INSTEAD OF FEAR BASED. ACCEPTANCE HAS REPLACED FEAR OF REJECTION. ASKING REAL CORE QUESTIONS TO SEE THE HEART & SOUL FROM THE HEART & SOUL HAS CHANGED FROM ASKING QUESTIONS THEN DILUTING THEM BEFORE RECEI-VING AN HONEST ANSWER OCCURS. KIND OF LIKE KISSING YOU IN MY DREAM THEN IMMEDIATELY WAKING UP BEFORE SEEING WHAT HAPPENED NEXT. THAT IS STILL OBVIOUSLY IMPRINTED IN MY SUBCONSIOUS AND THAT IS OK AS IN ACTUAL "WOKE" (SMILING? I HOPE SO) LIVING THESE THINGS ARE BECOMING FASTLY @ THE FOREFRONT OF CHANGE. ⇒♡⇒ (10:23pm) WELL ANGEL... MY HEART IS ABSOLUTELY FILLED TONIGHT IN MULTIPLE WAYS. TALKING TO MY GIRLS, EVEN THOUGH EMOTIONS RUN UP & DOWN BECAUSE OF MY ETERNAL LOVE FOR THEM, I FIND POSITIVETY AND DRIVE TOWARDS A BETTER LIFE, FRAME OF MIND, AND AWARENESS OF SELF AND OTHERS. TALKING TO YOU W/FROM MY HEART HAS OPENED A DOOR IN WHICH HEARING YOUR HEART HAS CONNECTED ME TO YOU. I TRUST YOU AND THAT SPEAKS VOLUMES. A TRUST W/OUT HESITATION OR RESERVATIONS. TO ME UMMMMM... ITS KIND OF A BIG DEAL (☺) ← NOT SURE WHY I PUT

⑫

THAT INTO BRACKETS. ALSO WHAT IMPACTED THE MOST WAS THE PURCHASE OF NON-VIOLENT COMMUNICATION (NVC). THAT IS AN ABSOLUTE HEART MELTER. IM EXCITED FOR YOU AS THAT BOOK [redacted] HELPED ME/HELPS ME GROW AND I HOPE IT GIVES YOU WHAT IT GIVES TO ME. [redacted] I FEEL BLESSED TO BE ABLE TO SHARE AND COMMUNICATE ON A DEEPER HIGHER LEVEL W/ YOU AS WE PROGRESS ON THIS JOURNEY OF GETTING TO KNOW ONE ANOTHER W/ A COMMON LANGUAGE CREATING A MUCH DEEPER BOND & CONNECTION. YOU ARE MY BEST FRIEND ANGEL AND MY LOVE FOR YOU IS GROWING/EVOLVING IN SUCH BEAUTIFUL WAYS. ♡ IN THE FUTURE I LOOK VERY MUCH FORWARD TO HOLDING YOU IN MY ARMS ONCE AGAIN, HOLDING YOUR HANDS, AND LOOKING INTO YOUR MOST GORGEOUS EYES WHILE CONNECTING. GOODNIGHT [redacted] SWEETGIRL, I LOVE YOU W/ ALL MY HEART & SOUL Z X Z O Z X Z O Z X Z O Z X Z O Z X Z O Z

2022-06-22

HELLO GORGEOUS GIRL. I AM VERY MUCH LOOKING FORWARD TO CALLING YOU AT 6PM. (4PM NOW) ONLY 2 MORE HOURS. TODAY HAS BEEN GOOD. WORK WAS SLIGHTLY BORING AS WE ARE JUST STANDING AROUND WATCHING/"LEARNING". LIFERING WAS DECENT. OUR HOUSE IS A TAD BIT AWKWARD ATM. THE WEATHER IS SUPPOSED TO BE A SCORCHER FOR THE NEXT FEW DAYS SO ILL WORK ON MY TAN SHIRTS OFF. ALL DAY MY THOUGHTS HAVE BEEN ON YOU BUYING THAT BOOK. I FUCKING ADORE YOU!!! ⇒ ♡ ⇒

(13)

(7PM) WELL THE AWKWARDESS HAS PASSED LOL. WHEN I CALLED YOU WERE AT YOUR FRIENDS HOUSE I COULD HEAR THE KIDS IN THE BACKGROUND. YOU SOUNDED SO HAPPY AUNTY ANGEL. I FELT HAPPINESS KNOWING HOW HAPPY YOU ARE AROUND KIDS. YOU'LL BE SUCH AN AMAZING MOM ONE DAY DUDE!!! TONIGHT THERES NOTHING GOING ON HERE SO MY WRITING WILL BE BOOOOOORING. I SAW THE I.P.O EARLIER AND ALL LOOKS AS IT SHOULD FOR DAY PAROLE SO FAR. ILL BE EXSTATIC TO HAVE THAT OVER DONE AND MAINTAIN BEING HUMBLE NOW, DURING, AND FOR THE REST OF MY LIFE AFTER THIS IS ALL SAID AND DONE. LIFE IS/HAS BEEN/ALWAYS WILL BE A BEAUTIFUL JOURNEY IN THESE EYES FROM HERE ON OUT. I ALSO JUST FILLED OUT A REQUEST TO MAIL YOU THE SHIRT I MADE THE OTHER NIGHT, SO FINGERS CROSSED ON THAT ⇒ (10:45) BEDTIME SWEETHEART. THANK YOU FOR ALL THE LONG CHATS RIGHT UP UNTIL BEDTIME LOCKDOWN. ALL THE TIME YOU HAVE GIVEN ME MAKES ME FEEL LOVED AND CARED FOR. I HOPE YOU TRULY KNOW EXACTLY HOW AMAZING YOU ARE ANGEL. DAY BY DAY TIME CLOSES IN UNTIL I CAN BE W/ YOU... ITS LIKE A DREAM REALITY WHERE SEEING EACHOTHER IN DREAMS BECOMES AN IN PERSON REALITY. TODAY IS DAY 240 OF MY TIME AWAY. IF GETTING TO KNOW MYSELF IN HERE HELPED GET TO KNOW YOU ON THE LEVEL ITS BECOME. WELL IT WAS WORTH IT 100%. SELF IMPROVEMENT CAN COME TO US IN VERY DIFFERENT WAYS. THIS JOURNEY HAS BEEN ONE FOR THE STORY BOOKS THAT IS PHÖ SHIZZLE (PHÖ PUN INTENDED... ALSO SORRY FOR SUBJECTING YOU TO THE PUN. I HOPE YOURE PH. OK w/ IT lol)

(14)

(TBH PLEASE DONT LAUGH AT THAT, IM EMBARASSED ITS WRITTEN AND CANT BE ERASED P.F.S ← — PHÖ. FUCK. SAKES. OK. OK ILL STOP NOW)

I LOVE YOU SO MUCH SWEETGIRL. WARM HUGS ALL NIGHT XOOXOXO♡ Z Z Z Z Z Z Z Z Z

2022-06-23

(7:30am) GREAT MORNING GORGEOUS. TODAY THE BIRDS ARE SINGING. WAKING UP THIS MORNING WAS FILLED W/ A CALM PEACE-LIKE STATE OF MIND. OUR CONVO LAST NIGHT LEFT A REAL FEELING OF BEING LOVED INSIDE. LOVE TANK FULL. I AROSE FROM BED AWAKE AND WELL RESTED HAPPY AND READY FOR ANOTHER DAY GETTING ME THAT MUCH CLOSER TO YOU!!! AS SLEEP CREPT IN LAST NIGHT HAVING YOU IN MY ARMS WAS ALL THAT I COULD THINK ABOUT. I COULD FEEL YOU AGAINST ME W/ OUR FINGERS IN ONE ANOTHERS HANDS. I HOPE YOUR SLEEP FELT THE SAME. WELL IM OFF TO WORK AND WILL CALL AT 10:30am ♡ ⇒ XO♡ ⇒ (4pm) JUST SPEECHLESS. I AM OVER THE MOON W/ HOW SPECIAL IVE BEEN MADE TO FEEL BY YOU TODAY. THERE IS NOT ENOUGH WORDS TO DESCRIBE THE HAPPINESS HAPPENING INTERNALLY & EXTERNALLY. I FUCKING ADORE YOU SWEETGIRL. YOU ARE TRULY THE SWEETEST OF GIRL AND SO MUCH MORE. EVERYTHING ABOUT YOU IS SEXY AND YOUR HEART & SOUL ARE ONE OF A KIND. MY HEART IS FOREVER YOURS ♡ ⇒ ♡ ⇒ I LOVE YOU ANGEL [redacted] ⇒ ♡ ⇒ THIS AMAZING DAY HAS COME TO AN END. THAT MOMENT TOGETHER HAS BEEN FROZEN IN TIME FOREVER. TALKING ABOUT AFTERWARD SEEMED LIKE WE FEEL/FELT THE EXACT SAME WAY.

(15)

RIGHT AT THIS MOMENT I WISH I WAS LAYING NEXT TO YOU HOLDING & KISSING YOU. BEING ABLE TO LOOK INTO THOSE MOST STUNNING EYES AND FEELING YOUR LIPS PRESSED AGAINST MINE, ~~AND~~ HAVING YOUR BODY UP AGAINST MINE, LEGS AND ARMS INTANGLED. (UMMM... YEP... HOT & BOTHERED JUST A BIT). TODAY WAS VERY SURREAL AND SPECIAL, I HOPE WE SHARE THAT MANY MORE TIMES IN THE FUTURE. I AM VERY ATTRACTED TO YOU ON ALL LEVELS SWEETGIRL. SEXY IS AN UNDER-STATEMENT. I MOVED YOUR PHOTO (THE ONE OF JUST YOU W/ NO SUNGLASSES) TO BESIDE MY BED SO I CAN LOOK AT YOU WHILE I FALL ASLEEP. FOR NOW IT IS THE CLOSEST THING I HAVE TO BEING NEXT TO YOU WHEN I FALL ASLEEP & WHEN I WAKE UP. I FEEL BLESSED TO HAVE THIS ♡. HEART MELTED FULLY!!!. GOODNIGHT SWEETGIRL... I LOVE YOU W/ ALL MY HEART Z x Z O Z x Z Z O Z x Z x Z O Z O Z♡

2022-06-24

GOOD MORNING SWEETHEART. TODAY IS AN AMAZING DAY. I FELL ASLEEP NEXT TO YOU AND WOKE UP THE SAME. YESTERDAY STILL RESONATING LEAVING A FEELING AS IF WE ARE STILL EMBRACING ONE ANOTHER. I FEEL TRULY BLESSED TO HAVE YOU IN MY LIFE. YESTERDAY FEELS LIKE A DREAM SO MUCH SO, I MAY NEED TO PINCH MYSELF A FEW TIMES TO MAKE SURE THAT WAS NOT A DREAM. WAKING UP TO THE SOUND OF NATURE, THE BRISK MORNING AIR, AND SUNSHINE GOT ME OUT OF BED AT 7AM, HALF HOUR BEFORE THE ALARM. I AM SO GRATEFUL BECAUSE OF ALL THIS AND MORE SO BECAUSE I WOKE UP TO THE

(16)

MOST BEAUTIFUL ANGELIC FACE IVE EVER SEEN.
HOPEFULLY ONE DAY WE CAN DO THAT IN PERSON.
HAVE AN AMAZING DAY FILLED W/ LOTS OF LOVE
AND I LOVE YOU SO MUCH!!! ♡XO ⟹ ♡ ⟹ (11:30AM)
HOW IS YOUR DAY? GREAT I HOPE!!! I HOPE THAT YOU
CAN FEEL ME LIKE I DO YOU. ♡ TODAY I SIGNED
MORE DAY PAROLE PAPERWORK AND THE DAYS ARE
COUNTING DOWN. AS THEY DO THE EXCITMENT
BEGINS TO SET IN. THE THOUGHT THAT YOU MIGHT
BE OUTSIDE WAITING FOR MAKES MY EMOTIONS
HIGHTENED IN SUCH POSITIVE WAYS. WORK HAS
GONE BY SO FAST ALSO HAS BEEN SUPER FUN &
FUNNY. AFTER WORK ILL GO WALK OUT BACK W/
CHARLES AND TRY TO TAN/BURN SHIRTS OFF.
MY MIND IS STILL/CONSTANTLY THINKING ABOUT
YOU, WHAT GOT US TO YESTERDAY, AND THE
CONNECTION WE SHARED/SHARE. YOU ARE VERY
BEST FRIEND DIAMOND ANGEL. (← JUST RAN
OUT ANOTHER PEN) ⟹ (4PM) WOW IT IS HOT OUT.
ITS REALLY NICE. CHARLIE & I WENT FOR A WALK
AROUND THE POND AND OUT BACK. WE TALKED
ABOUT OUR KIDS, GETTING OUT OF HERE, VISITING
EACH OTHER, ABOUT HIS RELATIONSHIP, AND I
TALKED ABOUT YOU ♡. AS I SIT HERE AND LOOK
AT THE PHOTOS YOU SENT I AM SO GRATEFUL
(THIS PEN IS ALMOST OUT FFS LOL.) NEW PEN ☺
MY SHIRT STILL SMELLS LIKE YOU AS WELL
♡XOXO♡. I CANNOT WAIT TO SEE YOU AGAIN!!!
(OR HAVE MORE & MORE PHOTOS. ILL BE KEEPING THESE W/ ME
FOREVER). ⟹ (10PM) OFFICIALLY DAY OVER. ONE
DAY CLOSER TO YOU ♡. WE TALKED ALL NIGHT
FROM 6-7 THEN 7:40-9:57. THAT REALLY MEANS

(17)

THE WORLD. THERE IS NOTHING I WANT MORE THAN TO SPEND QUALITY TIME W/ YOU. OBVIOUSLY I FEEL THE SAME ABOUT THE GIRLS [redacted], IT FILLS MY HEART WHEN YOU TALK ABOUT SPENDING TIME W/ THEM. I KNOW HOW MUCH THEY LOVE YOU. THATS THE ONLY OTHER THING ON MY PRIORITY LIST. THEM AND YOU. MY FEELINGS FOR YOU ARE GROWING STRONGER. MY SHIRT SMELLS LIKE YOU STILL AFTER TODAY ♡. I WISH IT WOULD STAY LIKE THAT UNTIL WE'RE TOGETHER AGAIN. GOODNIGHT SWEETGIRL. I WILL FOREVER BE IN LOVE W/ YOU. THANKS FOR BEING MY BEST FRIEND AND SOMEONE I TRUST AND CAN SHARE MYSELF FULLY W/. HAVING THIS PICTURE BESIDE ME AT NIGHT IS AMAZING. GORGEOUS & SEXY MORE THAN WORDS CAN DESCRIBE. ALWAYS FEEL FREE TO SEND MORE PHOTOS ♡ Z

Z x Z o Z x Z o Z x

2022-06-25

(11:08am) GREAT MORNING SO FAR MY LOVE. UP AT 7am TO HAVE COFFEE. WAKING UP NEXT TO YOU AGAIN WAS SO NICE I LOOK FORWARD TO ACTUALLY WAKING AND HAVING YOU IN MY ARMS. AT 8am I CALLED YOU BEFORE WORK. I AM VERY GLAD I DID. HEART FILLED!!!. AFTERWARDS CHARLIE WAS WOKEN UP TO GO WALKING MUAHAHAHA. HIM AND I WALKED BACK N FORTH SOCIALIZING W/ PEOPLE AS WE PASSED BY. SO FAR THE DAY HAS BEEN INCREDIBLE. WHAT A BLESSING TO HAVE BEGAN IT HEARING YOUR VOICE ♡ ⇒ ♡ ⇒ (7pm) HOW LOVELY TO TALK ONCE AGAIN FOR THAT LONG

(18)

THAT PHONE BOOTH WAS SOOOO HOT... WELLLLL WORTH IT THAT IS FOR SURE (100%(+HUNDO P)) ♡ HAVE FUN W/ [redacted] TONIGHT SEXY GIRL. IM HEADING TO N.A. TIL 8:30PM, THEN TO THE GYM UNTIL WE TALK AGAIN. ⇒♡⇒

(11PM) ANOTHER DAY OVER ☺ IT WAS VERY NICE TO HEAR [redacted] & [redacted] VOICES. IT HAS BEEN A LONG TIME. MAYBE THE 4 OF US CAN GO ON A DOUBLE DATE SOMETIME. OUR TALK WAS GREAT AS ALWAYS ♡. THE THOUGH OF US WRAPPED AROUND ONE ANOTHER ENTANGLED W/ AS MUCH SKIN SURFACE TOUCHING AS POSSIBLE. WHEN THIS HAPPENS I HOPE IT NEVER ENDS. GOOD-NIGHT SWEETGIRL. MY HEART IS YOURS ♡

x Z o Z x Z o Z x Z o Z

2022-06-26

(3:42am) HELLO MY LOVE ♡. IT WAS NICE TO LEAVE A MSSG AND TALK BRIEFLY DURING THE DAY. OUR MORNING CHAT MADE FOR AN AMAZING START TO THE DAY. THIS MORNING WE WALKED OUT BACK AFTER THE GYM. MOU HAD ME MAKE THE SHISHUKA THIS MORNING AGAIN, I CAN'T WAIT TO MAKE IT FOR YOU. AFTER THAT I WENT TO THE GYM AGAIN. I DREAM OF THE DAY YOU CAN RUN YOUR PERFECT HANDS OVER MY CHEST AS I HOLD YOU EVER SO TIGHTLY. DAYS HAVE BEEN SO BRIGHT LATELY BEING LOVED BY YOU. I CAN FEEL THE SINCERITY IN YOUR HEART. IVE NEVER TRULY FELT THIS WAY OR BEEN ABLE TO FULLY UNDERSTAND BEING LOVED BY ANOTHER PERSON. THAT HAS ALL CHANGED IN THE WAY THAT I CAN ACCEPT LOVE W/ OUT DOWN PLAYING MYSELF BECAUSE OF MY OWN INTERNAL

(19)

CONFLICTS. THOSE HAVE FADED WHICH HAS MADE
ME VULNERABLE TO YOU AND FOR THE FIRST TIME
IN MY LIFE I'AM NOT ONLY OK W/ IT. INFACT IT
FEELS AMAZING TO FINALLY HAVE LET MY GUARD
DOWN FOR THE FIRST TIME W/ OUT HESITATION
OR RESERVATION. I TRUST YOU AND YOU ARE
MY BEST FRIEND 5·13·9·12·25 !!! ♡⇒♡⇒
(10:41Pm) WORK TOMORROW. WE JUST ATE SOME
CHEESECAKE AND HAD COFFEE. IT WAS GREAT
TALKING W/ YOU SO MUCH TODAY. TOMORROW
IS VIDEO VISIT DAY. WHEN WE ENDED OUR CONVO
I COULD HARDLY WALK. TONIGHT ILL FALL
ASLEEP THINKING ABOUT YOU ON TOP OF ME
MOANING WHILE I HOLD YOU BY THE HIPS SLID-
-ING BACK N FORTH GUSHING ALL OVER ME.
GOODNIGHT SWEET GIRL. I LOVE YOU ALWAYS

I'M MAILING THIS IN THE AM. CAN YOU PLS
SEND A BUNCH MORE PICS OF YOURSELF FOR
AROUND MY BED FOR ME TO SLEEP BESIDE?
♡♡ (NO PRESH OR EXPEKT). THIS PHOTO OF YOU
IN YOUR DRESS IS GETTING "LOOKED" AT TONIGHT.
(~~IF YOU KNOW WHAT~~ (IF YOU PICK UP WHAT IM
PUTTING DOWN ☺ ♡)
SO F-ING SEXY MY LOVE. CANT WAIT TO UNDRE
-SS YOU AND FEEL ALL OF YOU. NIGHT SWEETHEART

11

Endurance

"Some days you do not rise — you just keep standing."

After a while, the noise faded into something like stillness. The same count, the same meals, the same cold mornings—they stopped feeling like punishment and started feeling like lessons. I began to see how peace could live inside repetition. It was not about change anymore. It was about presence.

Writing became a kind of prayer. I would sit with the page, breathe slow, and listen. Sometimes the words came easy, sometimes not at all. But even the silence started to mean something. I learned to thank God for small mercies—the sound of rain through the vents, a laugh from down the range, a moment where my thoughts didn't run wild.

Endurance stopped being about toughness. It became about trust. Trust that time would move the way it needed to. Trust that I was still being shaped into something better, even when I couldn't see it. Some days I didn't rise with strength, I just stayed standing—and that was enough.

(1)

2022 - 06 - 27

GOOD MORNING MY LOVE ♡ THIS MORNING IS ANOTHER BEAUTIFUL ONE. TODAY I FEEL SUCH GRATITUDE FOR EVERYTHING THAT IS UNFOLDING BETWEEN US. SOMETIMES QUICKLY SOMETIMES SLOWLY... (I KNOW YOURE THINKING THE REST LOL). WHO KNEW THAT WORKING ON MYSELF WOULD OPEN UP ALL OF THESE INCREDIBLE THINGS. AFTER OUR CALL I WAS TOLD THAT THERE IS NO WORK TODAY... SO... IM LITERALLY WAITING TO SEE YOU AT 5:15 ☺ I SAT ON THE PORCH DRINKING COFFEE AND TALKING W/ THE DUDE I WORK W/ FOR A BIT AND THEN WALKED AROUND THINKING ABOUT HOW AMAZING YOU ARE. YOU HUNDO P HAVE ALL OF MY HEART ♡. AS I SIT IN MY CHAIR LOOKING AT YOUR BEAUTIFUL FACE AND THE PIC OF YOU IN THAT SEXY DRESS I AM BESIDE MYSELF AND MAY HAVE TO "LOOK" AT IT JUST A BIT LONGER (UMMM... MORE PICS PLEASE.. NO PRESH OR ____ ... EXPEKT LOL) (DID YOU FILL IN THAT BLANK W/ EXPEKT LOL... I HOPE YOU ARE SMILING) ⟹ ♡ ⟹ (10:28) THE IS DONE ENDING IT W/ YOU IS WHAT MAKES IT COMPLETE. TOMORROW IS 1 YEAR OF SOBRIETY FOR YOU. THAT IS SO AMAZING SWEETHEART ♡ GOODNIGHT SWEETGIRL. I LOVE YOU Z Z Z Z x Z o Z x Z o Z x Z

2022-06-28

TODAY IS SUCH A BLESSING. CONGRATULATION ON 365 DAYS OF SOBER LIVING. I AM SO PROUD OF YOUR ACCOMPLISMENT AND EXTREMELY HAPPY FOR YOU. YOU ARE SUCH AN AMAZING PERSON W/ SO MANY AMAZING QUALITIES. WORDS

(2)

CANNOT DESCRIBE HOW BEAUTIFUL YOU ACTUALLY ARE INSIDE AND OUT. ITS BEEN AN ABSOLUTE BLESSING TO SEE YOU GROW AND GROW ALONG SIDE YOU/W/ YOU. I FEEL YOUR CHANGE HAS ALSO HELPED MY CHANGE. BECAUSE OF YOU AND SHARING THE TIME WE HAVE HAS BEEN THE BEST GIFT ONE COULD EVER ASK FOR. BEING LOVED AND CARED FOR BY SOMEONE AS UNIQUE AND SPECIAL AS YOU IS LIKE A VIVID DREAM THAT I HOPE NEVER ENDS. YOU DESERVE THE WORLD AND EVERYTHING GREAT IT HAS TO OFFER. YOU DESERVE TO BE LOVED & APPRECIATED & HAVE YOUR NEEDS FULFILLED ON EVERY LEVEL. TODAY I PRAY THAT YOUR LOVE TANK IS FULL, THAT COLORS ARE MORE COLORFUL, BRIGHTNESS IS BRIGHTER, AND THAT YOURE OVERFLOWED W/ LOVE & HAPPINESS. MY HEART IS FULL ~~[illegible]~~. I SEE YOUR HEART W/ ~~MINE~~ MY HEART AND I AM ALL YOURS!!! IN EVERY WAY POSSIBLE!!! ♡⟹ ♡⟹ ♡⟹ ♡⟹

(10:21pm) THE DAY IS FINALLY OVER. TODAY MY EMO-TIONS WENT UP & DOWN A BIT. I AM VERY GLAD I UNDERSTAND THEM FULLY NOW AND ACCEPT THAT IT IS OK TO HAVE FEELINGS. OUR CHAT WAS VERY NICE TONIGHT. I AM STILL PROCESSING SOME THINGS SO I AM GOING TO GO TO BED NOW. I LOVE YOU VERY MUCH SWEETGIRL Z Z Z Z XOX Z Z Z Z

2022-06-29

(10:10pm) HELLO SWEETGIRL. TODAY HAS BEEN A BIT OF AN ON & OFF DAY BUT THAT IS O.K.

(3)

THIS MORNING I FELT A BIT SAD. THAT IS BOUND TO HAPPEN OCCASIONALLY. WE CAN'T HAVE GOOD DAYS EVERY DAY. AFTER SOME REFLECTION I FOUND THAT I WAS JUST IN NEED OF SOME RE-ASSURANCE THAT I AM ON THE RIGHT PATH. I KNOW I SHOULD NOT BE IN NEED OF THAT BUT SOMETIMES WE/I NEED IT ONCE IN A BLUE MOON. WORK ENDED EARLY, AFTER 2 DAYS OF NO WORK (4 DAYS OFF W/ THE WEEKEND). MAYBE HOW I WAS FEELING DUE TO THE SHIFT IN PATTERN/SCHE-DULE. I THINK BECAUSE EVERYTHING IS SO ROUTINE IN HERE. I HAD A DRUMSTICK ICECREAM CONE AFTER WORK AND FOR A SPLIT SECOND I FORGOT WHERE I WAS. THE WEEKEND IS SOON AMONG US AND IT IS FILLING UP W/ ACTIVITIES ☺. IM SURE THEY'LL ALL GET WRITTEN ABOUT. THE GYM TODAY WAS A GREAT ONE. 5 MORE WEEKS TO REALLY GO FOR IT. THE GOAL IS SOME MORE MAJOR PROGRESSION (NOT PERFECTION LOL) OUR CHAT TONIGHT WAS VERY NICE. I APPRECIATE EVERY SINGLE SECOND OF IT. CHARLIE IS OUT OF HERE VERY SOON WHICH IS AWESOME. ONE STEP CLOSER TO HIS FAMILY. AS HAPPY AS I AM TO SEE HIM GO I AM SAD TO HAVE HIM GO AS I WILL MISS HIM VERY MUCH. HE HAS BECOME A REAL FRIEND AND ADMIRE ALL THE GROWTH HE HAS ACCOMPLISHED IN HIMSELF. I LOOK FOR-WARD TO THE DAY WE MEET AGAIN!!! I HAVE A TON OF LOVE FOR CHARLES. HE IS A GREAT PERSON. HE HAS A HEART OF GOLD AND I WOULD DO ANYTHING FOR HIM. IN LIFE WE HAVE SO MUCH TO BE APPRECIATIVE FOR AND IT MAY COME

(4)

IN THE MOST RANDOM FORMS AND RANDOM
TIMES. ITS SOMETHING THAT WILL ALWAYS
RESONATE IN ME UNTIL THE DAY I DIE.
EVERYTHING EXPERIENCED DURING THIS TIME
WILL CONSTANTLY BE A LIFELONG REMINDER
OF WHAT IT WAS LIKE, WHAT ITS LIKE NOW, AND
WHAT LIFE CAN BE IF WE WORK FOR IT. BELIEVE
ME, I WILL FOREVER WORK TOWARDS BEING A
BETTER PERSON IN EVERY WAY I CAN. LIFE
IS SO BEAUTIFUL. I KNOW SOMETIMES I CAN
BE OVERWHELMING SO ILL TONE IT DOWN FROM
NOW ON. I COULD TELL SOMETHING CHANGED
A LITTLE BIT SINCE YOU HAD THAT TALK W/
FRIEND. I DONT WANT TO PUSH YOU AWAY BUT
JUST KNOW MY FEELINGS HAVE NOT CHANGED.
I AM JUST THE TYPE OF GUY THAT WHEN I AM
IN LOVE & FEEL LOVED I BECOME ALL-IN.
BEING IN HERE HIGHTENED MY FEELINGS A BIT
AND IVE LEGIT NEVER MET SOMEONE AS UNIQUE AND
SPECIAL AS YOU ARE. WELL SWEETGIRL IT IS
BEDTIME. GOODNIGHT & I LOVE YOU SO VERY
MUCH ♡ Z X Z O Z X Z O Z X

2022-06-30

GOOD MORNING BEAUTIFUL GIRL. TODAY IS A REALLY
GREAT DAY. SO FAR... ICE CREAM BANANA CAKE,
CANTEEN, CHEESIES, AND NICORETTE GUM HAS
BEEN HAD. I APOLOGIZE FOR WAKING YOU. YOUR
VOICE SOUNDED SO SOFT & SWEET. THE S.P.O IS
WORKING ON OUR GATE PASS WHICH IS SUPER
EXCITING. ITLL BE A VERY HAPPY DAY WHEN
YOU CAN RECEIVE THEM ♡. WORK HAS BEEN GREAT
TODAY AS WELL AND GOING BY SUPER FAST.

(5)

YOU HAVE BEEN ON MY MIND ALL DAY AND YES... I AM STILL SUPER INTIMIDATED BY YOU (IN A GOOD WAY) THE WEATHER IS AMAZING TODAY W/ A SLIGHT COOL BREEZE, RANDOM CLOUDS, AND LOADS OF SUNSHINE. THE GEECE ARE EVERYWHERE AND THEIR YOUNG GOSLINGS ARE GETTING BIG VERY FAST. THE GRASS HERE HAS ALL BEEN FRESHLY CUT MAKING THE AIR SMELL GREAT. AFTER WORK CHARLIE & I ARE GOING TO WALK AND TAN OUT BACK RIGHT LIFERING DOMAINS. I CHERISH THE LITTLE TIME THERE IS LEFT TO SPEND W/ HIM AS HIM BEING GONE HAS BEEN ON MY MIND & HEART A LOT LATELY. EVERY SO OFTEN THROUGHOUT THE DAY I GET HEART SHOTS OF EMOTIONS AS THE TIME COUNTS DOWN. I GET EXCITED, ANXIOUS, HAPPY, AND SOMETIMES SAD AS LIFE HAS CHANGED SO MUCH. AS I READY MYSELF TO RE-EMERGE INTO THE WORLD AGAIN I WONDER HOW I WILL FEEL. ALL I KNOW IS THAT I AM ON THE RIGHT PATH. MY FEELINGS FOR YOU ARE CONSTANTLY GROWING AND I CANT WAIT TO SEE YOU & THE GIRLS AGAIN. WALKING OUT OF HERE TO THE ABSOLUTE MOST WONDERFUL PERSON IVE EVER MET/KNOWN. (FYI I AM GOING TO CRY ON THAT DAY TEARS OF JOY OBVIOUSLY) THANK FOR BEING MY VERY SPECIAL/BEST FRIEND ANGEL AND I HOPE YOU KNOW EXACTLY JUST HOW AMAZING & SPECIAL YOU ARE!!! ♡ ⟹ ♡ ⟹ (4PM) TODAYS LIFERING WAS VERY DIFFICULT. WE TALKED ALL ABOUT OUR CHILDHOODS WHICH IS HARD FOR ME. ESPECIALLY WHEN IT COMES TO THE RELATIONSHIP I HAD W/ MY DAD. A LOT OF STUFF CAME TO THE

⑥

SURFACE. SOME OF IT I SHARED WHILE OTHER PARTS WOULD HAVE BEEN WAY TOO TOUGH. SOME STUFF, WHEN I THINK OR TALK ABOUT IT MAKES MY EYES WELL UP W/ TEARS, AND I CHOKE UP TO A POINT THAT WORDS WON'T COME OUT W/OUT CRYING. AS MUCH AS THOSE MEMORIES CAUSE A GREAT DEAL OF PAIN, I AM GRATEFUL TO REFLECT UPON THEM. I TOLD CHARLES THAT I LOVE HIM LIKE A BROTHER AND HOW I FELT ABOUT HIM. HE FELT THE SAME. THIS NEXT MONTH IS GOING TO TOUGH BUT ALSO VERY EXCITING. WHILE I WAS AT LIFERING MY NAME GOT CALLED TO VISITS. THE LADY TOLD ME MY DADS VISITS/VIDEO HAS BEEN APPROVED EARLIER SHE HAD TOLD ME THE PAPERWORK HAD BEEN LOST. ONCE IT HAD BEEN FOUND SHE RUSHED IT THROUGH. WHEN MY NAME GOT CALLED I RAN THERE THINKING IT WAS YOU. EVEN THOUGH IT WASNT I WAS STILL STOKED ON THE NEWS. NEXT WEEK MY DAD AND I WILL FINALLY SEE ONE ANOTHER FOR THE FIRST TIME IN 8 MONTHS ♡ ☺. WELL SWEETGIRL IT IS NOW TIME FOR A SHIRTS OFF WALK W/ CHARLIE UNTIL I CALL YOU ♡ ⟹ ♡ ⟹ GOODNIGHT SWEETGIRL

Z Z Z Z Z

2022-07-01 (5 WEEKS LEFT)

HAPPY CANADA DAY!!! I HOPE YOUR DAY IS AMAZING DUDE. WE HAD A HUGE CHINESE BRUNCH MADE FOR US WHICH WAS SIIIIIIICK!! THE WEATHER IS AWESOME. TONIGHT IS OUR POTLUCK, A.A, AND THE GYM (IF IM NOT TOO FULL LOL). ANYHOW I JUST WANT YOU TO KNOW THAT I LOVE YOU TONS ⟹

⟹ ♡ ⟹

(7)

SO FAR TODAY HAS BEEN GREAT. POTLUCK WAS AMAZING, A.A WAS GOOD AS ALWAYS, SUNTAN IS GOING TO SET IN NICELY (A.K.A THOURGHLY BURNT), HEADING TO THE GYM IN AN HOUR FOR A MON-STROUS CHEST WORKOUT, THEN IM LOOKING FORWARD TO TALKING TO YOU FOR A BIT. THE WEATHER HAS BEEN PHENOMENAL TODAY SO FAR AND THIS BEAUTIFUL WEEKEND HAS JUST BEGUN. TODAY THE GIRLS WENT TO A PARADE AND A PETTING ZOO. THEY WERE SO EXCITED TO HOLD ANIMALS AND RIDE A MINI PONY FOR THE VERY FIRST TIME. IT MELTED MY HEART TO HEAR THEM TALK ABOUT IT. I CALLED MY GOOD FRIEND DOUGY WHICH WAS NICE. HE SAID HE MISSED ME AND WILL COME VISIT ME AT [redacted] AS SOON AS I TELL HIM HE CAN. HIM AND I HAVE BEEN FRIENDS FOR OVER 15 YEARS NOW. HES LIKE A BROTHER I ALWAYS WANTED BUT NEVER HAD. ITLL BE SUPER NICE TO CHILL AND CATCH UP W/ HIM LATE NEXT MONTH ☺

⇒ ♡ ⇒ ♡ ⇒ WELL GORGEOUS GIRL ITS THAT TIME ONCE AGAIN. OUR CHAT TONIGHT WAS A REALLY GOOD ONE. I FEEL CONFIDENT THAT WE ARE HEADED IN THE RIGHT DIRECTION OF COMMUN-ICATION. I APPRECIATE YOU SO MUCH [redacted] ♡ GOODNIGHT SWEETGIRL. I LOVE YOU VERY MUCH

Z ♡xo Z ♡xo Z ♡xx Z ♡xo Z ♡xo

2021-07-02

GREAT MORNING GORGEOUS GIRL. AS I SIT DOWN TO WRITE ABOUT THE MORNING SO FAR I LOOK AT A PHOTO OF A GIRL W/ THE MOST BEAUTIFUL FACE IVE EVER SEEN. HER EYES ARE ABSOLUTELY

(8)

STUNNING (HEART MELTING). I LOVE THIS PERSON DEARLY♡!!! THIS MORNING CHARLES AND I HAD COFFEE THE WENT AND PLAYED BEACH VOLLEY BALL. IT HAS BEEN 20+ YEARS FOR ME SINCE IVE PLAYED AND IT WAS FUN AF. NOW WE AWAIT COUNT CLEAR AT NOON AND ILL FINISH THE HOUSE CLEANING. TODAY IS BRIGHT W/ A SLIGHT BREEZE ROLLING DOWN FROM THE MOUNTAINS IN THE DISTANCE. AS TIME PASSES US BY I LONG FOR MOMENTS LOST TO BE RE-GAINED W/ A COMPLETELY CHANGED PERSPECTIVE & LEASE ON LIFE. THE FUTURE IS VERY PROMISING. I AM EXCITED TO FACE THE CHALLENGES LIFE WILL BRING, FACING THEM ALL W/ POSITIVITY & ACCEPTANCE. THE PASSION BUILDING UP IS AMAZING AND THE FEELINGS OF HAPPINESS SETS IN CONSTANTLY W/ EVERY BREATH (EVEN IN TOUGH TIMES). BREATHE IN & BREATHE OUT, THEN OPEN THE HEART AND SOUL AND REPEAT. ⟹♡⟹♡⟹ WELL IT IS ALMOST 4PM. BBQ IS WARMING UP AND ALL THE FIXINGS ARE PREPPED AND READY TO GO. EVERYONE IN THE HOUSE IS HAPPY, LAUGHING, AND SET FOR THIS FEAST. HOW IS YOUR DAY? AS USUAL YOU HAVE BEEN IN MY THOUGHTS CONSTANTLY. CANT WAIT TO CALL YOU AT 9PM ⟹♡⟹ SO. THERE IS DESTINYS CHILD & TLC... BEYONCÉ HERSELF MAY BE BIGGER THAN THE SPICE GIRLS (SG) ON HER OWN, BUT... HER BAND NOT SO MUCH. TLC WAS ONLY BIG FOR ONE ALBUM AND BECAUSE LEFT EYE DIED.. HOWEVER.. NOT IN THE SAME BALL FIELD AS SG... BESIDES—

(9)

THEM THERES NOT ANY OTHER GIRLS BAND WHO CAME CLOSE... VERDICT IS SPICE GIRLS FOR THE WIN LMAO... CHARLIE & I TALKED ABOUT IT AND THATS WHAT WE CAME UP W/. YOU AND YOUR BRO SOUNDED LIKE YOU WERE HAVING FUN ♡. TONIGHT WE PLAYED 3 GAMES OF BEACH VOLLEYBALL AND HAD SOME ICE CREAM VANILLA BANANA CAKE... THAT SHIT WAS BANANAS B.A.N.A.N.AS (IF YOU THE SONG THEN IM SURE YOU SANG IT AND ARE SMILING BEAUTIFULLY ♡) FOR THE REST OF TONIGHT ITS T.V. & LAYING DOWN. I MISSED YOU TODAY. THE DAY WAS AWESOME AND WENT BY FAST W/ A TON OF ACTIVITIES. TOMORROW WILL MOST LIKELY BE THE SAME. I WISH I COULD BE AT YOUR CAKE ANGEL AND AM SO INCREDIBLY PROUD OF YOU AND PROUD TO KNOW YOU/ GETTING THE CHANCE TO KNOW YOU ♡!!! TOMORROW WILL BE SUCH A BEAUTIFUL EXPERIENCE/MOMENT FOR YOU SWEETHEART. GOODNIGHT TO YOU THE SWEETEST MOST AMAZING PERSON IVE EVER MET. I TRULY DO LOVE YOU MORE THAN ONE PERSON COULD POSSIBLY LOVE ANOTHER PERSON. ♡ ♡ ♡ ♡ ♡ ♡ ♡ ♡ ♡ ♡ ♡ I CANNOT WAIT TO HOLD YOU IN MY ARMS AGAIN

Z Z Z Z Z Z

2022-07-03

HELLO LOVELY GIRL. WHAT A GREAT MORNING (BESIDES THE RAIN). I WAS SO EXCITED TO BEGIN THIS DAY W/ YOU. I HOPE YOUR CAKE IS AMAZING, IM SURE IT WILL BE. WHAT A WONDERFUL MOMENT IN YOUR LIFE ANGEL SO FAR TODAY CHARLIE, JESSE, AND I SAT ON THE PATIO DRINKING COFFEE AND LAUGHING. AFTER COUNT

(10)

AT 11am ITS SHOWER TIME. AT NOON I AM DOING A HEAD SHAVE AND BEARD TRIM WHICH IS ALWAYS FUN. I REALLY ENJOY DOING IT AND THE DUDE IS VERY APPRECIATIVE. I WILL BE SENDING YOU LOVE ALL DAY TODAY. ONCE AGAIN AS I SIT HERE AND GAZE AT THE STUNNING PHOTOS OF YOU I CAN FEEL YOUR LOVE ♡♡ ⇒ ♡ ⇒ ♡ (10:21pm) SO LOVELY TO HEAR YOUR VOICE ANGEL. YOUR DAY SOUNDED SO VERY BEAUTIFUL IN EVERY WAY. YOU DESERVE IT IN EVERY WAY. THIS WORLD NEEDS MORE OF YOUR HEART SHINING ON IT. GETTING TO KNOW YOU AND FALLING IN LOVE W/ YOU HAS BEEN AN ABSOLUTE PLEASURE. HAVING SOMEONE AS SPECIAL AS YOU IN MY LIFE HAS TAUGHT ME SO MUCH ABOUT LIFE, LOVE, & COMMUNICATION, NOT TO MENTION EVERYTHING ELSE THAT HAS BEEN EXPERIENCED ALONG OUR JOURNEY TOGETHER SO FAR. I LOVE YOU W/ ALL MY HEART ANGEL [redacted]. GOODNIGHT SWEETGIRL. YOU ARE BEAUTIFUL IN EVERY WAY!!! ♡xox♡ Z Z Z Z Z ♡ Z ♡ Z ♡ Z ♡ Z

2022-07-04

GOOD MORNING BEAUTIFUL GIRL. THE BOSSES NO SHOWED ONCE AGAIN SO NO WORK. THE INSTITUTION IS AWAITING A LOAD OF SAND SO US VOLUNTEERS CAN MAKE SAND ~~FOR~~ BAGS FOR THE LOCAL AREAS FOR FLOOD PREVENTION. OTHER THAN THAT THE C.A. FORM HAS BEEN SUBMITTED AND WE HAVE DONE THE MORNING SMUDGE/CLEANSE CEREMONY. THE WEATHER IS SLIGHTLY MIST LIKE RAIN AND FULL OVERCAST. I HOPE YOUR BEAUTIFUL DAY YESTERDAY

(11)

HAS OVERFLOWED INTO TODAY. YOU DESERVE ALL
THAT YOUR BEAUTIFUL HEART & SOUL DESIRES. I AM
NOT SURE WHAT THE REST OF THIS DAY HAS IN
STORE BUT IM SURE YOULL HEAR OR READ ABOUT
IT. I LOVE & ADORE YOU DIAMOND ANGEL. ⇒♡
⇒♡⇒ WELL... THE VOLLEYBALL GAME DIDNT
HAPPEN SO I CAME HOME AND HAD A LONG HOT SHO-
-WER. I THOUGHT ABOUT PRESSING YOU UP AGAINST
THE WALL AND PULLING YOUR HIPS UP TO MINE
W/ MY HAND ON YOUR LOWER BACK AND ONE PULL-
-ING YOUR HAIR TIGHT WHILE I KISSED YOUR NECK
AND LIPS, THEN BITTING YOUR LOWER LIP SOFTLY.
THEN HAVING YOU TURN AROUND AND BACK INTO ME
WHILE I MANHANDLED YOUR HIPS BACK AND FORTH
AS I THROB INSIDE YOU. ILL GRIP YOUR BODY SO TIGHT
W/ MY HANDS AND HEAVY PET YOU UP AND DOWN.
ID WRAP MY ARMS OVER YOUR SHOULDER AND
AROUND YOUR STOMACH PULLING YOUR SHOULDERS
INTO MY CHEST AND PUSH AS DEEP INTO AS I CAN
UNTIL ITS TIME TO MOVE TO THE BED STILL WET AND
LICK YOU UNTIL YOU CUM. WHAT WOULD WE DO NEXT?
IM GOING TO READ THIS TO YOU IN THE A.M. ILL
BE FANTASIZING ABOUT YOU BEFORE I FALL AS-
-LEEP TONIGHT. YOU TURN ME ON SO MUCH. FUCK
YOU ARE SO INCREDIBLY SEXY!!! ♡ GOODNIGHT
SWEETGIRL. I LOVE YOU ♡ Z Z Z
Z ♡ Z ♡ Z ♡ Z ♡

2022-07-05

GREAT MORNING BEAUTIFUL GIRL. IT WAS AWESOME
TO HEAR YOUR VOICE THIS MORNING. TODAY IS
FULL EVEN THOUGH MY BOSSES NO SHOWED ONCE
AGAIN. CIRCLE EARLIER, SAND BAGS AT 2PM, N.A.

(12)

AT 5:30PM, GYM AFTERWARDS UNTIL 7PM, SEE YOU AT 7:45PM (HIGHLIGHT OF THE DAY), THEN EITHER CALL YOU AFTER, GO TO THE GYM, OR PLAY BEACH VOLLEYBALL, THE "THINK" ABOUT YOU BEFORE SLEEPTIME (AND ALSO ACTUALLY THINK ABOUT YOU AND LOOK AT YOUR PHOTOS). (← HOPEFULLY YOURE SMILING & BLUSHING) ⇒♡⇒♡⇒ TONIGHT WAS INCREDIBLE. THE GYM WAS CRAZY AS IT HAS BEEN TAKEN TO YET ANOTHER LEVEL OF INTENSITY HAVING A LONG VIDEO CHAT W/ YOU WAS VERY REFRESHING AND DEFINATELY A HEART WARMER. TALKING ON THE PHONE AFTERWARDS VERY CALMING AND SERENE. SOON WE WILL BE IN EACHOTHERS ARMS. WE WILL BE ABLE TO CONNECT INTENSLY GRINDING ONE ANOTHER. PRESSED UP AGAINST EACH-OTHER W/ AS MUCH SKIN SURFACE TOUCHING AS POSSIBLE. HOT N HEAVY AS WE REMOVE OUR CLOTHES ONE PIECE AT A TIME EXPLORING EVERY SINGLE INCH W/ OUR HANDS AND MOUTHS. W/ YOUR LEGS WRAPPED AROUND ME PULLING ME IN WHEN YOURE READY, I WILL PLANK OVER TOP OF YOU AS YOU FEEL MY ARMS, CHEST, AND BACK, PULLING ME W/ YOUR HEELS UNTIL I AM DEEP INSIDE YOU. SLOWLY BACK N FORTH SO WE CAN FEEL EVERY BIT OF THE CONNECTION. ILL RUN MY HANDS UP AND DOWN YOUR CHEST, RIBS, HIPS, AND UP YOUR LEGS AS YOU SQUEEZE ONTO ME. KISSING AND LOOKING AT EACHOTHER. AFTER YOU CUM ALL OVER ME ILL PULL YOU ON TOP OF ME. ♡ ITS YOUR TURN TO TELL ME WHAT YOULL DO NEXT ♡. ♡

GOODNIGHT SWEETGIRL. I LOVE YOU. Z Z

Z Z Z Z

12

Always & Forever

"Love doesn't end — it just changes shape."

I stopped counting the days. Not because I forgot, but because they didn't own me anymore. The clock still ticked, the doors still clanged, but time lost its edge once I stopped fighting it. What mattered was how I spent it—who I thought of, what I wrote, how I carried myself when nobody was watching.

Love became something different in there. It was no longer about touch or presence. It was about the people who changed me and the lessons that stayed. She did that for me. So did my girls. They gave me a reason to stay soft in a place built to turn men hard. Even on the loneliest nights, when the lights buzzed and the air felt heavy, I could still feel them close, like a pulse I carried inside.

By the end, I had learned more from the quiet than I ever did from the noise. I learned that patience is strength, that silence can be a kind of peace, and that love can reach through anything, even concrete and time. The cell didn't take those things from me—it showed me how deep they ran.

I do not know what waits beyond the walls, but I know who I am because of them. Not perfect. Not fixed. Just real. And that's enough. Because the love that made it this far, the love that kept me breathing and believing, is still here.

(1)

2022-07-06

(4PM) WORK IS DONE, LIFEGING IS DONE, DAY IS DONE. I HUNDO P CHERISH BEGINNING THE MORNING OFF HEARING YOUR VOICE. AFTER COUNT VOLLEYBALL IS HAPPNIN'. THERES NOT A LOT GOING ON TONIGHT AND AS USUAL I AM PASSING TIME AND WAITING TO CALL YOU. AT 530PM. I WILL CALL THE GIRLS TO ASK THEM ALL ABOUT SUMMER CAMP WHICH IS SOMETHING TO LOOK FORWARD TO ☺ ⇒ ♡ ⇒ ♡ ⇒ OMG (AND YES I JUST USED "OMG" LOL) WHEN I CALLED THE GIRLS YOU WERE W/ THEM. MY HEART INSTANTLY MELTED. YOU TRULY ARE THE MOST BEAUTIFUL PERSON IN THIS WORLD. AFTERWARDS I PLAYED VOLLEYBALL FOR 2 OR SO HOURS AND WAITED TO CALL YOU ⇒ I WONT BE SAYING GOODNIGHT AS IM WRITING THIS LAST BIT AT 7:16AM JULY 7TH DUE TO BEING SO TURNED ON AFTER OUR CALL I CAME STRAIGHT HOME AND "HANDLED" IT (GET IT... "HANDLED"! I HAD A "HANDSOME" LOL I HOPE YOURE LAUGHING OUT LOUD ♡) SO. HOT

2022-07-07 (MY MOMS BDAY)

GOOD MORNING SWEETGIRL. I LOVE YOU ♡ ⇒ ♡ ⇒ (11PM) LUNCHTIME. I AM GLAD I WAS ABLE TO CALL YOU. THE BOSS SAID WE WOULD STAY UNTIL LUNCH COUNT, UMMMM NOO ... I HAD SOMEONE VERY VERY VERY IMPORTANT TO CALL!!! SO I WORKED SO FAST WE FINISHED 30MINS OF WORK IN 10 MINS, THEN I RAN TO THE PHONE ☺ ♡. NO ITS JUST WAIT TIL NOON TO GO BACK AND WORK ⇒ ♡ ⇒ ♡ ⇒ WHAT A BUSY DAY ☺ JASON

(2)

AND I CRUSHED WORK THIS AFTERNOON. THE INSTITUTION BROUGH IN A VOLUNTEER TO LIFE--RING TODAY, EVERYONE INCLUDING THE S.P.O WAS SUPER STOKED. IT MEANS ANOTHER TURN--ING POINT FOR DIFFERENT OUTLETS/SOURCES TO SOBRIETY FOR INMATES HERE. AFTER LIFERING AT 7:45Pm MY DAD AND I HAD OUR FIRST VIDEO VISIT IN 8 MONTHS. ALSO THE FIRST TIME SEEING ONE ANOTHER. MAN O MAN HIS HAIR TURNED WHITE. AT 8:30 CHARLES AND ME HIT THE GYM. I DID LEGS, BACK, AND LOTS OF SKIP ROPE... THEN THE BEST PART OF THE EVENING WAS THE OPPO--RTUNITY TALK TO THE LOVELIEST PERSON I KNOW... YOU!!! WEDNESDAY IS COMING SOON.. SOOOO EXCITING. ALSO... YOU TOLD ME SOME MORE PHOTOS ARE COMING. ☺ ♡ YOUR VOICE TONIGHT WAS SO CALM & SOFT IT WARMED MY HEART FULLY. WHEN YOU ANSWERED W/ "HELLO MY LOVE" MY HEART OVERFLOWED. I CAN FEEL THAT YOU LOVE ME AS MUCH AS I DO YOU♡. TONIGHT AS SLEEP SETS IN AND AFTER MY PRAYERS I WILL IMAGINE YOUR BODY AGAINST MINE CUDDLING WHILE WE MAKE EACH OTHER LAUGH. GOODNIGHT SWEETGIRL, I LOVE YOU W/ ALL MY HEART!!! ♡ Z Z Z Z Z Z Z Z

2022-07-08

(6:45Am) GOOD MORNING LOVE OF MY LIFE. TODAY IS A GREAT DAY. THE WEATHER IS/LOOKS MILD W/ ALL DIFFERENT KIND OF CLOUDS IN THE PATCHY BLUE SKY. THE BIRDS ARE WHISTLING/CHIRPING AND

(3)

FAINT SOUNDS OF AIRPLANES PASS BY OCCASSIONA-
-LLY. MY CUP IS FILLED W/ BLACK COFFEE (A.K.A.
JET FUEL LOL) WAITING TO COOL DOWN SO IT CAN
BE CONSUMED (← I USED "CONSUMED" BECAUSE I WAS
NOT SURE IF "DRANK" OR "DRUNK" ~~WAS~~ SHOULD BE
USED, OR WHICH TO USE LOL). WAKING UP AND
BEING ABLE TO LOOK AT YOUR FACE VERY FIRST
TO BEGIN THE DAY ALWAYS FILLS MY HEART
W/ HAPPINESS & LOVE. ITS A FUNNY THING TO
BE INCARCERATED BUT HAPPIER AND FULL IN
EVERY WAY LIKE NEVER BEFORE. JUST FOR
TODAY, I WILL KEEP LOVE & ACCEPTANCE IN MY
HEART AND BE GRATEFUL FOR LIVING GODS
WILL AND NOT MY OWN. JUST FOR TODAY I
WILL SHOW COMPASSION & UNDERSTANDING
TOWARDS OTHERS AND MYSELF... AND JUST FOR
EVERYDAY FOR THE REST OF MY LIFE I WILL
UNCONDITIONALLY LOVE YOU ANGEL W/ ALL
MY HEART & SOUL ♡♡⇒♡⇒ (11Am) WORK IS
COMPLETE ☺ OUR BOSS WAS SO HAPPY HE GAVE US
THE AFTERNOON OFF. WHAT AN AMAZING START
TO THE WEEKEND AND ANOTHER DAY CLOSER TO
HOLDING YOU ♡. I HOPE YOUR DAY IS GREAT AND
GOES EXEPTIONALLY WELL. I LOVE YOU ANGEL!!!
⇒♡⇒♡⇒♡⇒ (7pm) COUNT TIME... THEN
I GET TO CALL YOU, SWEETHEART. EARLIER I HIT
THE GYM, CHILLED W/ CHARLES, AND A BUNCH OF
US PLAYED VOLLEYBALL FOR 2 HOURS. TODAY
WENT BY SO QUICKLY. NOW FOR THE BEST PART
OF EVERY DAY... YOU!!! ♡. I'VE THOUGHT ABOUT
YOU ALOT TODAY, ALSO LOOKED AT YOUR PHOTOS
... MY HEART IS SO CONTENT & FULL ♡♡♡♡♡

(4)

⇒♡⇒♡⇒ (10PM) JUST GOT OFF THE PHONE W/ YOU..... UMMM... SPEECHLESS. THAAAAAT WAS UNNNNNNNREAL!!! I WILL BE IMAGINING EXACTLY WHAT WE TALKED ABOUT!!! I HOPE YOU "FINISH" HARD & WET AF. GOODNIGHT SWEETGIRL. YOU ARE EXTREMELY SEXY.. I LOVE YOU MORE THAN WORDS♡ Z Z Z Z Z Z Z Z

2022-07-09

GOOD MORNING MY LOVE. I HOPE YOUR EVENING WAS AS AMAZING AS MINE (IF YOURE PICKING UP WHAT IM PUTTING DOWN 😛). I WISH YOU AN AWESOME DAY. THIS A.M. I MADE COFFEE AT 7AM, LEFT THE HOUSE, WENT AND PULLED CHARLIES CURTAINS DOWN LETTING LIGHT INTO HIS DARK ROOM (MUAHAHA), THE WOKE ROB AND CHILLED ON THE PATIO UNTIL NOW (11AM). IM NOT SURE WHAT TODAY HOLDS BUT I AS USUAL AWAITING OUR CALL AT 6PM. ♡⇒ (I LOVE) ♡⇒ (YOU) ♡⇒ I LOVE YOU SO MUCH♡ TONIGHT WE ATE SO MUCH MEXICAN FOOD MM MMM... N.A WENT WELL AND AS ALWAYS REALLY REFRESHING. CHARLES AND I HIT THE GYM FOR AN HOUR THEN WE TALKED BRIEFLY. YOU MENTIONED YOU HAD A HEADACHE. SOON ILL BE ABLE TO TAKE OF YOU AND BE YOUR SUPPORT WHEN YOURE NOT FEELING WELL. I WOULD DIM ALL THE LIGHTS AND PUT A MOVIE ON THAT MIGHT CALM YOU. THEN I WOULD EVER SO GENTLY RUB MY HANDS ALONG YOUR BACK AND SIDES UNTIL YOU FELL ASLEEP. ID BE SO ATTENTIVE TO ALL YOUR NEEDS IN ANY WAY YOU NEEDED. YOU DESERVE TO BE TAKEN CARE OF WHEN

(5)

YOURE NOT FEELING WELL. I WOULD DO ANYTHING AND EVERYTHING NEEDED TO SOOTHE YOUR DISCOMFORT IN A HEARTBEAT. ILL ALWAYS BE HERE FOR YOU MY LOVE!!! GOODNIGHT SWEET GIRL AND I UNCONDITIONALLY LOVE YOU W/ ALL MY HEART ♡. ♡. ♡. ♡ ♡ ♡ ♡ ♡ ♡ ♡ ♡
(THESE ONE LOOK ↗ ↗ ↗ KINDA FUNNY)

Z x Z O Z x Z O

2022-07-10

GOOD MORNING MY LOVE. THIS MORNING HAS BEEN SERENE AND REFLECTIVE. I AWOKE AT 7AM THINKING ABOUT YOU AND ~~YOU~~ HOW YOU MIGHT BE FEELING, AND IF IT WASN'T WELL DUE TO YOUR HEADACHE, HOW I MIGHT BE OF SERVICE TO YOUR NEEDS. I SAT ON THE PATIO AND WATCHED THE SPRINKLER I SET OUT WATER THE LAWN AND READ MY BOOK. CHAPTER 9 (NVC) AS I HIGHLIGHTED CERTAIN AREAS THAT HIT HOME I PONDERED LIFE AND ALL THE THINGS PUT IN THIS JOURNEY THAT HAVED HELPED MY GROWTH AS A HUMAN BEING. I HAVE AN INCREDIBLE AMOUNT OF LOVE & APPRECIATION FOR YOU AND THE TIME YOU'VE SET ASIDE FOR ME DURING ALL OF THIS ♡ YOU ARE EVERYTHING TO ME SWEETGIRL ♡. AS I SAT THERE PASSERS-BY STOPPED BY TO CHAT. I FIND DEEP APPRECIATION FOR THIS "PRISON" AS PRISON HAS IN ITS OWN WAY SET ME FREE ⟹ ♡ ⟹ ♡ ⟹ DURING BEING SET FREE I FOUND THE LOVE OF MY LIFE (YOU). ⟹ ♡ ⟹ ♡ ⟹ (4PM) WELL MY LOVE... JUST TALKED FOR AN HOUR & A HALF W/ YOU ... UNBELIEVABLY SEXY... LEGIT THE BEST PHONE CALL I'VE EVER HAD IN MY LIFE [redacted] (HUBBA HUBBA)

(6)

I THINK WE WILL BOTH REMEMBER THAT CALL FOR THE REST OF OUR LIVES ♡♡♡ xox... ⇒♡⇒♡⇒

HELLO LOVE... TONIGHT WAS CALM & QUIET WHICH WAS NICE. I ENJOYED OUR GOODNIGHT CHAT ONCE AGAIN. NOW IT IS TIME FOR BED. GOOD-NIGHT BEAUTIFUL BEAUTIFUL GIRL. I LOVE & APPRECIATE SO MUCH MORE THAN I THINK YOU KNOW. I LOOK FORWARD TO SHOWING MY FEEL-INGS TO YOU IN PERSON IN THE VERY CLOSE FUTURE. GOODNIGHT SWEETIE ♡♡♡♡♡♡

x Z x O Z x O Z x O Z x

2022-07-11

GOOD MORNING MY LOVELY ANGEL. I HOPE TODAY IS FULFILLED W/ LOVE & HAPPINESS ♡. MY DAY HAS BEEN. IM VERY EXCITED TO SEE YOUR MOST BEAUTIFUL FACE IN 2 DAYS ♡. WORK HAS BEEN DECENT SO FAR TODAY WHICH IS GOOD. ♡⇒♡⇒♡⇒ WELL THIS DAY IS DONE. IT WAS UNEVENTFUL (OTHER THAN A BABY CROW FALLING FROM IT NEST IN OUR YARD) AND CASUAL. GOOD-NIGHT SWEET GIRL I LOVE YOU ♡♡♡♡♡

Z x O Z x O Z x O Z x O Z

2022-07-12

(4PM) GOOD AFTERNOON SWEETHEART. TODAY HAS BEEN PASSING QUICKLY. I PRESSURE WASHED AT WORK ALL DAY. AFTERWARDS I DROPPED YOUR SHIRTS OFF FOR TOMORROW ☺ ♡. I AM SO INCREDIBLY HAPPY TO SEE YOU TOMORROW. I FUCKING LOVE YOU!!! ♡⇒♡⇒ (7) HOW IS YOUR NIGHT/TIME IN THE CITY? TONIGHT HAS BEEN EXCEPTIONALLY CHILL THUS FAR. MOU MADE STEW & RICE, SIMON & I WENT FOR A WALK AND NOW AM JUST WAITING

(7)

TO THE GIRL WHO HAS MY HEART (YOU). THIS EVENING ILL CHILL W/ BIG ROB & PLAY VOLLEY BALL UNTIL OUR CALL. MY HEART IS SO FULL ATM AND EXCITED TO PRESS AGAINST YOURS ONCE AGAIN ♡ ⟹ ♡ ⟶ TONIGHT I WAITED TO CALL YOU. YOU WERE FEELING UPSET DUE TO YOUR FRIEND BEING UPSET. AT THE END OF THE CONVO I WAS TOLD ABOUT YOUR NEED FOR REASSURANCE. I ALSO HAVE THAT SAME NEED. I WILL ALWAYS PAY THE UTMOST ATT-ENTION TO ALL YOUR NEEDS AS IT IS VERY IMPORTANT NOT JUST AS FRIENDS BUT FUTURE PARTNERS IN LIFE. I WANT TO BE W/ YOU FOR A VERY LONG TIME AND CONTINUE TO GROW INDIVIDUALLY AND TOGETHER ON EVERY LEVEL. I WANT TO PERSERVERE THROUGH LIFE AS A TEAM & ALSO A BEST FRIENDS FOREVER (I WOULDVE WROTE B.F.F BUT I DIDNT WANT IT TO BE TAKEN AS A JOKE BECAUSE I DO MEAN IT FOR REAL) I AM IN THIS FOR KEEPS AND AM RESERVED FOR ONLY YOU. I AM INTIMIDATED BY YOU (IN A GOOD WAY) AND AM ALSO DEVOTED TO YOU MENTALLY, PHYSICALLY, & SPIRITUALLY AND THAT WILL NOT CHANGE. YOU ARE EVERTHING TO ME ANGEL AND I TRULY HOPE THAT YOU ACTUALLY FEEL IT DEEP IN YOUR HEART. MY HEART IS ALL YOURS AND EVEN THOUGH IT LEAVES ME VULNERABLE TO YOU (WHICH SOMETIMES TERIFIES ME) I CHOOSE TO OPEN MYSELF W/ OUT RESERVATION TO YOU AND HOPE YOU FEEL THE SAME. I WILL BE FOREVER GRATEFUL FOR YOUR FRIENDSHIP.

(8)

IM DEDICATED TO MEETING YOUR NEEDS AND BEING WHAT YOU DESERVE BY BEING EXACTLY WHO I AM AND WHAT I AM ABOUT. I CANNOT TELL YOU IN WORDS AND WILL SHOW YOU EVEN IF IT TAKES 100 YEARS. I CANT TAKE AWAY YOUR WORRIES W/ WORDS AND I ASSURE YOU IT IS MY ACTIONS THAT WILL SOLIDIFY AND INCOMPASS EXACTLY HOW MY FEELINGS ARE FOR YOU. I TRULY DO LOVE YOU MORE THAN YOU CAN IMAGINE. I KNOW THIS BECAUSE AS MY FEELINGS GROW I AM LEARNING A LEVEL OF TRUE LOVE I DID NOT KNOW EXISTED. YOUR NEEDS ARE ALSO MY NEEDS. GOODNIGHT SWEETGIRL. ♡... ALSO... YOU ARE THE SEXIEST PERSON I HAVE EVER SEEN, MET, AND GOTTEN THE OPPOR-TUNITY OF GETTING TO KNOW ON A LEVEL THIS DEEP (ALSO THE SEXIEST SOUNDING TO A POINT MY MIND AND IMAGINATION HAS BEEN BLOWN XXOXX)

I LOVE YOU Z Z Z Z

2022-07-13 (VISIT DAY ♡)

♡ ♡ ♡ ♡ ♡ ♡ ♡ ♡ ♡ ♡ ♡ ♡ ♡ ♡

TODAY DIAMOND ANGEL IS ALL LOVE. YOU ARE THE LOVE OF MY LIFE!!! ♡ ⇒ ♡ ⇒ MMMMM... WHAT A NIGHT!!! (INSERT STORY HERE WHEN WE'RE TOGETHER) WORDS HONESTLY DO NOT DESCRIBE HOW SEXY YOU ARE AND HOW ATTRACTED TO EVERYTHING ABOUT YOU I AM ♡. TODAYS SWEAT WAS A COOKER THATS FOR SURE. OTHER THAN THAT I AM SPEECHLESS ABOUT BEING W/ YOU EARLIER. I 100% LOOK FORWA-RD TO SHOWING YOU HOW I FEEL ABOUT YOU IN THE NEAR FUTURE. I LOOK FORWARD TO THE

(9)

OPPORTUNITY OF BEING ABLE TO APPRECIATE YOU ON EVERY LEVEL IN PERSON. I LOVE YOU ANGEL W/ ALL OF MY HEART, MIND, BODY, AND SOUL. I FEEL SUCH A DEEP LEVEL OF CONNECTION W/ YOU INTERNALLY & EXTERNALLY ♡ GOODNIGHT SWEETGIRL ♡ I AM ALWAY THINKING ABOUT YOU!!! ♡ Z Z Z Z Z

2022-07-14

GOOD MORNING MY LOVE. I GOT CALLED AWAY FROM WORK BEFORE LUNCH AND PUT INTO QUARANTINE. I KNOW IT WILL MAKE YOU SAD, JUST KNOW THAT I LOVE YOU AND WE CAN GET THROUGH THIS TOGETHER. ALL THIS DOES IS CEMENTS MY FEELING OF LAYING IN BED EVERY NIGHT W/ YOU AND WAKING UP NEXT TO YOU. TONIGHT I WILL CALL AT 6PM. IT'LL BE SO NICE TO HEAR YOUR SWEET VOICE SWEETHEART → ♡ ⇒ I JUST GOT WORD THAT CHARLIE GOT DAY PAROLE. IT IS UNFORTUNATE THAT WE CANNOT HANGOUT BEFORE HE LEAVES. EITHER WAY YOU ARE ALWAYS MY #1 PRIORITY ALONG W/ THE GIRLS. FRIENDS COME AND GO (ESP-ECIALLY IN HERE) BUT BEST FRIENDS & TRUE LOVE MAY ONLY HAPPEN ONCE. IT IS NOT SO BAD BEING ISOLATED INTO SOLITUDE BECAUSE I CAN FEEL/HEAR/LOVE/THINK OF YOUR BEAUTY THE ENTIRE TIME... AND I WILL. THIS IN MY MIND IS JUST ONE MORE THING WE WILL HAVE OVERCOME THAT BRINGS US CLOSER & MAKE OUR CONNECTION STRONGER. ABSENCE MAKES THE HEART GROW FONDER IN THESE MOMENTS. ALTHOUGH THIS SUCKS, WE BOTH

(10)

KNOW THERE HAS BEEN A LOT TOUGHER TIMES
IN THE LAST 8½ MONTHS. ONCE THIS IS
DONE AND WE DONT HAVE TO BE APART ILL
NEVER LET YOU GO. ILL LOVE YOU UNCOND-
-ITIONALLY AND APPRECIATE EXACTLY WHO
YOU ARE FOREVER & EVER. TOO BAD WE
COULDNT ISOLATE ALONE TOGETHER FOR
THE 11 DAYS. FOR WORKOUT ILL DO LOTS
OF PUSH UPS, SQUATS, DIPS, LUNGES, & ABS
NOT TO MENTION EAT SUPER HEALTHY. THE
BOYS IN HERE ALL MADE SURE ID HAVE MORE
THAN I NEED AND BROUGHT THE PHOTOS
OF YOU DOWN TO ME. THE ONE AT THE POOL
IS IN AN ENVELOPE HIDING AS THAT ONE IS
FOR MY EYES ONLY. I GOT THE 2 CAKE ONES
AND THE 2 HEADSHOTS NO GLASSES. AT LEAST
IN ISOLATION I CAN STILL SLEEP NEXT TO
YOU MY LOVE. TO KEEP MY MIND SUPER
POSITIVE I IMAGINE WHAT WE HAVE TALKED
ABOUT AFTER I AM RELEASED FROM HERE.
BEING ABLE TO WALK HAND IN HAND OUTDOORS
LOOKING AT YOUR HAIR BLOW IN THE WIND,
WATCHING YOU SMILE, MAKING EACHOTHER
LAUGH, HUGGING AND JUST ENJOYING THE
TRUE SIMPLICITY OF WHAT WE MEAN TO ONE
ANOTHER. IVE NEVER FELT THIS WAY BEFORE.
IT MAKES MY HEART MELT KNOWING THAT
YOU FEEL SEXY WHEN WE ARE TOGETHER.
YOU ARE THE ABSOLUTE SEXIEST PERSON I
HAVE EVER MET/KNOWN. I AM
SO GLAD WE TALKED. I DO APOLOGIZE THAT
THIS HAS CREATED SADNESS INSIDE OF YOU

(11)

HUN. THAT BREAKS MY HEART THAT YOURE UPSET. HEARING YOU ALMOST TEAR UP W/ FRUSTRATION REALLY MADE ME AWARE OF HOW IMPORTANT YOU ARE AND HOW I DONT EVER WANT YOU TO FEEL SADNESS BECAUSE OF ME AGAIN. THANK-YOU FOR THE KIND WORDS YOU HAD ME WRITE DOWN. ONE DAY I WILL MARRY YOU ANGEL, I TRULY BELIEVE THAT. ONCE WE HAVE GOTTEN PAST ALL THIS THERE WILL NOTHING WE WONT BE ABLE TO ENDURE. OUR STORY IS ALREADY AMAZING (A BEAUTIFUL ROM-COM LOVE STORY... MAYBE SANDLER CAN PLAY ME AND BARRYMORE CAN PLAY YOU ♡) OUR ROMANCE AND LOVE IS ONE FOR THE AGES. I AM SO GRATEFUL THAT IT IS W/ YOU. AND THATS WHY OUR BEGINNING HAS BEEN SO SPECIAL. ONE DAY WE WILL REFLECT UPON ALL OF THIS AND BE IN AWE OF WHAT WE WENT THROUGH TO BE IN LOVE. I PROMISE YOU ANGEL IT WILL BE WORTH IT!!! ♡♡♡ ⟹ ITS CRAZY HOW FAST WORD TRAVELS HERE. EVERY GUARD TALKS TO ME ABOUT BEING IN THE "PENALTY BOX" AND ASKS HOW I FEEL (LIKE A DOLT). THEY ALL REASSURE ME TO NOT BEAT MYSELF UP OVER THIS ALL THAT MUCH. THE THOUGHT OF NOT BEING ABLE TO SEE YOU ON THE 30TH IS A BUMMER HOW-EVER PAROLE IS SHORTLY AROUND THE CORNER. RIGHT NOW I CAN HEAR LAUGHTER OUTSIDE WHERE PEOPLE ARE SOCIALIZING ON THEIR BALCONIES. TONS OF PEOPLE HAVE STOPPED BY TO TELL ME TO "HANG IN THERE" WHICH IS NICE. CHARLES TOLD ME HE WILL FREEZE A TON

(12)

SPAG SAUCE FOR ME. MY C.O.[2] JUST DROPPED ME OFF ALL MY STUFF AND CAME IN LAUGHING AT ME SHAKING HIS HEAD. HE ALSO TOLD ME NOT TO BEAT MYSELF UP OVER IT. ALTHOUGH I FEEL LIKE AN IDIOT ILL JUST FOCUS AND USE THIS TIME TO WRITE & REFLECT ON THE PAST 9 MONTHS. WHAT LIFE WAS LIKE IN THE PAST, WHAT ITS LIKE NOW, AND THE FUTURE TO COME. I AM MADLY (HAPPILY) IN LOVE W/ YOU ANGEL ⟹ ♡ ⟹ ALL THE BOYS POPPED BY TO SAY GOODNIGHT. I MISS YOU TONS RIGHT NOW. I JUST FOUND OUT SIMON GOT FULL PARO-LE AND GET TO GO HOME (NO ½ WAY HOUSE) TOM-ORROW AFTER 6 YRS IN AMERICAN CELLS AND 2 MNTHS HERE. HIM AND I WALKED TOGETHER. HE WAS THE ONE SAYING FUNNY STUFF TO ME PASSING BY WHILE YOU AND I TALKED ☺ IT IS VERY HOT N STUFFY IN THIS HOUSE AND IT WILL ONLY BE GETTING HOTTER & HOTTER. I HOPE YOURE DOING O.K. RIGHT NOW SWEETHEART. I WILL BE SENDING A TON OF LOVE YOUR WAY!!! ♡ ⟹ ♡ ⟹ (10PM) DAY (1) QUARANTINE OVER. I AM ADJUSTED TO BEING ALONE ALOT FASTER THAN I THOUGHT. THE MIND DOES FUNNY THINGS SOMETI-MES. I AM TRULY GRATEFUL FOR YET ANOTHER EXPERIENCE WHERE I CAN USE/SEE THE TOOLS INGRAINED FROM THE TIME, DEDICATION, & HARD WORK IVE BEEN ABLE TO DO IN HERE. I AM ALSO EXTREMELY TO HAVE HAD AN OPPORTUNITY FOR AN ANGEL TO BE HERE ALONGSIDE ME THIS ENTIRE TIME (YOU). YOUVE HELPED ME FIND MYSELF IN WAYS I WILL NEVER FORGET. LIFE IS SO BEAU-

(13)

-TIFUL IN SO MANY WAYS. HARDSHIPS HAVE NO LONGER BEEN HARD. LOVE & ACCEPTANCE IS THE ONLY WAY TO LIVE. LESSONS TRULY DO COME IN ALL FORMS/SHAPES. HIDING EMOTIONS IS NO LONGER A WAY OF LIFE. COMMUNICATION IN HEALTHY WAYS [redacted] W/ EMPATHY, COMPASSION, AND AN OPEN HEART SEEMS TO COME NATURALLY NOW. THE PAIN I USED TO FEEL [redacted] HAS BECOME AN ALL TIME LOW INTERNALLY. I FEEL LOVED ON A LEVEL I'VE NEVER ACCEPTED/FELT BEFORE. MY SOUL IS OPEN AND OPENING MORE AND MORE IN WAYS I PREVIOUSLY HADN'T KNOWN POSSIBLE. RIGHT NOW I CAN PICTURE YOU IN OUR 28 BD SHIRT SNUGGLED INTO YOUR BED. WHICH MEANS I AM ALL WRAPPED AROUND YOU ♡. I FEEL SO SPECIAL KNOWING THAT THERE IS AN ANGEL (THE MOST STUNNINGLY BEAUTIFUL ANGEL) OUT THERE WHO LOVES ME POSSIBLY AS MUCH AS I DO HER ♡. WHAT A BLESSING YOU ARE. TONIGHT I AM WATCHING "ALONE" UNTIL 11:30PM AND THEN ILL LAY DOWN AND LOOK AT YOUR PHOTOS BEFORE BED. I FEEL SO UNBELIEVABLY FORTUNATE TO HAVE PHOTOS OF YOU HERE. SOLITUDE MAY HELP ME SETTLE INTO THIS FINAL PHASE OF INCARCERATION AND CEMENT MY APPRECIATION FOR LIFE, LOVE, & AND THE SIMPLE PLEASURES THAT THE WORLD STRIPS OUT OF PEOPLES LIVES. LIFE IS WAY TOO SHORT TO WASTE ON ANYTHING OTHER THAN LOVE & HAPP-INESS. ⇒ R ♡ ⇒ I HAVE A FEELING THAT THIS NOTEPAD IS GOING TO GET WRITTEN IN A TON OVER THE NEXT 10 DAYS. WRITTING HAS BEEN SO →

(14)

PROMINENT ALONG THIS JOURNEY. ITLL BE NICE TO SIT W/ YOU AND READ IT ALL ONE DAY. CERTAINLY EMBARRASMENT WILL BE FELT BUT ALSO SOME VERY PROFOUND THOUGHTS/WORDS AS WELL. I CAN ONLY IMAGINE WHAT THEY ALL SAY. ALSO BEING ABLE TO RECALL SOME FORGOTTEN MOMENTS ALONG THE WAY. WHAT A TRIP. GOODNIGHT MY BEAUTIFUL ANGEL, THANK YOU SO MUCH FOR BEING EXACTLY THE PERSON YOU ARE. I LOVE ALL OF YOU!!! ♡♡♡ Z x Z o Z x Z o Z x Z o Z x Z o Z x

2022-07-15

GOOD MORNING MY LOVE. TODAY IS DAY 2 OF ISOLAT--ION. I HAD A DECENT SLEEP LAST NIGHT. THE BED HERE IS A LOT MORE COMFORTABLE THAN WHAT I HAVE BEEN USED TO FOR THE LAST 8.5 MNTHS THATS FORSURE. AT SOME POINTS I WAS SLEEPING ON BASICALLY METAL PANS AS WIDE AS A PARK BENCH. I REMEMBER THOSE PLACES BEING SO INCREDIBLY COLD AT NIGHT I WOULD WAKE UP SHIVERING AND FEELING SO ALONE. IN HERE I HAVE 4 PHOTOS OF YOU NEXT TO MY BED AND SOME NICE WORDS YOU HAD ME WRITE WHICH IVE READ LOTS ALREADY AND THEY HELP SO MUCH. I MANAGED TO FALL IN AND OUT OF SLEEP LONGER THAN USUAL AND GOT OUT OF BED AT 10AM. NORMALLY ID BE WATERING MY LAWN AT 7AM AND WAKING UP CHARLIE FOR COFFEE ON WEEK--ENDS. TODAY I WILL WATCH T.V., DO WORKOUTS, WRITE TO YOU LOTS, READ, AND AS PER USUAL WAIT TO CALL THE LOVE OF MY LIFE ♡. TODAY I WILL BE WONDERING HOW YOU ARE FEELING ALL

(15)

DAY. I HOPE YOU'LL STILL FEEL THE SAME FEELINGS FOR ME AFTER ALL OF THIS. IN MY HEART I ALSO KNOW OUR CONNECTION IS SO DEEP THAT WE CAN GET THROUGH ANYTHING TOGETHER. THE WEATHER IS REALLY NICE OUT TODAY. I WAS TOLD THAT I CAN GO ONTO THE BACK PATIO BETWEEN THE 11-12 LUNCH LOCKDOWN. I WILL HAVE A SKIP ROPE BROUGHT DOWN SO I CAN AT LEAST GET SOME GOOD CARDIO IN WHILE I AM HERE. THE THOUGHTS OF US TOGETHER AFTER ALL OF THIS FILLS MY HEART AND HELPS ME MAINTAIN FOCUS. A PERSON TRULY DOES NEED MENTAL STRENGTH TO GET THROUGH ALL OF THE TIMES INCARCERATED, ESPECIALLY TO CONTINUE TO SEE POSITIVITY IN ALL THE UPPS & DOWNS THAT COME W/ IT. I LOVE YOU MORE THAN I KNEW THAT I WAS CAPABLE OF FEELING. YOU'VE TAUGHT ME SO MUCH ABOUT LIFE, LOVE, FRIENDSHIP, COMMUNICATION, FEELING, SELF WORTH/LOVE AND SO MUCH MORE. KNOWING THAT YOU'RE IN LOVE W/ ME MAKES ME ASPIRE TO CONSTANTLY WORK ON BEING A BETTER PERSON. ONE DAY IN THE NOT SO DISTANT FUTURE I WILL BE ABLE TO SHOW YOU EXACTLY HOW I FEEL AND HOW TRULY SPECIAL YOU ARE TO THIS WORLD ♡ THE UNIVERSE NEEDS WAY MORE SPIRITS LIKE YOURS SWEETHEART!!! I JUST SAW GEO & CHARLES WALK BY AND FELT A BIT SAD THAT I COULDN'T WALK W/ THEM OR BE W/ CHARLES FOR HIS LAST DAYS BUT MY MIND IS SOLELY FOCUSED ON GETTING HOME TO YOU & MY GIRLS. AS I LOOK AT THE TATTOO OF YOU

(16)

ON MY ARM AND SEE HOW MUCH IT ACTUALLY RESEMBLES YOU, I THINK THAT MY HEART & SOUL HAS BEEN SEARCHING FOR YOUR HEART & SOUL FOR A VERY LONG TIME. WHEN I LOOK AT PHOTOS OF YOU I DO SEE A HALO & WINGS. 9 MORE HOURS UNTIL OUR CALL ♡ ⟹ ♡ ⟹ (5PM) HELLO SWEETHEART. TODAY SO FAR IVE SKIPPED ROPE FOR AN HOUR & WALKED BACK N FORTH IN THESE HALLWAYS, IVE READ N.N.C., I PUT A LAWN CHAIR IN THE ~~BATH~~ SHOWER AND SAT UNDER THE WATER THINKING ALL ABOUT US TOGETHER, AND NAPPED WHILE WATCHING T.V. THE GUARDS TALK TO ME WHEN THEY PASS THROUGH EVERY ONCE IN AWHILE WHICH IS NICE. FOR THE MOST PART TIME CRAWLS BY IN HERE. THANKFULLY I HAVE PHOTOS OF YOU AND GET TO CALL YOU AT NIGHT. IT WOULD NOT BE THE SAME W/ OUT THOSE COMFORTS. I HOPE YOUR DAY HAS BEEN OK FOR YOU AND THAT YOURE NOT SAD. I LOVE YOU ANGEL ♡!!! BEING COMPLETELY ALONE IS NOT THE WORST THING IVE EXPERIENCED IN THIS TIME. MY FORMER SELF DIDNT ENJOY BEING ALONE WHATSOEVER. I AM HAPPY I HAVE FOUND SELF WORTH & SELF LOVE AGAIN. MY HEART IS FULL. I DO MISS YOU A TON RIGHT NOW THOUGH ⟹ ♡ ⟹ ♡ ⟹ (6PM) MY EMOTIONS ARE A BIT UP & DOWN A.T.M AS THOUGHTS OF NOT GETTING PAROLE ENTER MY ~~THE~~ MIND. NOT BEING W/ YOU OR MY GIRLS FOR ANOTHER YEAR WOULD BE SO DIFFICULT. I CAN TELL MY NEXT 10 DAYS WILL BE FILLED W/ UPS & DOWNS LIKE THIS. IF MY P.O. DOESNT SUPPORT ME DUE TO THIS I WILL STILL GO FOR DAY PAROLE ON THAT DATE AND PRAY FOR A POSITIVE OUTCOME.

(17)

THIS TIME IN ISOLATION UNKNOWING WHAT THE REPROCUSSIONS MAY BE, REALLY SETS IN ALL THE PEOPLE I CARE ABOUT. I'D MISS YOU SO MUCH AND COULD NOT EXPECT YOU TO WAIT FOR ME, AND IT BREAKS MY HEART AT THE THOUGHT OF LOSING YOU BECAUSE OF THIS ♡. I AM TRYING TO KEEP A POSITIVE OUTLOOK AND MAINTAIN OPTIMISM, ITS DIFFICULT WHEN THERE IS NO ONE TO TALK W/. THE INMATES ARE WORRIED, THE STAFF SEEMS TO LAUGH, SO I DO NOT KNOW WHAT TO THINK RIGHT NOW. HEARING YOUR VOICE WOULD BE SO NICE MY LOVE. SOMETHING ABOUT YOU IS SO CALMING AND SERENE. BEING AWAY HAS BEEN SO DIFFICULT FOR ME EVEN THOUGH PERSONAL GROWTH CONTINUES. ASPECTS OF ISOLATION CAN SEEM LIKE TORTURE OF THE MIND BECAUSE THOUGHTS CAN BE VERY VERY HAUNTING. ISOLATION TIME RUNS IN SLOW MOTION AND WHEN TROUBLING THOUGHTS CREEP IN TIME LITERALLY STANDS STILL. THIS IS ALL MY FAULT! ⇒♡⇒♡ (10PM) THE EVENING IS WINDING DOWN FINALLY... THAT WAS A VERY LONG DAY THAT IS FOR SURE. AFTER MY LAST ENTRY I JUST SAT AT THE KITCHEN TABLE AND READ NVC UNTIL I CALLED YOU AT 9PM. I FELT BETTER WHILE INGULFED IN A BOOK. AS USUAL HEARING YOUR VOICE WAS THE MOST MEANINGFUL PART OF THE DAY. FEELING LOVE FROM THE PERSON I LOVE IS VERY SPECIAL. I LOVE THAT YOU ARE WEARING THOSE SHIRTS AT NIGHT ♡. I CAN ONLY IMAGINE HOW AMAZINGLY GORGEOUS YOU LOOK IN THEM!!! FOR THE REST OF TONIGHT I WILL JUST LAY ON THE COUCH (MORE LIKE AIRPORT WAITING ROOM BENCH) ⟶

(18)

AND WATCH THE HISTORY CHANNEL. AND THEN REPEAT IT ALL FOR 9 MORE DAYS. ISOLATION IS MOST DEFINATELY AN AMAZING WAY TO PUNISH A PERSON 100%. ILL REMAIN GRATEFUL FOR EVERY EXPERIENCE AND KEEP GROWING & WORK-ING TOWARDS BETTERMENT (& NOT SURE IF THATS ACTUALLY A WORD). I REFUSE TO BECOME BROKEN BY THIS AS THERE IS ALWAYS AN UNDERLYING LESSON TO BE LEARNED. WE WILL MOST LIKELY SEE THE EMOTIONAL SHIFTS DURING THIS GO UP & DOWN. I WILL CONTINUE TO JOURNAL THEM ALL FOR THE FUTURE. A FUTURE W/ YOU IS THE LIGHT AT THE END OF THIS TUNNEL MY LOVE ♡. ON ANOTHER NOTE I AM FIGHTING MYSELF ON WHETHER OR NOT TO MAKE SPAGHETTI TONIGHT AND BINGE EAT IT LOL. I HAVE ALL THE INGREDIENTS TO MAKE IT TOO... TO FAT KID OR NOT TO FAT KID THAT IS THE QUESTION LOL. RIGHT NOW IM ALSO IMAGINING LAYING ON MY BACK ON A NEW COUCH WHILE YOU LAY ON MY CHEST W/ MY ARM AROUND YOUR BACK AND THE OTHER HAND GENTLY RUNNING MY ALONG YOUR FACE & THROUGH YOUR HAIR AND KISSING YOUR HEAD. HOW NICE THAT WOULD BE RIGHT NOW ♡. I LOVE YOU ANGEL. GOODNIGHT SWEETGIRL, I LOVE EVERYTHING THAT IS YOU. FOR SOME REASON I AM COMPELLED TO WRITE THE WORD "ORGAAAANIC" FOR NO REASON OTHER THAN I HOPE YOU BURST INTO LAUGHTER

NIGHT ♡♡♡♡ Z O Z X Z X Z O Z
Z X Z O Z ♡ Z X Z O Z X Z
Z ♡ Z X Z X Z ♡ Z X Z Z
X Z O Z X Z O Z X Z

(19)

2022-07-16

GOODMORNING MY LOVE. IT IS DAY 3 ISOLATION.
LAST NIGHT I FELL ASLEEP ON THE COUCH THEN
MANAGED TO CRAWL INTO BE AROUND MIDNIGHT.
I FELL ASLEEP W/ YOU ON MY MIND. IT IS 9:40am
AND THE DAY IS DRAGGING BY. 11 MORE HOURS
WAITING TO CALL YOU. I AM PASSING TIME BY
WATCHING T.V. ATM. I HAVE A POT OF SPAGHETTI
SAUCE SIMMERING WHICH IS MAKING THE
HOUSE SMELL AMAZING. BEING DECLINED
FOR DAY PAROLE IS WEIGHING HEAVY ON MY
HEART. GETTING TO KNOW YOU HAS BEEN ONE
OF THE HAPPIEST TIMES OF MY LIFE AND
LOSING YOU BREAKS MY HEART. MY GIRLS
WOULD HAVE TO GO ANOTHER YEAR W/ OUT
THEIR DADDY AND THAT ALSO BREAKS MY
HEART. ISOLATION IS TORTURE!!! ♡⟹ ♡⟹
I LOVE YOU SO MUCH ANGEL, ITS ALL I CAN THINK
ABOUT. I WILL BE DEVASTATED IF I CANT HOLD YOU
IN MY ARMS ANYMORE. IVE NEVER FELT A REAL
CONNECTION LIKE THIS BEFORE. YOU MEAN THE
ABSOLUTE WORLD TO ME♡. I CAN ONLY IMAGINE
WHAT YOURE GOING THROUGH, JUST KNOW THAT
MY LOVE FOR YOU IS FOREVER UNCONDITIONAL
AND ILL ALWAYS BE HERE FOR YOU AND YOUR
NEEDS AS LONG AS I AM ALIVE. BEING IN HERE
AWAY FROM YOU IS EXTREMELY DIFFICULT. I AM
A GOOD PERSON. I HAVE A GOOD HEART AND CAN
ONLY PRAY THAT MY SUPPORTS CAN GIVE ME A
CHANCE TO SHOW THE WORLD WHAT I HAVE TO
OFFER. I WANT TO INSPIRE OTHERS TO FACE
THEIR DEMONS AS I HAVE AND FIND ACCEPTANCE

(20)

OF THEMSELVES. ITS A HARSH WORLD BUT THERE IS STILL A TON OF GOOD OUT THERE. IN LIFE I HAVE SUFFERED A LOT OF LOSSES AND STR--UGGLED IMMENSELY. I LOST MYSELF FOR A VERY LONG TIME. SOBRIETY HAS BEEN THE ABSOLUTE BEST THING THAT HAS EVER HAPP--ENED. BEING SOBER THIS YEAR HAS BEEN THE BEST YEAR EVEN THOUGH SIMULTANEOUSLY THE TOUGHEST BY FAR. HAVING HAD THE ABI--LITY TO DISCOVER ALL THE POSITIVE ATTR--IBUTES ABOUT MYSELF HAS BEEN A TRID THATS FORSURE. FOR THE FIRST TIME EVER I LOVE ME. IN FINDING ME I ALSO HAD THE OPPORTUNITY OF A LIFETIME, FINDING MY ANGEL. A PERSON SO WONDERFUL AND KIND THAT IT SOMETIMES FEELS LIKE A DREAM SO VIVID ID STAY IN ~~THAT~~ THIS DREAM FOREVER. I HAVE A LOT TO OFFER AND MY HEART FINALLY HAS NO WALLS, RESERVATION, OR BARRIERS. THANK YOU FOR BEING YOU!!! I AM NOT SURE IF I COULD BE VULNERABLE TO ANYONE ELSE AS THERE IS NO ONE ELSE LIKE YOU♡. I TRULY BELIEVE WE WERE BROUGHT TOGETHER FOR A REASON AND CAN ONLY PRAY THAT DAY PAROLE ACCEPTANCE ALLOWS US TO EXPLORE, GROW, AND PROGRESS INTO DEEPER LEVELS OF OUR ALREADY DEEP CONNECTION. ⇒♡⇒

(28)⇒ (11AM) WELL THE SPAG SAUCE W/ EGG NOODLES IS COMPLETE. IT DOESNT HAVE ALL THAT MUCH FLA--VOR AS ISOLATION SUPPLIES ARE VERY LIMITED. JUST ENOUGH TO NOT GO HUNGRY, UNLESS I RATION MEALS INCORRECTLY. HOURS SEEM LIKE DAYS

(21)

IN HERE. AFTER THE GUARDS WALK THROUGH I WILL DO PUSH UPS & JUMP ROPE FOR AN HOUR TO PASS TIME AND WORK ON "YOUR VIEW"♡. ISOLATION IS A REMINDER OF ALL THE OTHER TIME I SPENT IN RRAC & LOCKDOWNS PREVIOUSLY. I DO NOT WISH INCARCERATION ON ANYONE. ALTHOUGH I AM SOLELY RESPONSIBLE FOR BEING IN THE "PENALTY BOX" I DO FEEL I AM STILL A GREAT CANDIDATE FOR DAY PAROLE AT HALFWAY HOUSE. I DO LONG FOR THE DAY I BECOME FREE OF THIS BURDEN I CAUSED IN MY FORMER LIFE, THAT LIFE HAS BEEN GONE FOR ALMOST 14 MONTHS, HOWEVER THERE ARE REPROCUSSIONS DUE TO ACTIONS OF MINE, ACTIONS FROM 4 YEARS AGO. ONCE THIS IS ALL IN THE PAST I WILL ONLY LOOK BACK TO REMIND MYSELF TO STAY LOOKING FORWARD AT ALL THERE IS TO BE GRATEFUL FOR. I AM TRULY GRATEFUL / APPRECIATIVE TO ALL THOSE WHO CARED FOR ME AND CONTINUED TO BE BESIDE ME THROUGHOUT MY JOURNEY. THERE ARE VERY FEW LEFT. MY DAUGHTERS ARE ALL SO PRESIOUS AND FULL OF KINDNESS & LOVE, MY FAMILY WHO NEVER GAVE UP ON ME, MY FEW FRIENDS WHO ALWAYS KNEW WHO I WAS WHEN I WAS LOST, AND MY BEST FRIEND, MY ANGEL, MY LOVE (YOU). I CANNOT WAIT TO HEAR YOUR VOICE THIS EVENING ANGEL. YOUVE BEEN THE LIGHT FOR ME SO MANY TIMES I AM FOREVER GRATEFUL ♡⇒♡⇒ SO APPARENTLY THE WORD IS I MIGHT BE GETTING SHIPPED TO MEDIUM WHICH MEANS I MAY BE DENIED PAROLE ♡. THE WORST PART WOULD TO LOSE THE LOVE OF MY LIFE

(22)

AND HAVE MY KIDS BE HURT BY ME ALL OVER AGAIN. I AM HAVING SUCH A HARD TIME W/ THIS ALL RIGHT NOW. BEING ALONE DEFINATELY DOES NOT HELP AT ALL. IT WAS THE CREEPY GUARD THAT SAID IT. HOPEFULLY HE IS JUST FUCKING W/ ME. IT HURTS ME TO THINK ABOUT HOW THIS MAY AFFECT YOUR FEELINGS. THIS WAS ALL MY FAULT!!! UGH!!! EVEN THOUGH I AM STRUGGLING HUGE I WILL TRY TO STAY POSITIVE AND HOPE FOR THE BEST. I LOVE YOU SWEETGIRL♡!!! ⇒ (2PM) TO PASS THE REST OF TODAY I WILL READ THE BIG BOOK TO FURTHER THIS JOURNEY INTO RECOVERY. I APPRECIATE THE OPPORTUNITIES THIS INSTITUTION HAS GIVEN ME AND WILL 100% RESPECT THEIR DECISION TO SHIP ME NEXT DOOR. ITS NOT THEIR ~~ELA~~ FAULT IT IS SOLELY MY OWN. THE STAFF HERE HAS BEEN SO AMAZING ESPECIALLY MY C.O.2 ANDREW, MY P.O. GARRY, AND VERONICA AT V&C. I FEEL SO DISAPPOINTED THAT I LET EVERYONE WHO HAS BEEN HERE FOR ME DOWN. I WILL PRACTICE BEING EMPATHETIC ON MYSELF AND BE EASY ON MY EMOTIONS. THROUGHOUT THIS TIME ISOLATED MY LOVE & DETERMINATION ONLY GROW STR-ONGER. MY LOVE FOR YOU WILL KEEP GROWING EVEN IF YOU DECIDE TO MOVE ON♡. MY LOVE IS TRULY UNCONDITIONAL AND NO MATTER WHAT HAPPENS JUST KNOW OUR TIME TOGETHER WILL ALWAYS FILL MY HEART♡. ⇒ ♡ ⇒ (7:30PM) EARLY THIS EVENING I HAVE BEEN TRYING TO SLEEP TO PASS THE HOURS UNTIL OUR CALL♡♡. TIME IS VERY SLOW ATM. I FIND EVENING EASIER ON MY MIND.

(23)

I AM NOT EXACTLY SURE WHY BUT IT SEEMS JUST SO. THERE ISNT MUCH ON T.V. I HAVENT ALREADY SEEN AND IVE READ A TON TODAY. I WISH FALLING ASLEEP WAS EASIER. I DONT GET AS FATIGUED WHEN I AM NOT OUT DO PHYSICAL ACTIVITIES. AH WELL I GUESS... ONLY 1.5 HOURS UNTIL OUR CALL ♡ ⟹ ♡ 45 MORE MINS UNTIL OUR NIGHTLY CALL ♡. I ALSO JUST FOUND OUT THAT IS NO TALKING THRU THE WINDOW WHATSOEVER. I FULLY UNDERSTAND AS THIS IS A PUNISHMENT. MORE CLOTHES, EGGS, CHEESCAKE, & BAKED SPAG (SPAG & CAKE FROM CHARLES) ARE WAITING FOR ME RIGHT OUTSIDE THE DOOR. NOW TO WAIT UNTIL A C.O. WALKS THROUGH. CHARLES IS SUPER GLAD HE WILL BE LEAVING THIS WEEK. HIS DAD IS COMING TO PICK HIM UP. ITLL BE SUPER NICE TO BE ABLE TO WEAR SWEATPANTS IN HERE, THE JEANS ARE NOT AT ALL COMFORTABLE. THE HOUSE WAS NOT SO HOT THIS AFTERNOON WHICH WAS NICE. I DIDNT GO OUT-SIDE OVER 11 COUNT, I JUST SKIPPED INSIDE AND DID PUSH-UPS... THE CHEESECAKE WAS AMAZING!!! ⟹ ♡ ⟹ ♡ (10PM) THE DAY HAS PASSED, SLOWLY, BUT SURELY. IT WAS A SEMI EMOTIONAL DAY TODAY. MY THOUGHTS KEPT WONDERING HOW YOU WERE FEELING & NEEDING. YOUR FEELINGS & NEEDS ARE VERY IMPORTANT TO ME. BEING VULNERABLE W/ ONE ANOTHER HAS BECOME THE BEAUTIFUL FOUNDATION OF OUR FRIENDSHIP. THAT VULNE-RABILITY IS SO VERY IMPORTANT. IT KEEPS OUR COMMUNICATION AND BOND STRONG. TALK-ING TO YOU WAS VERY NICE. THANK YOU FOR ALL YOUR KIND WORDS & LOVE YOU SHOW ME.

(24)

I LOVE YOU SO MUCH ANGEL. I ALSO ADMIRE THE PERSON THAT YOU ARE, SUCH BEAUTY RESO-NATES OUT OF YOU IN EVERY DIRECTION. I FEEL SO LOVED BY YOU, IT IS SO SURREAL. I TRULY HOPE THAT YOU FEEL MY WORDS OF LOVE & SOON TO BE ACTIONS. I WILL APPRECIATE THIS FRIEND-SHIP FOREVER!!! ♡. TONIGHT I WILL TRY TO NOT OVERTHINK ABOUT POTENTIAL OUTCOMES AND FOCUS ON THE LOVING BOND THAT WE HAVE COME TO SHARE. WHATEVER HAPPENS WILL HAPPEN AS OUR HIGHER POWER INTENDS FOR IT TO HAPPEN. GOODNIGHT MY LOVE. KNOW THAT I LOVE YOU SWEETGIRL W/ ALL MY HEART ♡♡ = Z ♡ Z Z Z
XOX Z X Z ♡ Z O Z X Z

2022-07-17

(4:50PM) DAY 4 ISOLATION ⇒. TODAY I RESTED AND WATCHED T.V LITERALLY ALL DAY. I HAVENT EATEN ALL THAT MUCH. I THOUGHT A LOT ABOUT US ALL DAY, AND OVERCOMING THIS ENTIRE EXPERIENCE W/ SUCH A BEAUTIFUL SOUL/ANGEL ALONGSIDE ME. IT MEANS MORE THAN YOU COULD EVER IMAGINE ANGEL. I BELIEVE WE CAN OVERCOME ANY OBSTACLE IN LIFE TOGETHER W/ POSITIVITY, COMMUNICATION, & GRACE. I HAVE SO MUCH RESPECT FOR YOU!!! ♡ ONE DAY I WILL MARRY YOU SWEETHEART. I ALSO WOULD LOVE TO BE THE FATHER OF YOUR CHILD/CHILDREN. WHEN I AM FREE I WILL SECURE ABSOLUTE STABILITY AND FINANCIAL SECURITY AND FOCUS ON GROWING ALONG A PATH W/ YOU TOWARDS A FUTURE TOGETHER HAPPILY ♡. I HAVE NEVER IN MY LIFE WANTED TO HAVE THIS OPPORTUNITY SO BADLY. THE FACT THAT

(25)

OUR FRIENDSHIP HAS GROWN TO WHAT IT HAS, HAS BEEN SO NATURAL (ORGANIC♡) I BELIEVE IN MY HEART THAT ALLOWING OURSELVES TO GROW TOWARDS ONE ANOTHER W/ OUT FORCING IT HAS BEEN THE REASON OUR JOURNEY IS SO UNBELIE--VABLY BEAUTIFUL ON ALL LEVELS. CONTINUING TO LET IT BE NATURAL AS WE FURTHER OUR GETTING TO KNOW EACHOTHER IS SO ESSENTIAL. I WILL ALWAYS REMAIN OPEN TO YOUR NEEDS ON EVERY LEVEL, MENTALLY, SPIRITULLY, PHYSI--CALLY, EMOTIONALLY, OR ANY NEED THAT NEEDS TO BE HEARD, FELT, COMMUNICATED, OR LISTENED TO. I AM IN LOVE W/ YOU ANGEL IN WAYS EVEN I HAD NEVER EXPERIENCED BEFORE. YOU ARE MY BEST FRIEND FOREVER. MY HEART WILL ALWAYS BE YOURS. ALSO... YOU ARE THE SEXIEST PERSON IVE EVER MET IN EVERY SINGLE WAY♡!!!♡⇒ ⇒ I WILL ALWAYS BE HERE FOR YOU!!!♡⇒♡⇒ ♡⇒(7PM) TWO MORE HOURS UNTIL OUR 30MIN CALL. I AM EXCITED TO HEAR YOUR BEAUTIFUL VOICE. YOU ARE WHAT KEEPS ME GOING THROUGHOUT THESE LONG DAYS WHICH SEEM TO BE ENDLESS. I WAS JUST STANDING IN THE BEDROOM LOOKING AT YOUR PHOTOS, I TELL THEM/YOU HOW MUCH I AM IN LOVE W/ YOU AND HOW AMAZING YOU ARE INSIDE & OUT. I AM ALWAYS STUNNED BY HOW INCREDIBLY GORGEOUS YOU ARE. AS IVE GOTTEN TO KNOW WHO YOU ARE YOUR TRUE BEAUTY CONSISTANTLY SHINES BRIGHTER AND BRIGHTER. 7 MORE DAYS OF ISO--LATION, THIS WEEK I WILL SURELY BE TOLD THE CONSEQUENCES TO MY ACTION. I AM FULLY IN ACCE--PTANCE AND READY FOR DISCIPLINE. I DO HOPE

(26)

THEY CAN SEE ALL THE GOOD I HAVE TO OFFER THIS WORLD. I CAN USE THIS STORY TO HOPEFULLY INSPIRE OTHERS THAT THE WORLD IS WHAT WE MAKE IT. ALSO I FEEL THAT TRUE LOVE & ROMANCE IS VERY REAL AS I HAVE FOUND BOTH W/ YOU♡!!! TRUE LOVE IS 100% UNCONDITIONAL AND FOR THE VERY FIRST TIME I KNOW WHAT UNCONDIT-IONAL IS. I HAVE FOUND IT W/ MY BEST FRIEND (ANGEL "THE DIAMOND")♡ ⟹ ♡ ⟹ (10pm) YET ANOTHER DAY DOWN. TONIGHTS CALL WAS VERY NICE. FOR THE REST OF THE EVENING I WILL RELAX & WATCH T.V. UNTIL BEDTIME. I WILL BE THINKING/IMAGINING BE AT HOME W/ YOU AT NIGHT CUDDLED ON THE COUCH W/ YOUR HEAD MY LAP WHILE I RUB MY FINGERS THROUGH YOUR HAIR & HOLD YOUR HAND♡. GOODNIGHT SWEETGIRL. I LOVE YOU W/ ALL MY HEART♡

Z x Z o Z x Z o Z

♡ 2022-07-18 ♡

GOODMORNING MY LOVE♡. TODAY IS DAY 5 ISOL-ATION. I AM SURE I WILL BE GETTING TALKED TO FROM THE ADMINISTRATION TODAY AND AM READY TO FACE JUDGEMENT. MY MOOD IS POSITIVE & HOPEFUL. I AM A GOOD PERSON AND ALSO HAVE AN ABOVE PAR INMATE IN EVERY PRISON/INSTITU-TION THAT I HAVE BEEN TO. MY HOPES ARE FOR THE FUTURE AND OUR HIGHER POWER ALWAYS HAS A PLAN IN STORE FOR US. I KEEP MY FAITH IN THE CREATOR AND CONTINUE TO PRAY FOR OTHERS. 7pm IS THE TIME I AM MOST LOOKING FORWARD TO TODAY AS THAT WILL BE OUR TIME TOGETHER. THIS MORNING ALL I COULD THINK ABOUT IS YOU

(27)

PICKING ME UP IN A LONG FLOWY SUMMER DRESS.
SUCH A BEAUTIFUL THING TO HAVE IN MY IMAGINA-
-TION. I CAN PICTURE YOU SO CLEARLY SMILING
AND READY FOR A HUG & KISS. ONCE WE DRIVE
AWAY FROM HERE I WILL HAVE TEARS OF JOY WHILE
I LOOK AT YOU AND HOLD YOUR HAND EVER SO
TIGHTLY. THIS DAY WILL BE A DREAM COME
TRUE♡THE WEATHER OUTSIDE TODAY IS WET &
DINGY. I'D STILL RATHER BE WORKING THAN IN
HERE ALONE. WELL MY LOVE FOR NOW I WILL GO
SIT IN THE CHAIR INSIDE THE SHOWER LETTING HOT
WATER BLAST DOWN ON ME WHILE I THINK OF YOU
RIDING ME ♡♡♡⟹♡⟹(11AM) SO FAR TODAY HAS
BEEN DECENT. I'VE READ THE BIG BOOK, WATCHED T.V.,
LOOKED AT YOUR PHOTOS, AND WRITTEN TO YOU.
FOR THE NEXT HOUR I WILL SKIP ROPE, DO PUSH-UPS,
AND WALK BACK N FORTH IN THE HALLWAYS. EGGS
HARD BOILED WAS BREAKFAST, SIMPLE BUT DELICI-
-OUS. I WAS TOLD THAT EVERYTHING WILL BE O.K.
BUT I AM GOING TO BE HAVING A LONG TALK W/
THE ELDER. MY MIND HAS BEEN FOR THE TIME
BEING, HOWEVER I AM FULLY ACCOUNTABLE AND
RESPECT THE REPROCCUSIONS. WHATEVER THE OUT-
-COME IS I WILL CONTINUE TO SHOW GRATITUDE.
FACING PROBLEMS W/ AN OPEN HEART, MIND, &
SOUL W/ LOVE IS WHAT MY HEART FEELS IS THE
ONLY WAY OF LIVING. TODAY IT IS RAINING QUITE
A BIT WHICH MAKES ME HAPPY KNOWING OUR LAWN
IS GETTING THE WATER IT DESPERATELY NEEDS.
I DO WISH I WAS AT WORK AS I ENJOY THE PHYSICAL
NATURE OF IT AND SOCIALIZING W/ THE DUDES
THERE. I WILL HONESTLY MISS DOING LABOR W/

(28)

[redacted] & [redacted]. WE GET A TON ACCOMPLISHED TOGETHER, PLUS ITS A FUN, LIGHT-HEARTED, POSITIVE ENVIRONMENT. WE ALL HAVE SUCH STRONG YET DIFFERENT SKILLSETS AND STRONG WORK ETHICS, IT SHOWS W/ HOW WE SOLVE PROBLEMS & GET THE TASKS ACCOMPLISHED. THE BOSSES OF [redacted] ARE ALSO REALLY GOOD DUDES AND REALLY EASY TO WORK W/. ALSO TODAY I AM THINKING ABOUT HOW MY GIRLS ARE DOING AS I MISS THEM ALL SO MUCH. ONE DAY SOON DADDY WILL BE BACK AND A BETTER DAD THAN EVER BEFORE, IN EVERY WAY ♡. IT IS SO CRAZY HOW MUCH A PERSON LEARNS ABOUT THEMSELVES IN ISOLATION. THE EXPERIENCE IS SOMETHING QUITE DIFFERENT THAN WHAT MOST PEOPLE COULD REALIZE UNLESS THEY'D GONE THROUGH IT. AS "SICK" PEOPLE WE ALL FEEL ISOLATED & LONELY AT ONE POINT OR ANOTHER. FOR US WHO PUSH THROUGH IT SEEMS LIKE A MIRACLE THAT WE MAKE IT. I AM SO GRATEFUL TO HAVE SPIRITUALITY & SOBRIETY BEFORE THE DURATION OF THIS TIME AWAY. W/OUT IT I DONT KNOW WHAT IT WOULD HAVE BEEN LIKE. HAVING FOUND MY BEST FRIEND (YOU) HAS BEEN/MEANT THE ABSOLUTE WORLD. IT TRULY TAUGHT ME THAT THERE IS LIGHT IN THE DARK IF YOUR HEART REMAINS OPEN AND A CONSIOUS CONTACT W/ GOD (OF OUR UNDERSTANDING) REMAINS OPEN. NEVER IN A MILLION YEARS OF MY FORMER SELF, WOULD I EVER THINK GOD WOULD BE SO PROMINENT IN MY LIFE TODAY. HE HAS ALSO SHOWN ME THAT ANGELS DO

(29)

EXIST♡(2)⇒♡(3)⇒ (3:30PM) TODAY HAS BEEN GOING BY VERY SLOWLY. ILL SURELY BE GLAD WHEN ISOLATION IS COMPLETED. FORREST GUMP IS ON T.V. ATM, ONE OF MY ALL-TIME FAVORITES☺. I LOOK FORWARD TO THE DAYS I CAN LAY AND WATCH SHOWS NEXT TO YOU. THIS MOVIE IS SO CLASSIC, I LOVE ALL OF HIS CATCH PHRASES LOL. WHILE IT PLAYS IN THE BACKGROUND I AM READING THE BIG BOOK. I AM TRYING TO USE THIS TIME TO FURTHER MY RECOVERY, COMMUNICATION SKILLS, AND REFLECT ON ALL THE EMOTIONS RUNNING THROUGH ME ALL THROUGHOUT THE DAYS. AT TIMES IT IS VERY DIFFICULT IN HERE. I FEEL LIKE IVE LET YOU DOWN A BIT. I CANT STRESS ENOUGH AT HOW HAPPY I WILL BE TO HAVE ALL OF THIS BEHIND US♡!!! I THINK ABOUT THE ABILITY TO COME HOME AND HAVE A ONE YEAR CAKE FOR REAL. SOBER IS THE ONLY WAY TO LEAD A FULFILLING LIFE I FEEL. I CAN SEE WHY THE LONELINESS & BOREDOM LEADS PEOPLE TO ADDICTION IN HERE. ITS SAD FOR THOSE WHO FALL INTO THAT WORLD, ALL WE CAN DO IS PRAY FOR THEM ALL. WHEN I AM OUT OF ISOLATION I WILL SPEND A LOT MORE TIME IN MY ROOM READING. I WANT TO DISCONNECT FROM HERE AND FOCUS MORE ON WHAT IS IMPORTANT, FAMILY, SOBRIETY, EDUCATION, COMMUNICATION, AND YOU ESPECIALLY. FROM NOW ON ALL MY ENERGY WILL BE FOCUSED IN THAT DIRECTION AS THOSE THINGS ARE WHAT IS TRULY IMPORTANT TO ME. I LOVE YOU SO MUCH ANGEL ♡!!!♡⇒ ♡⇒ (6:30PM) WELL FOREST GUMP WAS A BIT OF A TEAR JERKER. FUNNY THAT IVE SEEN THAT MOVIES PROBABLY OVER 100 TIMES AND NEVER SHED A

(30)

TEAR NOT ONCE. THE FIRST TIME WAS WHEN THE WAR WAS OVER AND HE WAS DOING A SPEECH. HIM & JENNY RAN INTO THE MIDDLE OF THE POND & HUGGED EVER SO TIGHTLY. IT MADE ME THINK OF LEAVING HERE AND DOING THE SAME THING W/ YOU♡. THE SECOND TEAR JERKER WAS PRETTY MUCH EVERYPART AFTER HE FOUND OUT ABOUT LITTLE FORREST AND WAS SO PROUD. THATS HOW I FEEL ABOUT ALL MY BABIES AND ONE DAY OUR BABY/BABIES. I TRULY DO DREAM OF THAT FOR US♡. THIS MUCH TIME AWAY FROM YOU ALL MAKES EVERY MOMENT TO COME SO SPECIAL TO ME, ILL NEVER TAKE ANOTHER MOMENT FOR-GRANTED EVER AGAIN. LIFE IS WAY TOO SHORT TO NOT BE FILLED W/ LOVE. TODAY EMPATHY FOR MYSELF & OTHERS HAS BEEN ON MY MIND. I USED TO VIEW EMPATHY AS A WEAKNESS WHEN IN FACT IT IS A BEAUTIFUL STRENGTH. OVER THE NEXT FEW DAYS I WILL FOCUS ON COURAGE & FAITH. FAITH IS SUCH AN AMAZING ATTRIBUTE AND INCREASINGLY BECOMING SUCH A PROMINENT PART OF MY LIFE. BEING IN ISOLATION REALLY CEMENTS MY FAITH IN A HIGHER POWER, OPENING TO LET GOD GUIDE ME THROUGH HIS WILL. I FEEL HE WANTED US TO LEARN THIS LESSON AND SEE IF IT BRINGS US TOGETHER. IN MY HEART I BELIEVE ALL THIS IS HAPPENING FOR A REASON. LIKE YOUVE SAID BEFORE, ABSENCE MAKES THE HEART GROW FONDER. WELL... THAT IS DEFINATELY RESONATING W/ ME RIGHT NOW♡. ONLY 1 HOUR UNTIL OUR CALL☺ LAST NIGHT WHEN YOU SAID TO CALL EARLY THEN TOLD ME ABOUT YOUR SHOW

(31)

... THANK-YOU FOR THE REASSURANCE SWEETHEART.
THE FUNNY THING IS, IS THAT IF YOU HADN'T TOLD
ME I WOULDN'T HAVE HAD ANY BAD THOUGHTS. I
TRUST YOU AND LOVE YOU UNCONDITIONALLY AND
WOULD NEVER HOLD YOU BACK FROM BEING WHO
YOU ARE. W/ ME YOU ARE FREE. I WOULD'VE REASSURED
YOU THE SAME WAY HUN. I FEEL THAT W/ BOTH OF
OUR PAST EXPERIENCES THAT HONESTY, TRANSPARENCY,
OPENESS, UNDERSTANDING, EMPATHY, & COMMUNIC-
-ATION OF OUR NEEDS IS SUCH A CRUCIAL FOUND-
-ATION TO OUR FRIENDSHIP. I PROMISE YOU THAT
I WILL LIVE ALL OF THOSE THINGS (NATURALLY (ORGAAN
ICLY)). I FEEL WE BOTH LIVE ALONG THE SAME
PRINCIPALS & MORALS AND HAVE BEEN TAKEN
ADVANTAGE OF MANY OF TIMES. THOSE ARE ALL
TRAITS TO BE ADMIRED. LOYALTY IS AN ABSOLUTE
STRENGTH!!! ♡♡♡ ⇒ ♡♡♡ ⇒ NICE TO HEAR YOUR
VOICE SWEETHEART!!! ♡ 24HRS UNTIL OUR NEXT CALL.
ENJOY "4 HE BACHELORETTE" HUN. YOU SOUNDED
VERY VIBRANT THIS EVENING. I AM MISSING YOU
A LOT RIGHT NOW. FOR THE MOST PART MY SPIRITS
ARE LEVEL OR ABOVE PAR CONSIDERING ALL THAT
IS HAPPENING. I REMAIN HOPEFUL FOR THE FUT-
-URE AND DAY PAROLE ACCEPTANCE. IT'LL BE NICE
TO TALK LONGER THAN 30 MINS NEXT MONDAY.
AND THE ABILITY TO CALL MY SISTER & THE GIRLS
AGAIN. ♡ ALSO TO CALL MY DAD, DAVE, AND CHECK
THE MAIL / SEND THIS MONSTROUS LETTER TO
YOURS TRULY ♡. SHOWER (AGAIN) OR NOT TO SHOW-
-ER (AGAIN) THAT IS THE QUESTION. IF THE
SHOWER WAS W/ YOU, THEN, ABSOLUTELY WOULD
100% (HUNDO P) BE AN IMMEDIATE YES!!!

(32)

♡⇒♡♡⇒ (10pm) GOODNIGHT SWEETGIRL. I LOVE YOU ♡ Z x Z Z o Z Z x Z o Z Z x Z Z o Z

2022-07-19

(9:10am) GOODMORNING SWEETHEART. TODAY IS DAY 6 ISOLATION. I AM FEELING A LOT MORE ENTHUSIASTIC TODAY. MY MOOD IS VERY MELLOW, HAPPY, & LOVING. THE WEATHER IS SUPER SUNNY WHICH MAKES A HUGE DIFFERENCE I THINK. AT LUNCH I WILL GO OUTSIDE AND SOAK SOME OF IT IN. SORRY I HAVE BEEN A BIT OF A BUMMER THE LAST FEW DAYS AS I HAVE BEEN GOING THROUGH A LOT IN HERE. TODAY I WILL JUST TAKE IT EASY FOR THE MOST PART AND LET THE DAY BE WHAT IT IS GOING TO BE. THIS MORNING I "THOUGHT" ABOUT YOU, OHHH BOY! IS ALL I CAN SAY. AND ALSO WOW! MY [redacted] UNDILUTED IMAGINATION IS/WAS AMAZING. THANK-YOU FOR THAT!!! ♡♡♡⇒♡⇒ (11am) TIME FOR COUNT. AFTER THE GUARDS WALK THROUGH I WILL GO OUTSIDE AND SKIP ROPE & DO PUSH-UPS UNTIL NOON. I CAN FEEL/SEE MY MID SECTION SLIMMING DOWN. SKIP ROPE & MEAL RATIONS IS DOING WONDERS THIS WEEK. I THINK YOULL REALLY ENJOY WHAT YOU SEE. ITS ALL FOR YOUR EYES ONLY ♡!!! ON THE STOVE I HAVE CHICKEN BOILING, SO I CAN HAVE SOUP & CHICKEN SALAD FOR THE NEXT FEW DAYS. AFTER ISOLATION IS COMPLETE I PLAN TO SOCIALIZE A LOT LESS, I WILL FOCUS ON RECOVERY, SELF-GROWTH, FITNESS, AND COMMUNICATION. MY ONLY GOAL IS TO GET HOME TO YOU AND THE GIRLS. IT WAS ALWAYS THE GOAL ONLY NOW I WILL DOUBLE DOWN AND PROVE I AM WORTHY OF DAY PAROLE. AFTER THESE PAST FEW EMOTIONAL DAYS I FEEL

(353)

THAT MY ENERGY IS REVAMPED AND MY CONFID-ENCE IS BACK. I KNOW WHAT IS NEEDED TO BE DONE AND I WILL DO WHAT IT TAKES TO BE SUCC-ESSFUL IN THIS GOAL. I KNOW IT IS 100% O.K. TO HAVE A DOWN WEEK, HOWEVER, I WILL NOT LET THIS OCCURANCE KEEP ME DOWN!!! PERSERV-ERANCE IS KEY TO SUCCESS. A STRONG MINDSET AND DETERMINATION TO LIVE IN GODS WILL IS FLO-WING THROUGH MY VEINS. I AM A GREAT FATHER, FRIEND, SIBLING, AND PARTNER. MY LOYAL QUALITIES AND POSITIVE MINDSET WILL GET ME THROUGH ANYTHING. I WILL NEVER GIVE UP. I FUCKING LOVE & ADORE YOU ANGEL AND I CANNOT WAIT. TO SHOW YOU THE LOVE AND APPRECIATION IN PER-SON THAT I FEEL FOR YOU ♡♡ YOURE ARE THE MOST BEAUTIFUL PERSON I HAVE EVER KNOWN (OH STOP) ♡♡ ⟹ ♡ ⟹ ILL NEVER STOP TELLING YOU!!! ♡ ⟹ (4PM) HELLO SWEETGIRL. AS OF NOW I WILL CONTINUE TO RESIDE AT M.M INSTITUTION. I STILL MAINTAIN THE SUPPORT OF MY P.O. AS WELL. I NOW KNOW EXACTLY HOW TRANSPARENT I NEED TO BE W/ MY P.O. IVE LEARNED THAT AS SOON AS WE HAD FEELINGS MORE THAN FRIEND-SHIP (BEST FRIENDS) THAT I NEEDED TO FULLY DISCLOSE THOSE FEELINGS. NOW THAT I UNDER-STAND I WILL 100% DO THIS. I BREIFLY EXPL-AINED THE ENTIRETY OF OUR FRIENDSHIP UP UNTIL THE PRESENT. I EXPRESSED MY DESIRE TO CONTINUE THIS FRIENDSHIP AS IT HAS NOT BEEN LABELLED. I EXPRESSED THAT RECOVERY & PAROLE ABSOLUTELY COME FIRST AND THAT YOU SUPPORT ME/HAVE SUPPORTED ME THROUGHOUT THE ENTIRE

(34)

DURATION OF RECOVERY, INCARCERATION, AND WHAT IS TO FOLLOW UPON RELEASE. IT SUCH A BEAUTIFUL THING TO HAVE A BEST FRIEND LIKE YOU. THE INSTITUTION MAY SEE OUR ACTIONS AS IMPULSIVE, WHICH I UNDERSTAND, THE WAY WE HAVE GOTTEN TO THIS POINT HAS BEEN VERY SLOW AND DRAWN OUT. WE SPENT A LOT OF TIIME (2 ii'S NOT SURE WHY LOL) BECOMING BESTFRIENDS, SHOWING LOVE AND SUPPORT NON STOP IN EVERY SITUATION, THEN FALLING IN LOVE DEEPER THAN EITHER OF US MAY HAVE ANTICIPATED. I WILL FOREVER APPRECIATE ALL THE HOURS SPENT GETTING TO LEARN ABOUT EACH OTHER AND ABOUT OURSELVES W/ ONE ANOTHER. I KNOW THAT W/ DEDICATION THE POWERS THAT BE (P.O.) WILL SEE THAT THERE IS NO BETTER SUPPORT THAN YOU HAVE BEEN. MY FAITH REMAINS W/ OUR HIGHER POWER AND I WILL CONTINUE IN LIVING HIS WILL. THIS IS YET ANOTHER PAGE WRITTEN FOR THIS TIME AWAY, AND AS ALWAYS WAITING TO CALL HER (YOU) I PRAY THAT I WILL STILL BE ABLE TO WALK OUT OF HERE TO YOUR FACE. I LOOK FORWARD TO OUR CALL LATER THIS EVENING ⇒ ♡ ⇒ (6:30PM) HOLY JESUS IT IS HOT INSIDE THIS HOUSE!!! I JUST MAY HAVE TO HAVE A COLDISH TEMP SHOWER TONIGHT. THE SWELTERING HEAT MAKES IT DIFFICULT TO EVEN MOVE AROUND. AH WELL... IT IS ONLY SUPPOSED TO GET WARMER. YIKES! THE EXTREME SLOWS TIME EMMENSELY DURING AN ALREADY ~~GRE~~ GRUELINGLY SLOW TIME HERE IN ISOLATION. 5 MORE DAYS LEFT. I THOUGHT WORKING IN THIS HEAT WAS BRUTAL. AT LEAST

(35)

A JOB IS ENJOYABLE AND LETS ME GIVE BACK TO THE INSTITUTION. IT ALSO PASSES TIME TOO... IVE BEEN WONDERING HOW THE GIRLS ARE DOING A LOT TODAY. MAN'O' MAN ARE THEY LIL' CUTIE-PIES. I CANT WAIT TO GIVE THEM DADDY SNUGGLES AGAIN. I CLOSED ALL THE BLINDS AND POINTED A FAN DIRECTLY AT MYSELF. I HELPS THE SLIGHTEST BIT. 2 MORE HOURS UNTIL OUR 30 MINUTE CALL☺♡. "MIDWAY" IS THE MOVIE ON TV A.T.M. IVE SEEN PROBS ONCE A MONTH SINCE IVE BEEN "INSIDE", AND YET STILL ENJOY IT AS IT PASSES TIME ENTERTAININGLY (← NOT SURE IF THAT IS A WORD... IF NOT... NOW IT IS LOL). I WAS JUST LOOKING AT YOUR PHOTOS AND WHAT YOU HAD ME WRITE. I AM SO GRATEFUL TO HAVE THEM IN HERE W/ ME THATS FORSURE ♡!!! ⟹ ♡ ⟹ ♡ ⟹ IT WAS SO NICE TO HEAR YOUR VOICE SWEETHEART!!! MY HEART IS COMPLETELY FILLED. MY FEELING ARE OF HAPPINESS & LOVE KNOWING THAT YOU LOVE ME THE WAY I DO YOU. ALL MY NEEDS ARE FILLED BY YOU EXACTLY THE WAY YOU ARE HUN. I TRULY LOOK FORWARD TO WHATEVER COMES NEXT FOR US♡. THANK YOU SO MUCH FOR ALL THE SUPPORT ALONG THIS EYE OPENING, EMOTIONAL, LIFE CHANGING PATH. LIFE IS SO GREAT IN MYSTERIOUS & MAGICAL WAYS. GOD DOES EXIST AND I FEEL HIM GUIDING ME IN WAYS I NEVER KNEW POSSIBLE. THE HARDEST YEAR OF MY LIFE HAS ALSO BEEN THE MOST BEAUTIFUL. I WILL BE SO STOKED TO RE-READ ALL OF THIS FOR THE FIRST TIME AND POTENTIALLY PUBLISH THIS STORY OF →

(36)

LOVE, TRIUMPH, GROWTH, PERSEVERANCE, CONNECTION, PAIN, SUFFERING, AND COURAGE. DEFINATELY AN AMAZING JOURNEY FINDING MY BEST FRIEND. TITLED "WAITING TO CALL HER"... "THE ANGEL ON MY ARM" ♡ GOODNIGHT SWEETGIRL ♡ I MISS & LOVE YOU VERY MUCH ANGEL ♡♡ Z Z Z Z Z Z Z Z Z

2022-07-20

GOOD MORNING SWEETHEART. HOW ARE YOU, MY LOVE? I LAYED IN BED THIS MORNING FOR AN HOUR AFTER I WOKE AND THOUGHT ABOUT LIFE AFTER ALL THIS IS FINISHED. THE FUTURE IS BRIGHT ☺. RECOVERY WILL BE ANOTHER GREAT EXPERIENCE ALONG THIS PATH AND ST. LEONARDS WILL BE A GREAT PLACE TO LEARN & GROW YET AGAIN. I LIKE THE IDEA OF NORTH VAN UNTIL THE RETURN BACK TO THE ISLAND (ITS NOT AN ISLAND, ITS ATTACHED TO SQUAMISH, IT JUST SEEMS LIKE AN ISLAND CAUSE OF THE FERRIES. ITS A PENINSULA... GOD!!!) (I HOPE YOURE LAUGHING HUN) ♡ HAVE AN AMAZING DAY ONLY 11 MORE HOURS UNTIL OUR CALL ♡⟹♡⟹♡⟹ (11AM) WELL. THE BIG BOOK HAS BEEN READ & NVC. DO I READ THEM AGAIN. HMMMM. WE WILL SEE. TODAY I AM GOING TO HAVE A REST DAY. MY ENERGY IS LOW AS THE FOOD SUPPLY IS SEVERELY LIMITED. I DONT HAVE A LOT OF INGREDIENTS NOR AN IDEAL AMOUNT. CES LA VIE WHEN RULES ARE BROKEN. I PUT MYSELF HERE SO I HAVE NO COMP-LAINTS WHATSOEVER. LESSON LEARNED, NOW TO JUST MOVE FORWARD FROM HERE W/AN ATTITUDE OF GRATITUDE FOR THE PATH THAT HAS BEEN

(37)

CHOSEN FOR ME. LAST NIGHTS TALK WAS SO
NICE THE WAY YOU SHOW ME LOVE BY REASSUR-
-ING MY GOOD QUALITIES AND TELLING ME
HOW I MAKE YOU FEEL, MAKES ME FEEL REALLY
HAPPY AND PROUD. I APPRECIATE ALL THAT YOU
ARE!!! ♡ AFTER THE GUARDS WALK THROUGH I
WILL HAVE CHICKEN BROTH W/ RICE AND SOME
SMALL PIECES OF CHICKEN TO TIED ME OVER
TIL PROBABLY 3PM OR SO. I LOVE YOU ANGEL
♡♡⟹♡⟹ (3PM) HELLO LOVELYGIRL. ITS A SLOW
SLOW DAY TODAY. I WAS OUTSIDE IN THE SUN EARL-
-IER WATCHING THE BEES FLY FROM FLOWER
PICKING THROUGH THE HONEYSUCKLE FOR 30
MINS OR SO. IT WAS VERY HOT. A HAD A NAP
FOR AN HOUR AND FELL ASLEEP GAZING AT
YOUR GORGEOUS EYES. MY HEART IS VERY
CONTENT, I FEEL SERENE INTERNALLY AND
FULL OF LOVE AND FEEL LOVED. THERE ISNT MUCH
ON T.V. THAT I HAVENT SEEN, SO I AM WATCHING
"HOW ITS MADE." IT REMINDS ME OF MY DAD AS
HE USED TO WATCH IT WHEN I WAS YOUNG. I
REMEMBER SITTING NEXT TO HIM BEING HAPPY
TO BE W/ MY DAD. THIS EXPERIENCE HAS HELPED
ME REALIZE THAT CHILDREN JUST WANT TO
BE HAPPY W/ THEIR PARENTS. ILL KEEP THAT
W/ ME FOR WHEN THE TIME COMES FOR THE
GIRLS TO HAVE THEIR DADDY HOME AGAIN, AND
IN THE FUTURE WHEN NEWBORNS ARRIVE ♡XO♡
⟹♡⟹ (7PM) 2 MORE HOURS HUN. THERE HASNT
BEEN MUCH HAPPENING, WHILE I WAS BORED I WROTE
A RAP VERSE LOL. THERE ARE SO MANY SELF PROCL-
AIMED "RAP ARTISTS" IN HERE I FIGURED ID TRY

(38)

AND STUMP THEM. THE OTHER DAY ONE WAS TALKING ABOUT AN ARTIST, I DIDN'T KNOW WHO IT WAS, WHEN I ASKED I WAS TOLD I WOULDN'T KNOW BECAUSE THEY WERE FROM "BACK IN THE DAY". I ASKED IF IT WAS LIKE DR. DRE ERA OR EARLIER. TO WHICH THE REPLY WAS "NO." I THEN ASK "UMMMM... LIL WAYNE & DRAKE ERA," THE REPLY WAS..."NO.. NEWER." I REALIZED THE PERSON WAS 27, SO I SAID..."RIGIIGHT"... FOR A 27 YEAR OLD "BACK IN THE DAY"... "UMMMM... WERE THEY RELEASED LAST WEDN-ESDAY.".. I LAUGHED LOL... I WAS WAITING FOR HIM TO CORRECT HIS AGE W/..."AAAAND ACTUALLY IM [redacted] 27 ¼" HAHAHAHA.... ♡ THIS HOUSE IS FINALLY COOLING OFF ~~IN THIS HOUSE~~ WHICH IS NICE. I FEEL AS IF IM WEARING SARAN-WRAP A.T.M. THE AIR IS HUMID & STAGNANT UNFORTUNATELY. AS I SIT HERE I WONDER WHAT YOU'RE UP TO AND HOW YOUR DAY HAS BEEN. I HOPE YOU'RE HAPPY AND HAVE A FULL HEART ♥.

⇒ ♡ ⇒ Ⓑ Ⓑ ⇒ CHARLIE JUST POPPED BY BRIEFLY TO SAY HIS GOODBYES ☺. I WILL MISS HIM A LOT. HE SEEMS SO HAPPY, LIKE A HUGE WEIGHT OFF OF HIS SHOULDERS. I AM SUPER HAPPY FOR HIM!!! ♥ IF I GET DAY PAROLE I WILL BE SO EXCITED & HAPPY. I COULD FEEL THROUGH CHARLES WHAT HE WAS FEELING. I BET ITS AMAZING!!! HIS DAD ARRIVES AT 9AM TOMORROW TO TAKE HIM. I CAN'T WAIT FOR THAT TO BE "US" YOU SWEETHEART ♥♥♥

⇒ ♥ ⇒ GOODNIGHT SWEETGIRL, IT WAS SO VERY SWEET TO HEAR YOUR VOICE TONIGHT ♡ I COULD TELL THAT YOU WERE A BIT ANXIOUS AS YOU

(39)

TALK FAST, AFTER WE DISCUSSED SOME OF THE THINGS THAT WERE STRESSING YOU I COULD FEEL YOUR VOICE GET MORE CALMING. I WILL ALWAYS BE HERE TO BE AN EAR WHEN YOURE IN NEED HUN, I PROMISE YOU THAT. YOUR NEEDS ARE VERY IMPORTANT AND I AM BLESSED TO BE A PERSON IN WHICH YOU CAN COMMUNICATE THEM TO W/ AN OPEN HEART. YOUR FEELINGS ARE MY FEELINGS ♡♡ I LOVE YOU ANGEL Z Z Z Z Z Z Z Z

2022-07-21

(7:30am) GOOD MORNING BEAUTIFUL GIRL♡. I WOKE UP EARLY FOR SOME REASON. SLEEP WAS REALLY GREAT LAST NIGHT. TODAY WILL PROBABLY BE YET ANOTHER LONG ONE. IT IS VERY SUNNY OUT ALREADY SO MOST LIKELY ANOTHER HOT ON AS WELL. AS I SIT HERE WRITING TO YOU I THINK OF BEING BESIDE YOU AS YOU WAKE UP SO BEAUTIFUL IN THE MORNING AS I SLIDE YOU IN TIGHT FOR MORNING CUDDLES♡. TODAY CHARLES LEAVES. I AM GRATEFUL TO HAVE MET HIM & SPENT THAT MUCH TIME W/ HIM. MY BEST MEMORIES OF PHYSICALLY BEIN INCARCERATED ARE W/ HIM. WE HAD A LOT OF LAUGHS AS WELL AS MANY DEEP TALKS & ABOUT LOVE, LIFE, & FAMILY. ONE DAY WE WILL HAVE TO DRIVE TO REVELSTOKE SO YOU CAN MEET HIM. TODAY I FEEL COMPLETE, MY HEART IS VERY FULL. THE ROUTINE OF ISOLATION HAS BECOME NORMALIZED AS I ADAPT TO MY SURROU-NDINGS. PEACE, LOVE, & HAPPINESS COME FROM W/IN US. SEARCHING FOR SUCH THINGS EXTERNALLY WILL ALWAYS BE LOST. EXTERNAL HAPPINESS IS TEMPORARY AND OFTEN LEADS US BLINDLY ASTRAY AND SEARCHING

(40)

FOR SOMETHING THAT ALWAYS IS SO FAR AWAY. ALMOST LIKE THE WORLD CONSTANTLY DANGLES A CARROT AND USUALLY BY THE TIME WE REACH THAT CARROT IT WILL HAVE GONE BAD. NOT TO SAY THAT GOALS, MATERIAL ITEMS, ACHIEVEMENTS, ETC... CAN'T MAKE A PERSON HAPPY, BUT, IT WILL FADE AS WE ALWAYS MOVE RIGHT ALONG TO THE VERY NEXT THING... IF THAT MAKES SENSE. IF WE ARE FULFILLED INTERNALLY IN OUR NEEDS THEN ALL THOSE THINGS WILL BECOME IRRELEVANT AS WE SEE THAT THE ENTIRE JOURNEY IS THE BLESSING & NOT THE END RESULT. OUR THOUGHTS CAN BE THE TRAP YET ALSO THE KEY TO FREEDOM. THE SAYING "FOLLOW YOUR HEART" IS TRUE AS LONG AS WE KNOW WHAT WE FOLLOW MAKES OUR LIVES FEEL ENRICHED W/ GOODNESS AND THE POSITIVE NEEDS ARE BEING MET. DURING MY CHILDHOOD I HAD LEARNED THAT BACKWARDS AND MY NEEDS WERE NEGATIVE, IT LEFT ME SEARCHING ~~YET~~ EXTERNALLY WHICH GOT ME THIS POINT IN-PRISONED. THE TIME HERE HAS ACTUALLY SET ME FREE AS THE REAL PRISON WAS INSIDE MYSELF MY ENTIRE LIFE. INTERNAL INPRISONMENT LEFT ME SEARCHING FOR EXTERNAL FREEDOM, LITERAL EXTERNAL INPRIS-ONMENT MADE ME REALIZE/FIND INTERNAL FREEDOM ♡. WHAT A CONCEPT. ⇒♡⇒♡⇒ (10:30am)

AS I SIT HERE I GET WAVES OF EXCITEMENT ABOUT THE POSSIBILITY OF DAY PAROLE, I TRY TO MAINTAIN HUMILITY ~~IN~~ TOWARDS MY DRIVE TO STAY HUMBLE AND OPEN TO THE ROAD THAT LIES AHEAD. TODAY I WILL READ THE TRADITIONS OF N.A TO AGAIN FURTHER MY KNOWLEDGE TOWARDS AN ISSUE

41

THAT (THROUGH BAD LIFE CHOICES) BROUGHT ME TO THIS PLACE. AS HARD AS THIS HAS ALL BEEN ON MYSELF AND EVERYONE WHO CARES FOR ME THE FUTURE OUTCOMES, I BELIEVE, WILL HAVE THE ABSOLUTE BEST RESULTS, THERFOR I REMAIN GRATEFUL. THE PHRASE "ATTITUDE OF GRATITUDE" IS VERY REAL AND ENCOMPASES ALL THAT IS NEEDED FOR A BRIGHT FUTURE. I CAN GIVE ALOT OF APPRECIATION TO THE STAFF AT RRAC & M.M. INSTITUTION FOR TREATING ME W/ THE UTMOST RESPECT. THEY HAVE TAUGHT ME AN INCREDIBLE AMOUNT ABOUT ROUTINE, STRUCTURE, PLANNING, & CONSISTENCY. ALL THINGS I WILL BRING W/ ME THROUGHOUT THE REST OF MY LIFE. I FEEL EXCITEMENT AT THE POTENTIAL ABILITY OF TREATMENT AND ALL THE NEW LESSONS I CAN LEARN, BEING ABLE TO SHARE ALL OF THESE EXPERIENCES TO HOPEFULLY AID THOSE SIMILAR TO US SEE THAT THERE IS HELP WHEN WE'RE COMPLETELY READY TO RECIEVE IT. I BELIEVE IN MY ABILITIES TO RESONATE W/ OTHERS EMPATHETICALLY ALLOWING VOICES TO BE HEARD W/ AN OPEN HEART. ⇒ ♡ ⇒ ♡ I LOVE YOU MY SWEETHEART ♡ ⇒ HELLO MY LOVE. THE 11TH OF AUGUST IS MY DAY. 20 MORE DAYS. I LITERALLY JUMPED FOR JOY... THEN A WAVE OF REFLECTION HIT ME LIKE A TSUNAMI AND BEGAN TO CRY. I AM SO EXCEPTIONALLY GRATEFUL FOR THIS ~~[illegible]~~ OPPORTUNITY TO HAVE BEEN ABLE TO CHANGE MY ENTIRE LIFE ♡!!! LITERALLY EVERY SINGLE PART OF IT HAS CHANGED. THANK ~~[illegible]~~ YOU FOR ALWAYS BEING THERE FOR ME. I LOVE YOU FOREVER YOU ARE THE MOST PRECIOUS HUMAN BEING I HAVE

(42)

EVER MET!!! ♡♡♡ I HAVE UN-ENDING LOVE FOR
EVERY PART OF YOU♡. "[redacted], THE ANGEL ON MY
ARM". THAT ARM IS FOREVER YOURS. MY GIRLS CAN
FINALLY HAVE THEIR DADDY BACK♡!!! I FEEL SO
SPECIAL RIGHT NOW KNOWING THE LOVE THAT YOU
HAVE FOR ME♡!!! MY HEART & SOUL IS FOREVER
BONDED TO YOU [redacted]. I WILL ALWAYS BE YOURS!!!
♡♡♡ ⇒ (4pm) MY C.O.^{2} SAW ME CRYING EARLIER,
WE HAD A GOOD CHAT ABOUT THIS JOURNEY. ONLY
5 HOURS UNTIL OUR CHAT AND I CANNOT WAIT HUN
!!! ♡ THE THOUGHT OF HOLDING YOU DEEP IN MY
ARMS AND FEELING EACHOTHERS HEARTS BEAT
IS A DREAM TO ME. I WANT TO FEEL YOUR HEART
BEATING NEXT TO MINE FOREVER ♡ ON TOP OF ALL
THAT IS TRUE BEAUTY INSIDE YOU... YOU ARE SO
UNBELIEVABLY SEXY AND TURN ME ON IN EVERY
POSSIBLE WAY IMAGINABLE ☆ I AM SO EXCITED
TO HAVE YOU ON TOP OF ME AND ABLE TO MAN-HAN-
-DLE YOU IN EVERY POSITION POSSIBLE. GRIPPING
YOUR BODY FIRMLY MAKING YOU PANT AND MOAN.
SOAKED & DRIPPING ALL OVER ME WHILE I EXPLODE
INSIDE OF YOU FOR OUR FIRST TIME. LOOKING INTO
EACH OTHERS EYES WHILE YOU GO DOWN ON
ME AS I GET HARDER AND HARDER. THEN I CAN
LAY YOU ON YOUR BACK AND HOLD YOU DOWN
WHILE I FILL EVERY MILLIMETER OF YOU. SLOW
THEN FAST. I WANT YOU TO RIDE ME REVERSE
COWGIRL IN FRONT OF THE MIRROR AND REACH
BACK PUTTING YOUR HANDS ON MINE WHILE WE
SPREAD YOUR ASS CHEEKS APART FOR AS LONG
AS WE CAN LAST ♡♡♡☆ 1.5 MORE HOURS UNTIL
OUR CALL ☺♡ ⇒ ♡ ⇒ ♡ ⇒ ♡ xox ⇒

(43)

NICE CHATTING W/ YOU TONIGHT SWEETHEART.
23 HOURS UNTIL OUR NEXT CALL ♡. WHEN WE ARE
TOGETHER ID REALLY LIKE TO LISTEN TO SOME
OF YOUR PODCASTS W/ YOU. DRY N COLD →
WET N WARM LOL. I LOVE IT WHEN YOU BURST
INTO LAUGHTER. IT MAKE ME FEEL AMAZING TO
BE ABLE TO MAKE YOU LAUGH LIKE THAT. [redacted]
HAS A REAL AMAZING FRIEND, ALTHOUGH IT
SUCKS FOR HER TO HEAR THE TRUTH OF HOW YOU
FEEL I THINK SHE WILL APPRECIATE THE HONESTY
IN YOU ♡♡. AT LEAST SHE UNDERSTANDS HOW MUCH
YOU CARE ABOUT HER FEELINGS. WELL ITS TIME
TO WATCH "ALONE" ALONE IN ISOLATION ♡ GOODNIGHT
SWEETGIRL... I LOVE YOU SO VERY MUCH ♡♡♡
Z X Z O Z X Z O Zxxxx

2022-07-22

(7:44am)
GOOD MORNING MY LOVE ♡. TODAY AT 8AM I REC-
-EIVE A COVID MOUTHSWAP OR GARGLE. ONLY 3
MORE DAY LEFT IN HERE. I LOOK FORWARD TO
CALLING THE GIRLS ON MONDAY AND SPENDING
MORE THAN 30 MINS A DAY TALKING TO YOU
SWEETHEART ♡♡. I WOKE UP FACING YOU AND
I OPENED MY EYES I SAW THE MOST GORGEOUS
FACE I HAVE EVER SEEN.(YOURS). I AM VERY
HAPPY TO HAVE AN OPPORTUNITY LIKE THAT
IN MY LIFE. TODAY CONSISTS OF A LOT OF NOT ALL
THAT MUCH. AT LEAST THE WEATHER IS OVERCAST
SO IT WONT BE SO HOT IN HERE WHICH IS NICE.
I MAY JUST CUDDLE UP ON THE COUCH AND WATCH T.V.
ALL DAY (W/ THE EXCEPTION OF SHOWERS). WHEN I WOKE
UP I WAS HARD AS A DIAMOND (ROCK) THINKING OF YOU.
MY IMAGINATION RAN WILD FANTASIZING ABOUT

44

ALL THE EXPERIENCES WE ARE GOING TO HAVE TOGETHER SEXUALLY. OH THE POSSIBILITIES (OH BOY!) I CANT WAIT!!! ♡♡♡ ⇒ ♡ ⇒ (11AM) WELL HELLO MY LOVE, HOW IS YOUR DAY? BEAUTIFUL I HOPE!!! ♡ MY DAY HAS BEEN FAIRLY CALM & CHILL SO FAR. I ORGANIZED AND SQUARED UP ALL THE FURN-ITURE AND AM CURRENTLY BAKING CHICKEN BREASTS IN THE OVEN W/ SOME OIL & TEX-MEX TACO SEASONING (ITS ALL I HAVE). I CALLED IN ABOUT THE VEGGIES & DAIRY AS I AM AT THE POINT WHERE MEAT IS NO LONGER APPETIZING TO EAT. WHEN I AM RELEASED I MAY ASK YOU SOME QUES-TIONS ABOUT YOUR DIET AND POTENTIALLY MAKE THE DECISION TO SWITCH TO IT. FOOD IS A VERY INTIMATE WAY OF CONNECTION AND ANOTHER WAY FOR US TO BOND EVEN FURTHER IN OUR FUTURE TOGETHER. ♡ HEALTHIER CHOICES CREATE HEALTHIER LIFESTYLES WHICH IS WHAT ID LIKE TO SHARE W/ YOU. ONLY 10 MORE HOURS UNTIL I GET TO HEAR YOUR BEAUTIFUL VOICE (YOU TRULY MAKE MY HEART MELT ANGEL, I LOVE YOU SO VERY MUCH). ♡ ⇒ ♡ ⇒ ♡ ⇒ (4:30PM) I JUST WANTED YOU TO KNOW THAT IVE BEEN THINKING ABOUT YOU ALL DAY. I AM HEAD OVER HEELS IN LOVE W/ YOU. THIS IS A 44. CALIBER LOVE LETTER STRAIGHT FROM MY HEART (YEP!!! ALEXISONFIRE REFERENCE... IM CLEVER I KNOW ☺ ♡) (I HOPE YOURE SMILING) ♡. (ALMOST USED "YOUR" INSTEAD OF "YOURE")

♡ ⇒ ♡ ⇒

♡ ⇒ ♡ ⇒ ♡ ⇒ AS I LOOK OUT ~~THE~~ ONTO THE "GHETTO" STREETS, THEY ARE DISTITUTE. I HAVENT SEEN GROUPS GATHERING ALL WEEK. I LAUGH INSIDE KNOWING AS SOON AS I SEE BIG ROB

(45)

THAT ITLL BE HEAD SHAVE AND BEARD TRIM TIME. I AM LOOKING FORWARD TO WATERING THE LAWN BEFORE WORK DURING THE WEEK AND HAVING COFFEE W/ROB ON THE PORCH AT 7AM WHILE DOING SO. I HAVE NOT HAD COFFEE IN 8 DAYS AND AM ALMOST OUT OF FOOD COMPLETELY. I MAY BE LOOKING AT A DAY OF FASTING ON SUNDAY... AH WELL, CES LA VIE. TODAY TALKING TO YOU WILL BE AMAZING AS USUAL AND AS ALWAYS THE HIGHLIGHT ♥ ⇒ ♡ ⇒ X GAMES IS ON... YAAAY!!! THE TIME HAS BEEN FLYING BY BECAUSE OF IT. I HAD A THOUGHT ABOUT "THE SOBER SKULL" DESIGN.. SEEING THAT IT WAS MY IDEA, I THOUGHT OF PITCHING IT TO SKULL SKATES AND SEEING IF THEY WOULD SUPP-ORT/PRINT A SERIES OF THEM FOR US. WHAT DO YOU THINK? ♥ ⇒ ♥ ⇒ GOODNIGHT MY LOVE ♡♡♡

Z Z Z Z Z

2022-07-23

HELLO MY LOVE ♡. SORRY I DIDNT FINISH LAST NIGHTS LETTER. I THOUGHT ABOUT YOU ALL NIGHT. I FELT I NEEDED TO INTERNALIZE WHAT I WAS FEELING. AFTER ASSESSING WHAT ALL THE EMOTIONS WERE I WAS ABLE TO IDENTIFY THE NEEDS. I WAS THEN OPEN TO EMPATHIZE W/ [redacted] NEEDS AND HEAR HER W/ AN OPEN HEART. THANK YOU FOR BEING STERN THAT I CALL BOTH DAYS SWEETHEART. IT WAS NICE TO SEE MY ABILITIES TO COMMUNICATE W/ [redacted]. I HAVE DEFINATELY CHANGED A LOT. I WAS ALSO ABLE TO EXPRESS MYSELF PROPERLY AND I THINK WE BOTH FELT RELIEF. I RESPECT YOU ON SUCH A HIGH LEVEL ANGEL THAT I COULD REALLY TRUST YOUR THOUGHTS AND UNDERSTAND THEM FULLY

(46)

I CAN FEEL HOW MUCH YOU ACTUALLY CARE FOR ME W/ HOW YOU UNDERSTAND ME ON SUCH A HIGH LEVEL. I LOVE YOU ♡♡. YOU MEAN THE WORLD TO ME. AT THE END OF OUR CONVERSATION WE HAD SOME REALLY GREAT LAUGHS ABOUT POSITIONING YOUR PHONE SO MY EYES JUST POKED UP LMAO 😄 HAHAHAHAHAHA... STILL LAUGHING ABOUT IT. THINKING ABOUT YOU DOING THAT WHILE LOOKING AT MY PHOTO MAKES ME REALIZE EXACTLY HOW SIMILAR WE TRULY ARE. KNOWING YOU PUT A COUNTDOWN ON YOUR PHONE MELTS MY HEART & SOUL. YOU TRULY ARE THE ANGEL ON MY ARM. ♥♥♡ IM MISSING YOU ALOT TODAY AND WILL TOM-ORROW BUT ABSENSE DOES MAKE THE HEART GROW FONDER ♡ ⇒ ♡ ⇒ I APPRECIATE YOU SO MUCH HUN ♡ ⇒ ♡ ⇒ (4PM) HELLO HUN. TODAY HAS BEEN GO-ING BY FAIRLY QUICKLY, I AM MOST LOOKING FORW-ARD TO BED TONIGHT. THAT WILL MEAN ONLY 1 MORE DAY AND NIGHT. THE WEATHER OUTSIDE IS SUNNY W/ A BREEZE SO THE HOUSE IS JUST THE RIGHT TEMPERATURE IN HERE. I AM THINKING ABOUT HOW YOU ARE DOING AND HOW YOUR DAY HAS BEEN SO FAR, I HOPE ITS AMAZING AS THAT IS WHAT YOU DESERVE ♡!!! THE FIRST THING THATS GETTING DONE MONDAY IS MAILING THESE/THIS LETTER. I DREAM OF THE DAY WE GET TO CUDDLE & WATCH A MOVIE TOGETHER (I LOVE THAT FOR US). WHAT SHOULD WE WATCH MY LOVE? OR SHOULD WE JUST MAKE OUR OWN? (♡😎) (HUBBA HUBBA) ONE DAY IN THE ~~FUT~~ VERY NEAR FUTURE I BELIEVE WE ARE GOING TO BLOW EACHOTHERS MINDS & HEARTS & SOULS IN EVERY WAY MENTALLY & PHYSICALLY & EMOTIONALLY

(47)

CONNECTIVITY IS SO IMPORTANT AS WELL AS OUR COMMUNICATION ♡♡ ⟹ ♡ ⟹ (6pm) I CANNOT WAIT TO BE OUT OF ISOLATION AND THEN INCARCERATION. BEING HOME W/ YOU AND THE GIRLS IS ALL THAT IS ON MY MIND. I AM STOKED TO GO TO TREATMENT TO GAIN EVEN MORE SKILLS & EXPERIENCES TO ADD TO ANOTH-ER POINT FORWARD TOWARDS HAPPY/HEALTHY SIMPLE LIVING ♡!!! MONDAY 5:30 COULD NOT COME SOON ENOUGH LOL. ♡ ⟹ ♡ ⟹ (9pm) HOLY FUCK DO I WANT TO RAVAGE YOU SO BADLY RIGHT NOW YOU HAVE NO IDEA. YOU ARE SO SEXY AND TURN ME ON SOOO MUCH I AM HARD AS A ROCK RIGHT NOW THINKING ABOUT YOU, SITTING ON MY FACE MOANING, SHAKING, AND BREATHING HEAVY. I WANT TO EAT YOU OUT SO BADLY UNTIL YOU CUM ALL OVER ME MULTIPLE TIMES (OH' BOY!!!) I AM GOING TO FILL YOU W/ SO MUCH CUM AS I PULL YOUR HAIR, KISS YOU, AND SUCK YOUR NIPPLES. YOURE GOING TO SQUIRT ALL OVER MY COCK UNTIL THE MATTRESS IS SOAKING WET ♡♡ AND YOUR ENTIRE BODY IS SHAKING ♡♡♡ ⟹ ♡ ⟹ ♡ ⟹ ♡ ⟹ GOODNIGHT SWEETGIRL. I HOPE YOU WRAPPED IN ONE OF THE SHIRTS & SMELL LIKE ME. I LOVE YOU ANGEL ♡ Z x Z o Z x Z Z o Z x Z o Z x

2022-07-24 (9AM)

GOOD MORNING SWEETHEART ♡ LAST DAY ISOLATION. MY LOVE FOR YOU IS ORGANIC BRAH (ORG-AAAAHNIK BRAHH) ♡ ⟹ ♡ ⟹ ⟹ (11AM) I TALKED TO THE GIRLS, MAN O MAN ARE THEY SUCH BEAUTIFUL & LOVING HUMAN BEINGS. THEYRE SO FUNNY & KIND AND I AM SO UNBELIEVABLY PROUD TO BE THEIR LOVING DADDY, ONE DAY I WOULD

(48)

LOVING TO SHARE THAT EXPERIENCE W/ YOU. YOU WILL
100% (HUNDO P) BE THE BEST MOTHER & ROLE MODEL &
INSPIRATION, I ADMIRE ALL YOUR NATURAL MOTHER-
-HOOD ABILITIES. THE WAY YOU ARE W/ KIDS IS SO
HEART MELTING AND SPECIAL. I KNOW YOU MEAN
THE ABSOLUTE MOST TO DAUGHTER & DAUGHTER,
THEY JUST LOVE & ADORE YOU AS MUCH AS THEIR
DADDY DOES ♡♡♡ I LOOK FORWARD TO SPENDING
QUALITY TIME W/ EACH AND EVERY ONE OF YOU.
DAUGHTER TOO, WHEN THE TIME COMES. TODAY I REFLECT
ON EXACTLY HOW SPECIAL YOU ARE TO ME. WHEN
WE ARE FINALLY TOGETHER I WILL TELL YOU IN
WORDS EXACTLY WHAT I THINK AND HOW I FEEL,
ILL SHOW YOU MY HEART AND LOOK FORWARD TO LEARNING
MORE ABOUT YOU. ILL CHERISH, LOVE, RESPECT, &
AND ADMIRE YOU FOREVER. YOU ARE FOREVER
MY BEST FRIEND!!! ♡♡♡ YOUR NEEDS ARE
EXTREMELY IMPORTANT TO ME ANGEL, I LOVE YOU ♡
⇒ ♡ ⇒ ♡ ⇒ I WENT OUTSIDE DURING COUNT, MAN
IT IS HOT OUT THERE. WHILE I WAS OUTSIDE I SEAR-
-CHED FOR HEART SHAPED ROCKS AND WAS ABLE
TO FIND 2 ♡♡. IT MADE ME FEEL LOTS OF LOVE DUR-
-ING MY HUNT FOR THEM. I WENT SHIRT OFF AND GOT
TO SEE MY WHOLE UPPER BODY IN A WINDOW REFLEC-
-TION... I FELT REALLY SEXY AND CONFIDENT IN MY-
-SELF... IT HAS BEEN A TON OF DEDICATION & WORK
TO GET TO THIS POINT. THANK YOU FOR BEING THE
INSPIRATION I NEEDED TO KEEP ON PUSHING WHEN
I WASNT MOTIVATED. ITLL BE EVEN NICER TO HAND
LIPS, HANDS, EYES, HEART, & BODY UP AGAINST THIS
BODY IVE DEVELOPED ♡ (HUBBA HUBBA) ♡ ⇒
♡ ⇒ ♡ ⇒ ♡ ⇒ ♡ ⇒

(49)

♥ ⟹ (2:30) TODAY CONSISTED OF X-GAMES & TATTOO
SHOWS SO FAR. I HOPE YOUR DAY HAS BEEN GREAT
SO FAR. CHATTING ON THE PHONE FOR MORE THAN
30 MINS SEEMS LIKE A DREAM. EVEN THOUGH THE
LAST 11 DAYS HAS BEEN LONG I AM GRATEFUL FOR
THEM ALL. THERE HAS BEEN A LOT OF SELF GROWTH
AND ONCE AGAIN ANOTHER DIFFICULT SCENARIO TO
GET THROUGH W/ GRACE & HUMILITY. KEEPING FAITH
HAS BEEN HUGE AND HAVING YOU REALLY MADE ME
REALIZE WE CAN GET THROUGH ANYTHING TOGETHER ♥.
LOYALTY IS SO HUGE IN MY LIFE AND I AM ABSOLUTELY
LOYAL TO YOU IN EVERY WAY POSSIBLE. ITS NICE TO
TALK TO SOMEONE W/ THE SAME MORALS & VALUES
AS I HAVE, LOYALTY IS AN EXCEPTIONAL STRENGTH AND
SHOULD NEVER EVER BE TAKEN FORGRANTED. ONE
MORE ½ DAY AND A SLEEP... YAAAAAAAAAAAY!!!!!!!
HOPEFULLY IN THE NEXT FEW DAYS I CAN HEAR YOU CUM
ON THE PHONE ONCE MORE. YOU SOUND SO SEXY I JUST WANT
TO MAKE THOSE SOUNDS COME OUT OF YOU WHILE YOU
DIG YOUR NAILS INTO MY CHEST AND HEELS INTO MY
BACK SCREAMING FOR ME TO CUM INSIDE OF YOU ♡
ONCE WE FINISH ILL STAY INSIDE OF YOU WHILE MY
THROBBING COCK PULSATES AND YOUR PUSSY SQUEEZES
ALL OVER IT, SOAKED ♡♡♡ THEN HAVE YOU SUCK ME
[redacted] W/ MY FINGERS INSIDE YOU WHILE RUBBING YOUR
ASS & CLIT ♡♡♡ THEN WE CAN CONTINUE PLAYING
& TEASING EACHOTHER AND GO AGAIN & AGAIN
& AGAIN ♡ ⟹ ♡ ⟹ ♡ ⟹ (7PM) ALMOST THERE HUN
ALMOST THERE... I HAD A HALF NAP EARLIER... NOT
TO SURE IF I ACTUALLY SLEPT BUT DEFINATELY RELAXED
IN BED AND THOUGHT ABOUT YOU ♡. WE ARE ALMOST
THERE MY LOVE... ALMOST THERE SWEETHEART. →

(50)

ONE DAY CLOSER ☺. I COULD SURE GO FOR A WALK ON A BEACH RIGHT ABOUT NOW, HAVE A FIRE, EAT A MASSIVE CHARCUTERIE BOARD, THEN WATCH A MOVIE TOGETHER RIGHT ABOUT NOW. THE C.O.S JUST WALKED THROUGH AND ASKED ME IF THIS WAS MY FIRST "FED BIT" I TOLD THEM IT WAS MY ONLY "BIT" EVER... THEY THEN ASKED HOW MUCH PROVINCIAL TIME IVE HAD TO DO IN MY PAST... AAND WERE SHOCKED WHEN THEY LEARNED I HAD NEVER BEEN IN A JAIL & THIS WAS THE ONLY THING ON MY CRIMINAL HISTORY. ONCE AGAIN BASED ON A JUDGEMENT ON HOW I CARRY MYSELF AND THE WAY I LOOK... CES LA VIE, ITS COMES W/ THE TERITORY OF BEING THIS TATTOO-ED AND SEXY ☺ ♡♡♡ ⟹ ♡ ⟹ (8PM) 2-3 HOURS UNTIL BED (HALLELUJAH). ISOLATION DONE. HOLY FUCK THE PAST 11 DAYS HAS BEEN A TRIP. IT TAKES SOME SERIOUS MENTAL ENDURANCE TO GO THROUGH SO MANY EMOTIONAL UPS & DOWNS. LUCKILY MY HEART IS TRULY FILLED AND THERES A LIGHT SHINING SO BRIGHTLY AT THE END OF THIS TUNNEL (YOU & THE GIRLS). I WILL NOT BE HANGING OUT W/ PEOPLE AS MUCH STARTING TOMORROW, CHARLIE IS GONE SO ILL BE FOCUSED ON GROWTH BOTH MENTAL & PHYSICAL, MEETINGS, TALKING W/ YOU, AND MOSTLY JUST PREPARING FOR THIS DAY PAROLE HEARING. NO ONE HEAR MATTERS ANYMORE AND I AM FOCUSED SOLELY ON LEAVING HERE, WALKING OUT OF AND BEING ABLE TO HOLD ONTO YOU AND HAVING OUR FIRST KISS NO PRISON RESTRICTIONS. I LOVE YOU [redacted] ♡♡♡ ⟹ ♡ ⟹ (10PM) FINALLY ☺ ☺ ☺ ♡♡♡ ♡ ☺ ♡♡♡ ⟶

13

Counting Days

"Time doesn't move the same in here."

Some days dragged, some disappeared. You'd wake up thinking it was Monday and find out it was Thursday. Time in there didn't march forward—it folded in on itself. That's why I started counting. Not to mark how long I'd been gone, but to remind myself I was still moving through something, not stuck inside it.

I marked the small things—letters sent, workouts finished, nights I actually slept. I'd count the times I laughed, even the quiet ones that came from remembering something good. I thought about how long it had been since I last heard her voice, and somehow that number felt heavier than the sentence itself. But instead of letting it crush me, I used it as a measure of strength—another day I made it through without breaking.

Discipline saved me, but reflection changed me. The routine—push-ups, reading, writing—gave the day a frame, but thinking about what those days meant gave it color. I started noticing details again—the way light bent through the windows at certain hours, the smell of rain through the vents, the quiet that came just before count.

When it got still, I'd close my eyes and picture her beside me, the sound of her laugh mixing with the hum of the range. That's how I would measure time—not by clocks or calendars, but by the distance between us, and the hope that one day that distance would finally run out.

(1)

DEAR ANGEL ♡

TONIGHT I WRITE THIS LETTER TO
REMEMBER ALL THE AMAZING TIMES
WE SHARED. THE FIRST TIME I SAW
YOU WALK UP TO THE ROOMS I SAW
SOMETHING SO INCREDIBLY SPECIAL...
I WAS SO DRAWN TO YOU AS YOU WERE
TO ME. WE WOULD TXT ABOUT MOVIES
AND LOVED TRYING TO MAKE YOU LAUGH.
WATCHING YOU COLOR W/ MY GIRLS
ALWAYS MADE SMILE AND MELTED MY
HEART... AT BEACH MEETINGS THEYD
ALWAYS ASK ME IF THE COULD SIT W/YOU
..♡♡♡ I COULD THE LIGHT IN THEIR LITTLE
EYES AND HAPPINESS IN YOU... IT MADE
ME SO HAPPY... THE DAY WERE IN YOUR
CAR WHEN I GAVE YOU THAT CHIP I WAS
SO NERVOUS. I WAS SCARED BECAUSE I
KNEW I WAS GOING AWAY AND THOUGHT
I MAY NEVER SEE AGAIN. TALKING TO YOU
ON THE PHONE WAS ONE OF THINGS THAT
GAVE ME HOPE. YOU SAVED ME LIKE AN
ANGEL THAT GOD PUT IN MY PATH.....OVER
THE NEXT YEAR WE HAD TALKED ABOUT LOVE,
LIFE, STRUGGLES, JOYS, AND GETTING THAT
CHANCE WAS SUCH AN AMAZING TIME... I
REMEMBER TOUCHING YOUR SOFT HANDS W/
MINE AND NEVER WANTING TO LET THEM
GO... YOU LOOKED SO BEAUTIFUL... YOUR
BLUE EYES, PERFECT HAIR FILLED ME W/

(2)

SO MUCH LOVE... KISSING YOU FOR THE FIRST TIME AS YOU WRAPPED YOUR LEGS AROUND ME WAS A CONNECTION I HAD NEVER FELT BEFORE... AT THAT TIME I KNEW I WAS THE LUCKIEST MAN ALIVE ... I OFTEN THINK ABOUT US BEING INTIMATE AND WATCHING YOUR EYELIDS HALF SHUT AND YOUR VOICE SOFTEN... WHAT A BEAUTIFUL EXPERIENCE... I THINK OF HOW YOU LOOKED AT ME ~~WITH~~ WITH SUCH LOVE AND COMPASSION AND COULD SEE THE MAN THAT IS BURIED INSIDE ME... OUR HEARTS CONNECTED... WATCHING YOU DO THINGS AS SIMPLE AS COOKING AND BEING SUPER DORKY ALWAYS MADE ME SMILE... GOING OUT FOR DINNER KNOWING YOUD ORDER MULTIPLE THINGS TO SHARE MAKES ME SMILE ALOT STILL... YOU SURPRISING ME W/ VISITS AND GIFTS WAS SOMETHING NO ONE HAD EVER DONE FOR ME BEFORE ♡♡♡ WEARING MATCHING OUTFITS W/ THE GIRLS AND HOW EXCITED YOU WERE IN DOING SO IS SUCH AN AMAZING QUALITY ... THE WAY YOU ORGANIZE RIGHT DOWN TO WHICH WAY THE TOILET PAPER SAT ALWAYS MADE HAPPY... YOUR FRIENDSHIP AND LOVE FOR ME HAS GIVEN ME SO MUCH MORE THAN YOU REALIZE... YOUVE CHALLENGED TO BECOME A BETTER FATHER AND HUMAN BEING... YOUVE MADE REALIZE I NEED TO LISTEN MORE INTENTLY AND COMMUNICATE SOFTY... TAKE SPACE AND BE CALM

(3)

SO I CAN FEEL THE FEELINGS I AM SCARED OF... TO REACH DEEP INSIDE AND LOVE MYSELF THE WAY YOU AND THE GIRLS DO... YOUVE TAUGHT ME TO STICK TO ONLY A FEW PEOPLE I TRUST TO OPEN UP TO AND MAINTAIN PRIVACY AT ALL COSTS... YOUVE OPENED MY EYES TO WHAT TRUE LOVE ACTULLY IS AND NOT ALLOW MY PAST TRUAMAS TO OVERTAKE AND TAKE IT ALL AWAY. IVE BEEN ABLE TO FIND AND UNDERSTAND MYSELF MORE IN THE LAST TWO WEEKS THAN EVER BEFORE AND FOR THAT I AM GRATEFUL... ALL I EVER WANTED WAS TO BE HAPPY AND THROUGH THE PAINS OF NOT HAVING YOU I KNOW NOW TO FIND JOY IN WHAT MATTERS AND TO NOT TAKE THING FORGRANTED... I CAN PICTURE YOU IN ONE OF OUR SHIRTS AND THAT FILLS MY HEART... JUST KNOWING YOU CHERISH THOSE THINGS I MADE FOR YOU WHILE I WAS AWAY IS SUCH A SPECIAL MEMORY WE WILL SHARE FOR THE REST OF OUR LIVES. WHEN I WOULD WRITE YOU I WOULD LOOK AT YOUR PHOTOS AS IF YOU WERE THERE BESIDE ME... I MEANT EVERY SINGLE WORD IN THEM AND STILL DO... MAKING THAT "SKULL SUBTLE" DRAWING WAS FUNNY HOW I HAD TO TRADE MULTIPLE ITEM TO HAVE THAT DRAWN... WHEN I SAW THE ORIGAMI I KNEW I HAD TO BRING THEM TO YOU AND PROTECTED

(4)

AND SMUGGLED THROUGH 3 RANGES
2 LOCKDOWD A QUARANTEEN AND
2 PRISON TO GET THEM HOME
THE SHIRTS I MADE AT NIGHT WATCHING
"BING BANG THEORY" (THE WHOLE UNIVERSE
...) AND MADE STECILS NEXT TO YOU
AND SPRAYED BLEACH SO THEY TURN OUT
SO PERFECTLY IMPERFECT... TO HAVE
THEM RUSH RELEASED FOR OUR VISIT
I WAS TOLD THAT DOING THAT WASNT
ALLOWED BECAUSE OF THE BLEACH BUT
BECAUSE THEY WERE SO CREATIVE
THEYD ALLOW IT AS ARTS AND CRAFTS..
I SOAKED IN AFTER SHAVE SO YOU SMELL
ME.. (OH DID YOU FINISH THE BIG BANG
SONG IN YOUR HEAD.. I HOPE SO LOL ♡)
I WAS SO PROUD TO GIVE YOU THOSE
SHIRTS AND IT FILLS MY HEART YOU
STILL TREASURE THEM... WHEN I
WAS PUT IN THE DOG HOUSE FOR OUR
ROMANTIC BREACH (HOT AF BTW) I
WOULD PRAY FOR RELEASE, TALK TO
YOU AND KISS YOUR PHOTO MULTIPLE
TIMES A DAY... YOU WERE ALWAYS THE
ANGEL ON MY ARM AND I HAD KNOWN
YOU HAD FOUND ME IN A GODLESS PLACE
... THERE ARE SO MANY AMAZING MEMORIES
WE SHARED AND YOUVE MANAGED TO OPEN
MY HEART IN WAYS I DID NOT KNOW..
THOUGH SOME DARKNESS I CAN SEE LIGHT
AND IN DESPAIR THERE IS HOPE. I HAVE
FAITH IN GODS PLAN AND HIS TIME

(5)

ALL WILL BE RIGHT... IVE DONE SO
MANY THING WRONG WHICH HAS BROUGHT
TO A PLACE OF ACCEPTANCE TOWARDS
GODS LESSONS ALLOWING ME TO BE
HUMBLE AND FULLY ACCEPT ALL OF
MY FAULTS DEEP DOWN.. UNTIL NOW
I WAS UNABLE TO SEE SO CLEARLY
THE THINGS THAT I WAS RUNNING
AWAY FROM... I RUN TOWARDS THOSE
CHILDHOOD FEARS NOW IN ORDER TO
DISMANTLE WHY THEYRE ALL THERE...
THOUGHTS OF YOU MAKE HAPPY AND SAD
... HAPPY BECAUSE I HAD SUCH AN AMAZING
OPPORTUNITY TO HAVE LOVE BY YOU
PHYSICALLY, MENTALLY, EMOTIONALLY,
AND SPIRITUALLY.... SAD BECAUSE IT
TOOK LOSING YOU TO FIND ME... GOD
HAS A FUNNY WAY OF TEACHING US
VALUABLE LESSONS IN OUR LIVES... LIKE
YOU MY LIFE HAS NOT BEEN EASY...
THANK YOU FOR ALLOWING ME TO
LOVE YOU AND CARE FOR YOU OVER
THE LAST YEAR AND HALF AS YOU
DID ME... LOVING YOU IS TEACHING
SO MUCH MORE THAN YOULL EVER
REALIZE... I CANNOT CHANGE THE PAST
NOR WISH TO SHUT THE DOOR ON IT...
AS IT HOLDS THE KEYS TO LIFE CHANGE
AND A HAPPY FUTURE... I LOVE YOU
ANGEL... LOVE ALWAYS YOUR FRIEN
SEAN ♡2 ♡2 ♡2 ♡2 ♡2 ♡2

(6)

PLEASE PUT THIS W/ THE OTHER
LETTER AND THE PHOTOS I SENT
W/ THEM AS THEY WERE THE ONES
I WROTE TO THIS ENTIRE TIME
AND MEAN THE WORLD TO ME...
THEY SAVED ME SO MANY TIMES
YOULL NEVER REALIZE... THEY ARE
THE MOST BEAUTIFUL PHOTOS IN
THE WORLD AND I'LL NEVER FORGET
WHAT THEY LOOK LIKE... MY BLUE
EYED BLOND HAIRED TINY ANGEL...
– ESPECIALLY THE ONE I TRADED
36 ICE CREAM SANDWICHE TO HAVE
HAND DRAWN... WHAT AN INCREDIBLE
JOURNEY WE SHARED. FROM YOU
READING ME THE PROMISES TO MOST
LOVING CONNECTIONS... ALSO THE MOST
PHYSICALLY INTIMATE CONNECTE COMPATIB-
-ILITY WEVE EVER HAD... ILL NEVER
EVER FORGET, ANY OF OUR TIMES
TOGETHER!!!

TOMORROW MORNING I WILL MAIL THIS
LET AS MY FINAL CONTACT TO THE GIRL
WHO CHANGED ME FOR THE BETTER FOREVER
... IF GOD BRINGS US BACK TOGETHER I
PROMISED HIM ILL NEVER LET YOU GO AND
BE THE KIND, PATIENT, UNDERSTANDING, LOVING
MAN YOU DESERVE

Afterword

I made it. After all the nights staring at those walls, after all the days of waiting and writing, I'm finally standing on the other side of the gate. Free. Breathing air that doesn't taste like steel, feeling the sun without fences in the way. Living the life I used to only dream about in these pages.

To everyone who took the time to read my words, thank you. These letters carried me through the darkest place I have ever been, and now they have made their way into your hands. That means my struggle, my mistakes, my love—it all mattered. None of it was wasted.

I am out now. I hold my daughters, build real memories with them instead of dreaming about it from a cell. I have people who love me, and I love them back the best I can. Every day I wake up thankful, because I know how close I came to losing it all.

So thank you for walking this road with me, page after page. If you take anything from my story, let it be this: no matter how far you fall, love can still reach you. Hope can still carry you. And freedom—both inside and out—is always worth fighting for.

— Sean

Dedicated to a person I once knew.

"It was what it was."

DISCLAIMER

www.ingramcontent.com/pod-product-compliance
Lightning Source LLC
LaVergne TN
LVHW011915110626
841059LV00008B/22
* 9 7 8 1 0 6 9 8 9 5 8 1 3 *